Formulaic Language and New Data

Formelhafte Sprache
Formulaic Language

───

Edited by
Natalia Filatkina, Kathrin Steyer and Sören Stumpf

Advisory Board
Harald Burger (Zurich), Joan L. Bybee (New Mexico),
Dmitrij Dobrovol'skij (Moscow), Stephan Elspaß (Salzburg),
Christiane Fellbaum (Princeton), Raymond Gibbs (Santa Cruz),
Annelies Häcki Buhofer (Basel), Claudine Moulin (Trier),
Jan-Ola Östman (Helsinki), Stephan Stein (Trier),
Martin Wengeler (Trier), Alison Wray (Cardiff)

Volume 3

Formulaic Language and New Data

Theoretical and Methodological Implications

Edited by
Elisabeth Piirainen (†), Natalia Filatkina, Sören Stumpf
and Christian Pfeiffer

DE GRUYTER

The Open Access publication of the current volume was generously supported by the Interdisciplinary Research Unit "Patterns. Linguistic creativity and variation in synchrony and diachrony" established at Trier University in July 2019 within the framework of the research initiative of the Rhineland-Palatinate Ministry of Science, Professional Development and Culture.

ISBN 978-3-11-077772-7
e-ISBN (PDF) 978-3-11-066982-4
e-ISBN (EPUB) 978-3-11-066658-8

Dieses Werk ist lizenziert unter der Creative Commons Attribution-4.0 Lizenz.
Weitere Informationen finden Sie unter http://creativecommons.org/licenses/by/4.0/.

Library of Congress Control Number: 2019955411

Bibliographic information published by the Deutsche Nationalbibliothek
The Deutsche Nationalbibliothek lists this publication in the Deutsche Nationalbibliografie; detailed bibliographic data are available on the Internet at http://dnb.dnb.de.

© 2021 Elisabeth Piirainen, Natalia Filatkina, Sören Stumpf and Christian Pfeiffer, published by Walter de Gruyter GmbH, Berlin/Boston
This volume is text- and page-identical with the hardback published in 2020.
This book is published with open access at www.degruyter.com.

Printing and binding: CPI books GmbH, Leck

www.degruyter.com

Acknowledgments

The content of this edited volume has a complex origin and looks back at a long history. At its core, it combines selected talks presented at the international conference "Europhras 2016. Word combinations in the linguistic system and language use: theoretical, methodological and integrated approaches", which took place from August 1.–3. 2016 at Trier University, Germany. The Trier conference was attended by 220 scholars from 36 countries and continued the 23-year old tradition of the Europhras conferences organized by the Executive Board of the European Society of Phraseology (Europhras) every other year in different locations worldwide. This conference is a place of exchange for renowned and young scholars conducting research in various aspects of word combinations in the broadest sense of the word.

However, the 2016 conference showed that despite the long tradition and a vast variety of topics, research remains concentrated on only a few European standard languages with a rich literary tradition and a distinct written norm. The present volume suggests a shift of focus from these more traditional sources to what we call "new data". In this volume, the relatively small number of Europhras 2016 contributions which drew upon such data back then is supplemented by a number of invited papers.

We would like to thank both all the authors for their contributions and a frictionless cooperation and all the anonymous reviewers for their time and insightful comments. Thanks also to the German Research Foundation / Deutsche Forschungsgemeinschaft (DFG), Trier University and the European Society of Phraseology, which provided financial help in organizing the conference. We appreciate the highly professional support and patience of Daniel Gietz, Anna Rudolph and Albina Töws from the De Gruyter publishing house. In its final stage, the completion of the volume benefitted greatly not only from the English native language competence but also from the general linguistic knowledge of Angela Oakeshott. All the layout work was in the fast and reliable hands of Johanna Schäfer, whose dedicated and accurate efforts allowed the editors to concentrate on the content of this volume. Last but not least: It would not be possible to publish this volume in the Open Access format without the generous financial support of the interdisciplinary Research Unit "Patterns. Linguistic creativity and variation in synchrony and diachrony" established at Trier University in July 2019 within the framework of the research initiative of the Rhineland-Palatinate Ministry of

Science, Professional Development and Culture. Our sincerest thanks go to the Board of the Research Unit.

The initial idea of including new data in the Europhras 2016 conference program and drawing specific attention to it in the form of the current volume was inspired extensively by the remarkable research of our colleague **Elisabeth Piirainen**. Her ground-breaking and pioneering achievements at the crossroads of figurative language and "new data" paved the way for similar research on the part of many scholars, including the editors of and some contributors to the current volume. Almost two years after her unexpected and untimely death in December 2017, it is still hard to believe that Elisabeth was not able to take part in the final stages of the editing process and cannot hold the published volume in her hands. To continue what she started many years ago, we would like to dedicate this book to Elisabeth Piirainen, an open-minded, curious and tireless scholar and a supportive human being with a big heart.

Elisabeth Piirainen at the Europhras 2016 conference in Trier

Trier/Luxembourg, Trier/Princeton and Freiburg, in September 2019

Natalia Filatkina, Sören Stumpf and Christian Pfeiffer

Content

Acknowledgments —— v

Natalia Filatkina, Sören Stumpf & Christian Pfeiffer
Introduction: Formulaic Language and New Data —— 1

Part I: Lesser-Used and Areally Limited Languages

Elisabeth Piirainen
Lesser-Used Languages and their Contribution to the Study of Formulaic and Figurative Language —— 19

Stephan Elspaß
Areal Variation and Change in the Phraseology of Contemporary German —— 43

Zuriñe Sanz-Villar
An Analysis of Basque Collocations Formed by Onomatopoeia and Verbs in a Translational Corpus of Literary Texts —— 79

Part II: Languages Spoken outside Europe

Andreas Buerki
(How) is Formulaic Language Universal? Insights from Korean, German and English —— 103

Abdullah Eisa
***Marḥaban*: Reconsidering the Criteria of an Arabic Phraseme —— 135**

Muhammad A. Badarneh
Formulaic Expressions of Politeness in Jordanian Arabic Social Interactions —— 151

Part III: Linguistic Varieties Used in Spoken Domains and/or Regarded as 'Conceptually Oral'

Joanna Szerszunowicz
New Pragmatic Idioms in Polish: An Integrated Approach in Pragmateme Research —— 173

Mareike Keller
Compositionality: Evidence from Code-Switching —— 197

Part IV: Earlier/Historical Stages of Language Development

Marie-Luis Merten
Insights into a Changing Communal Constructicon. Legal Writing in the Late Middle Ages and Early Modern Period —— 225

Christian Pfeiffer & Markus Schiegg
Religious Formulae in Historical Lower-Class Patient Letters —— 249

Natalia Filatkina, Sören Stumpf & Christian Pfeiffer
Introduction: Formulaic Language and New Data

1 Preliminary Remarks: What Do We Know?

The existence of formulaic patterns in the widest sense (including phrasemes, constructions, non-literal units and/or other prefabs) has been hypothetically attested to all the languages in the world. Probably the most extensive attempt to grasp the complex nature of such utterances was undertaken within the framework of phraseology. The complexity was reflected already in the defining criteria of phrasemes. According to Burger (2015: 14–15), phrasemes are polylexical items that must consist of at least two constituents, have a more or less stable form in which they are frequently reproduced by speakers and can (but don't have to) be idiomatic in meaning. Research was traditionally focused mainly on one type of polylexical word combination, namely idioms such as *to spill the beans* or *to break the ice*, because they met all the criteria mentioned above and were therefore considered to be at the centre of the phraseological system.

But as newer linguistic theories such as usage-based approaches to Construction Grammar (Fillmore 1988; Goldberg 1995), corpus linguistics (Steyer 2013) or text and discourse studies (cf. most recently Stumpf and Filatkina 2018) show, the formulaic character of human communication reaches far beyond the items that can meet the criteria of phrasemes (Stein and Stumpf 2019). It encompasses single word conventionalised structures such as routine formulae like *and?, congratulations!, frankly (speaking)*, adverbial/prepositional constructions (*notwithstanding*), word formation, syntax on the one hand and formulaic text genres such as contracts, business correspondence, newsletters, recipes, announcements etc. on the other. Language acquisition (Tomasello 2003) and language loss (Wray 2008, 2012) are strongly interwoven with formulaic patterns. In second language teaching, too, formulaic items are now considered a key aspect of language competence (Lewis 1993). This new understanding of the constitutive role of formulaic patterns is the first central starting point of the current volume.

The second point concerns the notion of "new data". At first sight, the appeal for inclusion of "new empirical data" might seem to be not so new for modern linguistic research. It has been in demand since the development of corpus and computer linguistics in the 1960s. However, the appeal was restricted to the analysis of large text corpora that until now continue to consist (not exclusively but predominantly) of written data from standard languages. Even within the framework of the above-mentioned newer paradigms, systematic research has been focused on only a few European standard languages with a rich literary tradition and a predominantly written norm. It was on the basis of these data that the theoretical framework, classification criteria and methodological approaches of various research directions dealing with formulaic language were developed. The most recent proof of this statement can be found in Häcki Buhofer's introduction to volume 9 of the "Yearbook of Phraseology":

> Linguistic research has dealt with the semantics of lexics in general and of phraseology in specific time and again, and rightly so. The present volume offers the desired spectrum as far as the languages examined are concerned, by presenting articles on Russian, English and others. At the same time, studies on rare and small languages and languages in the process of getting extinct remain a continuing desideratum. While quite a number of studies have investigated such languages from a general point of view, only few have taken on a phraseological perspective.
>
> (Häcki Buhofer 2018: 1)

The current volume does not neglect the necessity and importance of corpus based approaches but it goes far beyond that and suggests a shift of focus by placing other new data at the center of scholarly research. Within the framework of this volume, the "new data" are understood as data from 1) areally limited and lesser-used languages, 2) languages spoken outside Europe, 3) linguistic varieties used in spoken domains and/or regarded as 'conceptually oral' and 4) data from the earlier/historical stages of language development. As first studies show, the systematic inclusion of these data challenges the existing postulates of research on formulaic patterns at both theoretical and methodological levels in a different way from the challenges that corpus-driven and corpus-based approaches brought decades ago. What we already know now is that, at the theoretical level, the challenges affect primarily the role of linguistic genetic affiliation, intertextuality, variation/modification, normatisation/codification, regularity/analogy and frequency in the process of formulaic language formation. In what follows, we give a short outline of available scholarly knowledge for each of these phenomena.

1.1 Genetic Affiliation and Intertextuality

The most extensive attempt to include "new data" into the research on formulaic language was Elisabeth Piirainen's project "Widespread Idioms in Europe and Beyond (WI)" (Piirainen 2012, 2016). It was dedicated to the classification of cultural phenomena in idioms of modern language varieties and had access to 78 modern standard and lesser-used languages from all language families as well as dialects. The project identified 470 idioms as similar and widely known. Currently, a similarly large-scale project devoted to dialects, spoken data and/or historical languages of the mediaeval and early modern periods does not exist.

Two results of the WI-project are of particular importance. Firstly, earlier ideas that the same genetic affiliation of two or more languages could explain a similarity on the level of idioms have been disproven. These ideas disregard the fact that the origin of the majority of idioms does not go back to a common "proto-language" of an early past. As becomes obvious, distribution crosses genetic boundaries. Secondly, the concept of a "common (European) cultural heritage", which was also often used for explanation of similarities in earlier works, requires a more detailed investigation. Until now, cultural traditions from Classical Antiquity, Christianity (the Bible), the Renaissance, Humanism, and the Enlightenment have been included in this term. Though the role of these domains remains central, other cultural domains such as folk narratives, jokes and legends appear to be significant as well, particularly for formulaic patterns in dialects, areally restricted, lesser-used and/or predominantly orally used languages. These domains have produced numerous widespread idioms (*to fight like cat and dog*, *to shed crocodile tears*) and have not yet been listed under the concept of "common (European) cultural heritage". Today's convergence of idioms is the product of an intense exchange of thoughts and ideas among educated language users that could only have been based on writing and reading books in historical times. This shared knowledge of widely disseminated written and oral texts led to and supported the establishment of cultural memory and many formulaic patterns such as idioms and proverbs. The WI-project described this phenomenon using the term *intertextuality* and called for its precise validation in individual languages, particularly those outside of Europe, as well as dialects and lesser-used languages (Dobrovol'skij and Piirainen 2005; Piirainen 2012: 520).

1.2 Variation and Modification

One of the major achievements of phraseological research in recent years is the understanding that even highly idiomatic units, such as *to cast pearls before swine*, are not as fixed as has previously been thought. As the first results of diachronic studies show, at the historical stages of a language, fixedness or stability can only be attributed to a basic structure underlying a formulaic pattern. The patterns that might be considered formulaic in a certain language at the current point in time are always products of a complex process of change, which is inherently enabled by variation. However, at the current state of international research, for the majority of languages, systematic studies into the diachronic processes of the emergence of what is considered formulaic in modern languages face methodological difficulties, a theoretical vacuum and most importantly a lack of empirical data (Filatkina 2012, 2013, 2018a, b, c). Since its establishment in the 19th century, historical linguistics was strongly focused on the description of various but single and isolated linguistic domains such as phonetics, grammar or the lexicon. The variation and change of formulaic patterns as one basic condition of human communication remain a fundamental research question for all languages without exception and are often completely neglected, even in publications claiming the status of reference works on language change (for a detailed overview cf. Filatkina 2018c: 57–96).

As shown in Filatkina (2013) and Piirainen (2000), formulaic patterns undergo diachronic changes at absolutely all levels: structure, semantics, pragmatics, ways of syntactic contextualization, distribution in texts, stylistic connotations, frequency of use, degree of familiarity, cultural image component and so on. However, the assumption that formulaic patterns emerge due to a decline in variation should be reconsidered. Though the pivotal role of the decline in variation has been most clearly demonstrated for orthographical (Kohrt 1998), phonetic (Kohrt 1998) and morphological (Werner 1998) norms, it does not appear to be relevant to formulaic patterns. On the contrary, variation can be an indication of the completion of a conventionalisation process and the establishment of a new utterance: Only after a pattern has reached a high degree of fixedness and conventionalisation, can it become subject to variation and/or modification by language speakers and still remain recognisable and understandable for them (cf. Burger 2012 for collocations in German).

Similar research results come from the first works on varieties, dialects and colloquial languages handed down orally, including that of Luxembourg, which is distinguished by its dialectal origin and the domain of orality. Piirainen (in this volume) sums up the findings very precisely:

> [They] showed deviations from the hitherto established theories, e.g. regarding the stability or variability of idioms, the so-called anthropocentrism, usage restrictions of idioms

(among them gender restrictions which are due to certain images), as well as specific pragmatic functions of conventional word plays, all of which up to that time had not been known to this extent.

Synchronic mechanisms of variation and/or modification have been studied in detail within the framework of phraseology, particularly using data from standard English(es), German, Russian, French, Italian and Spanish.[1] Despite the numerous studies, no theoretically viable distinction between variation and modification has been reached so far (Pfeiffer 2016, 2017, 2018, Pfeiffer and Schiegg, in this volume). The former is generally understood as a conventional and regular phenomenon that is independent of particular contexts and compatible with the norms of usage of a given language. The different variants are usually not only expected to occur with a certain frequency, but also to be stored in the mental lexicon and should thus be codified in dictionaries. By contrast, modification is defined as an intentional and conscious intervention by a speaker into a common form and/or meaning of a formula. Modifications represent an occasional phenomenon that occurs in a specific context. Thus, they allow for unexpected semantic-pragmatic effects on the part of the hearer and are used creatively as a favourable tool of wordplay, e.g. in mass media headlines, fiction or commercials. The functions and mechanisms of modifications have been described in detail for a relatively small number of written standard languages. Once again, however, lesser-used languages, oral communication and dialects (Piirainen 1995, 2007, 2008) continue to be underrepresented in this research area. The same holds for historical stages of modern languages (cf. however Pfeiffer and Schiegg, in this volume, for 19th century German lower class letter writing).

1.3 Normatisation and Codification

The decline of variation in the process of emerging phonetic, morphological and orthographic conventions in language use has often been attributed to the normative influence of dictionaries and grammar books. This is where the decline predominantly took place as the lack of variation was treated as a necessary characteristic of language norms in historical times. With regard to formulaic patterns, this does not hold true as dictionaries, historical collections of proverbs and idioms as well as chapters dedicated to formulaic patterns in early grammar

---

[1] For reasons of space, only a small selection of scholarly work can be given here: Burger (2015); Dobrovol'skij (2013); Dobrovol'skij and Piirainen (2009); Langlotz (2006); Pfeiffer (2018); Sabban (1998).

treatises have been compiled with rather different goals from that of a prescriptive establishment of norms (Filatkina 2016; Hundt 2000; Moulin 2016). Therefore, older texts and collections differ substantially with regard to the formulaic patterns they include (cf. Filatkina 2018c: 97–127 and 128–141 for Old High German). The same holds true for dialectal, areally restricted data and phrasemes in lesser-used languages where dictionaries and grammar books might not exist at all (Piirainen 2007, 2008).

1.4 Regularity and Analogy

In the same way, the explanation of the development of formulaic patterns and their variation just as a case of regularity and analogy would be a simplification of the actual state of affairs. Norm conflicts and preservation of lexical and/or grammatical constituents that have to be regarded as obsolete or irregular from the point of view of free language use are widespread phenomena in the formation of formulaic patterns. A corpus based attempt to prove the high degree of "regular irregularity" (in terms of norm conflicts and/or preservation of obsolete lexical/grammatical constituents) in the emergence of formulaic patterns is undertaken in Stumpf (2015, 2018, 2019) and based on data from standard modern German.

Within the framework of Construction Grammar, variation, regularity and analogy are considered intrinsic features of constructions (Goldberg 2003: 221–222). Variation is governed by the principles of inheritance, analogy and family resemblance, meaning semantic or phonological similarity between new and existing forms, relational knowledge and structural alignment. The conflict between these principles should allow for creativity, especially in predominantly oral communication, but this point has not yet been made clear. Bybee (2010: 58) uses the above mentioned principles for a fine-grained analysis of the variation potential of the construction *it drives me* $X_{adj.}$, but does not discuss a novel utterance like *it drives me happy* as a possible creative modification (a construct?) in certain contexts. In her eyes, it is just unlikely because – due to analogy and family resemblance principle – the *drives*-construction goes with adjectives and phrases indicating madness or insanity. Research into the micro-steps of variation and particularly the role of regularity, analogy and creative modifications[2] in new sources as defined in the current volume still requires a lot of attention in

---

2 From the constructionist point of view, the role of creative modifications is studied in Stumpf (2016) using data from modern German.

order to satisfy the far-reaching claim of Construction Grammar "to account for the full range of facts about language, without assuming that a particular subset of the data is part of a privileged 'core'" (Goldberg 2003: 219).

1.5 Frequency

Theories of language variation and change (morphological, typological, lexical and semantic) stress the pivotal role of frequency in any process of emergence of new items. It is a well known fact that in the process of lexicon expansion, for example, a sporadic innovation only has a chance of entering the lexicon if it is supported by a sufficient number of speakers, i.e. if they frequently use the item in a new form and/or meaning and function. It goes without saying that the emergence of formulaic patterns involves frequency. But another fact has to be taken into account as well: Formulaic patterns are constitutive elements of human communication only with regard to their type frequency; by contrast, their token frequency is generally low. In other words: A certain degree of formulaicity can be attested to absolutely any written text or oral communicative act because any of these sources contain different types of formulaic patterns (*type frequency*). The problem is that each type might occur only once (*token frequency*).

What seems to be a crucial factor for the emergence of formulaic patterns is not so much just the frequent use of a pattern but its frequent use in a specific situation of communication – oral or written! – as well as in a specific (cultural) text/discourse tradition (Stumpf and Kreuz 2016; Stumpf and Filatkina 2018). The link between a formulaic pattern and a context ensures that speakers resort to appropriate (even the most irregular!) units in respective situations. Evidence for such links has been already provided from different research perspectives and various modern languages (cf. Feilke 1994: 226 for German; Koch 1997 for French; Wray 2009: 36 and Wray and Perkins 2000: 7 for English), recently also within the fine-grained concept of construction discourse and the notion of discourse patterns in Östman (2005, 2015). The "new sources", particularly in the sense of spoken data, areally restricted or lesser-used languages, seem to support this evidence even more strongly. Therefore, more research needs to be forthcoming here.

2 Where Do We Go from Here? – This Volume

Departing from these briefly sketched already available research findings, the current volume tackles the following questions:
- What is formulaic in the "new types" of languages, varieties and dialects?
- Are the criteria developed within the framework of traditional phraseological research (e.g. fixedness, idiomaticity) applicable to "new data"?
- Can any specific types of formulaic patterns and/or any specific features (semantic, structural, pragmatic etc.) of regular (already known) types of formulaic patterns be observed and how do they emerge?
- What methodological difficulties need to be overcome when dealing with "new data"?

2.1 Lesser-Used and Areally Limited Languages

The first part of the volume brings together studies based on the data from areally limited and lesser-used languages. *Elisabeth Piirainen's* contribution provides the framework for this section and aims to bring together phraseological research and studies on formulaic and figurative language of lesser-used, mainly unwritten languages, from anthropology and ethnology. The term *lesser-used languages* is applied generically "for smaller and minority languages, which show a downward trend of influence" (Piirainen, in this volume) and which do not fulfill the criteria for their intergenerational transmission. In the context of the article, the term covers non-Western minority languages of the Austronesian language groups (Kilivila and Kewa), Basque as an isolate spoken in several varieties on both sides of the Western Pyrenees, Flathead Salish, a critically endangered American Indian variety in Montana, USA, and Inari Saami, a declining minority language on the edge of Northern Europe; some examples are taken from ethnic African languages. The study investigates body-part semiotizations, conceptual metaphors and pragmatic functions of figurative units in such languages. The results are threefold: Firstly, the inclusion of new, previously unresearched languages clearly shows that the symbolic value of semiotized body parts and inner organs is significantly different from that known in Western written languages. Secondly, the postulate of universality of such conceptual metaphors as TIME IS MONEY or UNDERSTANDING IS SEEING cannot be sustained. Thirdly, the entire complex of figurative secret languages, "veiled languages" and "tabooed languages" in Papua New Guinea appears to have no equivalent in the Western world.

Areal variation and change in oral modern German is studied by *Stephan Elspaß*. The novelty of this topic is remarkable as, at least to our knowledge, there is a complete lack of studies on phraseological change both in contemporary German and in any other modern language. Elspaß refers to data that has been obtained in three recent research projects on German areal linguistics: *Atlas zur deutschen Alltagssprache* (AdA) 'Atlas of colloquial German vernacular' (with internet survey data from mostly spoken regional vernaculars), *Variantenwörterbuch des Deutschen* (VWB) 'Dictionary of lexical variation in German' and the *Variantengrammatik des Standarddeutschen* (VG) 'Regional variation in the grammar of Standard German' (with data from large regionally-balanced corpora of the written Standard German in Germany, Austria and Switzerland). These new data are compared with data from the *Wortatlas der deutschen Umgangssprachen* (WDU) 'Word Atlas of colloquial German', collected in the 1970s and 1980s, and with the findings in Piirainen (2009). The study reveals a number of developments in the areal distribution of phrasemes both on the level of colloquial speech and in standard written German which have occurred in recent decades. In addition to his findings on phraseological change, Elspaß also shows a) that there are significant differences between awareness and actual usage of phraseological units and b) that the representation of areal phraseological variation in dictionaries is often misleading or even incorrect. This applies particularly to the phraseological dictionary edited by Duden (Duden 11), while the situation is considerably better for the VWB.

Basque collocations formed by onomatopoeia and verbs in a corpus of translated literary texts are the subject of investigation in *Zuriñe Sanz-Villar's* contribution. The Basque language has only a weak tradition of written literature and its standard variety only a short history. As Sanz-Villar notes, there has been no systematic research in the field of Basque phraseology and even less attention has been paid to the study of the translation of phraseological units from/into Basque. The benefit of the inclusion of Basque into research on formulaic language already becomes apparent at the typological level: Even though Basque phraseology still remains underinvestigated, previous research has already identified collocations formed by a partially or totally reduplicated onomatopoeia and a verb as a special type of formulaic pattern in Basque. Sanz-Villar selected 66 types and 162 tokens semi-automatically from her corpus and queried them in the TraceAligner program for the subsequent translation analysis. The translation analysis in its turn has shown that, despite the predominance of the translation option when the counterpart of the Basque collocation is a single verb in the German source text, the nuances hidden behind it are of great significance from a translation point of view; indirect translations are not an exception but rather a widespread reality in German-into-Basque translations.

2.2 Languages Spoken outside Europe

Three contributions in Part II of the current volume offer insights on formulaic language from the perspective of three languages spoken outside Europe: Korean (Buerki), Classical Arabic (Eisa) and spoken Jordanian Arabic (Badarneh).

Andreas Buerki tackles the questions how formulaicity may be understood across typologically different languages and whether indeed there is a concept of formulaic language that applies across languages. Using a new data set consisting of topically matched corpora in three typologically different languages (Korean, German and English) and a constructionist view of linguistic signs, this study proposes a quantitatively founded statement that formulaic language has to be regarded as a language-specific phenomenon. The conclusion results from the observation that though formulaic patterns are in evidence in a very large number of languages, their density of occurrence varies greatly between languages of different types. A cross-linguistically viable concept of formulaic language cannot be centred at any particular structural level (such as sequences of words, phrases or polylexicality) and has to incorporate more abstract elements specified at varying levels of schematicity. Buerki's broader view on formulaic language coincides with the perspective of the current volume regarding the place of formulaic patterns in overall theories of language: Such utterances cannot be ignored as insignificant grammatical exceptions or treated marginally as only random stylistic/aesthetic phenomena; rather, they should be recognised as equally prominent linguistic means of communication in an integrative model of language.

The contribution of *Abdullah Eisa* is based on similar ideas and demonstrates the difficulties that emerge when typological criteria of formulaic patterns established on the data of standard languages (English) are to be applied to Arabic phraseology. The criteria in question are the notion of word, polylexicality, flexibility, frequency, adjacency and idiomaticity/semantic unity. Even though these criteria have been described as problematic also in the framework of traditional research on the phraseology of standard written languages, Eisa's study makes it clear that "new data" shed light on more general issues and can illuminate what is required for a complete account of linguistic variety and complexity.

The third study in this part of the book explores the use of politeness formulaic expressions in everyday social interaction in colloquial Jordanian Arabic.

What makes the contribution of *Muhammad A. Bardaneh* interesting for the current volume is not only the novelty of the data set but also the results of the analysis. On the one hand, the studied formulaic expressions pose no theoretical problems for their description within the well-known concept of positive and negative politeness. Positive formulae in Jordanian Arabic are used in interactional and transactional contexts and emphasize solidarity and communal belonging in the same way as in other languages studied with regard to this; negative politeness formulae are concerned with showing deference and non-imposition. Furthermore, the study supports the notion that formulaic expressions are central elements of polite communication in colloquial Arabic in Jordan in a similar way to those in any other language. On the other hand, they are different with regard to the cultural and social traditions in which they are strongly embedded: According to Bardaneh, many of these formulae involve reference to God and emphasize the religious and fatalistic nature of the community they are used in. As the majority of formulaic patterns are oriented toward positive rather than negative face, Bardaneh concludes by emphasizing the positive politeness leanings of Jordanians and their concern with solidarity and acquaintance, collectivist satisfaction, and communal belonging, as opposed to individualism and personal space.

2.3 Linguistic Varieties Used in Spoken Domains and/or Regarded as 'Conceptually Oral'

Spoken data are at the center of the contributions in the third part of the current volume and demonstrate that formulaic patterns are dynamic linguistic utterances that emerge not only in language history but also in most recent times as a reaction to social, political, historical and cultural changes.

Joanna Szerszunowicz draws upon the notion of the so called new pragmatic idioms or pragmatemes in Polish and suggests an integrated approach to their study. The integrated approach means that the analysis is not restricted to linguistic aspects of pragmatic formulaic patterns, but also takes into consideration other factors, for instance, their cultural background and the cultural-historical context in which they emerge. Szerszunowicz's specific interest focuses on patterns that came into existence after 1989, the year of Poland's political and economic transformation. The analyzed idioms confirm the increasing influence of the English-speaking world on the Polish communicative style and changing language behaviors in the new reality, in which the quality of being friendly and nice gains a new dimension. Other examples can be traced back to the problems of budding Polish democracy or illustrate recent changes in social perception of the weekend.

In contrast, *Mareike Keller* uses recordings of German-English informal conversation not to study the emergence of new expressions but rather to address the issue of the storage and processing of phrasemes. Though this issue has been discussed extensively in the previous research, a consensus with regard to the degree to which phrasemes are stored and processed holistically or compositionally has not been reached so far. Spoken bilingual data appear to be particularly fruitful for the continuation of this dialogue on account of the large number of code-switching utterances that shed new light on both syntactic and semantic levels of patterns. As Keller states, they provide empirical evidence for the unitary storage of phrasemes at the conceptual level as well as for their compositional assembly in accordance with structural code-switching constraints during language production.

2.4 Earlier/Historical Stages of Language Development

The last part of the volume draws attention to data from historical stages of language development. *Marie-Luis Merten's* paper examines Middle Low German legal writing in the Late Middle Ages and the Early Modern Period (1227 until 1567) from a diachronic perspective. Despite a vast amount of research, Middle Low German can be still considered an underinvestigated historical language, especially from the point of view of its formulaicity. What is particularly remarkable about Merten's paper is her attempt to investigate historical data within the framework of construction grammar, a theory which has traditionally been dominated by synchronic approaches. Merten interprets evolving and changing constructions of legal writing in connection with the changing communal constructicon, i.e. a socio-cognitive network, a repertoire of constructions shared by legal writers of that time. For the analysis of diachronic formulaic patterns it is crucial to develop a theoretical framework that is capable of coping with phenomena of language in transition and both formulaic (lexical) expressions and more complex form-meaning pairs between fixedness and variability. This point was already made strongly at the beginning of the introduction to this volume and is emphasized by Merten. Approaches as shown by Merten can in their turn contribute significantly to the development of Construction Grammar as they include the cultural and historical context in the analysis of formulaic patterns, a perspective which is just starting to find its way into Construction Grammar.

Christian Pfeiffer and *Markus Schiegg* conclude the volume with a fine-grained study of sources that can be regarded as formulaic in a different sense from legal writings. They examine the use and functions of religious formulae in historical lower-class letters – a data set taken from the Corpus of Patient Documents (CoPaDocs), a new corpus of 19th- and early 20th-century texts written by patients in German psychiatric hospitals which has not yet been systematically investigated from the perspective of formulaic language. A factor that is of great importance for the current volume (and historical linguistics in general) is the fact that most of the letters were written by lower-class people with only a poor education. Hence, the letters permit an insight into the use of formulaic language by ordinary people in the 19th century opening up a wonderful perspective such as presents itself only rarely to scholars dealing with earlier periods in the history. The authors choose a functional approach and present an extensive analysis of the pragmatic functions of religious formulae in these texts. However, they also contribute to the above-mentioned challenge of differentiating between instances of variation and modification. A valuable contribution to the volume is the authors' conclusion that the tendency to use formulaic items creatively has a long tradition and is not a development of recent decades. The modifications they found do not seem to have the aim of wordplay but are most obviously produced to achieve particular communicative goals. Based on an exemplary intertextual analysis, the authors finally raise the question whether there exists something like a European tradition of letter writing and a common stock of formulaic items and call for further contrastive research on historical letter writing.

The contributions to this volume take, each in their different way, upon the scientific ideas of our colleague Elisabeth Piirainen. In the hope that Elisabeth's work will be continued we dedicate this volume to her.

References

Burger, Harald (2012): Alte und neue Fragen, alte und neue Methoden der historischen Phraseologie. In Natalia Filatkina, Ane Kleine-Engel, Marcel Dräger & Harald Burger (Hrsg.), *Aspekte der historischen Phraseologie und Phraseographie*, 1–20. Heidelberg: Universitätsverlag Winter.
Burger, Harald (2015): *Phraseologie. Eine Einführung am Beispiel des Deutschen.* 5 Auflage. Berlin: Erich Schmidt.
Bybee, Joan (2010): *Language, usage and cognition.* Cambridge: Cambridge University Press.
Dobrovol'skij, Dmitrij (2013): *Besedy o nemezkom slove/Studien zur deutschen Lexik* (Studia philologica). Moskva: Yazyki slavjanskoj kul'tury.
Dobrovol'skij, Dmitrij O. & Elisabeth Piirainen (2005): *Figurative language. Cross-cultural and cross-linguistic perspectives.* Amsterdam, Philadelphia: Elsevier.

Dobrovol'skij, Dmitrij & Elisabeth Piirainen (2009): *Zur Theorie der Phraseologie. Kognitive und kulturelle Aspekte.* Tübingen: Narr.

Feilke, Helmuth (1994): *Common sense-Kompetenz. Überlegungen zu einer Theorie „sympathischen" und „natürlichen" Meinens und Verstehens.* Frankfurt am Main: Suhrkamp.

Filatkina, Natalia (2012): „Wan wer beschreibt der welte stat/der muoß wol sagen wie es gat". Manifestation, functions and dynamics of formulaic patterns in Thomas Murner's „Schelmenzunft" revisited. In Natalia Filatkina, Ane Kleine-Engel, Marcel Dräger & Harald Burger (Hrsg.), *Aspekte der historischen Phraseologie und Phraseographie*, 21–44. Heidelberg: Universitätsverlag Winter.

Filatkina, Natalia (2013): Wandel im Bereich der historischen formelhaften Sprache und seine Reflexe im Neuhochdeutschen: Eine neue Perspektive für moderne Sprachwandeltheorien. In Petra M. Vogel (Hrsg.), *Sprachwandel im Neuhochdeutschen. Jahrbuch der Gesellschaft für germanistische Sprachgeschichte 2013*, 34–51. Berlin, New York: De Gruyter.

Filatkina, Natalia (2016): Wie fest sind feste Strukturen? Beobachtungen zu Varianz in (historischen) Wörterbüchern und Texten. In Luise Borek & Andrea Rapp (Hrsg.), *Vielfalt und Varianz interdiziplinär: Wörter und Strukturen*, 7–27. Mannheim: Institut für deutsche Sprache.

Filatkina, Natalia (2018a): Expanding the Lexicon through Formulaic Patterns: The Emergence of Formulaicity in Language History and Modern Language Use. In Sabine Arndt-Lappe, Angelika Braun, Claudine Moulin & Esme Winter-Froemel (eds.), *Expanding the Lexicon. Linguistic Innovation, Morphological Productivity and Ludicity*, 15–42. Berlin, Boston: De Gruyter Mouton.

Filatkina, Natalia (2018b): Historische formelhafte Wendungen als Konstruktionen: Möglichkeiten und Grenzen der diachronen Konstruktionsgrammatik. *Linguistik-online* 90 (3), special issue "Muster im Sprachgebrauch: Construction Grammar meets Phraseology", ed. by Alexander Ziem, 115–143.

Filatkina, Natalia (2018c): *Historische formelhafte Sprache. Theoretische Grundlagen und methodische Herausforderungen.* Berlin, Boston: De Gruyter.

Fillmore, Charles J., Paul Kay & Mary Catherine O'Connor (1988): Regularity and idiomaticity in grammatical constructions. The case of *let alone*. *Language* 64, 501–538.

Goldberg, Adele E. (1995): *Constructions. A construction grammar approach to argument structure.* Chicago, London: University of Chicago Press.

Goldberg, Adele E. (2003): Constructions: a new theoretical approach to language. *Trends in cognitive sciences* 7 (5), 219–224.

Häcki Buhofer, Annelies (2018): Editorial. *Yearbook of Phraseology* 9, 1–2.

Hundt, Markus (2000): *„Spracharbeit" im 17. Jahrhundert. Studien zu Georg Philipp Harsdörffer, Justus Georg Schottelius und Christian Gueintz.* Berlin, New York: De Gruyter.

Koch, Peter (1997): Diskurstraditionen: zu ihrem sprachtheoretischen Status und ihrer Dynamik. In Barbara Frank, Thomas Haye & Doris Tophinke (Hrsg.), *Gattungen mittelalterlicher Schriftlichkeit*, 43–79. Tübingen: Narr.

Kohrt, Manfred (1998): Historische Phonologie und Graphematik. In Werner Besch, Anne Betten, Oskar Reichmann & Stefan Sonderegger (Hrsg.), *Sprachgeschichte. Ein Handbuch zur Geschichte der deutschen Sprache und ihrer Erforschung.* 2. Auflage, 1. Halbband, 551–572. Berlin, New York: De Gruyter.

Langlotz, Andreas (2006): *Idiomatic creativity. A cognitive-linguistic model of idiom-representation and idiom-variation in English.* Amsterdam, Philadelphia: John Benjamins.

Lewis, Michael (1993): *The Lexical Approach: The State of ELT and the Way Forward*. Hove, England: Language Teaching Publications.
Moulin, Claudine (2016): „Nach dem die Gäste sind, nach dem ist das Gespräch". Spracharbeit und barocke Tischkultur bei Georg Philipp Harsdörffer. In Nina Bartsch & Simone Schultz-Balluff (Hrsg.), *PerspektivWechsel oder: Die Wiederentdeckung der Philologie. 2. Band: Grenzgänge und Grenzüberschreitungen. Zusammenspiele von Sprache und Literatur in Mittelalter und Früher Neuzeit*, 261–287. Berlin: Erich Schmidt.
Östman, Jan-Ola (2005): Construction discourse. A prolegomenon. In Jan-Ola Östman & Miriam Fried (eds.), *Construction grammars: Cognitive grounding and theoretical extensions*, 121–144. Amsterdam, Philadelphia: John Benjamins.
Östman, Jan-Ola (2015): From construction grammar to construction discourse ... and back. In Jörg Bücker, Susanne Günthner & Wolfgang Imo (Hrsg.), *Konstruktionsgrammatik V. Konstruktionen im Spannungsfeld von sequenziellen Mustern, kommunikativen Gattungen und Textsorten*, 15–43. Tübingen: Stauffenburg.
Pfeiffer, Christian (2016): *Frequenz und Funktionen phraseologischer Wendungen in meinungsbetonten Pressetexten (1911–2011)*. Baltmannsweiler: Schneider Verlag Hohengehren.
Pfeiffer, Christian (2017): Okkasionalität: Zur Operationalisierung eines zentralen definitorischen Merkmals phraseologischer Modifikation. *Yearbook of Phraseology* 8, 9–30.
Pfeiffer, Christian (2018): Zur Identifikation modifizierter Phraseme in Texten: ein Vorschlag für die analytische Praxis. In Sören Stumpf & Natalia Filatkina (Hrsg.), *Formelhafte Sprache in Text und Diskurs*, 49–84. Berlin, Boston: De Gruyter.
Piirainen, Elisabeth (1995): Mänden häbbt groote Aorne un könnt doch nich häörn. Zum usualisierten Wortspiel im Westmünsterländischen. *Niederdeutsches Wort. Beiträge zur niederdeutschen Philologie* 35, 177–204.
Piirainen, Elisabeth (2000): *Phraseologie der westmünsterländischen Mundart. 1. Band: Semantische, kulturelle und pragmatische Aspekte dialektaler Phraseologismen. 2. Band: Lexikon der westmünsterländischen Phraseologie*. Baltmannsweiler: Schneider Verlag Hohengehren.
Piirainen, Elisabeth (2007): Dialectal phraseology: Linguistic aspects. In Harald Burger, Dmitrij Dobrovol'skij, Peter Kühn & Neal R. Norrick (eds.), *Phraseology. An International Handbook of Contemporary Research*. Volume 1, 530–540. Berlin, New York: De Gruyter.
Piirainen, Elisabeth (2008): Phraseology from an areal linguistic perspective. In Maria Álvarez de la Granja (Hrsg.), *Beiträge zur Phraseologie aus kontrastiver Sicht*, 19–44. Hamburg: Dr. Kovač.
Piirainen, Elisabeth (2012): *Widespread idioms in Europe and beyond. Toward a lexicon of common figurative units*. Volume I. New York, Washington D.C.: Peter Lang.
Piirainen, Elisabeth (2016): *Widespread idioms in Europe and beyond. Toward a lexicon of common figurative units*. Volume II. New York, Washington D.C.: Peter Lang.
Sabban, Annette (1998): *Okkasionelle Variationen sprachlicher Schematismen. Eine Analyse französischer und deutscher Presse- und Werbetexte*. Tübingen: Narr.
Stein, Stephan & Sören Stumpf (2019): *Muster in Sprache und Kommunikation. Eine Einführung in Konzepte sprachlicher Vorgeformtheit*. Berlin: Erich Schmidt.
Steyer, Kathrin (2013): *Usuelle Wortverbindungen. Zentrale Muster des Sprachgebrauchs aus korpusanalytischer Sicht*. Tübingen: Narr.
Stumpf, Sören (2015): *Formelhafte (Ir-)Regularitäten. Korpuslinguistische Befunde und sprachtheoretische Überlegungen*. Frankfurt am Main: Peter Lang.

Stumpf, Sören (2016): Modifikation oder Modellbildung? Das ist hier die Frage – Abgrenzungsschwierigkeiten zwischen modifizierten und modellartigen Phrasemen am Beispiel formelhafter (Ir-)Regularitäten. *Linguistische Berichte* 247, 317–342.

Stumpf, Sören (2018): Formulaic (Ir-)Regularities in German. Corpus Linguistics and Construction Grammar Approaches. In Natalia Filatkina & Sören Stumpf (Hrsg.), *Konventionalisierung und Variation. Phraseologische und konstruktionsgrammatische Perspektiven*, 149–178. Frankfurt am Main: Peter Lang.

Stumpf, Sören (2019): Formelhafte (Ir-)Regularitäten. Theoretische Begriffsbestimmung und empirische Beispielanalyse. In Kauffer, Maurice & Yvon Keromnes (eds.), *Theorie und Empirie in der Phraseologie – Approches théoriques et empiriques en phraséologie*, 51–65. Tübingen: Stauffenburg.

Stumpf, Sören & Christian D. Kreuz (2016): Phraseologie und Diskurslinguistik – Schnittstellen, Fallbeispiele und Forschungsperspektiven. *Zeitschrift für Angewandte Linguistik* 65, 1–36.

Stumpf, Sören & Natalia Filatkina (Hrsg.) (2018): *Formelhafte Sprache in Text und Diskurs*. Berlin, Boston: De Gruyter.

Tomasello, Michael (2003): *Constructing a language. A usage-based theory of language acquisition*. Cambridge: Cambridge University Press.

Werner, Otmar (1998): Historische Morphologie. In Werner Besch, Anne Betten, Oskar Reichmann & Stefan Sonderegger (Hrsg.), *Sprachgeschichte. Ein Handbuch zur Geschichte der deutschen Sprache und ihrer Erforschung*. 1. Auflage, 1. Halbband, 572–596. Berlin, New York: De Gruyter.

Wray, Alison (2008): Formulaic sequences and language disorders. In Martin J. Ball, Michael R. Perkins & Nicole Müller & Sara Howard (eds.), *Handbook of Clinical Linguistics*, 184–197. Oxford: Oxford University Press.

Wray, Alison (2009): Identifying formulaic language: Persistent challenges and new opportunities. In Roberta Corrigan, Edith A. Moravcsik, Hamid Ouali & Kathleen Wheatle (eds.), *Formulaic language*. Volume 1, 27–51. Amsterdam, Philadelphia: John Benjamins.

Wray, Alison (2012): Patterns of formulaic language in Alzheimer's disease: implications for quality of life. *Quality in ageing and older adults* 13 (3), 168–175.

Wray, Alison & Michael R. Perkins (2000): The functions of formulaic language: An integrated model. *Language and communication* 20 (1), 1–28.

Part I: **Lesser-Used and Areally Limited Languages**

Elisabeth Piirainen
Lesser-Used Languages and their Contribution to the Study of Formulaic and Figurative Language

The Judeo-Christian tradition sees the profusion of tongues after the Tower of Babel as *a negative outcome punishing humans* for their presumption, and standing in the way of cooperation and progress. But the Warramurrungunji myth reflects a point of view much more common in small speech communities: that *having many languages is a good thing* because it shows where each person belongs.

(Evans 2010: 6; italics by E.P.)

Abstract: So far phraseology research has been carried out for a few major literary languages. In addition, there is a remarkable number of studies on formulaic and figurative language of lesser-used, mainly unwritten languages, anthropology and ethnology. Both spheres of research have, for the most part, the same object-linguistic data, but have so far little knowledge of each other. This paper is a sketchy report on some underestimated studies that can enhance our knowledge of phraseology and formulaicity. Three areas have been chosen which have often been the subject of research: body-part semiotizations, conceptual metaphors and pragmatic functions of figurative units. The inclusion of non-Western minority languages reveals various previously unknown peculiarities. The article aims to encourage scientists to include new data in phraseology and formulaic language research, i.e. to study languages which have not yet been investigated with regard to their phraseology and formulaicity, including varieties which exist merely in oral form.

1 Preliminary Remarks

Research on phraseology, with a focus on formulaic and figurative language, extends for the most part to a few current European standard languages, which all

---

Note: The article is published in the original version as written by the author. On account of her sudden and unexpected death, the editors of the volume have refrained from including the comments of two anonymous reviewers.

∂ Open Access. © 2020 E. Piirainen, published by De Gruyter. This work is licensed under the Creative Commons Attribution 4.0 License.
https://doi.org/10.1515/9783110669824-002

together account for less than one percent of the world's languages.[1] The data underlying European phraseology research and its results are quite coherent. These data are derived from some well-researched literary languages, above all from the Western cultural area. All these languages essentially fulfill the same communicative functions: they have developed for transregionally valid written and oral communication purposes of a complex modern society. The high degree of figurativeness of these standard European languages, as manifested in idioms and other figurative lexical units, appears equally uniform. It is not just the origin of many idioms from the so-called "common European cultural heritage", but the same metaphors and symbols, conceptualizations of abstract content that constitute these consistencies.[2]

Lesser-used languages have so far hardly been included in the phraseology research spectrum.[3] Two languages on the fringe of the European continent, namely Inari Saami and Basque constitute an exception. Both languages have been thoroughly investigated with regard to their figurative language, and these studies reveal metaphors and conceptualizations limited to their linguistic area, unparalleled by other European languages. These studies show very clearly how important it is to incorporate new language varieties: new data is urgently needed for phraseology research, especially from languages that are predominantly used in oral form. The subject of this article is lesser-used languages from the point of view of whether they could contribute to our knowledge of phraseology and figurative language.

But first let us look at the term *lesser-used language*. It will be used as a generic term for smaller and minority languages, which show a downward trend of influence. The term cannot be defined by linguistic criteria; rather, there exist extra-linguistic, political, social and economic factors which constitute this term. Here we refer to the explanations of relevant standard works, which instead of one definition give a bundle of criteria: When one of these criteria is met, it is a

---

[1] They belong to the Indo-European languages, the Finno-Ugric languages (Hungarian, Finnish, Estonian), some Turkic languages and Georgian, a South Caucasian language.

[2] Only on a concrete level of the source domains, such as national literature and history or natural environment and material culture, can some idiosyncrasies of idioms of these standard languages be observed.

[3] And vice versa: studies on lesser-used languages usually excluded phraseology. The 567-page volume *The Cambridge Handbook of Endangered Languages* (Austin and Sallabank 2011), for example, dedicates just ten lines to the topic "Idioms and proverbs", including commonplaces: "One might also wish to include idioms and proverbs because they reflect the culture of a speech community more than any other kind of linguistic unit; however, the explanation of their meaning and use can be difficult" (Austin and Sallabank 2011: 349).

question of a lesser-used language.⁴ The most important condition is that the intergenerational transmission of the language is not guaranteed. Further criteria are, among others: the language is restricted to a small area with few speakers; the number of speakers is obviously diminishing; the domains of usage are limited to unofficial situations; there is direct competition with the prestigious (national) language; standardization and written tradition are missing; the language exists mainly in oral form.

On the one hand, there would be no lack of research topics, as only less than one percent of the world's languages have been studied in terms of their phraseology and figurativeness so far – not to mention all modes of spoken language as they appear in the regional colloquial varieties and dialects around the world. On the other hand, there is extensive research on the stereotyped nature and figurativeness of non-literary languages, the data and results of which have hardly been noticed by traditional European phraseology research. A number of publications can be found on proverbs and other figurative or formulaic units in languages outside Europe, including lesser-used and indigenous unwritten languages.

For a hundred years, anthropologists and ethnologists have gathered data on the figurative and formulaic language of distant cultures on far-away continents, which were partly taken note of by (ethnology-oriented) paremiology, but not by linguistic phraseology research. When it comes to incorporating "new data" into research, it would be the first step to consider these studies. For in the area of stereotyped and figurative expressions, proverbs and metaphors, these studies are not only concerned with the study of phraseology, but also have the same linguistic elements as the object of their research. The same applies to the lesser-used minority languages in Europe, as well as to dialects that have only recently been added to phraseology research: they too have not been adequately considered, although they can certainly extend the knowledge of phraseology to date.

This paper is primarily a sketchy report on these underestimated studies. The following remarks are grouped around individual results: Section 2 deals with the results of the studies of languages distant from standard European varieties, including those of the Austronesian language groups, which have specific conceptualizations of certain internal organs and body parts, as well as concepts in

---

4 Cf. Allardt (1984); Fishman (1991); Hale et al. (1992); Matras (2003); Harrison (2007, 2010); Krauss (2007); Flores et al. (2010); Austin and Sallabank (2011); Lewis et al. (2014). Also, the definitions of the contrastive terms *standard language* or *literary language* must be omitted here and the literature be referred to (e.g. Lewis et al. 2014).

Basque which have no parallels in the standard European languages. Subsequently, some supposedly "universal" conceptual metaphors are considered. The inclusion of new, previously unresearched languages clearly shows that the postulate of universality cannot be sustained (section 3).

Pragmatic functions of proverbs and other figures of speech in several lesser-used, partly indigenous languages are the focus of the fourth section. The entire complex of figurative secret languages, "veiled languages" and "tabooed languages" in Papua New Guinea, for example, has no equivalent in the Western world. This topic is related to the classification of phrasemes or formulaic units. From the point of view of the languages outside Europe, the categories of the subject of investigation can be quite different from that of the European phraseology research. Sections 2–4 thus aim to confront the uniformity of the written European standard languages which have been studied so far with a diversity and dissimilarity outside this field, while section 5, Concluding remarks, provides references to current phraseology research.

2 Semiotized Concepts of Inner Organs and Body Parts

The far-reaching uniformity of European literary languages – as opposed to the diversity of lesser-used and non-European languages – can be demonstrated by the so-called "body part idioms".[5] From the beginning of phraseological research, the human body has been considered an extensive source domain and there has been a long tradition of analyzing *somatisms* (idioms with body part constituents). A wealth of publications on European standard languages provides a uniform picture of this group of idioms, especially of the symbolic functions of body part concepts such as, for instance, HAND, HEAD, EYE, TONGUE, etc. Internal organs are usually counted among the body parts. For example, HEART has been the subject of a large amount of phraseological work. These studies also show the strikingly close similarities in the area of symbolization (HEART is the imaginary organ of positive emotions in all standard European languages, without exception).[6]

---

[5] Compare the examples discussed in Piirainen (2016: 534–610).
[6] Only a few isolated relics may suggest that this was not always the case, cf. the idioms *to learn something by heart* and French *réciter par cœur* "to recite by heart" which reveal an earlier semiotization of HEART as the seat of mental activities.

That these Western languages are so consistent becomes particularly apparent when we turn our attention to languages of distant cultural areas. For some time, several East Asian standard languages have been the subject of phraseological research. They have significantly expanded our knowledge of symbolic functions of internal organs in figurative lexical units. As Yu (2003) points out, a wealth of Chinese idioms reflects the pre-scientific concept of GALL BLADDER, which is deeply anchored in the theory of internal organs in traditional Chinese medicine: the gall bladder serves to make judgments and decisions and determines the degree of a person's courage. According to Siahaan (2008), in Indonesian it is the LIVER (*hati*), among other things, that correlates with concepts such as HEART and MIND in European culture.[7] A key concept in Japanese culture called HARA, in turn, has no equivalent in Western languages. It is used mainly in male speech. Translations of *hara* as '(the inner part of the) belly', 'abdomen', etc. are only makeshift. HARA is regarded as the location of the mind, the center of mental energy and emotions, and emerges in a number of idioms (e.g. *hara wo warau* "to split the belly" 'to reveal one's thoughts, to tell the truth', cf. Hasada 2002, among others).

What these body-based concepts have in common and what distinguishes them from those in Western languages is not only the semiotized organs that seem to be unusual (GALL BLADDER, LIVER, BELLY).[8] Rather, these organs are seen as the seat of thoughts and/or emotions. Thus, the concepts do not comply with the common dichotomy in Western culture, the "Cartesian duality" of HEAD and HEART, i.e. the division between intellectual thoughts and emotions. A look at further languages of distant continents, but also at the Basque language, reveals the extent to which this Cartesian dualism is confined to the standard languages of Europe.[9]

---

7 LIVER as a semiotized concept is in fact much more widespread; it is documented in many languages of the East Asian and Pacific region (see, for example Franklin 2012: 189–190), but also known in European languages. There is a long cultural and historical tradition as to why the LIVER represents a special place of emotions; cf. Dobrovol'skij and Piirainen (2005: 127–128).
8 According to Sharifian et al. (2008: 6), this kind of *abdominocentrism* is characteristic of Southern Asian and Polynesian cultures while Chinese favors *cardiocentrism* (HEART as the seat of mind and emotion), and *cerebrocentrism* (HEAD as the seat of intellect) dominates West Asian, European and North African cultures. However, this is not entirely correct (cf. Ibarretxe-Antuñano 2012: 257; cf. also footnote 6).
9 Lutz (1987: 308) expressed the same ideas in her research on emotions of Ifaluk people (Micronesia): "[T]he dichotomous categories of 'cognition' and 'affect' are themselves Euroamerican cultural constructions."

2.1 Kilivila

A good example is Kilivila, an aboriginal Austronesian language spoken in the Trobriand Islands (Papua New Guinea), which, from a European perspective, has extremely unusual conceptualizations of body parts and internal organs. Cultural anthropologist Bronisław Kasper Malinowski carried out intensive field research on the island of Kiriwira, in the years 1915–1919, and managed to collect a large number of figurative units, including numerous magical formulae, and made them available in translation.

For the discussion of the somatic idioms, Malinowski's investigations on body-part terminology of the Trobriand Islanders are of great interest. The linguistic data presented in his famous book, *Argonauts of the Western Pacific* (1922), are fundamentally different from what was later written about European somatisms. His knowledge on how Trobriand Islanders speak about body and mind as well as his ethnophysical theory about the body and its role in emotions, knowledge, thoughts, memory, etc., however, received little attention on the part of phraseology research. In new field research, in the 1980s, Gunter Senft once again investigated the peculiarities of the Kilivila language, including the body-part terminology, and fully confirmed Malinowski's results.[10] The following quotation gives an insight into the way in which intellectual activities are conceptualized either by LARYNX or by BELLY, in the idioms of Kilivila:

> The mind, *nanola*, by which term intelligence, power of discrimination, capacity for learning magical formulae, and all forms of non-manual skill are described, as well as moral qualities, resides somewhere in the larynx. [...]. The memory, however, the store of formulae and traditions learned by heart, resides deeper, in the belly. A man will be said to have a good *nanola*, when he can acquire many formulae, but though they enter through the larynx, naturally, as he learns them, repeating word for word, he has to stow them away in a bigger and more commodious receptacle; they sink down right to the bottom of his abdomen.
>
> (Malinowski 1922: 316)

The Kilivila speakers have two body-based concepts that are located in different body parts and relate to different layers of intellectual activity. One of these concepts is located somewhere in the larynx – it comes close to what Europeans call "mind". In addition, there is a "deeper" concept, which is stored in the belly/abdomen – it is similar to what is understood in the Western world by "memory".

---

10 Compare Senft (1986, 1998), especially his "Appendix A: Kilivila body-part terms" (Senft 1998: 94–96) and "Appendix B: Speaking idiomatically about the body and the mind in Kilivila" (Senft 1998: 97–104).

This concept manifests itself in a series of idioms, in which words related to 'larynx', the central organ of voice and speech, are made into meanings like 'mind', 'intelligence', 'idea' or 'wants' (Senft 1998: 94, 100–104). Conversely, words for 'speech defect' stand for 'stupidity' (Senft 1998: 100). From a cultural point of view, this area of the mental activities is the more important, because it allows Trobriand islanders to memorize and fix in the mind the world of magical formulae that is central to their culture.[11] The "store of formulae and traditions" and the ability "to acquire many formulae" referred to in this passage leads us to the function of these idioms in the society and culture of the Trobriand Islanders.

2.2 Basque

Another example of unique conceptualizations comes from Basque, an isolate spoken in several varieties on both sides of the Western Pyrenees. Basque is the only remaining language of the oldest attainable stratum of Southwest European languages. Until the last century, it was used predominantly in oral communication and its written tradition is relatively young (older writings originated almost exclusively in a religious context). Basque has always been in contact with other languages and cultures, and indeed has been influenced by the dominant philosophical and religious movements throughout history. Nevertheless, the language has preserved some outstanding concepts, as outlined in the works of Ibarretxe-Antuñano (2008a, 2012). Her studies on external and internal body-part related concepts in Basque unveil certain conceptualizations that are deeply entrenched in this language and unparalleled in other European languages.

A dichotomy between the rational and irrational sides of the body as two separate entities is not unknown in Basque (i.e. BURU 'head' as the seat of intellect and BIHOTZ 'heart' as the seat of emotions) but is regarded as affected by global influences (Ibarretxe-Antuñano 2012: 266). In contrast, there is the concept GOGO which comprises both intellect and emotions and is truly unique to Basque. It is described "as a kind of 'primitive (irrational) thought', that is, an intellectual reasoning process based on intuition and emotion" (Ibarretxe-Antuñano 2008a: 122).

---

[11] Malinowski (1922: 317) reports how one of his informants answered the question whether he had any more magic formulas to produce. "With pride, he struck his belly several times, and answered: 'Plenty more lies there!' I at once checked his statement by an independent informant, and learned that everybody carries his magic in his abdomen."

Examples show the wide scope of meanings of GOGO in Basque figurative lexical units. On the one hand, intellect and thought can be to the fore, comparable to the functions of HEAD in other languages, as in the expressions *gogo argi* "gogo light" 'bright mind', *gogamen* 'intelligence', *gogoeta* 'thought' or *gogo-an izan* "gogo-LOC be.PFV" 'to remember'. On the other hand, emotions and feelings can be the focus, similar to functions of HEART, cf. Basque *gogoalai* "gogo.happy" 'jovial, cheerful', *gogo-a berotu* "gogo-ABS heat.PFV" 'to encourage', *gogo-ak izan* "gogo-ABS.PL have.PFV" 'to feel like', *gogohandi* "gogo.big" 'magnanimous, generous' and the like (cf. Ibarretxe-Antuñano 2012: 266–267).

> These examples show that *gogo* harmoniously unites these two apparent contrary concepts in one; in a way, *gogo* is a kind of *primitive thought* or *rational soul*, where there is an intellectual reasoning process, but one based on intuition and emotion; or to put it in another way, an intellectual reasoning process prior to any distinctions between feelings and thought – which, in fact, implies that reason and feelings are not differentiated at all.
> (Ibarretxe-Antuñano 2012: 267)

The old pre-Indo-European Basque tongue at the edge of Europe seems to preserve a unique "pre-Cartesian" worldview, since there are no parallels to the GOGO concept in languages other than Basque. However, this is surprising only against the background of the European standard languages investigated so far, whose images and conceptualizations are very similar to each other. Within the vast amount of literature on idioms containing somatic constituents, no attention has been paid to the peculiarity of Basque figurative language, as is also the case with phenomena demonstrated by the body-part terminology of Kilivila and other Aboriginal languages. This leads us to the next section.

3 Conceptual Metaphors and "Universality"

The so-called "universality" of conceptual metaphors, as supposed by Lakoff's "Cognitive Metaphor Theory" (e.g. Lakoff and Johnson 1980; Lakoff 1987), is one of to the principles of figurative language, which for a short time were regarded as irrefutable. It has been argued that certain particularly typical metaphors can be found in all languages and cultures. This assumption has been ascribed to the concept of "embodiment", the idea that body experiences underlie a number of conceptual metaphors, and to the sameness of human beings and their same physiological mode of operation across different cultures. However, these metaphors, postulated as ubiquitous, if not universal were discussed especially from an Anglocentric viewpoint and only on the basis of a small number of languages.

This theory, which was innovative at the time, has undoubtedly promoted the study of figurative language, but it has also drawn criticism from various sides. This is not the place to expand on this. Rather, some works on lesser-used, culturally distant languages which clearly disprove the universal character of these metaphors should be examined. These studies have been almost completely disregarded in traditional research on metaphors and figurative language.

3.1 TIME IS NATURE

A linguistic community which belongs geographically to Europe disproves the idea of "universal" metaphors. This language is Inari Saami, a declining minority language on the edge of Northern Europe, which does not fit into the system of widespread conceptual metaphors but displays completely independent images. The works on the phraseology of Inari Saami, a Uralic language spoken by about 350 people in Northern Finland, are of particular importance to the history of European phraseology. It was the Idiom Dictionary of Inari Saami (Idström and Morottaja 2006) which for the first time documented the figurative language of an indigenous population in its originality; it was followed by several other publications (Idström 2010, 2011, 2012).

The merit of this pioneering work is, on the one hand, the description of the methods used to make the older speakers of Inari Saami remember the authentic figurative expressions. On the other hand, results have been achieved for the theory of phraseology and metaphor research. The study shows that Inari Saami has its own conceptual metaphors – also created at a more concrete level – from the previous living conditions of an indigenous population which have no parallels in all other European languages studied so far. We will restrict ourselves to the well-known metaphoric model TIME IS MONEY and its parallels in Inari Saami.

According to Idström (2010), the traditional Inari Saami culture was polychronic. A metaphor such as TIME IS MONEY would have no place in the figurative language of the Saami.[12] Their culture was fundamentally different from that of most other societies in Europe. It was based on fishing, hunting and reindeer-husbandry in the harsh conditions of Lapland. Until the 1900s, the lifestyle of the Inari Saami community was determined not by the calendar but by the course of the seasons, the knowledge of nature and animal behavior. The Saami made every endeavor to predict the weather and timed their actions according to it.

---

12 Mueller (2015) discusses examples of other languages where the TIME IS MONEY metaphor did not exist but gained ground due to the "Westernization" of traditional non-Western cultures.

There was no preset schedule for determining actions such as fishing and hunting. It was important to know as exactly as possible what the weather and the snow conditions would be like.

> Time was not as strikingly objectified as in modern post-industrial cultures where the TIME IS MONEY conceptual metaphor seems to be prevalent. Traditional Inari Saami time was mainly contextual, not a centre of attention, and definitely not something worth money. Logically, the linguistic Inari Saami metaphors describe time systematically as nature or as something that happens in nature.
>
> (Idström 2010: 174)

The timing of human action was based on observations in the natural environment and spontaneous reactions to these observations. Based on a number of Inari Saami idioms, the author has reconstructed the conceptual metaphor TIME IS NATURE. For example, the 'beginning of autumn' is denoted by *riemnjis kamâs-iiðis koco* "fox is hanging up his legs" (as if the red leaves on the trees were the fox's legs or socks hung on the trees by him), and the 'period of the ongoing winter' is called *taan muottuu ääigi* "during the time of this snow" (SNOW referring metonymically to the time when the snow is on the ground).

In sum, the conceptual metaphor TIME IS NATURE is appropriate for the traditional polychronic Saami society, connected with the lifestyle in the arctic environment. This metaphor has no parallels in the hitherto analyzed standard European languages. This does not mean that it could not occur in other languages, for example, in languages of the Arctic region with the same climatic conditions (such as Komi or Tundra Nenets). However, any kind of investigation is lacking.

3.2 UNDERSTANDING IS HEARING

Other examples are the conceptual metaphors UNDERSTANDING IS SEEING and KNOWING IS SEEING, respectively, which are found in the standard European languages that have been examined so far, both in idioms[13] and in individual words, especially verbs of seeing (cf. *you see?* meaning 'do you understand?'). This metaphor has attracted the interest of Lakoff and Johnson (1980) and several of their successors. Perhaps the best known is the study by Sweetser (1990). Although her

---

13 Compare, for example, widespread idioms like *to bring something to light* 'to make something known that others would prefer remained unknown', *behind someone's back* 'without knowledge of another person': light is required for seeing and recognizing things in the environment, and what is behind someone's back remains hidden, therefore unknown (Piirainen 2016: 417, 485).

investigation is not concerned with idioms, her analysis of the semantic extension of perception verbs is highly regarding the above-mentioned metaphors.

Sweetser (1990) hypothesizes that vision has primacy, due to the human cognitive structure and the metaphorical and cultural aspects of this structure. Therefore, verbs of higher intellection, such as *to know* and *to think* are recruited from verbs of *seeing*. She suggests that verbs meaning 'to hear' would not take on these readings – an assumption which in her opinion applies to all languages and cultures. According to Sweetser, the meaning-extension from SEEING to KNOWING and, accordingly the metaphor UNDERSTANDING/KNOWING IS SEEING are universals.

The primacy of SIGHT has been questioned several times. Clear criticism came from Ibarretxe-Antuñano already in 1999, when she rejected this idea of "universality" – among other things – on the basis of Basque (cf. especially Ibarretxe-Antuñano 2008b). Looking at languages of distant cultures is particularly helpful in this context. Evans and Wilkins' (2000) study on perception verbs in Australian Aboriginal languages must be mentioned here. Based on the material of more than 60 languages, these hypothetical universals have been clearly disproved. It is exactly the opposite: Australian languages gain verbs of cognition like *to think* and *to know* from verbs meaning 'to hear', and not 'to see'. It can be inferred that the allegedly universal metaphorical concept UNDERSTANDING IS SEEING has no place in these languages but is replaced by UNDERSTANDING IS HEARING. Evans and Wilkins (2000: 580–586) provide convincing social and cultural reasons for the semantic extension of HEARING to KNOWING and THINKING in Australian Aboriginal societies, pointing to the role of oracy vs. literacy in privileging hearing in nonwriting cultures as opposed to sight in literate cultures.

Similar results also come from other regions of the world. Among the few works on metaphors in remote, non-Western languages that are available so far, some other languages have been found to be unfamiliar with the metaphor UNDERSTANDING IS SEEING. Let us look at Flathead Salish, a critically endangered American Indian variety in Montana, USA. Among the Salish metaphors collected by Sherris et al. (2015) the concept of UNDERSTANDING IS HEARING clearly emerges. Sherris et al. (2015: 122) point to the cultural weight given to SEEING or HEARING as a means of understanding and point to the orality of Salish as cause of the difference: "[I]n Salish culture, more importance is given to oral traditions, while in cultures that primarily speak English, more importance is often given to written traditions. However more data points would be required from other languages to make this assertion definitively."

The similarity of English metaphorical schemes with those of many other European languages and their absence in distant non-Western languages has long been pointed out by anthropological work on metaphors (cf. Keesing 1985). It has recently been confirmed by further research on lesser-used non-European languages, be it metaphors for DEATH in Māori (J. King 2015), TASTE metaphors in minor Papua New Guinean languages (P. King 2015) or body-based EMOTION metaphors in Safaliba (Schaefer 2015), a declining language spoken in Ghana. According to Schaefer (2015: 93)

> it seems prudent not to adhere too strongly to proposed "universals" unless they are supported by field research from diverse language families worldwide. Until a great many studies of conceptual metaphors are done on lesser-known languages, we will not even know what questions to ask about what such "universals" might really look like.

4 Pragmatic Functions

What has already been mentioned in sections 2 and 3 also applies to the pragmatic functions of the phrasemes: the European standard languages examined so far also appear remarkably consistent in this field. Pragmatics has long been a popular subject of phraseology. The numerous publications on this topic refer to general discussions within the framework of a theory valid for all current languages, and not to contrastive approaches that would elaborate interlingual differences.

The pragmatic functions attributed to phrasemes, especially to idioms, are of varied nature. Older traditional phraseology research regarded the "semantic surplus value" and the associated "higher expressivity" (Kühn 1985), later also the "communicative" or "connotative surplus value" as prominent features of phrasemes in contrast to non-phraseological word combinations. Later these views were qualified; it was found that a large number of idioms are rather unmarked in terms of their pragmatic, stylistic or connotative functions. Other pragmatic functions of idioms, well-known in many languages, consist of euphemistic allusions, often used in a humorous mental detour instead of directly naming what is meant (e.g. negative issues). But this is not the point here; we only want to note that European phraseology research has revealed no serious differences in the pragmatic behavior of phrasemes among the diversity of languages investigated so far.

The results would be different if historical linguistic layers were included. For example, didactic and educational or morally warning functions of paroemia and adages would play a much larger role (see, for example, Hallik 2007). Quite different dimensions of pragmatics can be observed if distant minority languages – far from the Western cultural area and used predominantly in oral form – are included. Several publications on figurative and formal language of non-European lesser-used varieties provide us with examples. We limit ourselves here to three complexes of pragmatic functions, which are distinctly different from the uniformity of the current European languages.[14]

4.1 "Secret Languages"

The first complex is intertwined with the veiling functions of euphemistic expressions, as they are known in the European languages as well, but which manifest themselves in a very different way. Recently, a few studies on endangered languages – mainly of the East Asia-Pacific region – have emerged which demonstrate the disguising potential of entire speech systems. What is interesting for the study of phraseology is the fact that these "secret languages" consist of idioms in the traditional sense, but the figurative expressions (used to veil tabooed concepts) are more obscure and occur in an abundance that permeates the entire language system: only insiders know the code; for outsiders, the language is incomprehensible.

Karl J. Franklin's outstanding work on Kewa (e.g. Franklin 1972, 1977, 2003, 2012) should be mentioned here as a representative of other studies. Franklin reports on different categories of veiled language such as *tabooed speech, intimate speech, ritualized speech, coded speech as warning and prohibition*, and *saa agaa*, the most salient and prototypical example of "veiled language":

> *Saa agaa* occurs in a variety of modes whose codes are interpreted according to the cultural communication setting. Although disguised speech is most often spoken, it may be shouted as a warning (*puri pane agaa*), a challenge (*yada malue agaa*), interpreted from song [...], expressed in courting (*remani agaa*), or even whispered (*mumu agaa*). The overall purpose and role of disguised speech is to leave the hearer with a certain amount of bewilderment, so it would defeat its purpose if the communication was completely transparent and not subject to interpretations.
>
> (Franklin 2012: 192)

---

[14] A unique function of formulas in non-written indigenous languages must be disregarded here for reasons of space. It is formulaicity as a prop in the memorization of oral literature. As Riesenberg and Fischer (1955: 9) put it for Ponapean (Micronesia), various stereotyped figures of speech "seem to be used solely as mnemonic devices for recalling the legends or lore to which they are attached [...]" – a function that connects them with literature of classical antiquity: mnemotechnical support has also been ascribed to the abundance of formulas in the Homeric poems (e.g. Lardinois 2001; Minchin 2001; Sale 2001).

An example is the Kewa idiom *rigi-areke lapo rata madi-ta aa*. It is glossed as "bamboo.knife1-2 two both carry-3.sg.prf man" and translated literally as "(be careful of) a man carrying both the *rigi* and *arege* bamboo knives". The figurative meaning discloses itself only if one knows the code and its components. The idiom is veiled because *one knife* would be adequate and here the figure of speech implies that if *two* are used the man is showy or pretentious, perhaps not to be trusted. The knives are codes for the inferred metaphorical characteristics of certain kinds of people (Franklin 2012: 191f.). Understanding such coding is a prerequisite for interpreting the Kewa metaphorical and pragmatic system.

Noteworthy are also other forms of the highly idiomatic tabooed Kewa language which are used almost exclusively by men, members of a particular group, while they are preparing for a cult or carrying out other kinds of joint works. A well-researched subcategory is the so-called *pandanus language*.[15] It is a secret contrived linguistic system which is used by men when they traditionally camp in the forest to harvest the pandanus nuts. Many ordinary Kewa expressions must be avoided and replaced by codes. "For example, when they took their dogs on such trips, the owners gave them a derisive and idiomatic name that was 'magical', following a code often found in 'disguised speech'" (Franklin 2012: 193). This is probably due to the idea that spirits in the deep forest of the mountains should not be disturbed by profane, non-ritual language.

4.2 "Authority"

4.2.1 Terminological Problem

Other complexes of pragmatic functions we want to look at are grouped around the aspect of "authority", which has been attributed to figurative and formulaic expressions. A high appreciation of proverbs – they were regarded as an embodiment of general truth – has been proved for several epochs of linguistic history and diverse regions and is still alive in some small speech communities around the world. The literature on the figurative aspects of lesser-used languages outside Europe gives many examples. However, a terminological problem must first be considered. Most languages do not distinguish between proverbs and related

---

[15] Cf. Franklin's (1972) detailed study on the Kewa pandanus language. Similar observations come from Kalam, a small language spoken in the Papua New Guinea Highlands: there, a special "'Pandanus Language' is used in the forest when on expeditions to harvest and eating pandanus nuts and when hunting or eating cassowaries" (Pawley 1993: 117).

elements of oral folklore. Often the same word applies to proverb, moral story, parable, riddle, and the like. In many publications, "wise words" is used as a generic term for these kinds of figurative speech. Deputizing for others let us look at Keith Basso's famous book entitled *"Wise Words" of the Western Apache*. Wise words are a "distinctive speech genre associated with adult men and women who have gained a reputation for balanced thinking, critical acumen, and extensive cultural knowledge" (Basso 1976: 99).[16]

"Wise words" may be used by the native speakers themselves, however, usually along with a differentiated terminology of the figurative expressions of their languages. Finnegan (1970: 390) gives examples of African languages:

> The Fulani term *mallol* for instance, means not only a proverb but also allusion in general, and is especially used when there is some deep hidden meaning in a proverb different from the obvious one. Similarly with the Kamba term *ndimo*. This does not exactly correspond to our term "proverb" but is its nearest equivalent, and really means a "dark saying" or "metaphorical wording", a sort of secret and allusive language.

We cannot go into every detail of manifestations of "proverbs" in the distant language communities which seem odd to us: proverbs can occur in chants, they can be sung, but can also be drummed: a very special category is created by the drum proverbs among Bantu ethnicities in Cameroon, which are performed by striking sequences on the wooden slotted drum (Piper 1989). All this seems to distinguish the concept of "proverb" in these languages clearly from its European counterpart. The terminological problem, therefore, must always be kept in mind when evaluating the functions of formulaic and figurative units of lesser-used languages outside the Western cultural area. What is referred to by "proverb" in these publications does not correspond to the definitions of *proverb* in European linguistics.[17]

These considerations are not trivial: they emphasize that the terms defined by European phraseology researchers are not valid worldwide, precisely in view of the prevalent orality of the languages considered here. If a term such as *proverb* is discussed or defined, the addition should always be made "this only applies to the standard languages that have been examined so far".

---

16 Cf. also the discussion on the definition of *proverb* against the background of African languages by Hansford (2003).
17 This reminds us of Grigory Permyakov's much discussed theories in his "Grammar of proverbial wisdom" (Пермяков 1979) which state: As a sign, the proverbs belong to language and as models to folklore (i.e. as cultural models they belong to the literature of folkloric provenance).

4.2.2 Authority as Judicial Argumentation

Let us return to the pragmatic functions grouped around the "authority" of proverbs and related figures of speech. As mentioned above, the purposes of using proverbs and other formulaic units are manifold, ranging from all kinds of rhetorical and didactic intensions to magical functions in performing rituals and ceremonies. The educational function is probably one of the most important.[18] Let us look at a function which, from a European perspective, seems to be uncommon: the use of proverbs as a part of legal procedure, as a method of gaining favor in court, as it is reported from several African ethnicities. There is an early contribution (Messenger 1959) on the Anang people (Nigeria). In the tribunals and hearings of the Native Court proverbs were skillfully introduced and influenced the actual decisions. From Gillian Hansford's investigations of the language of Chumburung people (Ghana) it can be seen that the practice of obtaining advantages with the help of proverbs is still common in present-day African speech communities (Hansford 2003: 73–75).

An episode from an Anang court negotiation described by Messenger (1959: 68–69) may serve as an example. It is about a notorious thief, who was again charged with theft. The plaintiff aroused antagonism towards the defendant by quoting the proverb *If a dog plucks palm fruits from a cluster, he does not fear a porcupine*. The rhetorical intention was to say that a chronic thief like the accused would not be afraid to steal time and again, just like a dog which can deal with the sharp needles of the palm fruit: it would be unafraid even of the porcupine's prickles. But that is not all, for the accused reacts with another proverb: *A single partridge flying through the bush leaves no path*.

> In using this proverb the accused likened himself to a single bird, without sympathizers to lend him support, and called upon the tribunal to disregard the sentiments of those in attendance and to overlook his past misdemeanors and judge the case as objectively as possible.
>
> (Messenger 1959: 69)

Both proverbs took a prominent place as authorities for the judicial decision – a function which is hardly conceivable in court negotiations in the West.

---

18 Taha (2011: 1) reports for Dongolawi Nubian, an endangered language spoken in Sudan, that "proverbs, often performed by the elderly, provide guidance, particularly to the young speakers. They generally recommend the adaption of the soundest course of action in life (as it pertains to the Nubian culture), and they warn of the consequences of bad and/or unreasonable choices."

4.2.3 Authority of Proverbial Knowledge

Let us conclude this section with another aspect of "authority", i.e. the fact that the use of proverbs and idioms can assume a completely different status of a person from that which would have been assumed from the viewpoint of standard European languages that have been researched so far. There is a remarkable article by the anthropologist Firth (1926) on Maori proverbs. Firth (1926) was one of the first to emphasize the need to take into account the context in which a proverb is used. His results included the observation of great authority attributed to the use of proverbial utterances. He reports that the ancestors of a Maori, particularly if men of high rank, were deeply venerated and great stress laid upon their last proverbial words on the deathbed:

> [...] they were quoted for years or even generations afterwards. From this, it is evident that the opinion expressed in any proverb, especially if known to have been uttered by some dead chief of high renown, was a matter of grave import, representing as it did the words and authority of the venerated past.
>
> (Firth 1926: 257–258)

Another example comes from Bété, one of the endangered languages spoken in the Ivory Coast (Zouogbo 2015). Bété figurative units are deeply rooted in the culture of Bété people, in their ideas of cosmogony and in oral narrative traditions.

Various expressions are based on "intertextuality", as they summarize the gist and moral of a well-known narrative. It is established that in for literary languages a large number of phrasemes originate from once well-known texts. The fact that this also applies to languages without a literary tradition may be surprising. However, here it is not written texts, but narrations, reports or legends of once important events which are passed down by word of mouth and provide the basis for figurative expressions in a series of lesser-used languages.

The use of figurative expressions is associated with particular social functions, as Zouogbo (2015) vividly explained. If someone presents a thought with the help of an idiom or a proverb, he shows that he is well acquainted with traditional culture. This, in turn, gives him recognition, power, and authority. For example, in order to be eligible for appointment as a village elder in a village community, the person concerned must prove that he has a full command of figurative expressions. Thus, transmitting a message by means of an idiom or a proverb indicates not only language competence but also knowledge of the traditional culture and therefore means authority.

These functions of idioms and proverbs differ significantly from those known in societies with literary traditions. Further studies on languages of preliterate communities are urgently needed to gain an overall picture of the occurrences and manifestations of phrasemes and formulas, not just based on a narrowly limited selection of languages (cf. the quotation from Nettle and Romain in the following section).

5 Concluding Remarks

In their remarkable book of 2000, *Vanishing Voices. The Extinction of the World's Languages*, Daniel Nettle and Suzanne Romaine report most vividly the extent to which the extinction of languages affects mankind's cultural knowledge of mankind. At the same time, the authors generally criticize linguistics, which does not seem to be interested in this cultural loss, and by no means tackles the investigation and documentation of endangered languages. The authors use a suitable comparison to illustrate the deficiency of linguistic research on more exotic languages:

> Linguists need to study as many different languages as possible if they are to perfect their *theories of language structure* and to train future generations of students in linguistic analysis. [...] *New and exciting discoveries* about language are still being made. There is every reason to believe that what we know now is but the tip of the iceberg. [...] Satisfying answers to many current puzzles about languages and their origins will not emerge until linguists have studied many languages. To exclude exotic languages from our study is *like expecting botanists to study only florist shop roses and greenhouse tomatoes and then tell us what the plant world is like.*
>
> (Nettle and Romaine 2000: 11; italics by E.P.)

Nettle and Romaine do not refer explicitly to phraseology or to studies of figurative and formulaic language in a broad sense. But how much more would their appeal apply to these areas! By analogy with the *theories of language structure* mentioned, the knowledge of the present theory of phraseology is founded on only a small fraction of the world's languages, on a very one-sided, limited material basis comparable to *the florist shop roses and greenhouse tomatoes* in Nettle and Romaine's figure of speech. As mentioned at the beginning, languages used only orally, minority languages of distant continents, as well as oral versions of otherwise well studied European languages, have been almost completely excluded from the study of phraseology. However, the few studies on the latter varieties have brought about *new and exciting discoveries*, to use Nettle and Romaine's phrase.

This article is therefore also an appeal to free phraseology, through new research approaches based on new, empirically obtained speech data, from the restriction of its own choosing. This appeal has two objectives: to incorporate both endangered minority languages and all modes of oral languages more intensely than hitherto into phraseology's research spectrum.

Concerning the first objective: In my opinion, it is the greatest task of contemporary linguistics to examine figurative and formulaic expressions of the endangered languages worldwide before they are lost forever in the near future. Figurative units of a language are vulnerable. All declining minor languages should be seen as cases of extreme urgency: the documentation of their idioms and formulas should be started immediately when a language becomes potentially endangered, be it under the pressure of a more dominant major standard language or endangered by other factors. "In such a situation metaphors and figurative nuances are the first to vanish, even if the language continues to exist" (Idström and Piirainen 2012: 18). The benefit of such studies for phraseology, linguistics and cultural sciences is obvious.

In the last few years, there has been a growth of research interest in linguistic diversity and declining minor languages; for some of them it was possible to record figurative elements in their originality, as shown above with individual examples. But for other regions of the world this is an impossible task. This is particularly evident in Aboriginal Australia. According to Evans (2007), language loss is more accelerated than in any other continent, with a 95 percent extinction rate expected to be reached during the course of the coming decades. Miller (2013: 405) speaks of at least 228 Indigenous languages in Australia, for which much work remains to be done with regard to figurative language. Such investigation needs to be conducted sensitively and with the help of competent native speakers.[19] Most of these languages will become extinct without their figurative expressions being recorded. Although this situation is regrettable, other projects could be carried out with ease, even in previously unexplored European language varieties.

Concerning the second objective: Phraseology research in recent decades has increasingly been oriented towards the written language. That was not always the case. Harald Burger (1979) reports on a project of the University of Zurich from the early days of Germanist phraseology research, when empirical data had to be collected in order to gain theoretical insights. Half of the data had to consist of written texts, and the other half of tape-recorded, oral texts. Even these initial research approaches yielded their own results, including the finding that idioms

---

19 Personal communication (April 18, 2017) by Julia Miller, Adelaide, president of AustraLex.

show a great variability in oral communication, a phenomenon that was to be "rediscovered" decades later – by the analysis of large text corpora.[20]

Already the first works on varieties, dialects and colloquial languages handed down orally, including that of Luxembourg, which was distinguished by its dialectal origin and the predominance of the oral domain, showed deviations from the hitherto established theories, e.g. regarding the stability or variability of idioms, the so-called anthropocentrism, usage restrictions of idioms (among them gender restrictions which are due to certain images), as well as specific pragmatic functions of conventional word plays, all of which up to that time had not been known to this extent. These results were recorded in the articles of the Handbook on Phraseology (HSK, Burger et al. 2007).[21]

The collection of linguistic data by means of survey research, that is, surveys of native speakers into their phraseological competence, proved to have an unimaginable advantage over research using exclusively written language data: it is not possible to ask the producers of written texts about their intention, e.g. whether they have used an idiom ironically or jokingly.

For some time now, phraseology, also on the part of the younger generation of researchers, has experienced a remarkable upswing. "New empirical data" are particularly in demand, which means corpus linguistic analysis. This, however, means not only a renunciation of all the oral phenomena of language, but also a further, self-imposed restriction of the linguistic material basis, not only to the literary language in general (the only possibility in the case of dead languages) but to a special kind of text, namely, the language of the press, which is currently dominant in the corpora of literary languages.

In contrast, all areas of the oral use of phrasemes are completely untapped. In German colloquial language alone, hundreds of idioms are in circulation, which have mostly penetrated the regional everyday language from local dialects, but which have not been lexicographically recorded at any point. The same applies to figurative lexicon units of all dialects and minority languages worldwide. Thus, this paper should be seen as an appeal to carry out new fundamental empirical research and to make greater use of linguistic reality, which can be achieved not only on the basis of written language corpora, but also by relevant information provided by the members of a speech community themselves, thereby expanding the theoretical framework of phraseology.

---

[20] Examples of variability of orally used idioms are open patterns like *not all X in the Y* meaning 'not to be in one's mind', which can even be regarded as the beginning of construction grammar (Burger 1979: 96–97).
[21] Cf. Moulin and Filatkina (2007); Piirainen (2007); Schmidlin (2007).

References

Allardt, Erik (1984): What constitutes a language minority? *Journal of Multilingual and Multicultural Development* 5, 195–205.

Austin, Peter K. & Julia Sallabank (eds.) (2011): *The Cambridge Handbook of Endangered Languages*. Cambridge, UK: Cambridge University Press.

Basso, Keith H. (1976): 'Wise Words' of the Western Apache: Metaphors and Semantic theory. In Keith H. Basso & Henry A. Selby (eds.), *Meaning in Anthropology*, 93–121. Albuquerque: University of New Mexico Press.

Burger, Harald (1979): Phraseologie und gesprochene Sprache. In Heinrich Löffler, Karl Pestalozzi & Martin Stern (Hrsg.), *Standard und Dialekt. Studien zur gesprochenen und geschriebenen Sprache. Festschrift für Heinz Rupp zum 60. Geburtstag*, 89–103. Bern, München: Francke.

Burger, Harald, Dmitrij Dobrovol'skij, Peter Kühn & Neal R. Norrick (eds.) (2007): *Phraseology. An International Handbook of Contemporary Research*. Berlin, New York: De Gruyter.

Dobrovol'skij, Dmitrij & Elisabeth Piirainen (2005): *Figurative Language: Cross-cultural and Cross-linguistic Perspectives*. Amsterdam, Philadelphia: Elsevier.

Evans, Nicholas (2007): Warramurrungunji undone: Australian languages in the 51st Millennium. In Peter K. Austin & Andrew Simpson (eds.), *Endangered Languages*. Linguistische Berichte Sonderheft 14, 19–44. Hamburg: Buske.

Evans, Nicholas (2010): *Dying Words: Endangered Languages and What They Have to Tell Us*. Oxford: Wiley-Blackwell.

Evans, Nicholas & David Wilkins (2000): In the mind's ear. The semantic extensions of perception verbs in Australian languages. *Language* 76, 546–592.

Finnegan, Ruth (1970): *Oral Literature in Africa*. Oxford: Clarendon Press.

Firth, Raymond (1926): Proverbs in the native life with particular reference to those of the Maori. *Folklore* 37, 135–153 and 245–270.

Fishman, Joshua A. (1991): *Reversing Language Shift: Theory and Practice of Assistance to Threatened Languages*. Clevedon, UK: Multilingual Matters.

Flores Farfán, Antonio José & Fernando Ramallo (eds.) (2010): *New Perspectives on Endangered Languages. Bridging gaps between sociolinguistics, documentation and language revitalization*. Amsterdam, Philadelphia: John Benjamins.

Franklin, Karl J. (1972): A ritual pandanus language of New Guinea. *Oceania* 43, 66–76.

Franklin, Karl J. (1977): The Kewa language in culture and society. In Stephen A. Wurm (ed.), *New Guinea area languages and languages study*, Volume 3: *Language, culture, society and the modern world*, 5–18. Canberra: Australian National University.

Franklin, Karl J. (2003): Tagmemic Insights on Kewa. Numbers and Names. In Mary Ruth Wise, Thomas N. Headland & Ruth Brend (eds.), *Language and Life. Essays in Memory of Kenneth J. Pike*, 247–261. Dallas, Texas: SIL International and University of Texas at Arlington.

Franklin, Karl J. (2012): Kewa figures of speech: understanding the code. In Anna Idström & Elisabeth Piirainen (eds.), *Endangered Metaphors*, 185–204. Amsterdam, Philadelphia: John Benjamins.

Hale, Ken, Michael Krauss, Lucille J. Watahomigie, Akira Y. Yamamoto, Colette Craig, LaVerne Masayesva Jeanne & Nora C. England (1992): Endangered languages. *Language* 68, 1–42.

Hallik, Sibylle (2007): *Sententia und Proverbium. Begriffsgeschichte und Texttheorie in Antike und Mittelalter*. Köln: Böhlau.

Hansford, Gillian F. (2003): Understanding Chumburung Proverbs. *Journal of West African Languages* 30 (1), 57–82.
Harrison, David K. (2007): *When Languages Die: The Extinction of the World's Languages and the Erosion of Human Knowledge.* New York: Oxford University Press.
Harrison, David K. (2010): *The Last Speakers. The Quest to Save the World's Most Endangered Languages.* Washington, D.C.: National Geographic.
Hasada, Rie (2002): "Body part" terms and emotion in Japanese. *Pragmatics & Cognition* 10, 107–128.
Ibarretxe-Antuñano, Iraide (1999): *Polysemy and Metaphor in Perception Verbs: A Cross-linguistic Study.* Unpublished Ph.D. thesis. University of Edinburgh.
Ibarretxe-Antuñano, Iraide (2008a): Guts, heart, and liver: The conceptualisation of internal organs in Basque. In Farzad Sharifian, René Dirven, Ning Yu & Susanne Niemeier (eds.), *Culture, Body, and Language. Conceptualizations of Internal Body Organs across Cultures and Languages*, 103–128. Berlin, New York: De Gruyter.
Ibarretxe-Antuñano, Iraide (2008b): Vision metaphors for the intellect: Are they really crosslinguistic? *Atlantis* 30 (1), 15–33.
Ibarretxe-Antuñano, Iraide (2012): The importance of unveiling conceptual metaphors in a minority language: The case of Basque. In Anna Idström & Elisabeth Piirainen (eds.), *Endangered Metaphors*, 253–273. Amsterdam, Philadelphia: John Benjamins.
Idström, Anna (2010): What Inari Saami idioms reveal about the time concept of the indigenous people of Inari. *Yearbook of Phraseology* 1, 159–177.
Idström, Anna (2011): Inari Saami metaphors of hunger. In Antonio Pamies & Dmitrij Dobrovol'skij (eds.), *Linguo-Cultural Competence and Phraseological Motivation*, 335–340. Baltmannsweiler: Schneider Verlag Hohengehren.
Idström, Anna (2012): Antlers as a metaphor of pride. What idioms reveal about the relationship between human and animal in Inari Saami conceptual system. In Anna Idström & Elisabeth Piirainen (eds.), *Endangered Metaphors*, 275–292. Amsterdam, Philadelphia: John Benjamins.
Idström, Anna & Hans Morottaja (2006): *Inarinsaamen idiomisanakirja* [Idiom dictionary of Inari Saami]. Inari: Sämitigge.
Idström, Anna & Elisabeth Piirainen (eds.) (2012): *Endangered Metaphors.* Amsterdam, Philadelphia: John Benjamins.
Keesing, Roger M. (1985): Conventional metaphors and anthropological metaphysics. *Journal of Anthropological Research* 41, 201–217.
King, Jeanette (2015): Metaphors we die by: change and vitality in Māori. In Elisabeth Piirainen & Ari Sherris (eds.), *Language Endangerment. Disappearing Metaphors and Shifting Conceptualizations*, 15–35. Amsterdam, Philadelphia: John Benjamins.
King, Phil (2015): Papua New Guinean sweet talk: Metaphors from the domain of taste. In Elisabeth Piirainen & Ari Sherris (eds.), *Language Endangerment. Disappearing Metaphors and Shifting Conceptualizations*, 37–64. Amsterdam, Philadelphia: John Benjamins.
Krauss, Michael (2007): Classification and terminology for degrees of language endangerment. In Matthias Brenzinger (ed.), *Trends in linguistics, studies and monographs: language diversity endangered*, 1–8. Berlin, New York: De Gruyter.
Kühn, Peter (1985): Phraseologismen und ihr semantischer Mehrwert. *Sprache und Literatur in Wissenschaft und Unterricht* 56, 37–46.
Lakoff, George (1987): *Women, Fire, and Dangerous Things: What Categories Reveal about the Mind.* Chicago, London: The University of Chicago Press.

Lakoff, George & Mark Johnson (1980): *Metaphors We Live By*. Chicago: University of Chicago Press.
Lardinois, André (2001): The Orality of Greek Proverbial Expressions. In Janet Watson (ed.), *Speaking Volumes. Orality and Literacy in the Greek and Roman World*, 93–107. Leiden: Brill.
Lewis, Paul, Gary F. Simons & Charles D. Fennig (eds.) (2016): *Ethnologue: Languages of the world*. 17th Edition. Dallas, Texas: SIL International. Retrieved from http://ethnologue.com.
Lutz, Catherine (1987): Goals, events, and understanding in Ifaluk emotion theory. In Dorothy Holland & Naomi Quinn (eds.), *Cultural Models in Language and Thought*, 290–311. Cambridge: Cambridge University Press.
Malinowski, Bronislaw (1922): *Argonauts of the Western Pacific: An Account of Native Enterprise and Adventure in the Archipelagoes of Melanesian New Guinea*. With a Preface by James George Frazer. London: Routledge & Kegan Paul Ltd.
Matras, Yaron (2003): Defining typical features of minor languages: with reference to Domari, a minor language of the Near East. In Joel Sherzer & Thomas Stolz (eds.), *Minor Languages. Approaches, Definitions, Controversies. Papers from the conference on 'Minor Languages: Coming to grips with a suitable definition', Bremen, June 2001*, 1–14. Bochum: Brockmeyer.
Messenger, John C. (1959): The Role of Proverbs in a Nigerian Judicial System. *Southwestern Journal of Anthropology* 15, 64–73.
Miller, Julia (2013): Phraseology Across Continents. In Joanna Szerszunowicz, Bogusław Nowowiejski & Katsumasa Yagi (eds.), *Research on Phraseology across Continents*. 2nd Volume. Białystok: University of Bialystok Publishing House.
Minchin, Elizabeth (2001): Similes in Homer: Image, Mind's Eye, and Memory. In Janet Watson (ed.), *Speaking Volumes. Orality and Literacy in the Greek and Roman World*, 25–52. Leiden: Brill.
Moulin, Claudine & Natalia Filatkina (2007): Phraseology of Luxembourgish. In Harald Burger, Dmitrij Dobrovol'skij, Peter Kühn & Neal R. Norrick (eds.), *Phraseology. An International Handbook of Contemporary Research*, 645–666. Berlin, New York: De Gruyter.
Mueller, Simone (2015): Time is money – everywhere? Analysing time metaphors across varieties of English. In Elisabetta Gola & Francesca Ervas (eds.), *Metaphor and Communication*, 79–104. Amsterdam, Philadelphia: John Benjamins.
Nettle, Daniel & Suzanne Romaine (eds.) (2000): *Vanishing Voices. The Extinction of the World's Languages*. Oxford: Oxford University Press.
Pawley, Andrew (1993): A language which defies description by ordinary means. In William A. Foley (ed.), *The Role of Theory in Language Description*, 87–119. Berlin, New York: Mouton de Gruyter.
Piirainen, Elisabeth (2007): Dialectal phraseology: Linguistic aspects. In Harald Burger, Dmitrij Dobrovol'skij, Peter Kühn & Neal R. Norrick (eds.), *Phraseology. An International Handbook of Contemporary Research*, 530–540. Berlin, New York: De Gruyter.
Piirainen, Elisabeth (2016): *Lexicon of Common Figurative Units. Widespread Idioms in Europe and Beyond*. 2nd Volume. In cooperation with József Attila Balázsi. New York: Peter Lang.
Piirainen, Elisabeth & Ari Sherris (eds.) (2015): *Language Endangerment. Disappearing Metaphors and Shifting Conceptualizations*. Amsterdam, Philadelphia: John Benjamins.
Piper, Klaus (1989): Zum Sprachgebrauch in den Sprichwörtern und in der Trommelsprache der Ewondo und der Bulu. *Afrika und Übersee* 72 (1), 1–16.

Riesenberg, Saul H. & John L. Fischer (1955): Some Ponapean Proverbs. *Journal of American Folklore* 68, 9–18.

Sale, Mary (2001): The oral-formulaic theory today. In Janet Watson (ed.), *Speaking Volumes. Orality and Literacy in the Greek and Roman World*, 53–80. Leiden: Brill.

Schaefer, Paul (2015): Hot eyes, white stomach: emotions and character qualities in Safaliba metaphor. In Elisabeth Piirainen & Ari Sherris (eds.), *Language Endangerment. Disappearing Metaphors and Shifting Conceptualizations*, 91–110. Amsterdam, Philadelphia: John Benjamins.

Schmidlin, Regula (2007): Phraseme in standardsprachlichen Varietäten des Deutschen/ Phraseological expressions in German standard varieties. In Harald Burger, Dmitrij Dobrovol'skij, Peter Kühn & Neal R. Norrick. (eds.), *Phraseology. An International Handbook of Contemporary Research*, 552–562. Berlin, New York: De Gruyter.

Senft, Gunter (1986): *Kilivila. The Language of the Trobriand Islanders*. Berlin, New York: Mouton de Gruyter.

Senft, Gunter (1998): Body and the Mind in the Trobriand Islands. *Ethos* 26 (1), 73–104.

Sharifian, Farzad, René Dirven, Ning Yu & Susanne Niemeier (2008): Looking for the "mind" inside the body. In Farzad Sharifian, René Dirven, Ning Yu & Susanne Niemeier (eds.), *Culture, Body, and Language. Conceptualizations of Internal Body Organs across Cultures and Languages*, 3–23. Berlin, New York: De Gruyter.

Sharifian, Farzad, René Dirven, Ning Yu & Susanne Niemeier (eds.) (2008): *Culture, Body, and Language. Conceptualizations of Internal Body Organs across Cultures and Languages*. Berlin, New York: De Gruyter.

Sherris, Ari, Tachini Pete & Erin Haynes (2015): Literacy and language instruction: Flathead Salish metaphor and a task-based pedagogy for its revitalization. In Elisabeth Piirainen & Ari Sherris (eds.), *Language Endangerment. Disappearing Metaphors and Shifting Conceptualizations*, 109–135. Amsterdam, Philadelphia: John Benjamins.

Siahaan, Poppy (2008): Did he break your *heart* or your *liver*? A contrastive study on metaphorical concepts from the source domain organ in English and Indonesian. In Farzad Sharifian, René Dirven, Ning Yu & Susanne Niemeier (eds.), *Culture, Body, and Language. Conceptualizations of Internal Body Organs across Cultures and Languages*, 45–74. Berlin, New York: De Gruyter.

Sweetser, Eve (1990): *From Etymology to Pragmatics. Metaphorical and Cultural Aspects of Semantic Structure*. Cambridge: Cambridge University Press.

Taha, Taha A. (2011): Proverbs in a Threatened Language Variety in Africa. *California Linguistic Notes* 36 (1), 1–19.

Watson, Janet (ed.) (2001): *Speaking Volumes. Orality and Literacy in the Greek and Roman World*. Leiden: Brill.

Yu, Ning (2003) Metaphor, Body, and Culture: The Chinese Understanding of *Gallbladder* and *Courage*. *Metaphor and Symbol* 18, 13–31.

Zouogbo, Jean-Philippe (2015): Idioms and proverbs in Bete language and culture: a metaphorical analysis of their aetiology, meaning and usage. In Elisabeth Piirainen & Ari Sherris (eds.), *Language Endangerment. Disappearing Metaphors and Shifting Conceptualizations*, 137–153. Amsterdam, Philadelphia: John Benjamins.

Пермяков, Григорий Л. [Permyakov, Grigori L.] (1979): Грамматика пословичной мудрости. In Григорий Л Пермяков [Grigori L. Permyakov] (ed.), *Пословицы и поговорки народов Востока*, 7–57. Москва: Наука.

Stephan Elspaß
Areal Variation and Change in the Phraseology of Contemporary German

Abstract: Areal variation and change in phraseology is still a remarkably underdeveloped area of research. Past studies of areal phraseology have either been restricted to small localities and regions, or have required considerable effort in data collection. There is a complete lack of studies on phraseological change in contemporary German. Recent research projects on German areal linguistics have used internet surveys, as in the case of the *Atlas zur deutschen Alltagssprache* (AdA) 'Atlas of colloquial German' (with data from mostly spoken regional vernaculars), or large corpora, in the case of the *Variantenwörterbuch des Deutschen* (VWB) 'Dictionary of lexical variation in German' and the *Variantengrammatik des Standarddeutschen* (VG) 'Regional variation in the grammar of Standard German' (with data from written Standard German). These new methods can be used to obtain reliable data on the areal distribution of phrasemes in contemporary German usage with relatively little effort. Moreover, a comparison of recent AdA data with data from the *Wortatlas der deutschen Umgangssprachen* (WDU) 'Word Atlas of colloquial German', collected in the 1970s and 1980s, can reveal developments in the areal distribution of phrasemes on the level of colloquial speech. This article aims to demonstrate the potential of such research approaches for the study of variation and change in phraseology and will use selected examples from the AdA and the VG for illustration.

1 Introduction

Diatopic variation and change are central research issues in modern variationist linguistics and historical linguistics. Phraseology, however, is comparatively marginal in this area of research. As for German, there is relatively little research on diatopic variation in phraseology.[1] After some studies on the phraseology of dialects and regiolectal varieties in the second half of the twentieth century,

---

1 Cf. Piirainen (2006) and Sava (2014) for overviews of the field of areal variation in the phraseology of German.

Open Access. © 2020 S. Elspaß, published by De Gruyter. This work is licensed under the Creative Commons Attribution 4.0 License.
https://doi.org/10.1515/9783110669824-003

mostly restricted to small localities or regions (cf. Hain 1951; Hünert-Hofmann 1991; Piirainen 2000),² it was Elisabeth Piirainen who carried out the first major survey on diatopic variation in the phraseology of contemporary colloquial German at the beginning of the new millennium. Unfortunately, the results of her study, based on about 3,000 written questionnaires from Germany, are only available through individual publications (see e.g. Piirainen 2003, 2006, 2009a, 2009b) rather than as a linguistic atlas of phraseology. Apart from and contrary to her own study, "[l]inguistic geographical studies on phraseology are usually restricted to aspects of the [!] German pluricentricity" (Piirainen 2006: 195). Piirainen demonstrates that the distribution of phrasemes is not limited to languages or so-called 'national varieties' of a language; they are sometimes distributed only in certain areas (of different sizes) within these countries, and phrasemes –idioms in particular – can be widespread across different languages (cf. Piirainen 2012). Piirainen (2009a) coined the term "areal phraseology" to encompass a linguistic concept which does not limit the consideration of diatopic phraseme distribution to individual languages or countries. The investigation of regiolectal phraseology in particular thus constitutes a research desideratum.³

Though the historical phraseology of German appears to be intensively researched today (see Friedrich 2007; Filatkina 2018 and the contributions to Filatkina et al. 2012), there is relatively little research on recent changes in the phraseology of German, particularly changes in areal phraseology.

The present article will therefore look at areal variation and change in the phraseology of contemporary German. Section 2 discusses some conceptual problems and issues of variation and change in phraseology. Case studies of areal variation in German phraseology are presented in section 3. Section 4 presents two examples of change in the areal variation of routine formulae in recent decades, and section 5 concludes with a brief summary.

---

2 Grober-Glück's (1974) study is an exception here, as it covers most of the German-speaking area. However, its primary interest is not linguistic; Grober-Glück's study on "motives and motivations in sayings and folk wisdom" is a by-product of the *Atlas zur deutschen Volkskunde* ('Atlas of German Folklore'), a large ethnographic project conducted in Germany and Austria from 1930 to 1935. Typically, phraseological comparisons (e.g. *dumm wie ein Schaf/eine Gans/Haferstroh* etc. 'thick as mince/a brick (etc.)') and sayings which are prompted by extralinguistic facts (e.g. 'What do people say when someone's nose itches?') are mapped.
3 In his 2018 plenary talk "Neue Wege der Regiolektforschung" ('New paths of research into regiolects') at the 6th congress of the *Internationalen Gesellschaft für Dialektologie des Deutschen (IGDD)* in Marburg, Michael Elmentaler identified phraseology as one of three prominent and particularly rewarding research fields in the future study of German regiolects.

2 Areal Variation and Change in Phraseology

For the purposes of this chapter, language variation and language change may be defined as follows (based on Pickl 2013: 39).
– Language variation occurs when more than one linguistic form is used to represent a linguistic function.
– Language change occurs when the association between linguistic function and linguistic form alters over time.

Areal variation in phraseology can thus be defined as the coexistence of different phraseological forms (or variants) representing the same linguistic function in a given area (e.g. in the German-speaking countries).

Phraseological change manifests itself in different ways, which may[4] be subsumed into three basic types:
– Type I: Phraseme A is replaced by phraseme B over time (cf. example 1).
– Type II: The internal structure of a phraseme variant is altered over time, either on a paradigmatic level (e.g. one constituent is replaced by another lexical form, cf. example 2, or by a different morphological form, e.g. a plural form of a noun by a singular form, cf. example 3), or on a syntagmatic level (e.g. a phraseme is shortened, cf. example 4, the word order is fixed, particularly in binomials, cf. example 5, or the constituents of a polylexical phraseme have moved together to form a monolexical expression, cf. example 6).
– Type III: The semantic or pragmatic function of a phraseme changes over time (cf. example 7).

(1) Middle High German *dâ gienc ez* (jmdm.) *ûz deme spil* > present-day German *da wurde es* (für jmdn.) *ernst* 'things become serious (for sb.)'

(Friedrich 2007: 1095)

(2) Early New High German (Luther) *Aus den aügen, aus dem hertzen.* > present-day German *Aus den Augen, aus dem Sinn.* 'Out of sight, out of mind.'

(Friedrich 2007: 1101)

(3) Middle New High German (Knigge) *in Reihe und Gliedern* > present-day German *in Reih und Glied* 'in formation'

(Burger 2015: 147)

---

4 This is a simplified typology. More elaborate classifications are presented by Friedrich (2007: 1100–1103), Dräger (2011: 63–170) and Burger (2015: 144–157).

(4) Middle New High German (Goethe) *seinen Platz nehmen* > present-day German *Platz nehmen* 'to take a seat'

(Burger 2015: 147)

(5) Old High German (Otfrid von Weißenburg) *arme joh riche / riche joh arme* > present-day German *Arm und Reich* 'the rich and the poor'.

(Hüpper et al. 2002: 91–95)

(6) Old High German *hiu tagu* > present-day German *heute* 'today'.

(Dal and Eroms 2014: 37)

(7) Middle New High German (Goethe) *im Augenblick* 'at that very moment' > present-day German *im Augenblick* 'now (from the speaker's perspective)'

(Burger 2010: 147–148)

In practice, the identification of phraseological variants faces several well-known problems. I will mention only five:

1. The definition of 'phraseme' as inherently involving polylexicality: Some compound verbs in German have two orthographic variants, such as *(jmdm. etw.) übel nehmen/übelnehmen* 'to hold sth. against sb.'. Is the discontinuous variant *übel nehmen* a phraseological unit?
2. The distinction between phraseological variant, phraseological modification, and phraseological error, e.g.: Is *etw. unter den Tisch kehren* (lit. 'to sweep sth. under the table') a modified phraseme (cf. Wotjak 1992: 171), an error (cf. Elspaß 2002), or by now a "canonical modified phraseological unit" (cf. Rodríguez Martín 2014), i.e. a variant, if it accounts for about a third of all occurrences in present-day German print?[5]
3. The distinction between structurally similar phraseological synonyms (e.g. *in letzter Minute/in zwölfter Stunde* 'at the last minute') and phraseological variants (e.g. the lexical variants *die Achseln/Schultern zucken* and the grammatical variants *die Achsel/Achseln zucken, mit der Achsel/den Achseln zucken* 'to shrug one's shoulders').
4. The low frequency of many phraseological types such as rarely used idioms: Even competent speakers can have trouble identifying such phrasemes or

---

[5] According to a quick search in the *Google Books Ngram Viewer*, conducted in November 2018 (cf. Pfeiffer 2017: 18–22). Stumpf (2016) points to another problem, i.e. the differentiation between modified phrasemes and phraseme schemata (or phraseological constructions) such as *X oder Y, das ist hier die Frage* ('X or Y, that is the question', built on *Sein oder Nichtsein, das ist hier die Frage* 'To be or not to be: That is the question!'), e.g. *Kaufen oder nicht kaufen* ('To buy or not to buy') / *Hart oder weich* ('Hard or soft') / etc., *das ist hier die Frage*.

judging what their 'normal' form is, and sometimes frequencies are too low even in large corpora to establish a 'normal' form.
5. The fairly limited usefulness of dictionaries in the investigation of variation and change of phraseological units due to either missing or unclear information on the underlying corpora and the lexicographic methodology.

3 Areal Variation in the Phraseology of Present-Day German

In section 2, I defined areal variation as the coexistence of different forms representing the same linguistic function in a given area. As for areal phraseological variation, Piirainen (2009a: 147–152) identifies six categories of distributional range. For the purpose of this paper, I will present a modified version of her classification, trimming the six categories down to four[6] and illustrating them with examples from Piirainen and from VWB (2016).

1. A phraseme is distributed in only a small region (sometimes within the range of just a few villages), e.g. the (West Low German) idiom *Klumpe nao Wessum dräägen* 'to carry coals to Newcastle' (lit. 'to carry clogs to Wessum'), which is (or was) only known and used in the dialects of a small region around Wessum, a Westphalian village that was known for its clog craft.
2. A phraseme is distributed within a larger area, e.g. the idiomatic saying *sie kommt nicht aus den Sträuchern* ('she isn't making (any) headway'), which is only known and used in the colloquial vernacular in Westphalia, as it is derived and translated from an idiom in the Westphalian dialects (*Se kümp nich uut de Strüüke*).
3. A phraseme is distributed within a standard variety of a larger region, e.g. *das ist gehopst wie gesprungen* (Northern German standard)/*das ist gehupft wie gesprungen* (Southern German standard) 'it's six of one and half a dozen

---

6 I omitted Piirainen's category „Verbreitung im Raum eines nicht mehr existierenden Staatsgebiets" ('distribution in the area of a defunct state territory'), because it only comprises phrasemes from the former GDR, which may be more appropriately subsumed under the (new) category 3 (phrasemes of areal standard German varieties), and the category „Verbreitung innerhalb des gesamten deutschen Sprachgebiets" ('dissemination within the entire German-speaking area'), because phrasemes falling into this category do not constitute areal variants.

of the other', or *es ist noch nicht im Topf, wo's kocht* 'it's still early days' (Eastern German standard, i.e. in the area of the former German Democratic Republic).
4. A phraseme is distributed within a standard variety of a country, e.g. *etwas gebacken bekommen* 'to get sth. done' (German Standard German, cf. section 3.1.1 below), *die Finken klopfen* 'to take to one's heels' (Swiss Standard German), or *es/etw. ist zum Krenreiben* 'it's a hoot' (Austrian Standard German).

This classification situates areal variation as encompassing variation in colloquial German, understood as usage in (mainly spoken) dialects and regiolectal varieties (categories 1 and 2), as well as variation in the (mainly written) standard language (categories 3 and 4). I will first concentrate on variation in colloquial German (3.1) and then on Standard German (3.2).

Based on Piirainen's concept of areal phraseology, and focusing on areal variation in the phraseology of German, this investigation is guided by the following research questions:
1. What does the areal distribution of phraseological variants look like in colloquial German vernaculars and in Standard German?
2. Is it possible to establish differences between awareness and actual usage?
3. How do dictionaries deal with areal variation?
4. Is it possible to establish changes in the areal phraseology of German?

RQ 3 can be subdivided into various sub-questions: Do dictionaries account for certain phrasemes at all? Do they account for the areal distribution of phrasemes or their variants? If yes, are these accounts reliable? Do dictionaries distinguish between awareness and usage? Duden 11, the main phraseological dictionary of Standard German, and VWB, the dictionary of areal variation in Standard German,[7] will be used to address RQ 3 and its sub-questions.

3.1 Areal Phraseological Variation in Colloquial German Vernaculars

3.1.1 Patterns of Distributional Range

The present chapter takes the definition of 'colloquial German vernacular' to be:

---

7 The VWB marks idiomatic expressions with an asterisk.

die Gesamtheit der Sprachformen, ‚die Sprecherinnen und Sprecher des Deutschen in der Alltagskommunikation verwenden', also ‚im sozialen und funktionalen („Nähe'-)Bereich des Privaten, des spontanen Gesprächs unter Freunden, Verwandten oder Bekannten oder auch im informellen Austausch unter nicht näher Bekannten aus demselben Ort, etwa im örtlichen Lebensmittelgeschäft'.
('registers and variants in everyday communication, i.e. in the social and functional domains of private life, of spontaneous speech among friends, relatives, acquaintances, or in informal situations among people from the same place who are not necessarily close to each other, e.g. in the local corner shop'.)

(Möller and Elspaß 2019, based on Möller and Elspaß 2014: 122)

This definition accounts for the different manifestations of everyday colloquial vernaculars in the German-speaking countries, which may include both dialectal and regiolectal varieties. In German-speaking Switzerland, Liechtenstein, and many regions in central and southern Germany, Austria, and South Tyrol, the vernacular language of everyday life is still dominated by local or regional dialects. In many other areas, however, everyday language is characterized by supra-regional varieties, such as regiolects.

Such colloquial vernaculars are the subject of the long-term *Atlas zur deutschen Alltagssprache* (AdA) ('Atlas of colloquial German') project (Elspaß and Möller 2003ff.). In 2003, an initial online questionnaire was distributed, aimed at eliciting everyday language, particularly as used by the younger generation in urban areas. The AdA is geared toward lexical variation, but also includes questions on morphosyntax, phonetics, and phrasemes (including routine formulae). This first survey was completed by 1,763 participants, and was followed by ten more surveys conducted at fairly regular intervals. Over the years, the number of participants snowballed; in the tenth survey, over 20,000 people provided data. As the data were collected in a crowd-sourcing approach, it was not possible to control the number of responses per location (though, in spite of this and rather surprisingly, the overall number of responses is almost balanced for gender). Responses were assigned to 500 cities and towns and then aggregated by location. The individual maps presented below show either one or two color-coded dots per location. In the latter case, the bigger dot represents the most frequently reported, i.e. the dominant, variant at the location. A smaller dot next to the big dot indicates that there is variation at the location and symbolizes the second most common variant there.

In the AdA surveys 1 to 11, data on 35 phrasemes were elicited and presented on 39 maps. A full list can be found in the appendix. I will present and discuss various examples here with regard to RQ 1.

Figures 1 and 2 show examples of phrasemes with a small-scale distribution. The routine formula *jmd. ist gut zufrieden* 'sb. is quite content' (figure 1) is used only in a small area in the northwest of Germany which borders the Netherlands. The similarity to (Standard) Dutch *iemand is goed tevreden* is obvious. Figures 2a/b present variants of the German equivalents for 'don't take offence' and 'you have to take things as they come': The Standard German variants are *nimm's mir nicht übel* and *man muss es nehmen, wie es kommt*. Only in a small area in the far west of Germany (Saarland and the western part of Rhineland-Palatinate), Luxembourg, and the southern part of East Belgium (around St. Vith) are the variants **hol**'s mir nicht übel (figure 2a) and *man muss es* **holen**, *wie es kommt* (figure 2b) common. These variants can be traced back to a general replacement of the German verb *nehmen* 'to take' by *holen* in the Moselle Franconian dialects (see RhWb 3: 759–760); as the two examples demonstrate, this also affects phrasemes.

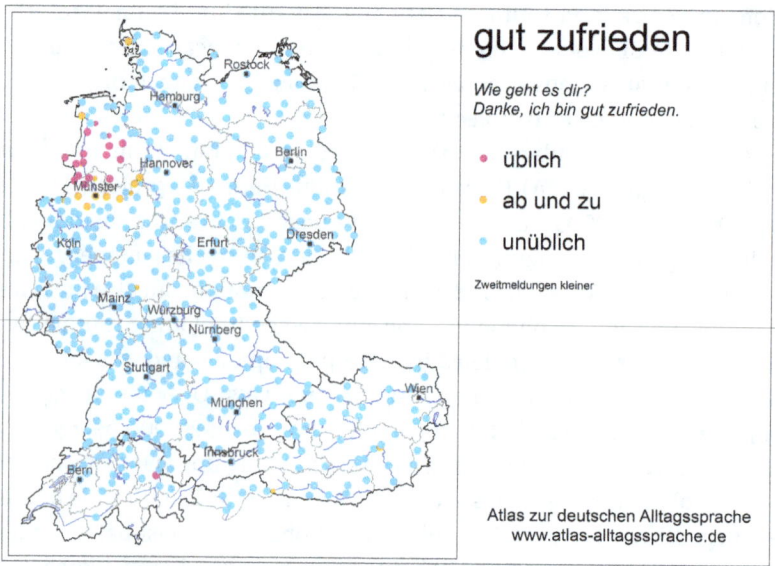

Fig. 1: Distribution of *gut zufrieden* 'quite content' (AdA VIII-6h)

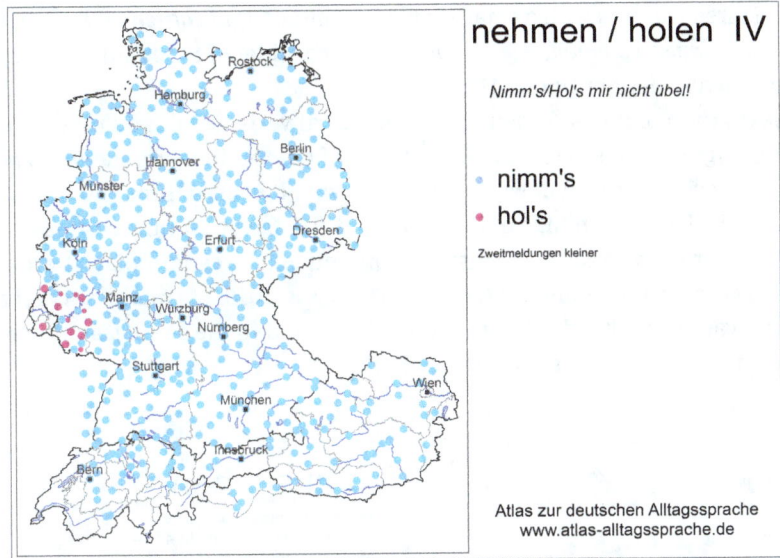

Fig. 2a: Distribution of *nimm's/hol's mir nicht übel* 'don't take offence' (AdA IX-6d)

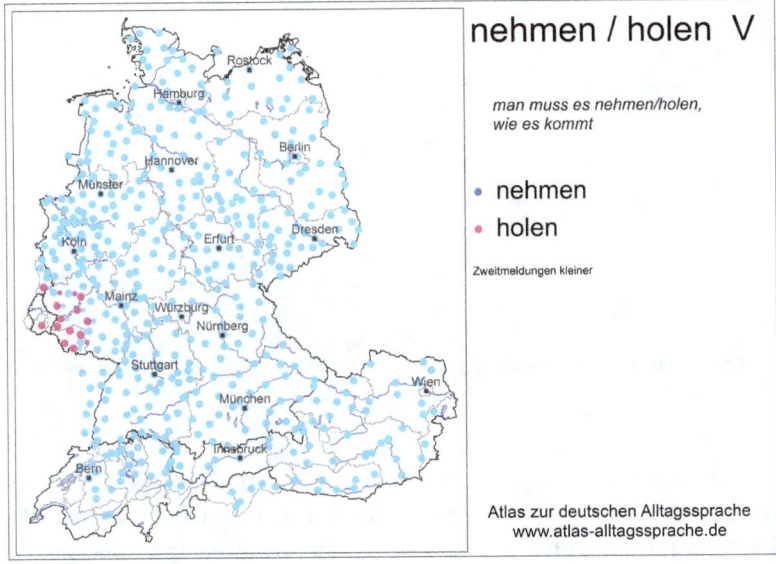

Fig. 2b: Distribution of *man muss es nehmen/holen, wie es kommt* 'you have to take things as they come' (AdA IX-6e)

None of the three variants with a small-scale distribution (*gut zufrieden*; *hol's mir nicht übel*; *man muss es holen, wie es kommt*) are considered Standard German, as they are listed in neither Duden 11 nor VWB.

The next group of maps presents phraseological variants with a large-scale distribution. Figure 3 illustrates the distribution of the routine formula *das geht sich [zeitlich] noch aus* 'this will work out (timewise)'. It is used throughout Austria, but also in Liechtenstein, South Tyrol, and the Bavarian dialect areas of southeastern Germany. Again, the distribution points to a certain dialect area. But it is also employed in Standard German: The VWB (2016: 65) marks *etw. geht sich aus* as a variant of Standard German in Austria and in the southeast of Germany. Duden 11, however, has no entry.

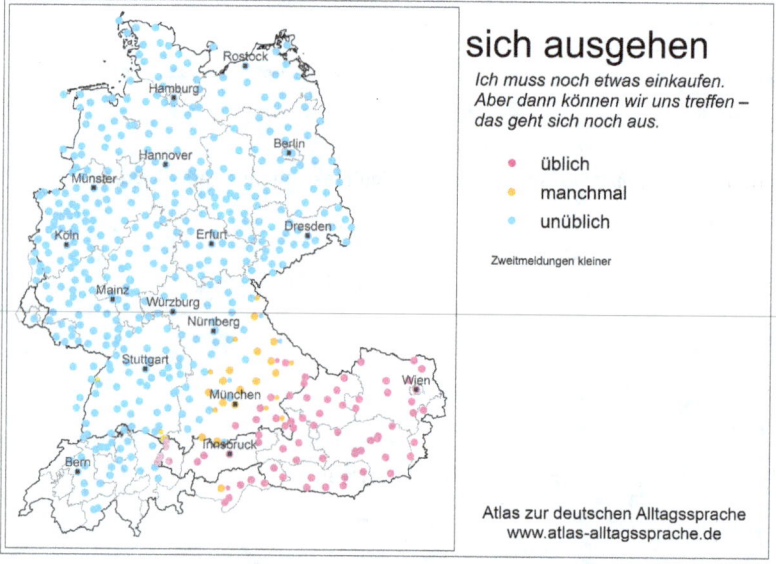

Fig. 3: Distribution of *das geht sich [zeitlich] noch aus* 'this will work out (timewise)' (AdA XI-3a)

The meaning of the variants in figure 4a is '(to do sth.) free of charge'. There are three main variants: *für umsonst* is the most widely distributed and is used as the standard form, *für umme* (a phonetically non-standard variant of *für umsonst*) is restricted to a small area in the Palatinate area in the southwest of Germany, and *für lau* – also considered 'non-standard' – is the dominant form in the north of Germany as well as the only non-standard variant mentioned in Duden 11.

Areal Variation and Change in the Phraseology of Contemporary German —— 53

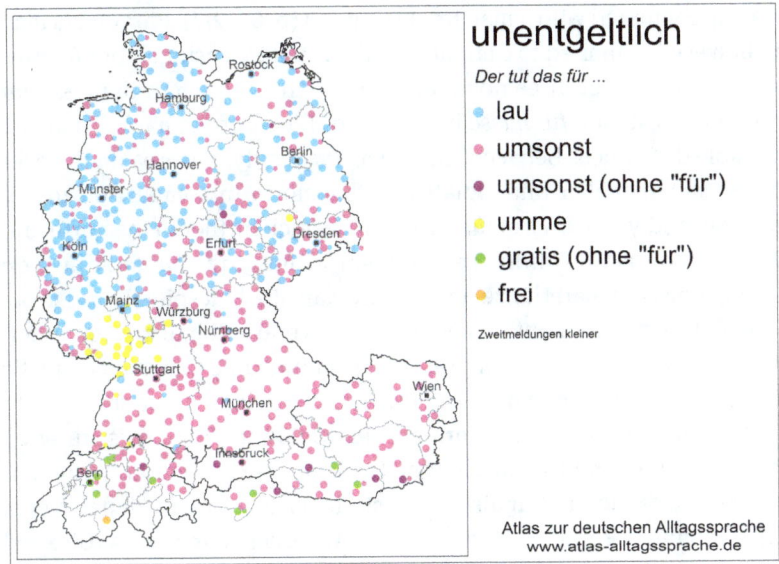

Fig. 4a: Distribution of variants for '(to do sth.) free of charge' (AdA VIII-4n)

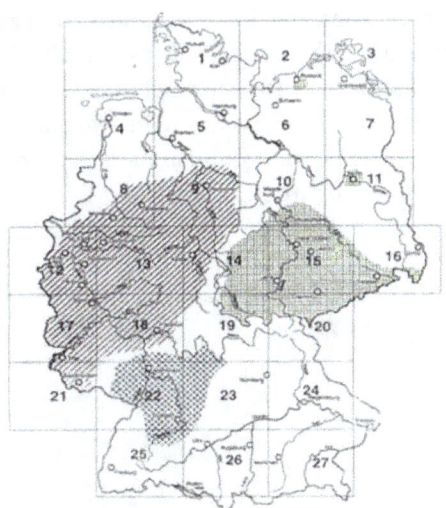

Fig. 4b: Variants for '(to do sth.) free of charge' from Piirainen (2006: 217)

Figure 4a can be compared with a map from Piirainen (2006: 217). Piirainen's map (figure 4b), however, is limited to Germany, and it is not extensional, but focuses on the distribution areas of three non-standard variants: *für lau* in the west, *für umme* in the southwest, and *für nasse* in the (central) east of Germany. There are three remarkable differences between the two maps. Firstly, the area on the AdA map for *für umme* is smaller and situated further north in comparison to Piirainen's map. Secondly, the area of *für lau* extends much further to the north and to the east on the AdA map. Thirdly, and most surprisingly, the *für nasse* area on Piirainen's map does not materialize on the AdA map at all, despite *für nasse* being at the top of the list of four optional variants (plus one optional box for 'other' variants) in the AdA online questionnaire. As it is improbable that such a drastic change has occurred within one decade,[8] these discrepancies are more likely to be due to the different numbers of informants (ca. 3,000 in Piirainen's study vs. 9,758 in the AdA study) and the different methods of data collection. While Piirainen targeted professional linguists and students at German departments throughout the country (Piirainen 2006: 210), the AdA questionnaire was directed at laypeople (see Möller and Elspaß 2015: 521–526 on the methodology of the AdA). Moreover, in contrast to the point-symbol maps of the AdA, Piirainen's area map does not show the distribution of responses.

Figures 5a and 5b map the distribution of two variants for the German phraseme for 'to get sth. done', one of which is considered non-standard (*etw. gebacken kriegen*) and the other standard (*etw. gebacken bekommen*). Clearly, the non-standard variant has a much wider distribution area (most of Germany, except the southeast) than the standard variant (the colour code on the two maps is as follows: Pink dots signify that the phraseme is 'very common in use', orange dots mean 'fairly common' and blue dots stand for 'utterly uncommon').

---

8 Piirainen collected her questionnaire data in 2000–2001, and the AdA data for '(to do sth.) free of charge' were collected in 2010–2011. There is also no evidence of significant age differences between Piirainen's informants and the AdA informants: About two thirds of Piirainen's respondents (Piirainen 2006: 210) and about half of the AdA informants were under 30 years of age.

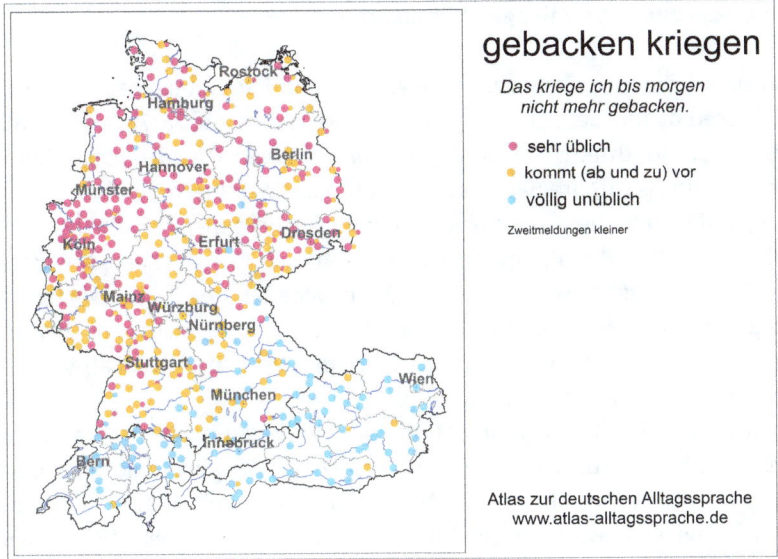

Fig. 5a: Distribution of *gebacken kriegen* 'to get sth. done [non-standard]' (AdA IV-21a)

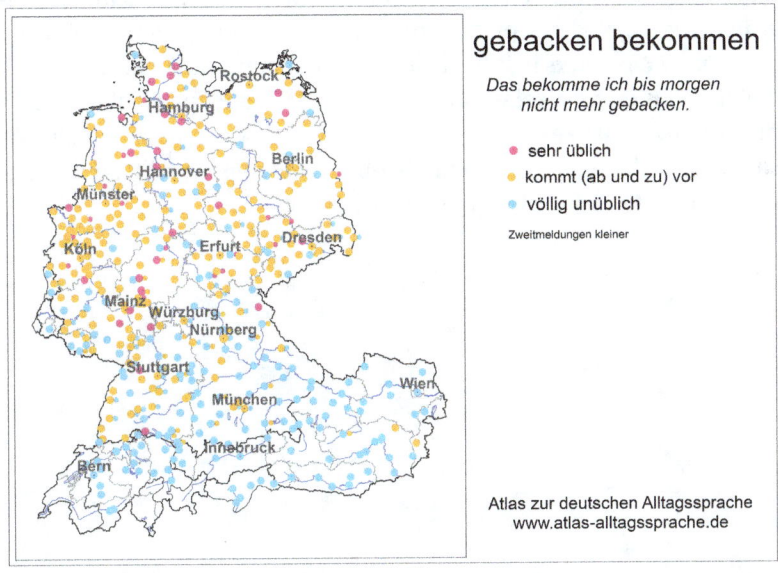

Fig. 5b: Distribution of *gebacken bekommen* 'to get sth. done [standard]' (AdA IV-21b)

3.1.2 Awareness and Actual Usage of Phrasemes

RQ 2, regarding differences between the awareness and actual usage of phrasemes, is addressed by this next group of variants. Figures 6a/6b, 7a/7b, and 8a/8b show pairs of maps for three phrasemes: *das geht dich einen Schmarren an* ('that's none of your business', figure 6a/b), *dicke Backen machen* ('to brag about sth.', figure 7a/b), and *mit etw./jmdm. ist kein Blumentopf zu gewinnen* ('you're not getting anywhere with this/them', figure 8a/b). In each case, the phraseme is widely known, but its actual usage is restricted to a much smaller area (pink dots in figures 6a, 7a and 8a stand for 'the phraseme is known' in the respective locality; in Figures 6b, 7b and 8b, pink dots mean 'the phrasem is used' in that locality. Blue dots signify 'unknown' or 'uncommon' respectively).

Dictionaries like VWB and Duden 11 do not distinguish between awareness and usage. Usually, they only mark the areas in which the phrasemes are used (cf. RQ 3). In view of figures 6b, 7b, and 8b, dictionaries' labels of areal distribution appear to be somewhat misleading. In Duden 11, *das geht Dich einen Schmarren an* is considered a 'southern German and Austrian' variant, and VWB marks it as being used in 'southeastern Germany and Austria'.[9] *Dicke Backen machen* is labeled as 'particularly northern German' by Duden 11, though it is apparently equally employed in the southwest. And *mit etwas/jmdm. ist kein Blumentopf zu gewinnen* is labeled as 'particularly used in the Berlin vernacular' by Duden 11, whereas VWB marks it as being used in 'Germany and Austria'. Neither matches the distribution as displayed on the map (Germany, particularly north and central Germany). These examples illustrate yet again the fundamental problems of lexicographic labels on the areal distribution of idioms, which Piirainen has pointed out repeatedly (e.g. Piirainen 2002).

---

[9] To be completely correct, South Tyrol should also be added. Both dictionaries consider this phraseme standard, although the online Duden dictionary marks *Schmarr(e)n* ('rubbish, tripe') as 'colloquial' (https://www.duden.de/rechtschreibung/Schmarren, accessed December 31, 2018).

Areal Variation and Change in the Phraseology of Contemporary German — 57

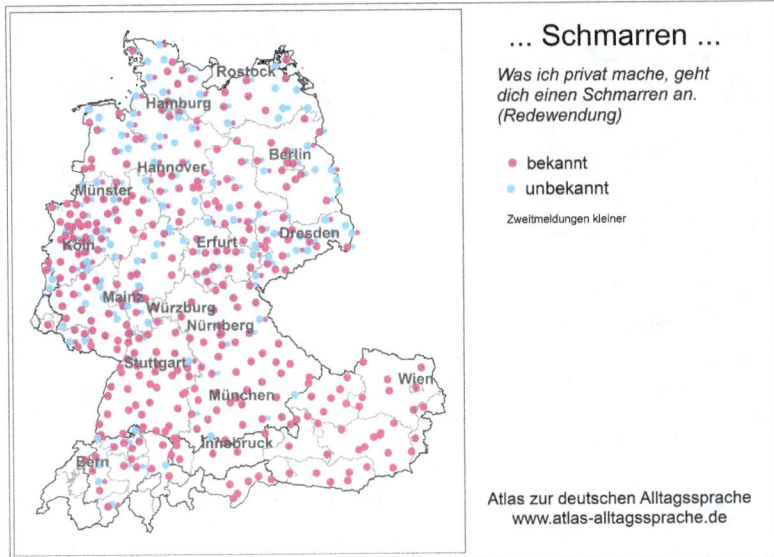

Fig. 6a: Distribution of awareness of *das geht dich einen Schmarren an* ('that's none of your business') (AdA IV-20a)

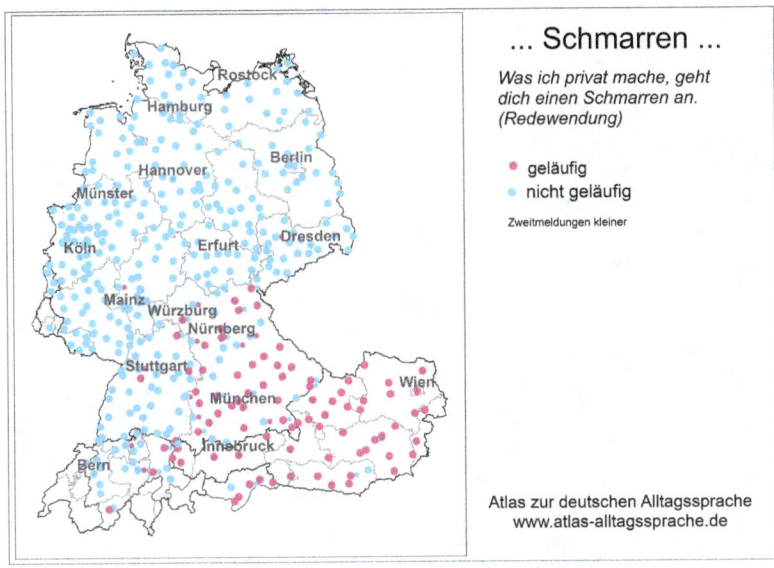

Fig. 6b: Distribution of usage of *das geht dich einen Schmarren an* ('that's none of your business') (AdA IV-20b)

58 — Stephan Elspaß

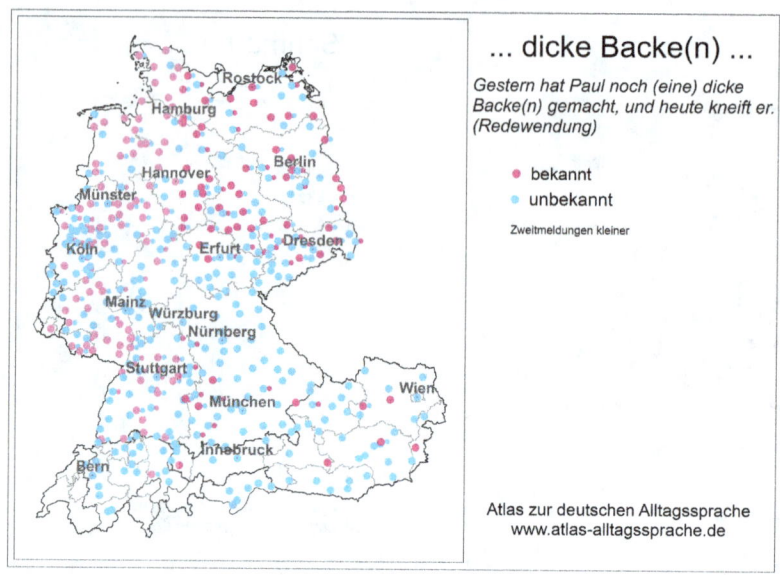

Fig. 7a: Distribution of awareness of *dicke Backen machen* ('to brag about sth.') (AdA IV-19a)

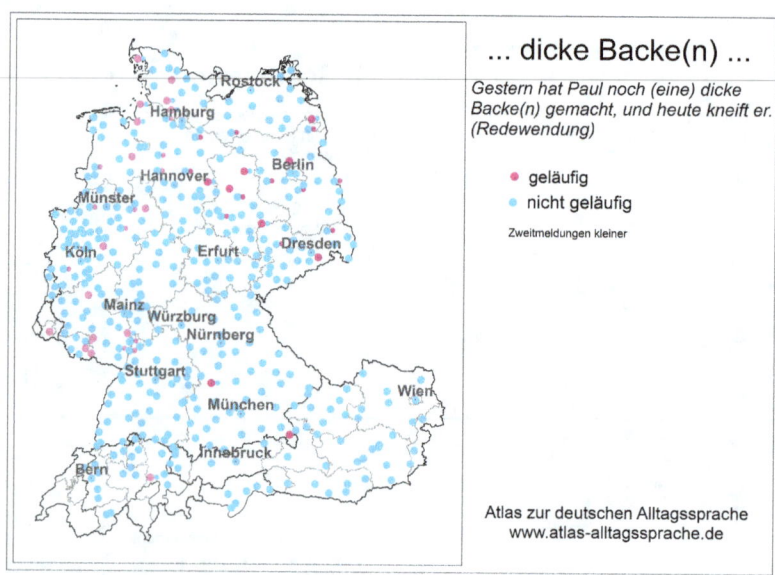

Fig. 7b: Distribution of usage of *dicke Backen machen* ('to brag about sth.') (AdA IV-19b)

Areal Variation and Change in the Phraseology of Contemporary German — 59

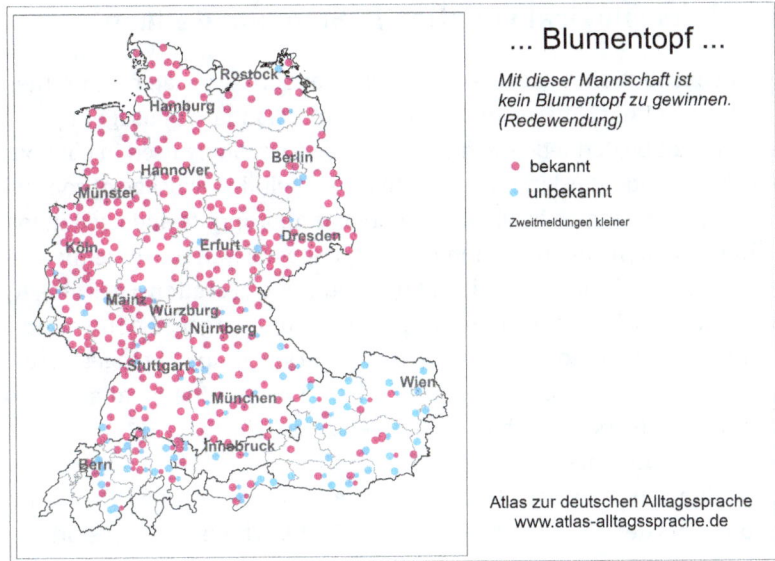

Fig. 8a: Distribution of awareness of *mit etw./jmdm. ist kein Blumentopf zu gewinnen* ('you're not getting anywhere with this/them') (AdA IV-18a)

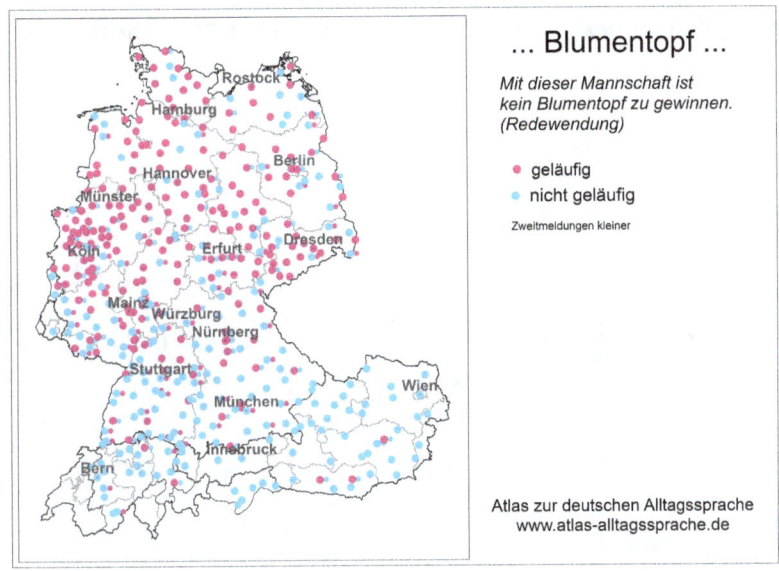

Fig. 8b: Distribution of usage of *mit etw./jmdm. ist kein Blumentopf zu gewinnen* ('you're not getting anywhere with this/them') (AdA IV-18b)

3.2 Areal Phraseological Variation in Standard German

In the present contribution, I use a definition of 'standard language' – or rather, 'standard varieties' – that is based on the concept of a standard of usage. Thus, a standard variety can be defined as a variety which is commonly used in contexts that are perceived as standard language.[10] This may include the usage of conceptually written language which is widely accepted as appropriate and used in formal and public situations in any region of a language area, in this case the German-speaking area. As the classification at the beginning of section 3 has already indicated, this standard variety can cover a country or a larger region within a country. In this respect, I follow a model of 'pluriareal standard languages' rather than 'pluricentric standard languages' in the sense of 'plurinational standard languages' (see Elspaß and Dürscheid 2017: 87–89; Elspaß et al. 2017: 70–74, for a discussion of the different concepts).

In this section, I first present three examples from the AdA and then three examples from a Master's thesis by Lisa Höller (2016), who based her study on two large electronic corpora of present-day Standard German.

Although the first three examples are taken from the 'Atlas of colloquial German' (AdA), the variants display variation that is also valid for the standard.

Figure 9 shows the results for the phraseological variants *eins gemerkt/eins im Sinn*/etc., 'to carry a digit over', as when a number greater than 9 (in this case 10) is transferred to the next position (in this case by adding "1" in the tens position).

---

[10] "Standard ist das, was in Kontexten, die als standardsprachlich aufgefasst werden, regelhaft in Gebrauch ist" (Elspaß et al. 2017: 71).

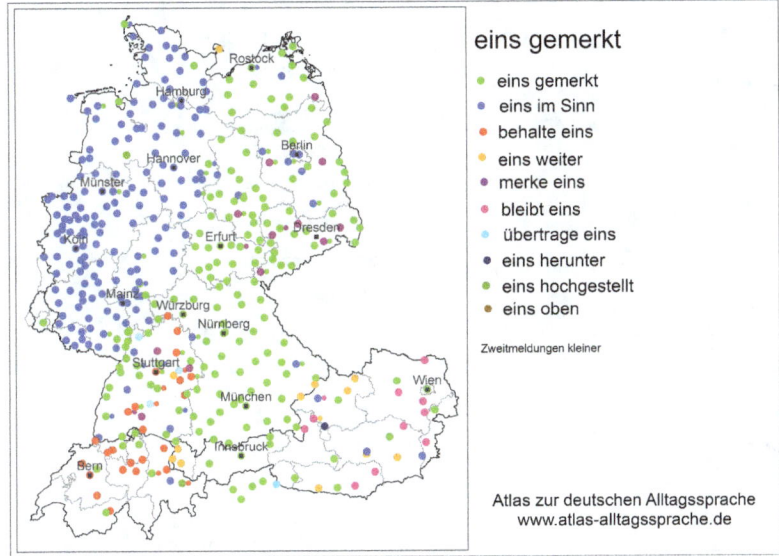

Fig. 9: Distribution of usage of *eins gemerkt/eins im Sinn/...* (lit. 'one in memory') (AdA I-19)

The map reveals a clear areal distribution of the two main variants *eins im Sinn*, which is the dominant variant in the north and the west of Germany, and *eins gemerkt*, which is used in the rest of the German-speaking countries. Some noticeable regional variants are *behalte eins* in the southwest, *merke eins* in the (north)east of Germany, and *bleibt eins* or *eins weiter* in some parts of Austria. These variants are not mentioned in Duden 11.

Figure 10 illustrates the distribution of the variants of New Year wishes in Standard as well as colloquial German. The distributional areas of four variants can basically be distinguished: *frohes* 'happy'/*gesundes* 'healthy'/*gutes* 'good' *neues (Jahr)* 'new (year)' and *Prosit Neujahr* (with the loan from Latin *prosit* 'may it benefit'). Duden 11 only lists *pros[i]t Neujahr*, with no indication as to its limited areal distribution.

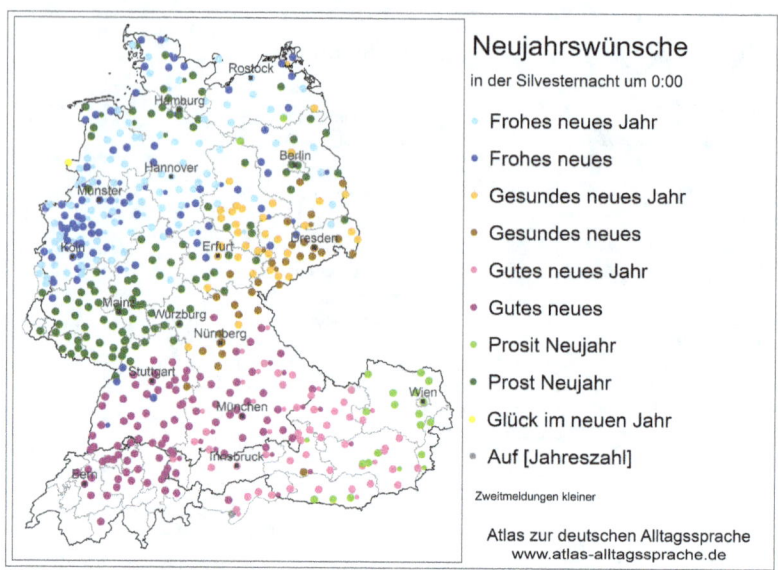

Fig. 10: Distribution of variants of New Year wishes (AdA VIII-1a)

Figure 11 is the only map which seems to identify a national variant, *jmdn. auf die Schaufel nehmen* ('to pull sb.'s leg'), which in colloquial language is only used in Austria (though not so much in the western parts of Austria[11]). The almost exclusive variant in the other German-speaking countries is *jmdn. auf die Schippe nehmen* (with *jmdn. auf die Schüppe nehmen* constituting merely a phonetic variant).

---

11 The grey dots on the map indicate that the idiom is not used at all – neither in this or the other variant – in many parts of Austria (and elsewhere).

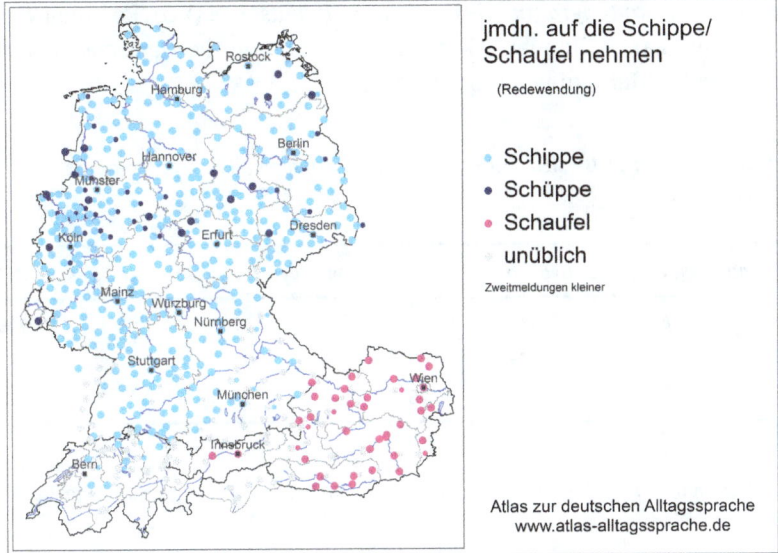

Fig. 11: Distribution of *jmdn. auf die Schippe/(Schüppe)/Schaufel nehmen* ('to pull sb.'s leg') (AdA, IX-3b)

The map appears to confirm the information given in VWB and Duden 11, which labels *jmdn. auf die Schaufel nehmen* as an Austriacism. A search in the Austrian newspaper corpus of the German reference corpus (DeReKo), however, paints a different picture.[12] Out of 1,125 cases in which the idiom was used, 191 (= 17.1%) have the variant *jmdn. auf die Schippe nehmen*.[13] In other words, in almost every sixth instance, an idiomatic variant is used in Standard German in Austria which has no basis in the Austrian spoken vernaculars – the lexemic variant *Schippe* is alien to colloquial varieties of German in Austria, as another map from the AdA confirms.[14]

The following three selected results, taken from Höller (2016), focus on areal standard variation in prepositions in phrasemes. Höller's study is partly based on

---

12 Search strings: "(auf die Schippe) /s0 &nehmen", "(auf die Schüppe) /s0 &nehmen" and "(auf die Schaufel) /s0 &nehmen".
13 There are no hits for *jmdn. auf die Schüppe nehmen*.
14 http://www.atlas-alltagssprache.de/schaufel/, accessed December 31, 2018.

the corpus of the *Variantengrammatik des Standarddeutschen* (VG) 'Regional variation in the grammar of Standard German' and partly on the *Deutsches Referenzkorpus* (DeReKo) 'German Reference Corpus'.

Tab. 1a: Distribution of *auf/zu Besuch fahren/kommen/sein/haben* (lit.: 'to go/come/be/have on (a) visit') in the VG corpus

	auf Besuch	*zu Besuch*	total	*auf Besuch* (%)	*zu Besuch* (%)
D	62	2,570	2,632	2.4	97.6
A	69	173	242	28.5	71.5
CH	23	105	128	18.0	82.0

Tab. 1b: Distribution of *auf/zu Besuch fahren/kommen/sein/haben* (lit.: 'to go/come/be/have on (a) visit') in the DeReKo

	auf Besuch	*zu Besuch*	total	*auf Besuch* (%)	*zu Besuch* (%)
D	1,015	41,366	42,381	2.4	97.6
A	1,328	4,185	5,513	24.1	75.9
CH	486	2,973	3,459	14.1	85.9

Tables 1a and 1b present results for variation in the prepositions *auf/zu* in the idiom *auf/zu Besuch fahren/kommen/sein/haben* (lit.: 'to go/come/be/have on (a) visit'). In order to provide a better overview, the results are summarized for Germany (D), Austria (A), and Switzerland (CH). With regard to the lexicographic representation of such standard variation, I will follow both the VWB's (2016: VIII) distinction between specific vs. unspecific variants and also Farø's (2005: 387) distinction between absolute vs. relative variants. A specific variant is used exclusively in a certain country and is a shibboleth of that country, whereas an unspecific variant is also used in other countries (but not in all countries and regions). Absolute variants are variants which are the (almost) only variants that occur in a speech community, whereas relative variants are those that occur frequently in a speech community, but are not the exclusive variants in the community.

Although the VG corpus is much smaller than the DeReKo (600 million word forms vs. 28 billion word forms[15]), the two corpus searches show similar results. The dominant form is clearly *zu Besuch* ..., while the variant *auf Besuch* ... is rarely used in Germany, more common in Switzerland, and accounts for about a quarter of all instances in Austria.

Tab. 2a: Distribution of *nach dem/zum Rechten sehen/schauen* ('to see that everything is OK') in the VG corpus

	nach dem Rechten	zum Rechten	total	nach dem Rechten (%)	zum Rechten (%)
D	975	0	975	100.0	0.0
A	56	1	57	98.3	1.7
CH	20	22	44	47.6	52.4

Tab. 2b: Distribution of *nach dem/zum Rechten sehen/schauen* ('to see that everything is OK') in the DeReKo

	nach dem Rechten	zum Rechten	total	nach dem Rechten (%)	zum Rechten (%)
D	13,569	15	13,584	99.9	1.1
A	1,100	1	1,101	99.9	1.1
CH	512	578	1,090	47.0	53.0

In tables 2a and 2b, Höller's results for the distribution of *nach dem/zum Rechten sehen/schauen* ('to see that everything is OK') are summarized for Germany (D), Austria (A) and Switzerland (CH). Again, both corpora render strikingly similar results. On the whole, *nach dem Rechten sehen/schauen* is the clearly dominant variant. In Switzerland, however, both variants are equally frequent in use; *zum Rechten sehen/schauen* can be considered a relative Helvetism. (The VWB simply marks it as a Helvetism.)

---

15 The numbers refer to the time of Höller's investigation. The size of the DeReKo has almost doubled since.

The last set of tables focuses on the variation of *auf dem* and *am*, which is not restricted to phrasemes (e.g. *Das Buch liegt auf dem/am Tisch* 'The book is on the table.'), but it is very noticeable in idioms such as
- *auf dem / am Laufenden sein/bleiben* 'to be/keep (oneself) up-to-date',
- *etwas auf dem / am Kerbholz haben* 'to have something (bad) on the tally',
- *auf dem / am Zahnfleisch gehen* ('to be on one's last leg').

The variants with *am* are usually presented as typical of Austrian usage, and *am* is often interpreted as a contraction of *an + dem* (e.g. Burger 2010: 208–209). Both assumptions require a revision. Firstly, *am* in these contexts most certainly originates in a contraction of *auf + dem* rather than a contraction of *an + dem* (cf. Höller 2016: 30), and secondly, as Höller's corpus studies show, the proportion of *am*-forms varies from phraseme to phraseme, cf. table 3.

Tab. 3: Proportion of *am/auf dem* in seven idioms in VG and DeReKo subcorpora 'Austria' (from Höller 2016: 53)

phraseme	% in VG corpus	% in DeReKo
am richtigen Weg sein	8	16
am Laufenden sein/bleiben/sich halten	18	25
am Prüfstand stehen	20	26
etw. am Kerbholz haben	26	26
jmdn. am falschen Fuß erwischen	27	45
am Boden der Tatsachen bleiben	40	28
am Zahnfleisch gehen	100	69

Here, some differences between the results of the corpus search in the VG and the DeReKo subcorpora are noticeable. All in all, because of the sheer size of the DeReKo its results are certainly more reliable. (For instance, the idiom *am Zahnfleisch gehen* appears only 5 times in the subcorpus 'Austria' of the VG corpus.)

To conclude, in none of the cases presented in this section could a variant be identified as a specific national variant (Germanism, Austrianism, or Helvetism) and at the same time an absolute variant. *Zum Rechten sehen/schauen* appears to be a specific idiom variant of Switzerland, but even this Helvetism is only a relative variant in the standard language corpora for Switzerland. Likewise, idioms with *am* are almost specific Austrianisms,[16] but none is an absolute variant in the corpora for Austria. *Eins im Sinn* is a 'Germanism' in the sense that it is only used in Germany, but here it is also a relative variant, and, more precisely, it shows a clear areal distribution in the northwest of Germany only. None of the other variants is nation-specific in Standard German. If they are absolute variants in one country, they are relative variants in another country. This appears to be a typical distributional pattern in the standard language varieties of German. From an empirical point of view, this kind of standard variation in the German-speaking countries may be more appropriately conceptualized as pluriareality rather than pluricentricity (in the sense of 'plurinationality', see Schmidlin 2006).

4 Changes in the Areal Variation of Colloquial and Standard German

In section 2, language change was defined as change in the associations between linguistic functions and linguistic forms over time. The present section investigates whether it is possible to establish changes in the areal phraseology of German (RQ 4). I will present two case studies of routine formulae in German. As in section 3, the examples are taken from atlases of colloquial German, but they also display variation in spoken registers of Standard German. Both case studies use a change in real-time framework (Chambers 2003: 212–215). More precisely, the findings come from a real-time panel study that uses the same questions and basically the same methodology. In both cases, areal distribution maps of routine formulae are compared. The older maps are based on data collected for the *Wortatlas der deutschen Umgangssprachen* (WDU) ('Word Atlas of colloquial German') in the 1970s, with data on the 'typical' expression at a given location provided by 1 or 2 informants per location. The AdA data were collected and presented in the manner explained in section 3.1 above, representing language use approximately one generation later than the WDU data.[17]

---

16 Some of them are also used in South Tyrol.
17 The hypothesis that the regional distribution of variants from colloquial language has changed in recent decades was first tested in Elspaß (2005). In this study, I compared the regional distribution of eleven WDU maps (nine lexical variables, two syntactic variables) from the first two volumes of the WDU (WDU I–II) to eleven equivalent maps from an online pilot study for the subsequent AdA conducted in 2002 – thus studying language change across a time span of c. 25–30 years.

Figures 12a and 12b illustrate the distribution of variants for 'a greeting formula which people would normally use when they enter a local shop in the afternoon'. The map in figure 12a is taken from the first volume of the WDU. Figure 12b shows the distribution of the same pragmatic variable about 25 years later, based on an online survey for the AdA. A comparison of the two maps reveals both similarities and differences, pointing partly to stability and partly to change. As for similarities, both maps display a north-south divide along the river Main, which has been identified as the main isogloss in the language geography of colloquial German (Durrell 1989; Möller 2003; Pickl and Pröll 2019). The dominant form south of the river Main is *Grüß Gott* (lit. '(may) God greet you-SG'), with its variant *Grüß Euch* ('(may God) greet you-PL', in South Tyrol and some parts of Austria) and the exclusively Swiss German form *Grüezi* (a phonetic variant of *Grüß Euch*). The dominant form north of the Main and along the river Rhine in the southwest of Germany was and is *Guten Tag*. The most obvious change is that in many places, particularly in the north of Germany, these polylexical routines have been joined or even replaced by the more informal monolexical *Hallo*. Although it exists natively in German (as an old imperative singular form of *holen* 'fetch', cf. Pfeifer 2003: 500), its rapid dissemination within one generation is certainly due to its status as an internationalism (cf. French *âllo*, English *hello*, Spanish *hola*, Dutch *hello*, etc.). Another striking change is the spread of *moin*, which is most probably the abbreviated form of the Low German and Frisian phraseme *mo(o)i(e)n dag* ('(I wish you/have a) nice day').[18]

---

[18] Today, *moin* is considered a salient marker of northern German regional identity. Anecdotal evidence has it that *moin* partly owes its rapid dissemination to the adoption of the expression as the title of a popular morning show of a private radio channel in the 1990s (https://de.wikipedia.org/wiki/Moin, accessed December 31, 2018).

Areal Variation and Change in the Phraseology of Contemporary German — 69

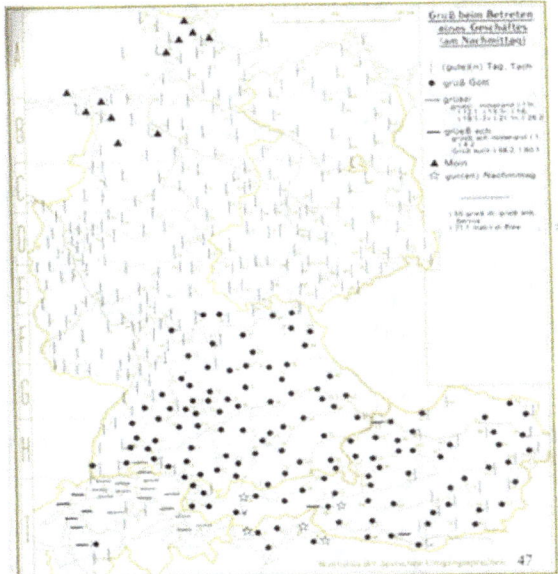

Fig. 12a: Distribution of variants of 'greeting when entering a local shop in the afternoon' (WDU I–47)

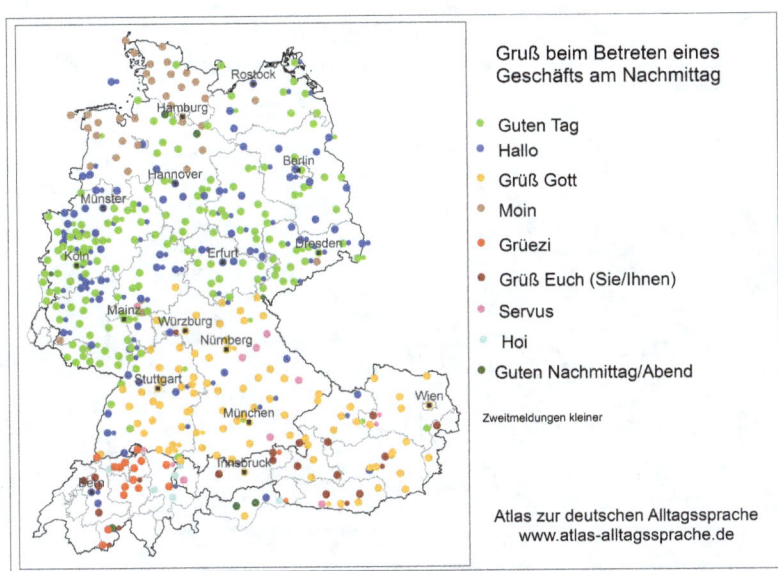

Fig. 12b: Distribution of variants of 'greeting when entering a local shop in the afternoon' (AdA II–1)

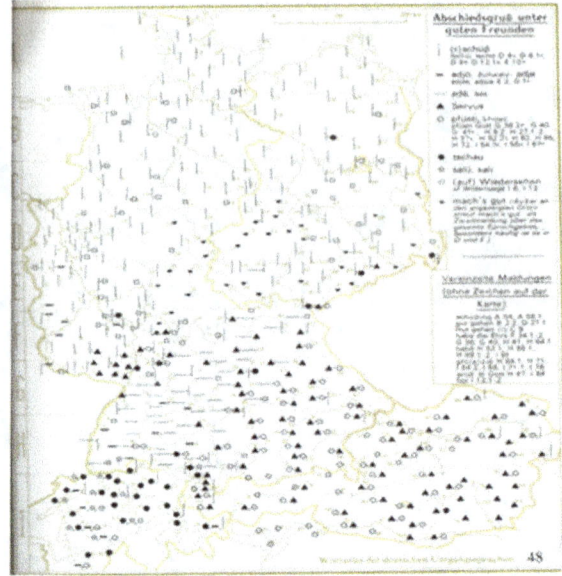

Fig. 13a: Distribution of variants of 'saying goodbye after meeting friends' (WDU I–48)

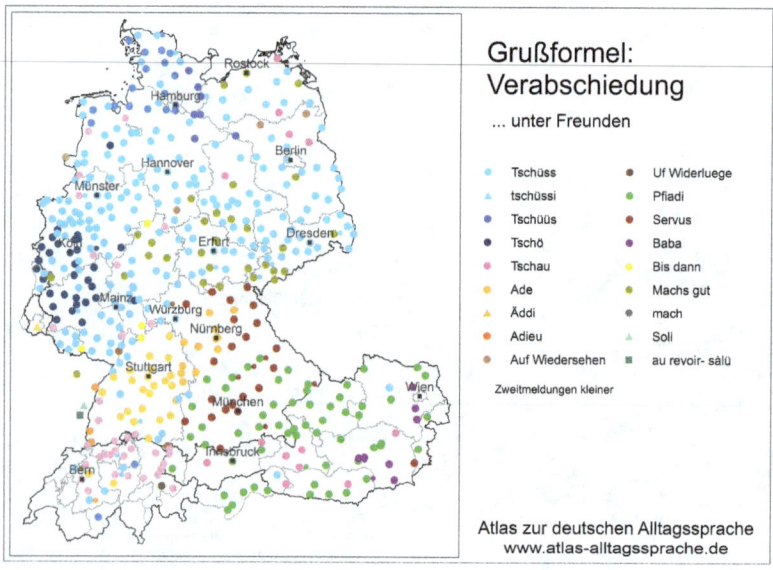

Fig. 13b: Distribution of variants of 'saying goodbye after meeting friends' (AdA X–17a)

Similar developments can be observed in the case of routine formulae for 'saying goodbye after meeting friends', a fairly informal situation (figures 13a and 13b).

I will confine my discussion to the only two phrasemes on these two maps. Whereas the distribution of *mach's gut* (lit. 'make-SG it good', mainly in Central East Germany) has remained relatively stable, the formal routine *Auf Wiedersehen* (lit. 'on seeing (you) again') has almost entirely been replaced by the more informal monolexical variants *Tschüss/Tschüüs/Tschö* in the north of Germany, again north of the river Main, which are shortened forms of *a tschüs(s)/a tschö* and all ultimately – via French *à dieu* or Spanish *adiós* – go back to Latin *ad deum* ('God be with you', cf. also *Ade* in Southwestern Germany), or by *Tschau* (cf. Italian *ciao*, from Venetian *sčiao* '(your) servant'). In present-day German, *Auf Wiedersehen*, including its southeastern variant *Auf Wiederschau(e)n* (and the Swiss German dialect form *Uf Widerluege*), are restricted to more formal contexts, as shown in figure 13c, the distribution of routines for 'saying goodbye to customers when they leave a local shop'.

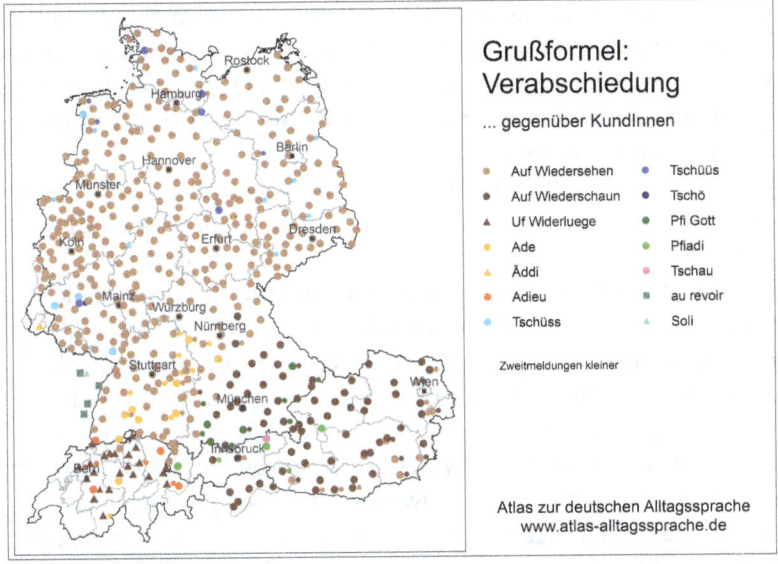

Fig. 13c: Distribution of variants of 'saying goodbye to customers when they leave a local shop' (AdA X–17b)

While both case studies include instances of long-term changes of form on a syntagmatic level (Type II change, e.g. *a tschüss* > *tschüss*, *mo(o)i(e)n dag* > *moin*), the most striking changes are Type I changes, i.e. polylexical routine formulae which are apparently perceived as rather formal have been or are gradually being replaced by monolexical informal expressions (e.g. *Guten Tag* > *Hallo*; *Auf Wiedersehen* > *Tschüss*).

5 Conclusion

This paper has identified areal variation and change as a still barely-researched subject in the phraseology of German. Case studies on variation and change in colloquial German have been presented, based on data from online surveys that aim to elicit spoken regional vernaculars and variation in Standard German (AdA), as well as from a regionally-balanced corpus of Standard German (VG).

With regard to RQ 1, the AdA has proven excellent for studying and presenting the areal distribution of phraseological variants in German as well as changes in their areal patterns. As in the lexis of colloquial German in general (cf. Pickl and Pröll 2019), neither traditional dialect boundaries nor contemporary political borders can fully account for the areal structure of phraseme variation in German. One of the most striking contrasts exists between the north and the south of the German-speaking countries, with the river Main as a prominent dividing line (see e.g. the salutations *Guten Tag* vs. *Grüß Gott*).

RQ 2 asked whether it is possible to establish differences between awareness and actual usage. Informants were asked (i) whether a certain phraseme is commonly known in their local town and (ii) whether it is commonly used. As expected, the three case studies showed that the phrasemes under investigation are widely known, but that their usage is restricted to a smaller area (see e.g. *das geht dich einen Schmarrn an* 'that's none of your business', which is known in all German-speaking countries, but is actively used only in Bavaria, Austria and South Tyrol.)

As for the representation of areal variation in dictionaries (RQ3), Piirainen already demonstrated in a number of essays that areal tags, even in phraseological dictionaries, are often sketchy and sometimes plainly incorrect. In many instances, dictionaries label areal variants of Standard German as simply 'colloquial' or 'regionally used', implying that they are non-standard. In the present paper, it has emerged that the tags given by VWB, a dictionary of areal variants in Standard German, are often more precise than those of Duden 11, the most prominent phraseological dictionary of German. The VWB, however, often does not differentiate between absolute and relative variants (see e.g. the figures for *zum Rechten sehen/schauen* 'to see that everything is OK' or *jmdn. auf die Schaufel nehmen* 'to pull sb.'s leg' in section 3.2).

Finally, a comparison of maps from two linguistic atlases of colloquial German, WDU and AdA, has revealed changes in the areal phraseology of German which have occurred in recent decades (RQ 4). In the case of the routine formulae examined here, the major finding was that polylexical formal routines have gradually been replaced by monolexical informal expressions (see e.g. *Guten Tag > Hallo*).

In methodological terms, the case studies have demonstrated the potential of both online surveys and corpus studies for gaining new insights into the areal variation of phrasemes and their change in German. Such new methods can help to advance this relatively young field of research, which Elisabeth Piirainen aptly coined 'areal phraseology' and to which she contributed some of her pioneering work.

References

AdA = Elspaß, Stephan & Robert Möller (2003ff.): *Atlas zur deutschen Alltagssprache (AdA)*. Retrieved from www.atlas-alltagssprache.de, accessed December 31, 2018.

Burger, Harald (2010): *Phraseologie. Eine Einführung am Beispiel des Deutschen*. 4. Auflage. Berlin: Erich Schmidt.

Burger, Harald (2015): *Phraseologie. Eine Einführung am Beispiel des Deutschen*. 5. Auflage. Berlin: Erich Schmidt.

Burger, Harald, Dmitrij Dobrovol'skij, Peter Kühn & Neal R. Norrick (eds.) (2007): *Phraseology. An International Handbook of Contemporary Research*. Berlin, New York: De Gruyter.

Chambers, J. K. (2003): *Sociolinguistic theory. Linguistic Variation and its Social Significance*. 2nd edition. Malden, MA et al.: Blackwell.

Dal, Ingerid & Hans-Werner Eroms (2014): *Kurze deutsche Syntax auf historischer Grundlage*. 4. Auflage. Berlin, Boston: De Gruyter.

DeReKo = *Deutsches Referenzkorpus* at the Institut für Deutsche Sprache, Mannheim. Retrieved from http://www.ids-mannheim.de/kl/projekte/korpora/, accessed December 31, 2018.

Dräger, Marcel (2011): *Der phraseologische Wandel und seine lexikographische Erfassung. Konzept des „Online-Lexikons zur diachronen Phraseologie (OLdPhras)"*. Ph.D. thesis Freiburg im Breisgau. Retrieved from https://freidok.uni-freiburg.de/data/8528, accessed July 15, 2019.

Duden 11 = Dudenredaktion (Hrsg.) (2013): *Duden. Redewendungen. Wörterbuch der deutschen Idiomatik*. 4. Auflage. Mannheim et al.: Dudenverlag.

Elspaß, Stephan (2002): „Alles unter den Tisch gekehrt" – Phraseologische Gebrauchsauffälligkeiten im Urteil von Sprachbenutzern. In Dietrich Hartmann & Jan Wirrer (Hrsg.), *„Wer A sägt, muss auch B sägen." Beiträge zur Phraseologie und Sprichwortforschung aus dem Westfälischen Arbeitskreis*, 127–160. Baltmannsweiler: Schneider-Verlag Hohengehren.

Elspaß, Stephan (2005): Zum Wandel im Gebrauch regionalsprachlicher Lexik. Ergebnisse einer Neuerhebung. *Zeitschrift für Dialektologie und Linguistik* 72, 1–51.
Elspaß, Stephan & Christa Dürscheid (2017): Areale Variation in den Gebrauchsstandards des Deutschen. In Marek Konopka & Angelika Wöllstein (Hrsg.), *Grammatische Variation – empirische Zugänge und theoretische Modellierung*, 85–104. Berlin, Boston: De Gruyter.
Elspaß, Stephan, Christa Dürscheid & Arne Ziegler (2017): Zur grammatischen Pluriarealität der deutschen Gebrauchsstandards – oder: Über die Grenzen des Plurizentrizitätsbegriffs. *Zeitschrift für deutsche Philologie* 136. Special issue: *Das Deutsche als plurizentrische Sprache. Ansprüche – Ergebnisse – Perspektiven*, hrsg. von Heinz Sieburg und Hans-Joachim Solms, 69–91.
Farø, Ken (2005): Plurizentrismus des Deutschen – programmatisch und kodifiziert. Zu: Variantenwörterbuch des Deutschen [...]. *Zeitschrift für Germanistische Linguistik* 33 (2/3), 380–395.
Filatkina, Natalia (2018): *Historische formelhafte Sprache. Theoretische Grundlagen und methodische Herausforderungen*. Berlin, Boston: De Gruyter.
Filatkina, Natalia, Ane Kleine-Engel, Marcel Dräger & Harald Burger (Hrsg.) (2012): *Aspekte der historischen Phraseologie und Phraseographie*. Heidelberg: Universitätsverlag Winter.
Friedrich, Jesko (2007): Historische Phraseologie des Deutschen. In Harald Burger, Dmitrij Dobrovol'skij, Peter Kühn & Neal R. Norrick (eds.), *Phraseology. An International Handbook of Contemporary Research*, Volume 2, 1092–1106. Berlin, New York: De Gruyter.
Grober-Glück, Gerda (1974): *Motive und Motivationen in Redensarten und Meinungen. Aberglaube, Volks-Charakterologie, Umgangsformeln, Berufsspott in Verbreitung und Lebensformen*. Marburg: Elwert.
Hain, Mathilde (1951): *Sprichwort und Volkssprache: eine volkskundlich-soziologische Dorfuntersuchung*. Gießen: Schmitz.
Höller, Lisa (2016): *Regionale Variation von Präpositionen in Phraseologismen der deutschen Standardsprache. Eine korpuslinguistische Untersuchung von Phraseologismen im Variantengrammatikkorpus und im Deutschen Referenzkorpus*. Unpublished Master Thesis Univ. of Salzburg. Retrieved from http://www.variantengrammatik.net/docs/MA-Arbeit_Hoeller.pdf, accessed December 31, 2018.
Hünert-Hofmann, Else (1991): *Phraseologismen in Dialekt und Umgangssprache*. Marburg: Elwert.
Hüpper, Dagmar, Elvira Topalović & Stephan Elspaß (2002): Zur Entstehung und Entwicklung von Paarformeln im Deutschen. In Elisabeth Piirainen & Ilpo Tapani Piirainen (Hrsg.), *Phraseologie in Raum und Zeit. Akten der 10. Tagung des Westfälischen Arbeitskreises „Phraseologie/Parömiologie" (Münster 2001)*, 77–99. Baltmannsweiler: Schneider Verlag Hohengehren.
Möller, Robert (2003): Zur diatopischen Gliederung des alltagssprachlichen Wortgebrauchs. Eine dialektometrische Auswertung von Jürgen Eichhoff: Wortatlas der deutschen Umgangssprachen (Bd. 1–4; 1977, 1978, 1993, 2000). *Zeitschrift für Dialektologie und Linguistik* 70, 259–297.
Möller, Robert & Stephan Elspaß (2014): Zur Erhebung und kartographischen Darstellung von Daten zur deutschen Alltagssprache online: Möglichkeiten und Grenzen. In Fabio Tosques (Hrsg.), *20 Jahre digitale Sprachgeographie*, 121–131. Berlin: Humboldt-Universität.
Möller, Robert & Stephan Elspaß (2015): Atlas zur deutschen Alltagssprache. In Roland Kehrein, Alfred Lameli & Stefan Rabanus (Hrsg.), *Regionale Variation des Deutschen – Projekte und Perspektiven*, 519–540. Berlin, Boston: De Gruyter.

Möller, Robert & Stephan Elspaß (2019): Die rezente Dynamik im arealsprachlichen Lexikon. In Joachim Herrgen & Jürgen Erich Schmidt (Hrsg.), *Sprache und Raum. Ein internationales Handbuch der Sprachvariation*. Bd. 4: Deutsch. Unter Mitarbeit von Hanna Fischer und Brigitte Ganswindt./*Language and Space. An International Handbook of Linguistic Variation*. Volume 4: German. In collaboration with Hanna Fischer and Brigitte Ganswindt, 758–783. Berlin, Boston: De Gruyter Mouton.

Pfeiffer, Christian (2017): Okkasionalität — Zur Operationalisierung eines zentralen definitorischen Merkmals phraseologischer Modifikationen. *Yearbook of Phraseology* 8, 9–30.

Pfeifer, Wolfgang (2003): *Etymologisches Wörterbuch des Deutschen*. 6. Auflage. München: dtv.

Pickl, Simon (2013): *Probabilistische Geolinguistik. Geostatistische Analysen lexikalischer Variation in Bayerisch-Schwaben*. Stuttgart: Franz Steiner.

Pickl, Simon & Simon Pröll (2019): Ergebnisse geostatistischer Analysen arealsprachlicher Variation im Deutschen. In Joachim Herrgen & Jürgen Erich Schmidt (Hrsg.), *Sprache und Raum. Ein internationales Handbuch der Sprachvariation*. Bd. 4: Deutsch. Unter Mitarbeit von Hanna Fischer und Brigitte Ganswindt./*Language and Space. An International Handbook of Linguistic Variation*. Volume 4: German. In collaboration with Hanna Fischer and Brigitte Ganswindt, 863–881. Berlin, Boston: De Gruyter Mouton.

Piirainen, Elisabeth (2000): *Phraseologie der westmünsterländischen Mundart*. Teil 1: *Semantische, kulturelle und pragmatische Aspekte dialektaler Phraseologismen*. Teil 2: *Lexikon der westmünsterländischen Redensarten*. Baltmannsweiler: Schneider Verlag Hohengehren.

Piirainen, Elisabeth (2002): ‚Landschaftlich', ‚norddeutsch' oder ‚berlinisch'? Zur Problematik diatopischer Markierungen von Idiomen. *Deutsch als Fremdsprache* 39 (1), 36–40.

Piirainen, Elisabeth (2003): Areale Aspekte der Phraseologie: Zur Awareness von Idiomen in regionalen Umgangssprachen. In Harald Burger, Annelies Häcki Buhofer & Gertrud Gréciano (Hrsg.), *Flut von Texten – Vielfalt der Kulturen: Ascona 2001 zur Methodologie und Kulturspezifik der Phraseologie*, 117–128. Baltmannsweiler: Schneider Verlag Hohengehren.

Piirainen, Elisabeth (2006): Phraseologie in arealen Bezügen: ein Problemaufriss. *Linguistik online* 27 (02/06), 195–218. Retrieved from www.linguistik-online.de/27_06/piirainen.html.

Piirainen, Elisabeth (2009a): Areale Phraseologie aus germanistischer Sicht. In Peter Durco, Ružena Kozmová & Daniela Drinková (Hrsg.), *Deutsche Sprache in der Slowakei. Festschrift für Prof. Dr. Ilpo Tapani Piirainen zum 65. Geburtstag. Internationale Fachtagung Piest'any, den 13.–15. Juni 2007*, 141–155. Trnava/Bratislava: Lehrstuhl für Germanistik, Philosophische Fakultät, Universität der Heiligen Cyril und Method.

Piirainen, Elisabeth (2009b): Phraseologie und Areallinguistik: ein interdisziplinärer Forschungsansatz. In Csaba Földes (Hrsg.), *Phraseologie disziplinär und interdisziplinär*, 361–372. Tübingen: Narr Francke Attempto.

Piirainen, Elisabeth (2012): *Widespread Idioms in Europe and Beyond: Toward a Lexicon of Common Figurative Units*. New York: Peter Lang.

RhWb = Müller, Joseph (Hrsg.) (1928–1971). *Rheinisches Wörterbuch*. Bonn, Berlin: Klopp. Retrieved from woerterbuchnetz.de/RhWB, accessed December 31, 2018.

Rodríguez Martín, Gustavo A. (2014): Canonical modified phraseological units: Analysis of the paradox. *Yearbook of phraseology* 5, 3–23.

Sava, Doris (2016): Areale Aspekte der Phraseologie. *Germanistische Beiträge* 38 (Lucian-Blaga-Universität Sibiu/Hermannstadt), 123–180. Retrieved from http://uniblaga.eu/wp-content/uploads/2016/04/38.2.1.pdf, accessed December 31, 2018.

Schmidlin, Regula (2007): Phraseological expressions in German standard varieties. In Harald Burger, Dmitrij Dobrovol'skij, Peter Kühn & Neal R. Norrick (eds.), *Phraseology. An International Handbook of Contemporary Research*. Volume 1, 551–562. Berlin, New York: De Gruyter.

Stumpf, Sören (2016): Modifikation oder Modellbildung? Das ist hier die Frage – Abgrenzungsschwierigkeiten zwischen modifizierten und modellartigen Phrasemen am Beispiel formelhafter (Ir-)Regularitäten. *Linguistische Berichte* 247, 317–342.

VG = *Variantengrammatik des Standarddeutschen* (2018). [A Grammar of Variation in Standard German]. An open access online reference work compiled by a team under the leadership of Christa Dürscheid, Stephan Elspaß and Arne Ziegler. Retrieved from http://mediawiki.ids-mannheim.de/VarGra, accessed December 31, 2018.

VWB = Ulrich Ammon, Hans Bickel & Alexandra N. Lenz (Hrsg.) (2016): *Variantenwörterbuch des Deutschen. Die deutsche Standardsprache in Österreich, der Schweiz und Deutschland sowie in Liechtenstein, Luxemburg, Ostbelgien und Südtirol*. 2. Auflage. Berlin, Boston: De Gruyter.

WDU I–IV = Eichhoff, Jürgen (1977 ff.): *Wortatlas der deutschen Umgangssprachen*. Bd. I/II: Bern [1977/78]; Bd. III: München et al. [1993]; Bd. IV: Bern, München [2000]: K.G. Saur.

Appendix: Phrasemes in AdA

Survey # Variable
1   *eins gemerkt/eins im Sinn/…* (Question 19)
2   Gruß beim Betreten eines Geschäfts am Nachmittag (Question 1)
     Antwort auf „Danke" (Question 2)
3   *etw. ist nicht nötig/etw. braucht's nicht* (Question 4b)
     Ach komm!/Ach geh! (Question 5d)
4   *mit jmdm. ist kein Blumentopf zu gewinnen* (Awareness) (Question 18a)
     mit jmdm. ist kein Blumentopf zu gewinnen (Usage) (Question 18b)
     (eine) dicke Backe(n) machen (Awareness) (Question 19a)
     (eine) dicke Backe(n) machen (Usage) (Question 19b)
     Das geht Dich einen Schmarren an (Awareness) (Question 20a)
     Das geht Dich einen Schmarren an (Usage) (Question 20b)
     Das krieg ich nicht gebacken! (Awareness) (Question 21a)
     Das krieg ich nicht gebacken! (Usage) (Question 21b)
7   Neujahrswünsche – in der Silvesternacht um 0:00 Uhr, wenn man auf das neue Jahr anstößt (Question 1a)
     Neujahrswünsche am 1. Januar (Question 1b)
     Wunsch in den Tagen vor dem 1. Januar (Question 1c)

dieses Jahr/heuer (Question 4d)
'unentgeltlich' (Question 4n)
gut zufrieden (Question 6h)

9   *jmdn. auf die Schippe/Schüppe/Schaufel nehmen* (Question 3c)
Verbreitung von *sich ausgehen*: Das geht sich noch aus. i.S.v. 'Es ist noch genug Geld/Zeit da' (Question 7g)
einen Purzelbaum machen/schlagen/schießen (Question 8c)

10   'Donnerstag vor dem Rosenmontag' (Question 1)
Verabschiedung unter Freunden (Question 17a)
Verabschiedung gegenüber KundInnen (Question 17b)

11   *Kalter Hund/Schwarzer Hund/...* (Question 1i)
hin ... zurück/hinzu ... rückzu/... (Question 2g)
Erwiderung auf *Schönes Wochenende!* (Question 2h)
Verbreitung von *sich ausgehen: Das geht sich (noch) aus.* [Wdh.] (Question 3a)
Verbreitung von *Du kannst doch nicht einfach hingehen und x tun!* (Question 3b)
Verbreitung von *Das war doch sowas von albern/dumm ...!* (Question 3e)
Verbreitung von *Das gehört geändert!* (Question 3f)
Verbreitung von „*Der kann das ab.*" (Question 3i)
20 geradeaus/genau/... (beim Zahlen) (Question 6a)
Haben Sie noch einen Weg?/(etwas) in der Nähe zu tun/erledigen? (Question 6b)
Das ist mir egal/gleich/wurscht!/Das kommt nicht drauf an. (Question 6c)
Wunsch beim Essen im Restaurant: *Guten Appetit!/Einen guten!/Mahlzeit!/...* (Question 6d)
Wunsch beim Essen in der Kantine: *Guten Appetit!/Einen guten!/Mahlzeit!/...* (Question 6e)
aufpassen wie ein Haftelmacher/Heftelmacher/Heftlmacher/Schießhund/Luchs/... (Question 6f)

Zuriñe Sanz-Villar
An Analysis of Basque Collocations Formed by Onomatopoeia and Verbs in a Translational Corpus of Literary Texts

Abstract: Collections of Basque proverbs and idioms have been compiled since the 16th century, but it was not until recently that interest in the study of phraseological units (PU) has arisen among researchers from different fields. This paper intends to analyze the use of a special type of phraseological unit – collocations formed by onomatopoeia and verbs – from a translational perspective in the language combination of German-Spanish-Basque. For that purpose, some introductory remarks will first be given regarding the realities of the Basque language and research on Basque phraseology. Then, the object of study will be presented, and the importance of Basque onomatopoeia will be highlighted. Since this is a corpus-based study, details on the compilation of the digitized, parallel, and multilingual corpus will be outlined, and it will be shown how these types of collocations were extracted from such a corpus in a semi-automatic way. In the translation analysis, it will be shown how one translation option stands out and how different factors (indirectness, for instance) influence Basque translations.

1 Introduction

The Basque language, spoken in the Basque Autonomous Community, Navarre, and the three provinces (Labourd, Basse-Navarre, and Soule) located within the French department of the Pyrénées-Atlantiques, is a minority language, not only due to the small number of speakers, but also because of the power relationships between the languages that coexist (i.e., the relationship between Spanish/French and Basque is not an equal, but a diglossic one), and this influences, among other things, translation activity in the Basque Country. The number of indirect translations made through Spanish versions instead of original (in this case, German) versions is, for instance, an obvious consequence, as will be shown later in this paper. At the level of language, Altzibar et al. (2011: 2) also mention that "Basque is currently undergoing a process of unification, standardisation, and adaptation to new uses. However, the influence of Spanish and

Open Access. © 2020 Z. Sanz-Villar, published by De Gruyter. This work is licensed under the Creative Commons Attribution 4.0 License.
https://doi.org/10.1515/9783110669824-004

French, especially through calque, is having an almost decisive influence on this process of renovation."

Indeed, "[i]n the last 30 years there has been an intense normalization effort in defining a unified form of Basque and in modernizing the language, as well as in extending its use from everyday affairs to high culture and science" (Uribarri 2011: 248). Although Basque has existed for centuries in many different dialects, the standard form, *Euskara Batua*, has a very short history of around 50 years, and its written literary tradition is short as well. The academic research on translation from/into Basque is very recent (Barambones Zubiria et al. 2015: 123); although authors have been compiling collections of Basque idioms and proverbs since the 16th century, not many researchers have devoted time and effort to the scientific study of phraseological Basque units.

From a contemporary and academic perspective, Aierbe (2008) analyzed the translation of phraseological units into Basque in administrative texts. An interesting conclusion she draws is the lack of fixation on the Basque language and phraseology, not only in the standard language, but also in specialized texts due to the fact that, as mentioned before, standard Basque was only recently established and because of the sociolinguistic situation of the language.

It has also been mentioned that another consequence of the diglossic situation of the Basque language is the creation and use of calques from other languages, namely Spanish and French. Some of these calques are collected on the webpage *Kalkoen Behatokia*[1] ("Observatory of Linguistic Calques"), where there is a special section on phraseological calques. During the last few years, members of this project have published papers on the use of phraseological calques in the Basque media (Alberdi et al. 2011), the use of collocations in the media (Altzibar 2004), Basque collocations (Altzibar et al. 2011), and Basque idioms (Altzibar and Bilbao 2016).

In the field of Natural Language Processing, within the IXA research group at the University of the Basque Country, authors such as Urizar (2012), Gurrutxaga (2014) and Iñurrieta et al. (2016) have worked on the automatic processing of Basque idioms and collocations.

Within Translation Studies, the author of this paper presented her PhD thesis (Sanz-Villar 2015) on the translation of phraseological units in the language combination of German-Spanish-Basque based on a parallel and multilingual corpus of literary texts. The analysis was limited to specific somatic phraseological units and binomials. The aim of the present article is to continue contributing to the field of Basque phraseological research from a translational perspective. For that

---

[1] http://www.ehu.eus/en/web/eins/kalkoen-behatokia, accessed March 28, 2018.

purpose, in the following section, the object of study will be presented: a specific type of phraseological unit, that is, Basque collocations formed by verbs and onomatopoeia, i.e. words with a more or less direct relationship between sound and meaning. Then, from a methodological perspective, the focus will be on the compilation of the corpus from which these collocations were extracted, and on the automatic extraction of these patterns. Once the collocations to be analyzed are selected and extracted, the translation analysis will be conducted and the author will conclude with some final remarks.

2 Basque Collocations Formed by Onomatopoeia and Verbs

Two approaches are usually distinguished when defining the boundaries of phraseology: the linguistic or phraseological approach and the statistical approach (Gurrutxaga 2014: 15). The former understands phraseology as a *continuum* with fixed phraseological units at the one end and flexible constructions at the other. The relation between the elements that constitute the phraseological unit is determined by their syntactic relationship and not the distance between them. According to Bernardini (2007: 1), "*[p]hraseological* approaches attempt to tell collocations apart from free combinations on the one hand, and from other lexical restriction phenomena on the other." At the same time, within the statistical approach, distance or window span plays a very important role as well as the co-occurrence between the elements. As stated by Moon (1998: 26), "[c]ollocation typically denotes frequently repeated or statistically significant co-occurrences, whether or not there are any special semantic bonds between collocating items." Word combinations are extracted from corpora and can be located in a *continuum* that goes from Sinclair's (1987) *idiom principle* to the *open choice principle*. Here, the concept of collocation is central because collocations are more frequent in the use of language than idioms.

Following the linguistic or phraseological approach, Altzibar et al. (2011) presented a taxonomy of Basque collocations (the first and only one to the author's knowledge) based on the well-known classification proposed by Corpas Pastor (1996) for Spanish. According to their morphosyntactic structure, Basque collocations are divided into three main classes: noun-based, adjective-based, and adverb-based. At the same time, each of them is made up of several subclasses. Among the adverb-based collocations, in the framework of this study the focus will be on one specific subclass, namely the type of collocations that are made up of an instance of onomatopoeia (in adverbial function) and a verb, such as *dinbi-danba jo* [to hit repeatedly, to fire a shot, to toll a bell], *zanga-zanga edan* [to drink with large gulps or with great desire], or *tipi-tapa joan* [to march/walk step by step], as exemplified in Altzibar et al. (2011: 10).[2] A conclusion drawn by the authors of the paper indicates that "an important number of the morphosyntactic patterns of Basque collocations are different to the Romance languages of the region" (Altzibar et al. 2011: 11). The collocation type "onomatopoeia + verb" is mentioned as one of those different patterns. Apart from this feature, it is worth mentioning that there is a large number of them in not only everyday but also educated language.

According to Ibarretxe-Antuñano (2006), the linguistic study of onomatopoeia has long been neglected. However, studies on onomatopoeia carried out in different languages have shown that they constitute an essential part of a language and that they are of considerable importance in terms of quantity.[3] Basque onomatopoeia are characterized by three features: total or partial reduplication, the use of unusual phonological and prosodic elements (for instance, *-dz*), and the association of certain sounds with certain meanings (Ibarretxe-Antuñano 2006: 151). According to Ibarretxe-Antuñano, the former feature does not appear very often in other European languages, but it is one of the most used strategies in Basque (not only with regard to onomatopoeia but also as a mechanism to express emphasis).

From a morphosyntactic point of view, different grammatical categories can be found (nouns, adverbs, verbs, adjectives, interjections) among Basque onomatopoeia, and, due to the fact that in Basque it is quite easy to create new words through derivation and composition, it is not unusual for new words to be created based on onomatopoeia (Ibarretxe-Antuñano 2006: 153). Semantically, they are mainly used in the following semantic fields: actions and activities, animals, plants, atmospheric phenomena, musical instruments, physical and mental features, tools, things, child language, large quantities, nature, and sexual terms. The first group is the largest among Basque onomatopoeia, and is divided into

---

[2] Ibarretxe-Antuñano (2006: 153), making reference to Etxepare (2003), refers to this type of collocation as "complex predicates" and adds that they are very common in languages with onomatopoeia. She also mentions that the verbs accompanying the onomatopoeia are usually "dummy verbs", i.e., verbs such as *(to) make, (to) say, (to) think*, and so on. Therefore, it is not the verb but the onomatopoeia that provides the real meaning of the construction (Ibarretxe-Antuñano 2012: 150–151).
[3] Referring to Basque, Schuchardt (1925: 18), for instance, says that "das Baskische ist sehr reich an deutlichen Schallworten", emphasizing the abundance of onomatopoetic constructions in Basque.

different categories: motion, communication, light, sound, beverage/food, destruction, hitting, boiling, emotions, body functions, and others (Ibarretxe-Antuñano 2012: 152–160).

The main limitation of Ibarretxe-Antuñano and Martinez Lizarduikoa (2006) is that it does not reflect the real use of these constructions, the onomatopoeia, since all the examples are extracted from different dictionaries and collections containing Basque multiword expressions.[4] Ibarretxe-Antuñano also concludes that studies regarding the translation of onomatopoeia constitute a field that requires further research in the future (Ibarretxe-Antuñano 2012: 171). This paper intends to make a contribution to filling this gap by analyzing the use of collocations formed by onomatopoeia in children's and adult literature texts translated from German into Basque.

3 Compilation and Features of the Corpus

In order to conduct such an analysis, it was first necessary to compile a corpus consisting of German-into-Basque literary translations. For that purpose, the following steps were taken: the creation and description of a catalog consisting of literary texts that have been translated in the language combination German-Basque, specification of the criteria for selection of the texts that would be part of the corpus, and (once the texts were selected) digitization, cleaning, tagging, aligning, and uploading the texts to a database.

The catalog, known as Aleuska, which was updated until 2013, includes 710 entries that can be divided into different text types: theater (1%), essay (8%), adult literature (8%), poetry[5] (20%), and children's literature (63%). The first decision in the selection of the texts was based on this distribution: Children's literature (CL) texts and adult literature (AL) texts were included in the corpus on the basis of their representativeness in the catalog. The chronological factor was another aspect that was taken into account when defining the selection criteria. In the catalog, as far as AL and CL texts are concerned, the number of translations published starts increasing from the year 1980 onwards. For this reason, the texts included in the corpus are translations published from that year on. In addition,

---

4 However, in the paper from 2012, Ibarretxe-Antuñano includes a section about the pragmatic functions of Basque onomatopoeia, and in this section the reader can find how these constructions are used in different contexts, such as oral literature, poetry, comics, and advertising.
5 Regarding poetry, it has to be mentioned that many entries in the Aleuska catalog consist of single poems.

the CL-AL sub-catalog includes texts by 126 different German authors and 127 different translators. Thus, source and target author diversity was another criterion to be considered when selecting the texts. The final factor that needs to be mentioned is the mode of translation; in other words, the fact that the CL and AL texts of the Aleuska catalog were identified as direct translations made from the German source text or as indirect translations carried out from an intermediary text (most of the time the Spanish version) was of great importance (not only for the compilation of the corpus but also for the translation analysis).

To sum up, the corpus is made up of 24 CL texts and 24 AL texts, which represents around 3.5 million words. As for author diversity, works from 30 different German authors and 28 different translators were selected; regarding the mode of translation, there are 34 direct translations and 14 indirect translations. With reference to this last feature, it is important to bear in mind that they should be regarded as *assumed* direct and indirect translations, since it was not always easy to obtain this information from the catalog.

For the compilation of the corpus, a tool called TAligner was used. The latest versions of this program were developed within the TRALIMA/ITZULIK research group[6] at the University of the Basque Country, and one of its strong points is that it allows the simultaneous alignment of not only two but various texts. This option was an indispensable condition for the compilation of the present corpus—indispensable in order to be able to align the indirect translations with their source and intermediary texts.

After all the bi- and tri-texts had been digitized, they were cleaned, tagged, and aligned. It can clearly be observed in Figure 1[7] that the tool contains all these functions—*limpiar* (clean), *etiquetar* (tag), and *alinear* (align)—and that it allows the simultaneous alignments of numerous texts, three in this case:

---

6 The website of the research group can be accessed via this link: https://www.ehu.eus/en/web/tralimaitzulik/home, accessed March 28, 2018.
7 Figures 1 and 2 represent the latest version of the tool, known as TAligner 3.0.

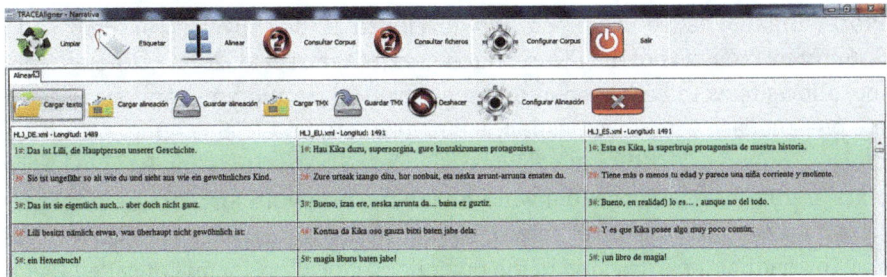

Fig. 1: Functions of the program TAligner 3.0

Once all the texts are aligned, the user can make queries by using the option *Consultar Corpus*. The example in figure 2, for instance, shows the search for the Basque collocation *kar-kar egin* [to laugh] in the corpus. In this case, the author was querying the whole corpus, but since metadata, such as author's name, translator, genre, and so on, was introduced when tagging the texts, the queries can be limited to words or word combinations in certain texts translated by certain translators or texts written by certain authors, just to mention some possibilities.

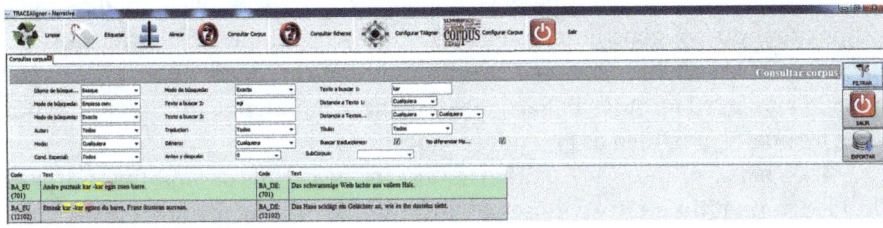

Fig. 2: Querying the corpus with the program TAligner 3.0

4 Extraction of Potential Collocations

The aim is to extract specific grammatical patterns from the corpus that may constitute collocations. For this purpose, it is necessary to tag the corpus at a part-of-speech (POS) level. This task was performed with the help of a Natural Language

Processing tool called IXA pipes[8] and developed at the University of the Basque Country by members of the IXA research group (Agerri et al. 2014). Although this tool allows texts to be tagged at different levels, the annotation options used in the present case were tokenization, lemmatization, and POS tagging. As for the process, only the TXT files of each text need to be annotated—the Basque target texts in this case—and the tool will provide the user with an output file in NAF format for each file that is tokenized, lemmatized, and tagged at the POS level.

To conduct the extraction of the potential collocations, a toolkit called Foma (Hulden 2009) was employed. Created by Mans Hulden, it is a free and open-source tool, and may be used to satisfy different goals within Natural Language Processing. For the purposes of the present study, a code to extract user-defined grammatical patterns based on the information of the NAF tagged files was defined[9] and then processed with Foma.

The number of patterns extracted was very large (48,296), a result which was expected considering the widespread use of these patterns as well as the size of the corpus. However, advantage was taken of a special feature of the Basque onomatopoeia under study: The fact that they contain a hyphen in the onomatopoeia part of the word combination helped reduce the initial list to 2,617 patterns. Then, with the help of a number of Unix commands (*sed*, *egrep*, and so on) and some manual work, unnecessary combinations were removed[10] and a list of 428 patterns was compiled. Many of those combinations were partial or total reduplications that do not constitute onomatopoeia. As mentioned in Ibarretxe-Antuñano (2012: 138), reduplications, constituting onomatopoeia or not, are a frequently employed resource in Basque. From the 428 patterns, 147 different types were manually identified as potential collocations.

Since many of those 147 patterns occur in the corpus several times, it was decided to limit the study to those patterns that, according to the semantic classification mentioned in section 2, represent the largest group among Basque onomatopoeia: the ones that describe the semantic field of actions and activities. All in all, 66 types and 162 tokens were selected and queried for the subsequent translation analysis.

---

8 http://ixa2.si.ehu.es/ixa-pipes/, accessed March 28, 2018.
9 I hereby thank the member of the IXA research group Iñaki Alegria for helping me to write the code.
10 Many of them constituted compounds, such as *gutun-azala ireki* [to open the envelope] and were easy to identify and exclude from potential collocations. Many other results indicated that unnecessary spaces were added between the constituents of a compound, and thus, only a part of the compound was extracted. For instance, in *monopoly-jolastu* [to play Monopoly], the word *game* or something similar is missing.

The ascription of semantic fields to the patterns found in the corpus was not always straightforward. While in some cases there was no doubt about the category a specific collocation belonged to (for instance, *mauka-mauka jan, dir-dir egin*[11]), other cases (such as, *plisti-plasta egin*[12]) were more controversial. Be that as it may, it is worth mentioning that the largest semantic field, in terms of occurrences, was the field expressing motion, with 44 occurrences. In fact, as for the group of onomatopoeia describing motion, Ibarretxe-Antuñano (2012: 153) mentions that it is one of the largest in Basque: "El grupo de las onomatopeyas que describen el movimiento es uno de los más numerosos en euskera."

Analyzing the verbs that accompany the onomatopoeia, it may be concluded that the most usual by far is the above-mentioned "dummy verb" *egin* [to do; to make] with 88 occurrences, followed by the verb *joan* [to go] with 14 occurrences. Thus, in the case of those dummy verbs, as mentioned in Ibarretxe-Antuñano (2012: 150–151), the onomatopoeia is the component providing the real meaning of the construction.

5 Translation Analysis

During the extraction of the collocations and the translation analysis, the main focus was on the target texts and culture, which is in line with the target-oriented approach established within Descriptive Translation Studies (Toury 2012). In other words, the queries were made based on the Basque target texts, and thus the Basque translations and their cultural context served as the starting point. Then, the target texts' outputs were compared to their German (and Spanish) source texts, and the following translation options were identified:
- *No PU-Collocation*: The counterpart of the Basque collocation is not a PU in the German source text; it is usually a single verb.
- *Collocation-Collocation*: A German collocation has been translated with another collocation in the Basque target text.
- *Idiom-Collocation*: The German equivalent of the Basque collocation is an idiom.

---

11 *Mauka-mauka jan* means 'to eat voraciously, greedily' and *dir-dir egin* 'to shine; to sparkle; to gleam; to glitter', and they clearly belong to the semantic groups *beverage/food* and *light*.
12 In *plisti-plasta egin*, the word *plisti-plasta* is the onomatopoeia of splashing water. Due to the sound created through the action of splashing water, it was ascribed to the semantic group of *sound*, but it may also belong to the semantic field expressing motion.

- *Ø-Collocation*: There is no counterpart in the German source text for the Basque collocation; the Basque collocation is an addition.

The examples in table 1 may serve for a better understanding of each of the translation options explained above:

Tab. 1: Examples of the different translation options found in the corpus

Source Text	Target Text	Translation Option
1. Ein gigantischer Fluss **schlängelt sich** behäbig seinen Weg. (HLJde)[13] [A gigantic river meanders its way slowly.[14]]	Ibai ikaragarri handi batek bere bideari jarraitzen dio **astiro-astiro, sigi-saga eginez**. (HLJeu)[15] [A gigantic river follows its way slowly, zig-zagging.]	No PU-Collocation
2. [...] Franz **geht mit kleinen Schritten** und weiß: (BAde)[16] [Franz walks in small steps and knows:]	[...] Franz **tipi-tapa doa** eta badaki: (BAeu)[17] [Franz walks pitter-patter and knows:]	Collocation-Collocation
3. Das schwammige Weib **lachte aus vollem Hals**. (BAde) [The spongy woman laughed loudly.]	Andre puztuak **kar-kar egin zuen barre**. (BAeu) [The swollen woman laughed loudly.]	Idiom-Collocation
4. Es gibt auch unter uns Zöglingen etwas wie einen aus Luft und Nichts herausgegriffenen Zeitungenklatsch. (JGde)[18] [There is also something like newspaper gossip plucked out of the air and nothing among us pupils.]	Ikasleon artean ere badabil zerbait, airetik eta hutsetik **bolo-bolo zabaltzen** diren egunkarietako hizkimizkien antzekorik. (JGeu)[19] [There is also something among us pupils, similar to the newspaper gossip that extends everywhere, plucked out of the air and nothing.]	Ø-Collocation

---

13 Knister (2003): *Hexe Lilli auf der Jagd nach dem verlorenen Schatz*. Würzburg: Arena.
14 All English translations are by the author of the paper. They are intended to show the literal meaning of the examples.
15 Knister (2003): *Kika Supersorgina altxorraren bila*. Bilbao: Gero (translator: Iñaki Aristondo).
16 Döblin, Alfred (1929): *Berlin Alexanderplatz*. Berlin: Fischer.
17 Döblin, Alfred (1929): *Berlin Alexanderplatz*. Berlin: Fischer (translator: Anton Garikano).
18 Walser, Robert (1909): *Jakob von Gunten*. Berlin: Cassirer.
19 Walser, Robert (2005): *Jakob von Gunten*. Donostia: Erein (translator: Edorta Matauko).

The first example shows how the equivalent of the German verb *sich schlängeln* ('to meander') and the Spanish verb *serpentear* is a collocation made up of the onomatopoeia *sigi-saga* [zigzag] and the verb *egin* [to make; to do]. The fact that a reduplication (*astiro-astiro*, 'slowly') appears in the same sentence in Basque makes this example even more interesting because it shows (together with other examples that were found in the corpus but cannot be mentioned in this paper due to space constraints) that not only onomatopoeia but also reduplications are a widespread resource in Basque, as mentioned in section 2. The translation of the German collocation *mit kleinen Schritten gehen* [to walk in small steps], as identified in the online collocation dictionary compiled by Häcki Buhofer et al. (2014)[20], is the Basque collocation *tipi-tapa joan* [to walk pitter-patter]. In the third example, the German idiom *aus vollem Hals* [loudly] is translated with the Basque collocations *kar-kar barre egin* [to laugh loudly]. In the last case, it can be observed that there is no counterpart for the Basque onomatopoeia *bolo-bolo* [everywhere] and that it rather serves to intensify the meaning of the two phraseological units *aus dem Nichts* [out of nothing] and *aus der Luft gegriffen sein* [something that is plucked out of the air].

The distribution of the above-mentioned translation options across the different subcorpora—children's literature direct translations (CL DI), adult literature direct translations (AL DI), children's literature indirect translations (CL INDI), and adult literature indirect translations (AL INDI)—is presented in tables 2 and 3. Before giving any interpretation of the figures, it is important to mention that the different subcorpora are not equal in size. The largest is AL DI (1,708,825 words), followed by CL DI (809,301 words); AL INDI (547,773 words) and CL INDI (463,634 words) are significantly smaller compared to the former. Therefore, it cannot be concluded that more collocations formed by onomatopoeia and a verb have been extracted from the AL DI subcorpus. Rather, the main conclusion that can be drawn from the figures in tables 2 and 3 is the predominance of the translation option *No PU-Collocation* in all subcorpora, and consequently the sporadic occurrence of the rest of the translation options.

---

20 http://www.kollokationenwoerterbuch.ch/web/, accessed March 28, 2018.

Tab. 2: Distribution of translation options across subcorpora (raw numbers)

	CL DI	AL DI	CL INDI	AL INDI	Total
No PU-Collocation	46	72	16	10	144
Collocation-Collocation	2	6	1	0	9
Idiom-Collocation	1	4	1	1	7
Ø-Collocation	0	1	0	1	2
	49	83	18	12	162

Tab. 3: Distribution of translation options across subcorpora (in percentages)

	CL DI	AL DI	CL INDI	AL INDI	Total
No PU-Collocation	93.88	86.75	88.89	83.33	88.89
Collocation-Collocation	4.08	7.23	5.56	0.00	5.56
Idiom-Collocation	2.04	4.82	5.56	8.33	4.32
Ø-Collocation	0.00	1.20	0.00	8.33	1.23
	100.00	100.00	100.00	100.00	100.00

Next, it is intended to go beyond these general figures and focus on the nuances of the different translation options as well as other interesting features observed during the translation analysis.

5.1 No PU-Collocation

Despite the undeniable predominance of this translation option, it is necessary to mention that it is not a homogeneous group and that it deserves more detailed attention. In some cases, for instance, there is no phraseological unit in the German source text, but instead verbs with a more or less evident onomatopoetic origin can be found, such as *schwabbeln* [to wobble], *plappern* [to chatter], *kitzeln* [to tickle], *plantschen* [to splash], *scheppern* [to rattle], *brummen* [to grumble], *knurren* [to growl], and so on. In the first example, extracted from an adult literature text, to express that Mieze is chattering, in the original text the verb *plappern* is used, and in the Basque text the onomatopoeia *tar-tar*, together with the dummy verb *esan* [to say], is employed. The second example is from a children's literature text, and the Basque onomatopoeia *mar-mar egin* was selected as a counterpart of the German onomatopoetic verb *brummen*.

Tab. 4: The use of verbs of onomatopoetic origin in the source texts

Source Text	Target Text
1. Und Mieze sitzt auf, faßt ihren Franz um und sieht ihm wonnig ins Gesicht und **plappert** so lauter süßen Quatsch und bettelt und bettelt: (BAde) [And Mieze sits up, takes her Franz and looks him in the face with delight and chatters, saying nothing but sweet nonsense and begs and begs.]	Eta Miezek bizkarra tentetu, besarkatu bere Franz eta begiratzen dio aurpegira bozkariotsu eta **tar-tar esaten** dizkio sekulako txorakeria goxoak eta arren eta arren: (BAeu) [And Mieze stiffens her back, hugs her Franz and looks at his face with joy and does not stop telling him some incredible sweet nonsense and begs and begs.]
2. "Ja, ja", **brummte** Tobi, der sich mindestens fünf Jahre zu alt für eine Holzeisenbahn fühlte. (SLHde)[21] ["Yes, yes," grumbled Tobi, who felt at least five years too old for a wooden train.]	"Bai, bai", **mar-mar egin** zuen Tobik, zeini zurezko trenekin jostatzeko gutxienez bost urte zaharregia zela iruditzen zitzaion. (SLHeu)[22] ["Yes, yes," grumbled Tobi, who felt at least five years too old to play with a wooden train.]

On other occasions, there is not just one verb, but two (of onomatopoetic or non-onomatopoetic origin) in the German source text, and the translators decided to use a collocation with onomatopoeia in the Basque target texts. Two different examples can be found in table 5: In the first example, the meaning of the German verbs *rappeln und rattern* [to rattle] is represented by the Basque word combination *triki-traka ibili* [to clatter], while in the second example, the above-mentioned verb *plappern* is repeated twice. The Basque translator decided to triplicate[23] the onomatopoeia by using *tar-tar-tar*, thus emphasizing that she does nothing but chatter.

---

21 Sommer-Bodenburg, Angela (1991): *Schokolowski. Lustig ist das Hundeleben*. Munich: Bertelsmann.
22 Sommer-Bodenburg, Angela (1996): *Txokoloski. Dibertigarria da txakurren bizitza*. Bilbao: Desclée de Brouwer (translator: Edurne Azkue).
23 Ibarretxe Antuñano (2012: 138) refers to this structural feature as *triplicación total* or total triplication.

Tab. 5: The use of two verbs of onomatopoetic origin in the source texts

Source Text	Target Text
1. Neben ihm **rappelte und ratterte** schon der Kompressor. (JVde)[24] [Beside him, the compressor was already rattling.]	Ondoan konpresorea **triki-traka zarataka zebilen** jada. (JVeu)[25] [Beside the compressor was already clattering.]
2. Sie **plappert, plappert,** legt den Kopf um seinen Hals, [...]. (BAde) [She chatters, chatters, puts her head around his neck.]	**Tar-tar-tar ari** da, jarri du burua mutilaren lepoan, [...]. (BAeu) [She does not stop talking, puts her head on the boy's neck.]

In many cases, the most natural, direct, and straightforward correspondent of the German verb is the collocation with onomatopoeia, but in other cases, the Basque translation option seems more phraseological or expressive than the original. As can be seen in table 6, the first example is extracted from an indirect translation. Both the German and Spanish texts contain a single verb (*trinken, beber,* 'to drink'), while the translator in the Basque version, with the use of the onomatopoeia, describes more exhaustively how the drinking is performed: *zanga-zanga* [in gulps]. A very similar situation can be observed in the second example: The equivalent for the German verb *essen* [to eat] is not just the Basque verb *jan*, but it describes how the fish is being eaten by Jasper: *mauka-mauka* [voraciously, greedily].

Tab. 6: Examples of more phraseological or expressive options in the target texts

Source Text	Intermediary Text	Target Text
1. Er schimpft, reißt den Kühlschrank auf, schnappt sich das Mineralwasser und **trinkt** direkt aus der Flasche. (HLJde) [He scolds, tears open the fridge, grabs the mineral water and drinks directly from the bottle.]	Dani abre la nevera de golpe y **bebe** directamente de la botella de agua mineral. (HLJes) [Dani opens the fridge at once and drinks directly from the bottle of mineral water.]	Danik hozkailua kolpetik ireki eta ur minerala **zanga-zanga edaten** du botilatik bertatik. (HLJeu) [Dani opens the fridge at once and drinks in gulps the mineral water directly from the bottle.]

---

24 Massanek, Joachim (2003): *Juli, die Viererkettte.* Frankfurt am Main: Baumhaus.
25 Massanek, Joachim (2010): *Juli, defensa onena.* Bilbao: Gero (translator: Nuria Sebrango).

Source Text	Intermediary Text	Target Text
2. Jasper fanden wir bei Mama in der Küche. Er **aß** den gestern verschmähten Tiefkühlfisch. (DAKde)[26] [We found Jasper in the kitchen with mum. He ate the yesterday spurned frozen fish.]		Jasper, amarekin sukaldean aurkitu genuen, bezperan nahi izan ez zuen arraina **mauka-mauka jaten**. (DAKeu)[27] [We found Jasper in the kitchen with mum, eating voraciously the fish he did not want yesterday.]

The following translation options in the Basque target texts extracted from indirect translations could be described as more phraseological if the original German text and the Basque translation were compared, but it is obvious from looking at the intermediary versions that the Basque translation has been influenced by the Spanish version. In the first example, the sun rests [*ruhen*] in the German text, while in the Spanish and Basque versions it sparkles [*centellear, diz-diz egin*]. In the second example, the path leads [*führen*] somewhere in the German original text, and in the Spanish and Basque versions it meanders or zigzags [*serpentear, sigi-sagan igaro*].

Tab. 7: Examples of the influence of the intermediary texts on the Basque translations

Source Text	Intermediary Text	Target Text
1. Wenn das liebe Tal um mich dampft, und die hohe Sonne an der Oberfläche der undurchdringlichen Finsternis meines Waldes **ruht**, und nur einzelne Strahlen sich in das innere Heiligtum stehlen […]. (DLWde)[28] [When the dear valley steams around me, and the high sun rests on the surface of the im-	Cuando el valle se vela en torno mío con un encaje de vapores; cuando el sol de mediodía **centellea** sobre la impenetrable sombra de mi bosque sin conseguir otra cosa que filtrar entre las hojas algunos rayos hasta el fondo del santuario;	Harana nire gainean lurrinezko mihiztaduraz barrandatzen denean; eguerdiko eguzkiak nire basoaren gerizpe sarkaitzaren gainean, hostoen artean eta santutegiko ostalderaino izpi batzu iraiztea baino lortu ez dela, **diz-diz egiten** duenean;

---

26 Nöstlinger, Christine (1982): *Das Austauschkind*. Weinheim: Beltz & Gelberg.
27 Nöstlinger, Christine (1991): *Ingeles bat etxean*. Lizarra: Elkar (translator: Xabier Mendiguren).
28 Goethe, Johann Wolfgang von (1774): *Die Leiden des jungen Werther*. Leipzig: Weygand.

Source Text	Intermediary Text	Target Text
penetrable darkness of my forest, and only single rays steal into the inner sanctum.]	(DLWes)[29] [When the valley veils around me with a lace of vapors; when the midday sun sparkles on the impenetrable shadow of my forest, achieving nothing but filtering some rays through the leaves to the bottom of the sanctuary.]	(DLWeu)[30] [When the valley lurks over me with a lace of steam; when the midday sun sparkles on the impenetrable shadow of my forest, achieving nothing but filtering some rays through the leaves and to the sanctuary's heaven.]
2. Dieser Weg, der direkte Weg nach Napoule, **führte** an den Ausläufern des Tanneron entlang durch die Flußsenken von Frayere und Siagne. (DPGMde)[31] [This path, the direct path to Napoule, led along the foothills of the Tanneron through the river valleys of the Frayere and the Siagne.]	Este camino, el camino directo a Napoule, **serpenteaba** por las estribaciones del Tanneron, cruzando las cuencas de Frayére y Siagne. (DPGMes)[32] [This path, the direct path to Napoule, meandered through the foothills of the Tanneron, through the basins of the Frayere and the Siagne.]	Bide hura, La Napoulera zuzenean zihoan bidea, **sigi-sagan igaro**tzen zen Tanneronen oinetik, Frayere eta Siagne ibaien arroetan barrena. (DPGMeu)[33] [This path, the direct path to Napoule, zigzagged through the foothills of the Tanneron, through the basins of the Frayere and Siagne rivers.]

5.2 Collocation-Collocation

A special case of this translation option is represented by the example in table 8. The Basque children's literature text has been translated indirectly through the Spanish text. However, in this case, the collocation is found in the German text (*laut klopfen*, 'to knock loudly') and not in the Spanish text, where a single verb has been used (*dar*, 'to knock'). Thus, given the indirect character of the Basque translation, it may be argued that, with the use of the word combination *kaska-kaska jo* [to tap] as an equivalent of the Spanish verb *dar*, a more phraseological target text is created.

---

[29] Goethe, Johann Wolfgang von (1835): *Las desventuras del joven Werther*. Barcelona: Apolo (translator: José -Mor de Fuentes).
[30] Goethe, Johann Wolfgang von (1987): *Werther*. Donostia: Kriselu (translator: Gotzon Lobera).
[31] Süskind, Patrick (1985): *Das Parfum*. Zürich: Diogenes.
[32] Süskind, Patrick (1985): *El perfume*. Barcelona: Círculo de lectores (translator: Pilar Giralt).
[33] Süskind, Patrick (2007): *Perfumea*. Irun: Alberdania (translator: Miren Arratibel).

Tab. 8: Example of the translation option *Collocation-Collocation* in an indirect translation

Source Text	Intermediary Text	Target Text
denn ein Gast **klopft laut** mit dem Messer ans Glas und will zahlen. (EDde)[34] [because a guest knocks loudly with the knife on his glass and wants to pay.]	porque un parroquiano **daba** con el cuchillo en la copa como el que quiere pagar. (EDes) [because a customer knocks with the knife on his glass as if he wants to pay.]	bezero bat, ordaindu nahi zuenarena eginez, aiztoarekin basoa **jotzen** ari bait zen **kaska-kaska**. (EDeu) [because a customer, as if he wanted to pay, was tapping his glass with the knife.]

5.3 Idiom-Collocation

In the example cited in table 9, which represents an indirect translation, the idiom is also found in the German source text (*wie Kraut und Rüben liegen*, 'to be higgledy-piggledy'), and not in the intermediary text from which the Basque translation originates. However, since the meaning changes in the Spanish version [to curl up] with respect to the original version, the Basque (which matches the meaning of the Spanish text) and German versions also differ semantically.

Tab. 9: Example of the translation option *Idiom-Collocation* with a difference in meaning due to indirectness

Source Text	Intermediary Text	Target Text
Die Jungen warfen sich zu Boden und **lagen wie Kraut und Rüben** durcheinander. (EDde) [The boys threw themselves to the ground and lay higgledy-piggledy.]	Y los chicos se tiraron al suelo y **se quedaron muy acurrucaditos**. (EDes)[35] [And the boys threw themselves to the ground and they were very curled up.]	Mutikoak etzan eta **kuzkur-kuzkur egin**da geratu ziren. (EDeu)[36] [The boys lay down and they were very curled up.]

In the next and final example, however, idioms can be observed both in the original and in the intermediary text: *mit vollen Backen (verzehren)* ('to eat with

---

34 Kästner, Erich (1929): *Emil und die Detektive*. Zurich: Atrium.
35 Kästner, Erich (1967): *Emilio y los detectives*. Barcelona: Juventud (translator: José Fernández).
36 Kästner, Erich (1991): *Emilio eta detektibeak*. Donostia: Elkar (translator: Tomás Sarasola).

stuffed cheeks') and (*devorar*) *a dos carrillos* ('gobble food down'). The Basque translator used a collocation formed by onomatopoeia and a verb (*mauka-mauka jan*, 'to eat voraciously, greedily') to represent the same meaning.

Tab. 10: Example of the translation option *Idiom-Collocation* with no difference in meaning

Source Text	Intermediary Text	Target Text
[...] und, wenn sie das gewünschte endlich erhaschen, es **mit vollen Backen verzehren** und rufen: "mehr!" (DLWde) [and when they finally catch what they desire, eat it with stuffed cheeks and shout: "more!".]	[...] cuando logran atrapar el manjar apetecido lo **devoran a dos carrillos** y gritan: "¡Más!" (DLWes) [and when they finally catch the desired delicacy, they gobble it down and shout: "more!".]	[...] gura izandako jatena harrapatzen lor dezatenean **mauka-mauka jan** eta "gehiago" deiadar egiten dutenak direla. (DLWeu) [when they finally catch the desired delicacy, they are the ones who eat it voraciously and shout "more".]

6 Conclusions

This paper has focused on specific phraseological units found in the Basque language. Basque has a weak tradition of written literature and a short history of its standard variety, which coexists diglossically with other major languages and is still in the process of standardization. Given these features, it is understandable that there has been no systematic research in the field of Basque phraseology and that even less attention has been paid to the study of the translation of phraseological units from/into Basque. However, as presented in the introduction of this paper, there are some projects worth mentioning (Aierbe 2008; Sanz-Villar 2015; Iñurrieta et al. 2016), and the objective of the present article has been to make a further contribution toward research in this field.

Altzibar et al. (2011) identified collocations formed by partially or totally reduplicated onomatopoeia and a verb as a special type of formulaic pattern in Basque, and the actual use of those collocations has been analyzed in this paper from a translational perspective. By doing so, we have encountered both theoretical and methodological challenges since there was no similar previous study that would have served as a reference. From a theoretical perspective, it has not always been easy to identify the onomatopoeia part of the collocation as actual onomatopoeia or to establish the boundaries between collocations and free word combinations. In this sense, the onomatopoeia dictionary of Ibarretxe-Antuñano and Martinez Lizarduikoa (2006) as well as Ibarretxe-Antuñano's papers (2006, 2012) on this topic were of great help and served as a constant reference.

Methodologically, the first challenge was to create a corpus from scratch that would meet the requirements to conduct German-into-Basque translation analyses of literary texts. Although at present there are a number of very diverse Basque corpora available to any user, the type of corpus we needed – a digitized, parallel, and multilingual corpus consisting of German original texts, intermediary versions in the case of indirect translations, and Basque target texts – not only needed to be built from scratch but also required creation of a specific tool,[37] which allowed for the simultaneous alignment of several texts. Due to the lack of precedent, another methodological challenge involved the extraction of the phraseological units under analysis. This was solved thanks to a lemmatization and POS-tagging tool developed by members of the IXA group that works, among others, with Basque, and an open-source tool that requires some knowledge of computational linguistics, but can be used with any language. The author is aware of the fact that the corpus probably contains more collocations formed by onomatopoeia that were not extracted using this method, because, for instance, the verb does not always appear right after the onomatopoeia. However, a great number of them were extracted, and this may be seen as a first attempt toward such an exhaustive analysis.

The translation analysis has shown that, despite the predominance of the translation option *No PU-Collocation*, the nuances that are hidden behind it are of great significance from a translational point of view. Sometimes the use of the collocations seemed to be the most natural way of rendering the content of the source text in the target text, but at other times, as exemplified in table 6, the use of the Basque collocations resulted in a more phraseological text. When analyzing somatic phraseological units (Sanz-Villar 2018), it was concluded that in the case of indirect translations there is "a tendency to deviate from the Spanish intermediary version and create more typical Basque texts." The examples in tables 6 and 8, as well as others that could not be presented in this paper, corroborate this hypothesis, but more examples should be analyzed. One thing is clear: during the whole process, from the creation of the catalog to the translation analysis, it was crucial to take into account that indirect translations are a reality in German-into-Basque translations.

---

[37] I hereby thank the computer technician Iñaki Albisua for his dedication to the alignment tool over the past years.

References

Agerri, Rodrigo, Josu Bermudez & German Rigau (2014): IXA pipeline: Efficient and ready to use multilingual NLP tools. *Proceedings of the 9th Language Resources and Evaluation Conference (LREC2014)*, 26–31.

Aierbe, Axun (2008): La traducción a la lengua vasca de las unidades fraseológicas especializadas del lenguaje administrativo. In María Isabel González (ed.), *A Multilingual Focus on Contrastive Phraseology*, 27–44. Hamburg: Dr. Kovač.

Alberdi, Xabier, Xabier Altzibar & Julio Garcia (2011): Calcos fraseológicos en euskera de los medios de comunicación. In Antonio Pamies, Lucía Luque Nadal & José Manuel Pazos Bretaña (eds.), *Phraseologie und Parömiologie. Multi-Lingual Phraseography: Second Language Learning and Translation Applications*, 215–224. Baltmannsweiler: Schneider Verlag Hohengehren.

Altzibar, Xabier (2004): Kolokazioak euskaraz. Zer axola duten kazetaritzan. *Euskarazko kazetaritzaren I. Kongresua. Kazetaritza Euskaraz: Oraina eta Geroa*, 383–395.

Altzibar, Xabier & Xabier Bilbao (2016): Locuciones en euskera: Necesidad y pautas para su recopilación y ordenación a partir de los corpus textuales existentes. In Gloria Corpas Pastor (ed.), *Computerised and Corpus-based Approaches to Phraseology: Monolingual and Multilingual Perspectives*, 24–31. Geneva: Editions Tradulex.

Altzibar, Xabier, Xabier Bilbao & Koldo Garai (2011): Collocations in Basque: A test for classification. *Proceedings of the 5th International Conference on Meaning-Text Theory*, 1–12.

Barambones Zubiria, Josu, Elizabete Manterola Agirrezabalaga, Zuriñe Sanz Villar, Ibon Uribarri Zenekorta & Naroa Zubillaga Gómez (2015): Itzulpen ikasketak eta euskara. Zenbait ekarpen Itzulpen Ikasketa Deskribatzaileei, eta haratago. In José Jorge Amigo Extremera (ed.), *Traducimos Desde el Sur. Actas del VI Congreso Internacional de la Asociación Ibérica de Estudios de Traducción e Interpretación*, 121–140. Las Palmas de Gran Canaria: University of Las Palmas de Gran Canaria.

Bernardini, Silvia (2007): *Collocations in Translated Language: Combining Parallel, Comparable and Reference Corpora*. Paper presented at the fourth Corpus Linguistics conference held at the University of Birmingham, 27–30 July 2007.

Corpas Pastor, Gloria (1996): *Manual de fraseología española*. Madrid: Gredos.

Gurrutxaga, Antton (2014): *Idiomatikotasunaren karakterizazio automatikoa: Izena+Aditza konbinazioak*. PhD thesis. University of the Basque Country.

Häcki-Buhofer, Annelies, Marcel Dräger, Stefanie Meier & Tobias Roth (2014): *Feste Wortverbindungen des Deutschen. Kollokationenwörterbuch für den Alltag*. Tübingen: Francke.

Hulden, Mans (2009): Foma: A finite-state toolkit and library. *Proceedings of the 12th Conference of the European Chapter of the Association for Computational Linguistics*, 29–32.

Ibarretxe-Antuñano, Iraide (2006): Estudio lexicológico de las onomatopeyas vascas: el euskal onomatopeien hiztegia: euskara-ingelesera-gaztelania. *Fontes Linguae Vasconum: Studia et Documenta* 101, 147–162.

Ibarretxe-Antuñano, Iraide (2012): Análisis lingüístico de las onomatopeyas vascas (Linguistic analysis of Basque onomatopoeia). *Oihenart: Cuadernos de Lengua y Literatura* 27, 129–177.

Ibarretxe-Antuñano, Iraide & Alfontso Martinez Lizarduikoa (2006): *Hizkuntzaren bihotzean: euskal onomatopeien hiztegia*. Donostia-San Sebastian: Gaiak.

Iñurrieta, Uxoa, Itziar Aduriz, Arantza Diaz de Ilarraza, Gorka Labaka & Kepa Sarasola (2016): Izen+aditz konbinazioen itzulpenaz eta tratamendu konputazionalaz. *Senez* 47, 237–249.
Moon, Rosamund (1998): *Fixed Expressions and Idioms in English*. Oxford: Clarendon Press.
Sanz-Villar, Zuriñe (2015): *Unitate fraseologikoen itzulpena: Alemana euskara. Literatur testuen corpusean oinarritutako analisia*. PhD thesis. Servicio Editorial de la UPV/EHU.
Sanz-Villar, Zuriñe (2018): Interference and the translation of phraseological units in a parallel and multilingual corpus. *Meta* 63 (1), 72–93.
Schuchardt, Hugo (1925): *Das Baskische und die Sprachwissenschaft*. Viena: Hölder-Pichler-Tempsky A.-G.
Sinclair, John (1987): The nature of the evidence. In John Sinclair (ed.), *Looking Up: An Account of the COBUILD Project in Lexical Computing*, 150–159. London: Collins.
Toury, Gideon (2012): *Descriptive translation studies and beyond*. Amsterdam, Philadelphia: John Benjamins.
Uribarri, Ibon (2011): Dialectics of opposition and construction: Translation in the Basque Country. In Dimitris Asimakoulas & Margaret Rogers (eds.), *Translation and Opposition*, 247–264. Bristol: Multilingual Matters.
Urizar, Ruben (2012): *Euskal lokuzioen tratamendu konputazionala*. PhD thesis. University of the Basque Country.

Part II: Languages Spoken outside Europe

Andreas Buerki
(How) is Formulaic Language Universal? Insights from Korean, German and English

Abstract: Items of formulaic language, also referred to as phraseological units or common turns of phrase, are in evidence in a very large number of languages. However, the extent to which languages feature such formulaic material is unclear. Similarly, how formulaicity may be understood across typologically different languages and whether indeed there is a concept of formulaic language that applies across languages, are questions which have not generally been discussed. Using a novel data set consisting of topically matched corpora in three typologically different languages (Korean, German and English), this study proposes an empirically founded universal concept for formulaic language and discusses what the shape of this concept implies for the theoretical understanding of formulaic language going forward. In particular, it is argued that the nexus of the concept of formulaic language cannot be fixed at any particular structural level (such as the phrase or the level of polylexicality) and incorporates elements specified at varying levels of schematicity. This means that a cross-linguistic concept of formulaic language fits in well with a constructionist view of linguistic structure.

1 Introduction

In this chapter, I set out to assess whether formulaic language (FL) can be regarded as universal in a comprehensive sense, and if so, what such a universal concept of FL looks like. To make this assessment possible, data from Korean, German and English are used – between them, these languages cover the spectrum of morphological typology, which is arguably the most pertinent typological classification when it comes to FL.

One way of characterising FL is to say that it represents habitual turns of phrase in a speech community (cf. Burger et al. 1982: 1; Coulmas 1979; Erman and Warren 2000; Fillmore et al. 1988; Howarth 1998: 25; Langacker 2008: 84; Pawley 2001). Such typical ways of putting things may include conversational formulae (e.g. *Thank you very much – not at all*), collocations (like *face a challenge*, or *utter*

∂ Open Access. © 2020 A. Buerki, published by De Gruyter. [CC BY] This work is licensed under the Creative Commons Attribution 4.0 License.
https://doi.org/10.1515/9783110669824-005

disgrace), multi-word terms (*open letter, contempt of court*) as well as other habitual sequences (*half an hour, no chance of X, behind closed doors*) and, to the extent to which they are in recurrent use within a community, idioms (like *get one's knickers in a twist*) and even proverbs (*garbage in, garbage out*).

FL is held to be of central importance to the functioning of language in a number of key ways. For example, besides making up a sizable portion of language in use (Altenberg 1998; Butler 2005: 223), knowledge of FL is thought a prerequisite for full proficiency in a language, register, dialect or sociolect. This is because habitual turns of phrase are crucially only a subset of all expressions that might be judged grammatical (e.g. Bally 1909: 73; Pawley and Syder 1983: 191; O'Keeffe et al. 2007: 60) and so knowledge of the boundaries of grammaticality alone is insufficient. FL is also thought to ease processing load during language production and thus it is nothing less than a key enabler of fluency in language (Nattinger and DeCarrico 1992, Pawley and Syder 1983, Wray and Perkins 2000). Further, research suggests that FL is key to successful mutual understanding in communication because items of FL activate a range of social, situational and cultural contextual cues (Erman 2007: 26; Feilke 1994, 2003: 213, Wray 2008: 20–21). Hence even in lingua franca communication among L2 speakers, communities move fast to establish a stock of FL to aid mutual understanding, as shown by Seidlhofer (2009). In short, much in language depends on FL.

It is likely that items of FL are found in languages universally (Colson 2008: 191). Previous phraseological research has established the existence of FL phenomena in very many different languages, including all major European languages and less widely spoken European languages and dialects (cf. overview in Burger et al. 2007: part XIV and the survey of 74 European and 17 non-European languages in Piirainen 2012) as well as Arabic (Abdou 2011), Catalan (Bladas 2012), Chinese (Shei and Hsieh 2012), Hebrew (Al-Haj et al. 2014), Hindi (Shama 2017), Japanese (Namba 2010), Korean (Kim et al. 2001), English as a Lingua Franca (Kecskes 2007; Seidlhofer 2009) and indeed artificial languages like Esperanto, Interlingua and Ido (cf. Fiedler 2007), to name only a few of the more recently investigated varieties (See also major comparative works including the recent Idström and Piirainen 2012; Benigni et al. 2015 and the large number of monolingual and multilingual phrasebooks and idiom dictionaries, e.g. anon. 2010; Cownie 2001).[1] Consequently, there is every reason to expect that languages

---

1 Arguably even programming languages feature items of FL that represent habitual ways of coding tasks in a programming language (cf. *programming idioms,* e.g. in Maruch and Maruch 2011: ch. 21).

that have not yet had their phraseology documented will nevertheless be shown to feature FL.

Crucially, however, the points made above regarding the importance of FL to the functioning of language in general require that FL is not only found in all languages but found in comparable measure in all languages (universality in the comprehensive sense): it would be difficult to maintain that some languages feature a greater density of habitual ways of expression than others (all else being equal) or that fluency and mutual understanding is better or more easily achieved in some languages than others by virtue of their higher rate of FL occurrence. To date, no quantitative cross-linguistic studies have confirmed whether FL is indeed found in similar measure across different languages or whether the degree of reliance on FL in fact varies between languages and language varieties, though results of some studies appear to point to non-universality of FL in the comprehensive sense (e.g. Kim 2009).

This is a matter of very considerable consequence for the study of FL: if it were found that different languages rely on FL to very differing degrees, widely-accepted theoretical claims about the importance and role of FL (such as those outlined above) would require a fundamental re-examination – there would be a strong possibility that FL may in fact be a mere epiphenomenon, a language-specific reflex of a more general, yet to be formulated principle that manifests itself differently in different languages, rather than a phenomenon of theoretical interest in itself. If, on the other hand, a coherent concept of FL can be formulated that is equally valid across typologically diverse languages, it would reaffirm the significance of FL in linguistic theory and contribute substantially to an understanding of FL that is able to sustain the continued expansion of phraseological research into new domains and its application to new data.

In the following, I will first outline some of the main ways in which FL has been understood. Then previous research relevant to the question of comprehensive universality will be reviewed, along with the relevant concepts of linguistic typology. The *data and procedure* section subsequently outlines how a trilingual, topic-matched corpus of around 80 million words of Korean, German and English was put together and how it was used to test the universality of the concept of FL. In the final two sections, results of this analysis are presented and their significance discussed.

2 Background

2.1 Formulaic Language

There is a range of current understandings of and approaches to FL and phraseological phenomena. This complicates any statements made about FL in general because it begs the question to which understanding of FL those generalisations apply. But the plurality of understandings is also a sign of the multi-faceted nature of the phenomenon at hand which invites a diversity of approaches and conceptualisations and it is an index of the vitality of research into FL which attracts scholars from diverse fields, and with diverse interests and research agendas.

At the risk of a degree of oversimplification, it is nevertheless possible to identify main strands of thinking on FL which I will do by reviewing three main approaches: the traditional phraseological, the psycholinguistic and the corpus linguistic. Traditional phraseology considers the criterion-triplet of polylexicality (i.e. items involving more than one word), idiomaticity (semantic and/or syntactic irregularity) and fixedness (or stability) of key importance in conceptualising FL (cf. Burger et al. 1982). While the criteria of polylexicality and fixedness are common to most concepts of FL, the prominence of the criterion of idiomaticity has meant that idioms and proverbial expressions, although shown to be comparatively infrequent in language use (Moon 1995: V, 1998: 81; Colson 2007), have tended to be a particular (and occasionally exclusive) focal point within this strand of thinking. In the second strand, here dubbed psycholinguistic, the aspect of mental processing features particularly prominently. Sinclair described relevant entities as "phrases that constitute single choices" (1991: 110), and the idea of prefabrication is prominent in this strand, as for example in Wray's definition of a formulaic sequence as

> a sequence, continuous or discontinuous, of words or other elements, which is, or appears to be, prefabricated: that is, stored and retrieved whole from memory at the time of use.
> (Wray 2002: 9)

Since processing occurs in individuals' heads, formulaicity in this view might be understood primarily as a feature of idiolect rather than of the shared language system. The final line of thinking focuses on the aspect of conventionality in relation to speech communities, as manifested in language use. This can be summed up in the characterisation of FL as expressions that represent habitual ways of putting things in a community. Early formulations referred to "combinations sanctioned by usage" (Bally 1909: 73, my translation), while more recent work in this line of thinking has described FL as conventional or institutionalised phrases (Pawley 2001: 122; Bybee 2010: 35, respectively; cf. also Howarth 1998: 25; Brunner and Steyer 2007: 2). In specifically corpuslinguistic work, conventionality is typically measured via variously modulated measures of frequency of occurrence, as in the pioneering study by Altenberg and Eeg-Olofsson (1990) that made clear that idiomatic sequences are vastly outnumbered by conventional, non-idiomatic sequences that should nevertheless be considered instances of FL.

While conceptions of FL and their associated terminologies are therefore diverse, they also coincide in key characteristics, such as their tendency to involve units larger than words that display stability of form across instances of use. Views diverge on the importance of idiomaticity and on whether the mental processing of individuals or the shared conventions of a language community are the most relevant aspects of FL. Although the approach followed in this study is an inclusive, corpus-linguistic approach of the third strand, the commonalities between strands ensure that conclusions drawn are relevant to FL in general.[2]

2.2 Universality and Typological Difference

Above it was pointed out that previous research has established the existence of items of FL in a diverse range of languages. It was also argued that if the well-established theoretical claims about FL are to be maintained, the mere existence of tokens of FL in the languages of the world provides insufficient support for the universality of the full concept of FL. Only evidence of comprehensive universality (i.e. of comparable levels of recourse to items of FL across languages) would confirm the central importance of FL to the functioning of language in general. In the following, therefore, the focus will be on previous research that throws light on aspects of this comprehensive type of universality.

Although generally the concept of FL is most often treated as cross-linguistically unproblematic in FL literature, a number of authors have overtly commented on aspects of *comprehensive universality* and cross-linguistic concepts of FL. Wray (2002), for example, offers comments about the influence of flexible word-order on the nature of FL and highlights the fundamental nature in which typological differences can affect FL:

---

2 Although, due to the rarity of narrowly idiomatic expressions among all items of FL, results will be less relevant to a conception of phraseology that is concerned exclusively with items displaying semantic and/or syntactic irregularity.

> While an English phrase might be fully fixed except for, say, the verb morphology, its German equivalent might need to contain two slots for the verb, with one or the other being filled according to the syntactic environment.
>
> (Wray 2002: 269; similarly Heid 2012 and others)

Like most theoretical works, however, Wray otherwise presents findings in terms of properties of language in general while drawing primarily on a single language. Although some theoretical treatments are more circumspect when suggesting generalisations across languages (e.g. Fellbaum 2007: 2), the discussion of cross-linguistic aspects is largely left to one side, leading to Colson's perceptive comment that "[o]n the basis of European syntax, we may have a slightly biased view of what phraseology looks like in other [i.e. non-European] languages" (Colson 2008: 193).

Specifically cross-linguistic studies have overwhelmingly focussed on strongly idiomatic items of FL (for overviews and discussion of contrastive phraseology see esp. Colson 2008; also Burger et al. 2007: part XIII; Földes 1997) and have uncovered findings particularly relating to the figurative semantics of idioms and their possible implications for universal tendencies in human cognition (e.g. Dobrovol'skij and Piirainen 2005) and how widely similar idioms are shared between languages (e.g. Piirainen 2012). Other studies discussing cross-linguistic aspects (e.g. Butler 1997, 2005; Cortes 2008; Granger 2014) have presented insightful comparisons of form and function in items of FL, typically across pairs of languages. Though none of these studies directly address the question of comprehensive universality or propose adjustments to the concept of FL based on their comparisons, Granger observes in relation to lexical bundles in French and English that "the overall number of n-grams may differ across languages" (2014: 61) and that

> a lexical bundle approach [to FL] is likely to generate more interesting results if the languages compared are sufficiently close morphologically, lexically and syntactically.
>
> (Granger 2014: 61)

However, Granger views this and similar issues caused by "typological differences between languages" (60) as methodological problems to which solutions need to be found rather than matters of theoretical importance. Similarly, Kim (2009) in a comparison of Korean lexical bundles of three-word length in conversation and academic texts, finds that "in Korean, [...] lexical bundles are generally rare overall due to the wide range and variety of word endings" and "[t]he findings of the current study [...] suggest that typological differences are obviously central to any explanation of these differences" (2009: 157). The fundamental questions this raises regarding the nature of FL are not discussed.

On the other hand, Durrant's (2013) study of formulaicity in Turkish offers important insights regarding the nature of FL in relation to language typology: based on extensive corpus evidence, he demonstrates formulaicity at the morpheme sequence level and suggests that in agglutinating languages, this may pick up the shortfall in the number of recurring multi-word items of FL. Durrant maintains that

> [s]ince individual word forms are rare, so too are high-frequency word combinations. [...] it may be that collocation is better described as relationships between lemmas, or between specifiable subsets of a lemma, or even between suffix combinations, abstracted from lexical roots.
>
> (Durrant 2013: 34)

Similar insight may be gleaned from treatments of FL in languages that do not mark word boundaries orthographically, such as Chinese. In Chinese orthography, characters represent single "syllables associated with a morpheme" (Sun 2006: 102) and are not grouped orthographically into words. Since morphemes are furthermore "more indeterminate with respect to their bound [or] free status" (Sun 2006: 46) the word "is neither a particularly intuitive concept nor easily defined" (Sun 2006: 46–49), creating immediate problems for the FL-criterion of polylexicality. Hence Shei and Hsieh, when describing items of FL in Chinese place the locus of formulaicity at the morphological level: they point out that "there are traditionally a huge number of four-morpheme units called *cheng2yu3* ([...] "established language", "idiom") [...] used to show erudition or simply for succinct meaning making" (2012: 327), but that the "issue of large habitually formed morpheme groups [...] is not so well investigated to date" (2012: 328). They then proceed to outline a "method which can separate idiomatic expression from ad hoc polysyllabic [i.e. polymorphemic] strings" (2012: 328), operating, again, at the morpheme level.

In summary, discussions of cross-linguistic aspects of FL, where they have occurred at all, have rarely engaged with the question of *comprehensive universality* or the concept of FL that might underlie it. The studies that have compared semantic, functional and structural aspects of items of FL have not, in general, commented on the effects of differing morphological behaviour among languages on the concept of FL or on quantitative aspects, leading to the apparent assumption that existing understandings of FL are unproblematically universal. Kim (2009), Granger (2014) and Durrant (2013) have shown, however, that this cannot be assumed and that models of FL as recurrent strings of word-forms, for example, are unlikely to be universal in the comprehensive sense. Consequently, the question of how recurrent complex units should be conceived of, across very different languages, has so far not been investigated at anything approaching the depth which would be necessary to support the ambitious research programme that is currently pursued in the area of FL, or indeed to safeguard the theoretical importance currently attached to the concept of FL. The next section lays out how the question of whether, and if so in what way, FL is comprehensively universal was assessed in this study.

3 Data and Procedure

How does one work out whether and how FL is universal in the comprehensive sense? The approach taken in this study is a quantitative, corpus-linguistic one involving three basic steps: in a first step, a novel genre, topic, structure and size-matched trilingual corpus of languages representative of the breadth of diversity found across morphological typology was compiled. Next, comprehensive automatic extractions of items of FL from each of the languages represented in the corpus were carried out, employing various candidate universal concepts of FL and measuring their effects. In the third and final step, the concept of FL that succeeded in yielding a closely comparable number of extracted items of FL across the three language sections of the corpus (thus simulating a comprehensively universal concept of FL) was assessed in terms of whether it is a theoretically viable concept of FL or one that does not form a plausible basis for the shape of a universal concept of FL. In the former case, the relevant simulated universal FL concept would furnish the basis for an explanation of how FL is universal; the latter case would suggest that FL is not universal in the comprehensive sense.

3.1 Corpus Compilation

In compiling a corpus for present purposes, a range of features needed to be considered to obtain valid results. The most fundamental of these was the choice of languages compared. Known factors likely to influence FL-density, including genre, topic and corpus size, also needed controlling across the different language sub-corpora.

The languages chosen for the comparison were Korean, German and English. Languages can be classified in various ways according to a multitude of features. Some of the more common linguistic typologies have classified languages according to word order, vocabulary or morphological type. While all of these criteria will influence FL to some extent, in this study, morphological classification was used as the basis for source data selection as this type of variation is clearly pertinent to FL (cf. below as well as Durrant 2013; Granger 2014).

The discussion of morphological typology in this section essentially follows Whaley (1997: 127–148). Morphological typology can be understood as a classification of the morphological behaviour of a language on two semi-independent continua. One is the continuum of synthesis (or morphemes per word ratio), with isolating languages (few morphemes per word) at one extreme and synthetic ones (many morphemes per word) at the other. The other continuum is that of fusion, with agglutinating languages (where individual morphemes remain recognisable as they are combined) at one end and fusional or (in)flectional languages where morphemes typically merge with one another, at the other extreme. Languages are placed at different points on the continua according to their tendencies which are, however, not necessarily uniform (Song 2001: 43). Korean, German and English take up different positions on the continua and therefore represent the breadth of diversity found across morphological typology: English is the most isolating language of the three, whereas German is more synthetic and also more fusional. Korean is yet more synthetic, though unlike German it is agglutinating (Sohn 2001: chapter 8). The situation is roughly sketched in figure 1.

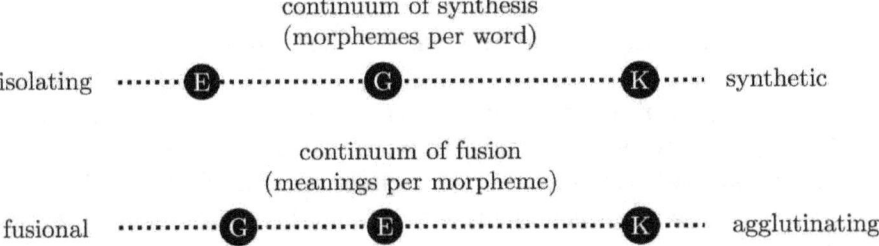

Fig. 1: Continua of synthesis and fusion. Note: E=English, G=German, K=Korean; placements are approximate

It is well known that genre and register influence the types of FL found, but crucially here, genres are also known to differ in the degree to which they rely on FL (Ädel and Erman 2012: 81; Biber 2006, 2009; Biber and Barbieri 2007; Biber et al. 2003; Kuiper 2009; Lenk and Stein 2011; Stein 2007). Topic may well have similar effects and it was therefore decided to control for topic as well as genre. To exclude possible effects of both, while avoiding the complications of translated texts, the sub-corpora for each language were drawn from Wikipedia articles, with 75% of articles in each language being on shared topics and 25% of articles on topics not covered by the respective other languages (see table 1 for an overview).³ A 100% match of topics would not have been feasible as article topics in some languages correspond to sections of more general articles in others and vice versa. It was also thought important to capture a proportion of language used to discuss indigenous topics, as it were, because shared topics would inevitably be more globalised in nature. Since several shorter texts may not be equivalent to a single text of the same total size in important respects, corpus structure in terms of number of documents was also matched across language sub-corpora. Where necessary, articles had random paragraphs removed in order to match sub-corpora in both overall size and in the number of documents included.

Tab. 1: Corpus composition. Note: SID = syllable information density; shared docs = documents with shared topics across languages

	total docs	shared docs	syll. count	word count	SID
Korean	63,075	40,545	67,164,785	25,021,576	1
German	63,075	40,349	55,840,652	28,636,204	1.203
English	63,075	40,501	48,004,421	29,077,310	1.4

Perhaps the most obvious factor to be controlled was sub-corpus size. Traditionally in corpus linguistics, size is measured in number of words. However, words are not cross-typologically stable units. As laid out in the above discussion on morphological typology, isolating languages tend to split morphemes into many words while synthetic languages pack many morphemes into single words resulting in situations where whole phrases in isolating languages like English are equivalent to single words in highly synthetic languages like Korean with obvious implications for measurements of corpus size.⁴ A measure of corpus size independent of the concept of 'word' was therefore required and a measure based on syllabic information density (SID) was chosen instead. SID (Pellegrino et al.

---

3 Translation across Wikipedia pages in various languages does occur, but "articles in the different versions are often written directly in the respective target-language" (Mc Donough Dolmaya 2015: 16). Warncke-Wang et al. (2012) found that of the 1,253,523 articles of the German Wikipedia, only 0.306% were as translations, and only 0.267% of the English Language Wikipedia. In any case, however, due to article creation and editing being collaborative and continuous, even articles with translation activity at a certain stage in their history are not likely to be translated texts in any conventional sense.

4 The concept of a word is problematic from a theoretical point of view, both within and even more so across languages (cf. Dixon and Aikhenvald 2002).

2011; Oh et al. 2013) measures the amount of information packed into a syllable and then allows for corpus size to be specified on the basis of a density-adjusted number of syllables, rather than words, leading to a balanced amount of language across sub-corpora.

To determine equivalent sub-corpus sizes based on SID, densities were first obtained for each language. This was done on the basis of a set of 825 sentences of Korean, German and English that were translation equivalents of each other and of mixed translation direction. The sentences were obtained from the Tatoeba database of sentence translations (Ho 2009). Information density was then calculated as the ratio of the total number of syllables found in the Korean sentences (baseline) to the number of syllables of German and English respectively. This resulted in the quotients given in the final column of table 1. These indicate that Korean has the lowest SID, followed by German and then English, which packs the most information into a single syllable. These figures were cross-validated against those obtained by Oh using different data (Oh et al. 2014; Oh, personal communication) and proved closely similar. Densities were then used to calculate the target number of syllables needed for each sub-corpus by dividing the baseline (Korean) syllable count by the SID for each of the other languages. The resulting figures are again shown in table 1. As the word counts of table 1 indicate, although Korean features the lowest SID (therefore requiring the highest number of syllables), Korean words contain the most syllables on average and so when measured in words, the Korean sub-corpus is the smallest, followed by the German and then the English language sub-corpus. The amount of language compared, however, is equivalent.

In terms of the actual process of corpus construction, the full Wikipedia dumps for all articles in Korean, German and English (as per February 2013) were downloaded, divided into one document per article and then cleaned and stripped of Wikipedia's XML and non-textual information using WikiExtractor (Attardi and Fuschetto 2012). The relevant documents as per table 1 were then compiled into a trilingual corpus, observing the target syllable and document counts as outlined above. Random paragraphs of some documents were left out in order to achieve the target syllable count within the necessary number of documents. To facilitate the subsequent analyses, a morphological annotation layer was added. For German and English, TreeTagger (Schmid 1994) was used to add part-of-speech, lemmas and morphological parsing; HanNanum (Park 2011) was used to add the same to the Korean sub-corpus, additionally annotating morpheme boundaries.

3.2 Identification of FL

This section describes the procedure employed in the identification of items of FL in corpus data and the options available within the procedure to simulate various underlying FL-concepts. Above, items of FL were characterised as expressions representing habitual ways of putting things in a speech community. The idea of conventional ways of putting things implies that there are both units of meaning (i.e. things to be 'put'), and linguistic forms conventionally associated with those meanings (i.e. ways of putting them). For the purposes of automatic identification and extraction, therefore, the operationalization in (1) was used:

(1) Frequent sequences of linguistic elements forming a semantic unit

Linguistic elements were taken to be word forms in the first instance (more specifically, white space delimited orthographic words) with the option to also consider lemmas (i.e. words abstracted away from features like case marking), morphemes (i.e. sub-lexical units of meaning) and combinations of these. Sequences of 2 to 9 elements in length were considered. Following the corpus-linguistic strand of thinking on FL, conventionalisation was measured via frequency of occurrence in corpus material; *frequent* was taken as minimally occurring twice per million words. A *semantic unit* was deemed a word sequence possessing the sort of semantic unity typical of words and structurally complete phrases. Semantic unity was also attributed to sequences that, while lacking this unity, can acquire it through the addition of a single, semantically or formally restricted variable element at either edge of the sequence (such as when *in search of* does not form a full semantic unit unless a variable element on the right is added, i.e. *in search of X* where *X* is restricted semantically to something prized that is being pursued). For reasons of practicality, the phenomenon of sequence-internal variable slots (such as *at the [young/early/average/premature] age of X*) was not specifically catered for as only continuous sequences of elements were extracted. There is no indication that this decision affected the three tested languages unequally, and the most frequent fillers of variable slots will be extracted in-situ as an additional sequence type (i.e. *at the age of X, at the early age of X* and *at the young age of X* as separate types). For a more detailed discussion of internal variability, see Buerki (2016).

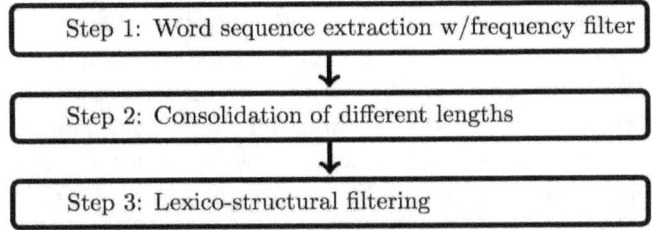

Fig. 2: Main steps of the identification procedure

The actual identification of items of FL from each sub-corpus was conducted in three steps (cf. figure 2). The extraction from each sub-corpus of all word sequences occurring at least twice per million words (step 1) was carried out using the N-Gram Processor (Buerki 2013). To aid accuracy, sequences across sentence and sentence-equivalent boundaries were blocked and an additive stop list was used. The stop list contained the 200 most frequent word forms of the respective language according to the Leipzig Corpus Portal (anon. 2001) and served to eliminate exclusively sequences that are made up entirely of stop-listed (i.e. very high-frequency) words.[5] In step 2, the various lengths of identified sequences had their frequencies consolidated and were combined into a single list using Sub-String (Buerki 2017). At step 3, lexico-structural filters were applied to the lists of sequences to remove sequences that were likely to lack semantic unity. One entry of the lexico-structural filter for English, for example, bars sequences ending in the word 'and' as most such sequences would fail to show semantic unity. A detailed discussion of the extraction procedure (applied to a different data set) is found in Buerki (2012).

Extraction accuracy was established as follows. A random sample (n = 300 types) of automatically identified sequences in each language was rated for compliance with the operationalisation in (1) by the author and independently by an L1 speaker of the respective language acting as a research assistant. Extraction accuracy at the baseline (i.e. using sequences of orthographic word forms exclusively) varied between languages and raters in the range of 72% to 75% of sequence types rated as operationalisation compliant. Recall (the comprehensiveness of an extraction) is difficult to assess in this scenario, but is typically inversely related to accuracy, that is, higher accuracy leads to lower recall and vice-versa (Manning and Schütze 1999: chapter 5). The accuracy figures achieved

---

[5] For German, a stop list based on the top 150 (rather than 200) most frequent words proved sufficient to yield comparable extraction accuracy to the other languages.

were therefore regarded as suited to present purposes. Notably, the achievement of a narrow range of variation in extraction accuracy between the three languages was critical because it means that comparability between extractions across languages was successfully maintained. A higher accuracy for one language, for example, would almost certainly have caused a lower number of sequences to be extracted for that language, thus introducing a bias. Thus a robust identification procedure was applied to enable the subsequent quantitative comparison of FL across the three languages studied.

3.3 Simulation of FL Concepts

As noted above, the first (baseline) FL-concept tested for universality employed orthographic word form sequences as the basic building blocks. This represents a traditional FL-concept in that it accepts the multi-word level as the relevant level at which formulaicity is manifested and it is also very conservative in terms of fixedness – it takes the view that all elements of a habitual turn of phrase are fully fixed such that, for example, the sequences in (2) are deemed separate types of sequences, each needing to satisfy FL-status on its own, rather than being tokens of one sequence.

(2) *consists of X*
     consisting of X
     consisted of X
     consist of X

Two exceptions to full fixedness applied even at the baseline level (in addition to allowing variable slots at either edge): all numbers (whether in figures or words) were replaced by the label NUM, and occurrences of the names for months of the year were replaced by the label NMONTH. This allowed the identification of sequences like those in (3) as a single type.

(3) *NUM days later (two/ten/21 days later)*
     in NMOUNTH of that year (in April/July/August of that year)
     in the early NUMth century (in the early twentieth/17th century)

Although adequate for many cases, previous studies have shown that as a general requirement, (almost) complete fixedness is not realistic as items of FL are subject to a substantial amount of variation (Wray 2002: chapter 14; Sinclair 2004: 161; Langlotz 2006; Dutton 2009). An exception here is the idea of lexical bundles

(Biber et al. 1999; Biber and Conrad 1999) which uniquely requires complete fixedness. Since there is no definition of lexical bundles independent of their operationalization (resulting in a conflation of theory and method) it remains unclear whether full fixedness is of theoretical importance to the idea of lexical bundles or simply a methodological expediency.

As reported in the next section and expected on the basis of previous research (Granger 2014; Durrant 2013; Kim 2009), the baseline concept of FL failed to produce comparable FL-densities in the three languages. Consequently, progressive changes were made to the FL-concept tested until approximate parity in FL-densities across the three languages was reached. In this iterative process, modifications to the FL-concept were progressively stepped up through aspects of fixedness to more fundamental alterations concerning the level at which formulaicity applies. While at each stage, modifications to simulated FL-concepts were made incrementally and with a view to maintaining plausibility as far as possible, it is important to recall that the goal was to take the simulation to whatever level necessary to produce approximate parity in FL-density across languages, and subsequently to assess whether the resulting comprehensively universal FL-concept is a plausible one or not. Thus it was never in doubt whether parity could be achieved (this is a relatively simple exercise), but rather what modifications would be necessary, to what extent alterations would be needed and whether the resulting concept was plausible. The results of this process are detailed in the next section.

4 Results

As a baseline for comparisons, the results of a FL-concept of (almost) complete fixedness and taking the orthographic (white space separated) word sequence as the level at which formulaicity is manifested, are presented in figure 3 and table 2. Several key observations result: first, the number of items of FL identified across the languages is vastly different (both in terms of types as well as tokens) and therefore the underlying concept of FL is clearly not universal in the comprehensive sense. It is evident, therefore, that an understanding of FL similar to the baseline concept used here has to be regarded as a language-specific phenomenon in that density of occurrence varies greatly between languages. Perhaps the most prominent such concept is the idea of lexical bundles, which is even more fixed and depends to a much greater extent on (ultra-high) frequency of occurrence as a defining characteristic than the baseline concept used here. A second immediate observation is that the number of items identified as FL in each language parallels the placement of the respective language on the continuum of synthesis (cf. figure 1). This confirms the dependence of the baseline concept of FL on typology – something distinctly undesirable for a concept of importance to language in general rather than certain languages only.

Tab. 2: Items of FL under the baseline FL concept

	FL-types	FL-tokens
Korean	10,617	1,480,862
German	19,114	2,677,999
English	25,712	3,727,071

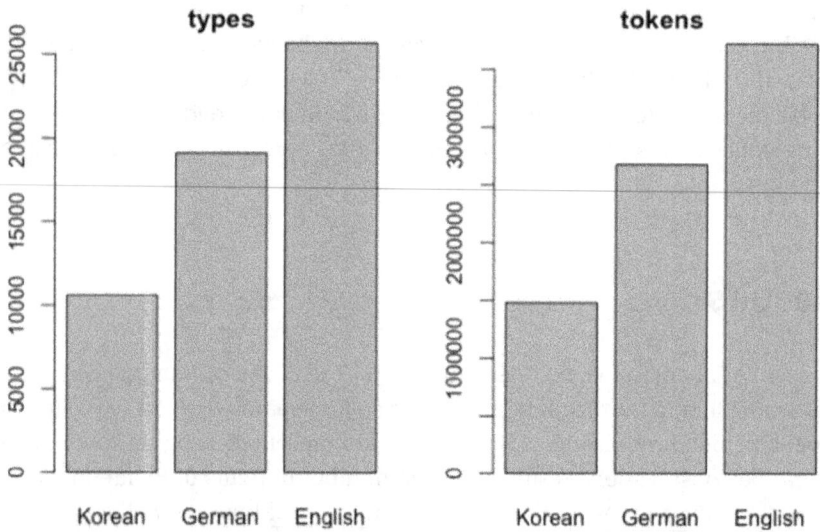

Fig. 3: Items of FL under the baseline FL

By contrast, the figures obtained by employing a simulated universal concept of FL are presented in figure 4 and table 3. These figures show that it is entirely possible to automatically identify a comparable number of items as formulaic in each of the languages. The question to consider is whether the underlying concept of FL is a plausible, coherent and sensible concept within the context of what is known about FL. To make this assessment, the changes to identification parameters implemented to move from the baseline concept of FL to the simulated universal concept are set out below, and subsequently assessed.

Tab. 3: Items of FL under the universal FL concept

	FL-types	FL-tokens
Korean	24,345	3,619,171
German	26,577	3,807,337
English	25,712	3,727,071

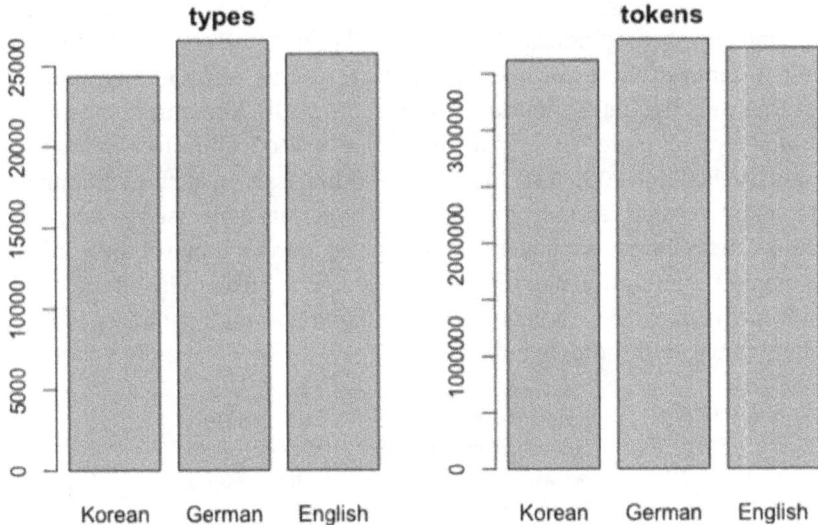

Fig. 4: Items of FL under the universal FL concept

4.1 Adjustments

The adjustments indicated below were implemented by adapting a version of the source corpus and then re-running the FL identification procedure with commensurate adjustments to stop lists and filters where necessary.

4.1.1 Fixedness

The first set of adjustments was made to the degree of fixedness: as pointed out above, phraseological research has long maintained that many items of FL require certain types of flexibility. Such flexible items could be said to be underspecified to a degree, or specified at a more schematic level than the word form sequence – and they require adjustments to fit contexts of use. One type of flexibility is the occurrence of variable slots as seen above. Others are alternations in word order and inflectional morphology. The effects of morphological typology seen in the results reported above suggest that inflectional morphology is pertinent to the differences observed in the data and so the first set of adjustments to the concept of FL was made to reduce fixedness in areas of inflectional morphology.

In Korean, this flexibility was simulated by removing case markers of subject (- 이/가 [i/ga]) object (- 을/를 [eul/reul]) and topic (- 은/는 [eun/neun]) as realised by the bound morphemes indicated, as well as all plural markers (- 들[deul]).[6] Notably, the absence of these markers does not necessarily result in ungrammaticality as they are "frequently omittable" (Sohn 2001: 231). Korean also possesses an elaborate system of verbal (and in some cases adjectival) inflection to mark politeness levels (Sohn 2001: 231–241), though other aspects, such as grammatical person, are not marked morphologically. The formal style used in texts like Wikipedia articles, however, means that only a very narrow range of these inflections is manifest, rendering intervention superfluous. To exemplify effects of adjustments made, items in (4) can be seen united under a single sequence type (5) as a consequence of the adjustments.

(4) 버스 정류장을   [beoseu jeongriujangeul]   bus stop-OBJ
    버스 정류장은   [beoseu jeongriujangeun]   bus stop-TOPIC
    버스 정류장이   [beoseu jeongriujangi]   bus stop-SUBJ
    버스 정류장   [beoseu jeongriujang]   bus stop
(5) 버스 정류장   [beoseu jeongriujang]   bus stop

Morphology to mark tense/aspect, mode and modality was left unadjusted – as in other languages (including German and English), these are expressed partly

---

6 There is some disagreement over whether these markers are more suffix-like (as assumed here) or more word-like (cf. Sohn 2001: 231). As current orthography does not typically afford these markers the status of orthographic word, they are taken as bound morphology here.

by inflectional morphology and partly periphrastically. The relaxation of fixedness would therefore not have contributed to addressing typological differences between the languages compared.

Methodologically, the adjustments mentioned were implemented by producing a version of the source corpus that had all items deleted that were marked by the morphological parser as instances of the Korean subject, object, topic and plural markers. The FL-identification procedure was then re-run to produce a new list of items of FL.

In the German sub-corpus, an equivalent reduction in fixedness was targeted by masking all verbal inflections for grammatical person (but tense/aspect, mode and modality was again retained as this is marked in all the languages under investigation and would therefore not target differences).[7] Further, all case and gender inflection was masked on definite and indefinite articles, adjectives and nouns (but number distinctions were retained as they occur in the English sub-corpus as well and were deemed an overly harsh generalisation for these languages). Again, to illustrate the effect of some of these adjustments, sequences in (6) appear united under (7) after the adjustments.

(6) *die Bundesrepublik Deutschland* the Federal Republic of Germany [nominative]
    der Bundesrepublik Deutschland the Federal Republic of Germany [dative/genitive]
(7) ARTDEF Bundesrepublik Deutschland

Similarly, after adjustments the nine attested sequence types in (8) appear under (9) as four generalized types.

(8) *zur Verfügung stehen*   be available   [1st/3rd pers. pl, pres. tense]
    zur Verfügung steht   be available   [3rd pers. sg/2nd pers. pl, pres. tense]
    zur Verfügung stehe   be available   [3rd pers. sg, subjunctive I]
    zur Verfügung stünden   be available   [1st/3rd pers. pl, subjunctive II]
    zur Verfügung stand   be available   [1st/3rd pers. sg, past tense]
    zur Verfügung standen   be available   [1st/3rd pers. pl, past tense]
    zur Verfügung stehende   available   [adjectival, case/number marked]
    zur Verfügung stehenden   available   [adjectival, case/number marked]
    zur Verfügung stehender   available   [adjectival, case/number marked]
(9) *zur Verfügung stehen_IndPres* [indicative, present tense]
    zur Verfügung stehen_IndPast [indicative, past tense]
    zur Verfügung stehen_Subj   [subjunctive]
    zur Verfügung stehend   [adjectival]

---

7 This was done by replacing finite verbs with lemmas marked for tense and mode.

As shown, distinctions in tense and mode are retained, but flexibility is introduced with regard to grammatical person (for verbs) and case/number marking on adjectival expressions. Notably, not all available forms of the respective inflectional paradigms are attested in the corpus (*zur Verfügung stehen* [be available] does not occur in the data with inflection for first or second person singular, for example) and some forms occur only a few times. This is partly due to the particularities of the corpus, of course, but is also a manifestation of a degree of fixedness of the expression. Therefore, even when extensive flexibility in terms of inflection is introduced, this does not necessarily lead to the identification of as many more items of FL on the basis of heightened recurrence as might be expected. The examples also show that the range of inflectional morphemes is further limited by the fusion of morphemes – the last three forms in (8) represent all possible combinations of case and number marking.

Methodologically, these adjustments were again achieved by modifying a copy of the source corpus in which all German verb forms, adjectival forms, forms of the definite and indefinite article and noun forms were replaced with the respective lemma (plus the added information on mode, tense, number, etc. that was to be retained) as seen in (9). The FL-identification was then re-run.

In English, an equivalent level of flexibility is inherent due to the absence of some of the equivalent inflectional morphology on the one hand and the isolating morphology on the other. The effect of the latter is seen in (6), where English would require the addition of the free morpheme *of* for genitive case marking in the second line, but this would still leave the recurring 5-element sequence *the Federal Republic of Germany* intact (and easily identifiable) in both lines of (6).

Although further flexibility could have been introduced to the simulated FL concept, this was not deemed judicious because the adjustments introduced already cover the aspects of flexibility that are pertinent to the typological differences in morphology present in the data set: there would have been little gain, for example, in such sweeping adjustments as a complete generalisation over tense marking because morphological tense marking is not a feature on which the three languages differ categorically.[8] Despite little further room for sensible reductions in fixedness, checks at this stage of the simulation indicated that a

---

[8] While the focus of this study is on morphological differences, it is likely that a simulated generalisation over aspects of word order would reduce differences in this regard between Korean and German as languages with more word order variation on the one hand and English with less word order variation on the other (although, of course, there is some word-order variation in English as well; cf. Heid 2012). It has to be left to future studies to ascertain the magnitude of the impact of these differences.

comprehensively universal concept of FL was not yet achieved. The simulation was therefore stepped up to comprise another area to which previous research has drawn attention: the level(s) at which formulaicity operates.

4.1.2 Levels of Focus

The final step to the universal concept of FL that produced the figures of table 3 required adjustments to the levels at which constituent elements of FL are recognised, to include certain units at the morpheme level. In Korean, 14 common bound morphemes occurring word-finally (the translation equivalents of which are generally free morphemes in German and English), were separated from their hosts so that they became eligible for recognition as independent constituents of formulaic sequences. The morphemes concerned are: -의 ([ui] of); -에서 ([eseo] from); -에 ([e] at); -로/으로 ([ro/euro] towards); -과/와 ([gwa/wa] and); -하고 ([hago] and); -고 ([go] and); -에게 ([ege] to); -도 ([do] too), -부터 ([buteo] from); -까지 ([kkaji] until); -만 ([man] only); -마다 ([mada] every); -지 ([ji] not). This was implemented by identifying all instances of the named morphemes in a copy of the source corpus and isolating them from their hosts through the insertion of white space characters. Identification occurred with the help of part-of-speech tags supplied by the morphological parser, as many of the forms involved, being single or double syllables, also occur as constituents of other lexical items, or as homographs).

In German, compounds consisting of common words were separated so their constituents become eligible for recognition as independent constituents. Although both Korean and English feature compounds as well, German is particularly noted for its use of compounding and the length of its compounds (cf. Russ 1994: 221–225), making this an important area where formulaicity remains unrecognized in one language but picked up in others due only to differences in morphological typology. In addition, German compounds are typically single orthographic words where many English and some Korean compounds consist of multiple orthographic words (hyphens were treated as separate words in all languages, resulting in hyphenated compounds like *open-minded* being treated as 3-element expressions). In example (7) above, the cross-linguistic effect of German compounds is drawn into focus as the German expression consists of three elements, whereas the English gloss consists of five. After compound-separation, (7) appeared as in (10) featuring four elements.[9]

---

[9] *Deutschland* might also be split but was left whole by the splitting software (s. below).

(10) ARTDEF Bundes republik Deutschland

jWordSplitter (Naber 2015) was used to divide German compounds in a copy of the source text and the FL-identification procedure was repeated. jWordSplitter divides noun compounds and some verbal and adjectival compounds. Due to necessarily limited coverage of the morphological dictionaries used, jWordSplitter is in practice most effective splitting compounds that consist of common word forms, giving it a fairly light touch that turns out to be well suited for the level of adjustments required in the present case.

As before, no equivalent adjustments to the English language data was necessary as the adjusted Korean bound morphemes are already independent in English (as well as German) and the adjustment to German compounds now approximated the state of compounds in English (and Korean). A sample of identified items of FL, including items identified only after adjustments (marked with an asterisk), is shown in table 4.

Tab. 4: Sample of identified FL. Notes: * items resulting from an adjusted FL-concept; X = variable slot; NUM = numbers; ARTDEF = definite article

	items of FL	gloss
Korean	어느 정도 [eoneu jeongdo]	roughly, to some extent
	영어 로* [ieongeo ro]	in English
	지금 도* [jigeum do]	even now
	X 과 함께* [X gwa hamkke]	together with X
	박사 학위[를] 취득하였다 [baksa hakwi[reul] chwideukhaeotta]	received [their] PhD
	유럽 연합 의* [yureop yeonhap ui]	of the European Union
	X 후 곧바로 [X hu gotbaro]	right after X
	X 때 마다* [X ttae mada]	always when X
	그 다음 에* [geu daeum e]	after that
	X 에 따라 달라진다* [X e ttara dallajinda]	differ depending on X
	X 있는 것으로 알려져 있다 [X inneun geoseuro allyeojyeo itta]	it has become known that there is X
	첼로 협주곡 [chello hyeobjugok]	cello concerto
	X (으)로 인하여* [(eu)ro inhayeo]	because of X
	X 와 같이* [X wa gachi]	with X
	오래 된 [orae doen]	old (lit. long been)
	X 에 대한 지원* [X e daehan jiwon]	support for X
	NUM 살 의 나이 로* [NUM sal ui nai ro]	at the age of NUM
German	aus diesem Grund	for this reason
	zu diesem Zeit punkt*	at this point in time

	items of FL	gloss
	ARTDEF Stadt zentrum*	the city centre
	in diesem Sinne	in this way/sense
	anhand von X	by means of X
	Tage buch*	diary (day book)
	auch sonst	at any rate / anyway
	immer größer	bigger and bigger
	dazu führen, dass X*	lead to the outcome that X
	siehe unten	see below
	miteinander verbunden	connected to each other
	wie zum Beispiel X	as for example X
	DEFART so genannte/r/n X*	the so-called X
	bis zu seinem Tod NUM	until his death in NUM
	hinzu kommen/kommt, dass X*	added to this, X
	nach dem Krieg	after the war
	bereits im NUMten Jahrhundert	going back to the NUMth century
	in Frage gestellt	questioned
	stehen/steht unter Denkmal schutz*	be listed (i.e. be a listed building)
English	X was released in NUM	
	until his death in NUM	
	large amounts of X	
	natural resources	
	mainland China	
	Member of Parliament	
	internal combustion	
	consistent with X	
	open to the public	
	the Olympic Games	
	on several occasions	
	science and technology	
	in the US state of X	
	by the early NUMs	
	special effects	
	it is thought that X	
	incompatible with X	
	on the grounds of X	
	in a NUM – NUM victory over X	
	due to the fact that X	

4.2 Assessing the Simulated Concept of FL

Having reviewed the underpinnings of the simulated universal concept of FL that underlies the figures presented in table 4, we can now outline its main features: with regard to fixedness, the universal concept of FL allows flexibility minimally in the areas of inflectional morphology to do with case marking, marking of agreement and if necessary marking of number to allow items of FL that specify these aspects at a more schematic level than the word form. Additionally, the universal concept of FL used is flexible with regard to the locus of formulaicity and recognizes formulaicity at the morpheme level.[10]

It is important to note that in this context *flexibility* does not mean that in all cases items of FL must be pitched at the most schematic level: the results discussed suggest that many items may be pitched at that level, but others are not and there will be different elements of the same item at differing levels of schematicity. For example, the German item of FL *eines Tages* (some day, at some point in time; lit. *of a day*) is fixed in the genitive case, but the more schematic *ARTINDEF Tag*[11] (a day) is still a common turn of phrase forming a semantic unit regardless of case marking. Similarly, the Korean phrase 예를 들면 *[iereul deulmeon]* (*for example*, lit. *if [we] take an example*) invariably specifies the object case marker – 를 *[-reul]*, including in all 1,214 occurrences of the expression in the corpus, despite case marking in general often being omitted, as discussed above). Similar examples are mentioned by Granger (2014: 60) (see also Tognini-Bonelli (2001) for a defense of the word form as relevant unit). In this sense, the identification of items of FL carried out above was a *simulation* of a flexible FL concept; an actual identification based on a flexible FL concept would identify items at

---

10 It may be argued that instead of the flexibility claimed to be necessary, it may be sufficient (or at least partially sufficient) simply to adjust the minimum frequency level for less isolating languages as part of the identification procedure (as Granger 2014 suggests), or that, in effect, the need for flexibility is created artificially by using frequency as part of the operationalization of FL. But this argument would be problematic: frequencies would have to be lowered very substantially from an already low threshold to get a similar effect because unlike in certain other procedures, frequency is only one element of the operationalization of FL used. A substantial lowering of threshold frequency would result in a much lower accuracy of identification (unless replacement filtering devices are used), meaning that the additional items would be unlikely to be bona fide items of FL in the sense used in this study. More fundamentally, frequency bears theoretical significance as it is used to operationalize conventionality and so is a fundamental, rather than accidental, aspect of FL according to the understanding of FL put forward. Consequently, adjustments to take account of this are justifiable.
11 ARTINDEF is the label used for a lemma of the indefinite article.

their most relevant level(s) of schematicity, which might well differ for each constituent element.

It can now be considered whether the universal concept of FL described is plausible. There are two main considerations that strongly suggest that this universal concept of FL, besides succeeding empirically, also forms a coherent and sensible concept from the point of view of theory. First, the features of increased flexibility in levels of schematicity and locus of formulaicity are not novel features, but have been suggested, albeit more tentatively, by previous studies as outlined above. This analysis has principally added an indication of their scope and necessity. Second, specification at various and mixed levels of schematicity (with some elements highly fixed in all aspects and others much less so) and the loss of the significance of the distinction between the word and morpheme levels are features that are not unusual: if we turn to constructionist approaches to grammar (also known as Construction Grammar and noted for their tight interfacing with phraseological theory and data, cf. Van Lancker Sidtis 2015; Buerki 2016), these features are not only accommodated but predicted as features for linguistic structures across language (Hilpert 2014; Hoffmann and Trousdale 2013). In constructionist theory, all of language consists of constructions that are specified at the full range of levels of schematicity from fully substantive (lexically fixed) to fully schematic. For example, the fully schematic ditransitive construction in (11) is as much a bona-fide construction as the partially lexically substantive construction in (12) or the fully substantive construction in (13).

(11) <Subj V Obj1 Obj2> (e.g. I handed her the book)
(12) <the Xer the Yer> (e.g. the bigger the better)
(13) <blue jeans>

Further, in constructionist theory, constructions exist from the level of single morpheme or morpheme group to that of phrase without a theoretically significant distinction between word and morpheme level constructions (cf. table 1.1 in Goldberg 2006: 5). Consequently, constructions like <*prebook*> or <*over-V*> (as in *overeat, oversleep*, etc.) are as much constructions as <*blue jeans*> or phrase-level constructions (11) and (12). From a constructionist viewpoint it therefore comes as no surprise that a universal concept of FL should admit items that are specified at various and mixed levels of schematicity, such as specification of the exact word form for all elements as in (14), specification at word form level for all but one element in (15) where the second element is specified at a more schematic level that allows case marking flexibility, specification at a fairly abstract level as in (16), which only contains two fully substantive elements, or indeed (17) which is formulaic at the morpheme sequence level.

(14) eines Tages (one day)
(15) 박사 학의(를) 취득하였다 *[baksa hakwi(reul) chuieukhaeotta]* (received [their] PhD)
(16) X [was/is to be/will be/is due to be] released in NUM
(17) Tagebuch (diary, lit. book of days)

The comprehensively universal concept of FL outlined above therefore not only succeeds in demonstrating its comprehensive universality across the three languages in our data, but also presents itself as a plausible concept of FL, taking previous phraseological research and insights from constructionist theory into account.

5 Discussion and Outlook

The results of this study fall into three general areas of significance. The first concerns the concept of FL and in what sense it is applicable universally to different types of languages. Here results show that it is possible to construct a concept of FL that applies in equal measure to isolating languages such as English with a low morpheme-per-word ratio, languages like German that feature a vast array of case, gender and agreement morphology, as well as polysynthetic, agglutinating languages like Korean, where individual words are often equivalents of whole phrases in more isolating languages. This is significant, because although the existence of FL is documented in a wide range of languages, previously FL was not subject to large-scale cross-linguistic comparison of quantitative aspects and such comparisons as have been conducted have yielded stark cross-linguistic differences in the number of items of FL identified. This posed fundamental challenges to the adequacy of the theoretical claims outlined above, most principally to the central importance of FL to the functioning of language in general, but these claims have now been safeguarded by the presentation of a plausible universal concept of FL.

Second, results crucially also reveal that this cross-linguistically viable concept of FL must incorporate two key aspects that have hitherto not been prominently discussed or applied: on the one hand, the inclusion within the concept of FL of more flexible, more schematic forms that require fine-tuning at time of use (as well as fully substantive forms that do not) is a requirement for a plausibly universal concept of FL, not an optional or marginal feature. While some items of FL are best identified as fully substantive forms that allow their use in context without any further adjustments, more schematic forms that require morphological fine-tuning must equally be recognised as FL. In the data, this fine-tuning typically consists of adjustments for case, number, or person, but may include other aspects. The point here is that without the ability to stipulate schematic forms, many individual, fully substantive forms will on their own be too rare to be reasonably considered common turns of phrase in their own right and this shortfall has vastly more serious consequences for languages that use, for example, case marking than for languages that do not, resulting in vastly different amounts of FL being detected between such languages. On the other hand, an adjustment of a more radical nature is required if the notion of FL is to be a universal one: the traditional fixation on FL as sequences of words needs to be relativized and sequences of sub-word-level linguistic items need to be eligible for recognition as legitimate items of FL. Again, the data indicate that this is necessary for the notion of FL become universally applicable. Thus results indicate that a universal concept of FL is viable but absolutely requires the admission of sequences that need a degree of fine-tuning at the time of use, and further requires a discounting of the importance of the word level that has hitherto been a prominent feature in conceptualisations of FL.

Third, results also suggest adjustments to the place of FL in an overall theory of language. In terms of theories of linguistic structure (i.e. syntax and morphology), notionally, FL can be integrated into various frameworks (cf. Wray 2008: chapter 7) or it may be envisaged as a completely separate module or "subsystem" (Dobrovol'skij 1992: 279) of the grammar. However, the requirement for a universal concept of FL to discount the significance of the word level, and the inclusion of sequences at differing levels of schematicity, strongly support and integrate with constructivist approaches to grammar. These approaches place linguistic constructions (from fully substantive phrases to fully schematic constructions), rather than words and rules of combination, at the centre of theoretical thinking. Items of FL function in this view as constructions of a particular, namely a predominantly substantive, type. Therefore, a universal concept of FL suggests a natural integration with constructivist theories of language where FL is able to take up an important place, commensurate with its importance in accounting for how language operates.

There are of course also a number of limitations to consider: only some, though arguably the most pertinent, aspects of how languages vary have been considered in this study. Detailed consideration of other aspects, such as the effects of freer word orders in some languages, and other features of languages not investigated in this study will no doubt add further important detail to a universal concept of FL. In its outline however, the concept put forward is unlikely to change dramatically.

Overall, results obtained offer strong evidence for a cross-linguistically robust notion of FL and how it fits into a larger theoretical context. This advances the field of research into FL by placing it on a firmer footing and by affirming its importance in accounting for how language works. This firmer footing can sustain current interest in the phenomenon and contribute to stimulating further research into theoretical as well as applied aspects of FL.[12]

References

Abdou, Ashraf (2011): *Arabic idioms: A corpus based study*. London: Routledge.
Al-Haj, Hassan, Alon Itai & Shuly Wintner (2014): Lexical Representation of Multiword Expressions in Morphologically-complex Languages. *International Journal of Lexicography* 27 (2), 130–170.
Altenberg, Bengt (1998): On the phraseology of spoken English: The evidence of recurrent word-combinations. In Anthony Paul Cowie (ed.), *Phraseology: Theory, analysis and applications*, 101–122. Oxford: Clarendon Press.
Altenberg, Bengt & Mats Eeg-Olofsson (1990): Phraseology in Spoken English: Presentation of a Project. In Jan Aarts & Willem Meijs (eds.), *Theory and Practice in Corpus Linguistics*, 1–26. Amsterdam: Rodopi.
anon. (2001): *Word lists*. Retrieved from http://wortschatz.uni-leipzig.de/html/wliste.html, accessed April 30, 2015.
anon. (2010): *Get the Hang of it. 3000 Redewendungen in fünf Sprachen*. Köln: Anaconda.
Attardi, Giuseppe & Antonio Fuschetto (2012): *WikiExtractor 2.2* [computer programme].
Ädel, Annelie & Britt Erman (2012): Recurrent word combinations in academic writing by native and non-native speakers of English: A lexical bundles approach. *English for Specific Purposes* 31 (2), 81–92.
Bally, Charles (1909): *Traité de stylistique française, premier volume,* Paris: Librairie C. Klincksieck.
Benigni, Valentina, Paola Cotta Ramusino, Fabio Mollica & Elmar Schafroth (2015): How to apply CxG to phraseology: a multilingual research project. *Journal of Social Sciences* 11 (3), 275–288.
Biber, Douglas (2006): *University language: a corpus-based study of spoken and written registers*. Amsterdam, Philadelphia: John Benjamins.
Biber, Douglas (2009): A corpus-driven approach to formulaic language in English: Multi-word patterns in speech and writing. *International Journal of Corpus Linguistics* 14 (3), 275–311.
Biber, Douglas & Federica Barbieri (2007): Lexical bundles in university spoken and written registers. *English for Specific Purposes* 26 (3), 263–286.
Biber, Douglas & Susan Conrad (1999): Lexical bundles in conversation and academic prose. *Language and Computers* 26, 181–190.

---

[12] The work was supported in part by the Swiss National Science Foundation under Grant P2BSP1_148623.

Biber, Douglas, Susan Conrad & Viviana Cortes (2003): Lexical bundles in speech and writing: an initial taxonomy. In Andrew Wilson, Paul Rayson & Tony McEnery (eds.), *Corpus Linguistics by the Lune: A Festschrift for Geoffrey Leech*, 71–92. Frankfurt am Main: Peter Lang.

Biber, Douglas, Stig Johansson, Geoffrey Leech, Susan Conrad & Edward Finegan (1999): *Longman grammar of spoken and written English*. Harlow: Pearson.

Bladas, Òscar (2012): Conversational routines, formulaic language and subjectification. *Journal of Pragmatics* 44 (8), 929–957.

Brunner, Annelen & Kathrin Steyer (2007): Corpus-driven study of multi-word expressions based on collocations from a very large corpus. *Proceedings of CL2007, University of Birmingham, UK, 27–30 July 2007*. Retrieved from http://corpus.bham.ac.uk/corplingproceedings07/paper/182_Paper.pdf, accessed September 21, 2012.

Buerki, Andreas (2012): Korpusgeleitete Extraktion von Mehrwortsequenzen aus (diachronen) Korpora. In Natalia Filatkina, Ane Kleine-Engel, Marcel Dräger & Harald Burger (Hrsg.), *Aspekte der historischen Phraseologie und Phraseographie*, 263–292. Heidelberg: Universitätsverlag Winter.

Buerki, Andreas (2013): *N-Gram Processor 0.4* [computer programme].

Buerki, Andreas (2016): Formulaic sequences: a drop in the ocean of constructions or something more significant? *European Journal of English Studies* 20 (1), 15–34.

Buerki, Andreas (2017): Frequency consolidation among word n-grams: A practical procedure. In Ruslan Mitkov (ed.), *Computational and corpus-based phraseology*, 432–446. Cham: Springer.

Burger, Harald, Annelies Buhofer & Ambros Sialm (1982): *Handbuch der Phraseologie*. Berlin, New York: De Gruyter.

Burger, Harald, Dmitrij Dobrovol'skij, Peter Kühn & Neal R. Norrick (eds.) (2007): *Phraseology: an international handbook of contemporary research*. Berlin, New York: De Gruyter.

Butler, Christopher S. (1997): Repeated word combinations in spoken and written text: some implications for functional grammar. In Christopher Butler, John H Connolly, Richard A Gatward & Roel M. Vismans (eds.), *A fund of ideas: recent developments in functional grammar*, 60–77. Amsterdam: IFOTT.

Butler, Christopher S. (2005): Formulaic language: an overview with particular reference to the cross-linguistic perspective. *Pragmatics and beyond. New series* 140, 221–242.

Bybee, Joan L. (2010): *Language, usage and cognition*, Cambridge: Cambridge University Press.

Colson, Jean-Pierre (2007): The World Wide Web as a corpus for set phrases. In Harald Burger, Dmitrij Dobrovol'skij, Peter Kühn & Neal R. Norrick (eds.), *Phraseology: an international handbook of contemporary* research, 1071–1077. Berlin, New York: De Gruyter.

Colson, Jean-Pierre (2008): Cross-linguistic phraseological studies. In Sylviane Granger & Fanny Meunier (eds.), *Phraseology: an interdisciplinary perspective*, 192–206. Amsterdam: John Benjamins.

Cortes, Viviana (2008): A comparative analysis of lexical bundles in academic history writing in English and Spanish. *Corpora* 3 (1), 43–57.

Coulmas, Florian (1979): On the sociolinguistic relevance of routine formulae. *Journal of Pragmatics* 3 (3/4), 239–266.

Cownie, Alun R. (2001): *Dictionary of Welsh and English idiomatic phrases*. Cardiff: University of Wales Press.

Dobrovol'skij, Dmitrij (1988): *Phraseologie als Objekt der Universalienlinguistik*. Leipzig: Enzyklopädie.
Dobrovol'skij, Dmitrij (1992): Phraseological universals: theoretical and applied aspects. In Michel Kefer & Johann van der Auwera (eds.), *Meaning and grammar: cross-linguistic perspectives*, 279–301. Berlin, New York: De Gruyter.
Dobrovol'skij, Dmitrij (2000): Contrastive idiom analysis: Russian and German idioms in theory and in the bilingual dictionary. *International Journal of Lexicography* 13 (3), 169–186.
Dobrovol'skij, Dmitrij & Elisabeth Piirainen (2005): *Figurative Language: Cross-cultural and cross-linguistic Perspectives*. Oxford: Elsevier.
Durrant, Philip (2013): Formulaicity in an agglutinating language: the case of Turkish. *Corpus Linguistics and Linguistic Theory* 9 (1), 1–38.
Dutton, Kelly (2009): *Exploring the boundaries of formulaic sequences: a corpus-based study of lexical substitution and insertion in contemporary British English*. Saarbrücken: VDM.
Erman, Britt (2007): Cognitive processes as evidence of the idiom principle. *International Journal of Corpus Linguistics* 12 (1), 25–53.
Erman, Britt & Beatrice Warren (2000): The idiom principle and the open choice principle. *Text* 20 (1), 29–62.
Feilke, Helmuth (1994): *Common sense-Kompetenz: Überlegungen zu einer Theorie des „sympathischen" und „natürlichen" Meinens und Verstehens*. Frankfurt am Main: Suhrkamp.
Feilke, Helmuth (2003): Textroutine, Textsemantik und sprachliches Wissen. In Angelika Linke, Hanspeter Ortner & Paul R. Portmann (Hrsg.), *Sprache und mehr. Ansichten einer Linguistik der sprachlichen Praxis*, 209–230. Tübingen: Niemeyer.
Fellbaum, Christiane (2007): Introduction. In Christiane Fellbaum (ed.), *Idioms and collocations: corpus-based linguistic and lexicographic studies*, 1–22. London: Continuum.
Fillmore, Charles, Paul Kay & Mary O'Connor (1988): Regularity and idiomaticity in grammatical constructions: the case of *let alone*. *Language* 64 (3), 501–538.
Granger, Sylviane (2014): A lexical bundle approach to comparing languages: Stems in English and French. *Languages in Contrast* 14 (1), 58–72.
Goldberg, Adele E. (2006): *Constructions at work: the nature of generalization in language*. Oxford: Oxford University Press.
Heid, Ulrich (2012): German noun+verb collocations in the sentence context: morphosyntactic properties contributing to idiomaticity. In Thomas Herbst, Susen Faulhaber & Peter Uhrig (eds.), *The phraseological view of language: A tribute to John Sinclair*, 283–311. Berlin, New York: De Gruyter.
Hilpert, Martin (2014): *Construction grammar and its application to English*. Edinburgh: Edinburgh University Press.
Ho, Trang (2009): *Tatoeba Project*. Retrieved from http://tatoeba.org, accessed December 1, 2014.
Hoffmann, Thomas & Graeme Trousdale (eds.) (2013): *The Oxford Handbook of Construction Grammar*. Oxford: Oxford University Press.
Howarth, Peter (1998): Phraseology and second language proficiency. *Applied Linguistics* 19 (1), 24–44.
Idström, Anna & Elisabeth Piirainen (eds.) (2012): *Endangered metaphors*. Amsterdam: John Benjamins.
Kecskes, Istvan (2007): Formulaic language in English Lingua Franca. In Istvan Kecskes & Laurence R. Horn (eds.), *Explorations in pragmatics: Linguistic, cognitive and intercultural aspects* (Volume 1), 191–218. Berlin, Boston: De Gruyter.

Kim, Seonho, Juntae Yoon & Mansuk Song (2001): Automatic extraction of collocations from Korean text. *Computers and the Humanities* 35 (3), 273–297.

Kim, You-Jin (2009): Korean lexical bundles in conversation and academic texts. *Corpora* 4 (2), 135–165.

Kuiper, Koenrad (2009): *Formulaic Genres*. Houndmills: Palgrave Macmillan.

Langacker, Ronald W. (2008): Cognitive Grammar as a Basis for Language Instruction. In Peter Robinson & Nick C. Ellis (eds.), *Handbook of cognitive linguistics and second language acquisition*, 66–88. Abingdon: Routledge.

Langlotz, Andreas (2006): *Idiomatic creativity: a cognitive-linguistic model of idiom-representation and idiom-variation in English*. Amsterdam: John Benjamins.

Lenk, Hartmut E. H. & Stephan Stein (Hrsg.) (2011): *Phraseologismen in Textsorten*. Hildesheim: Olms.

McDonough Dolmaya, Julie (2015): Revision history: Translation trends in Wikipedia. *Translation Studies* 8 (1), 16–34.

Manning, Christopher D. & Hinrich Schütze (1999): *Foundations of statistical natural language processing*. Cambridge, Mass.: Massachusetts Institute of Technology Press.

Maruch, Stef & Aahz Maruch (2011): *Python for dummies*. Chichester: Wiley.

Moon, Rosamund (1995): Introduction. In John McH Sinclair (ed.), *Collins COBUILD dictionary of idioms*, iv–vii. London: HarperCollins.

Moon, Rosamund (1998): Frequencies and Forms of Phrasal Lexemes in English. In Anthony Paul Cowie (ed.), *Phraseology: theory, analysis and applications*, 79–100. Oxford: Clarendon Press.

Naber, Daniel (2015): *jWordSplitter* [computer programme].

Namba, Kazuhiko (2010): Formulaicity in code-switching: Criteria for identifying formulaic sequences. In David Wood (ed.), *Perspectives on formulaic language: Acquisition and communication*, 129–150. London: Continuum.

Nattinger, James R. & Jeanette S. DeCarrico (1992): *Lexical phrases and language teaching*. Oxford: Oxford University Press.

Oh, Yoon Mi, François Pellegrino & Edigio Marsico (2014): La complexité des langues du monde. *Pour la Science* 82, 66–71.

Oh, Yoon Mi, François Pellegrino, Egidio Marsico & Christophe Coupé (2013): A Quantitative and Typological Approach to Correlating Linguistic Complexity. *Proceedings from the 5th Conference on Quantitative Investigations in Theoretical Linguistics (QITL) Leuven, 12-14 September 2013*, 71–75. Retrieved from http://citeseerx.ist.psu.edu/viewdoc/download;jsessionid=8B48B870A6ECAF02510C5D8B364DAC33?doi=10.1.1.398.7882&rep=rep1&type=pdf, accessed November 22, 2014.

O'Keeffe, Anne, Michael McCarthy & Roland Carter (2007): *From corpus to classroom: language use and language teaching*. Cambridge: Cambridge University Press.

Park, Sangwon (2011): *HanNanum* [computer programme].

Pawley, Andrew (2001): Phraseology, linguistics and the dictionary. *International Journal of Lexicography* 14 (2), 122–134.

Pawley, Andrew & Frances Syder (1983): Two puzzles for linguistic theory: nativelike selection and nativelike fluency. In Jack C. Richards & Richard W. Schmidt (eds.), *Language and communication*, 191–226. Harlow: Longman.

Pellegrino, François, Christophe Coupé & Egidio Marsico (2011): Across-Language Perspective on Speech Information Rate. *Language* 87 (3), 539–558.

Piirainen, Elisabeth (2012): *Widespread idioms in Europe and beyond: toward a lexicon of common figurative units*. New York: Peter Lang.
Russ, Charles (1994): *The German language today: a linguistic introduction*. London: Routledge.
Schmid, Helmut (1994): *Probablistic Part-of-Speech Tagging Using Decision Trees. Proceedings of the International Conference on New Methods in Language Processing, Manchester, UK*. Retrieved from http://www.cis.uni-muenchen.de/~schmid/tools/TreeTagger/data/tree-tagger1.pdf, accessed April 20, 2015.
Sharma, Sunil (2017): Happiness and metaphors: a perspective from Hindi phraseology. *Yearbook of Phraseology* 8, 161–180.
Shei, Chris & Hsun-Ping Hsieh (2012): Linkit: a call system for learning Chinese characters, words, and phrases. *Computer Assisted Language Learning* 25 (4), 319–338.
Seidlhofer, Barbara (2009): Accommodation and the idiom principle in English as a Lingua Franca. *Intercultural Pragmatics* 6 (2), 195–215.
Sinclair, John McHardy (1991): *Corpus, Concordance, Collocation*, Oxford: Oxford University Press.
Sinclair, John McHardy (2004): *Trust the text*. London: Routledge.
Sohn, Ho-Min (2001): *The Korean Language*. Cambridge: Cambridge University Press.
Song, Jae Jung (2001): *Linguistic typology: Morphology and syntax*. Harlow: Pearson Longman.
Stein, Stephan (2007): Mündlichkeit und Schriftlichkeit aus phraseologischer Perspektive. In Harald Burger, Dmitrij Dobrovol'skij, Peter Kühn & Neal R. Norrick (eds.), *Phraseology: an international handbook of contemporary research*, 220–236. Berlin, New York: De Gruyter.
Sun, Chaofen (2006): *Chinese: A linguistic introduction*. Cambridge: Cambridge University Press.
Tognini-Bonelli, Elena (2001): *Corpus linguistics at work*. Amsterdam: John Benjamins.
Van Lancker Sidtis, Diana (2015): Formulaic language in an emergentist framework. In Brian MacWhinney & William O'Grady (eds.), *The handbook of language emergence*, 578–599. Chichester: Wiley-Blackwell.
Warncke-Wang, Morten, Anuradha Uduwage, Zhenhua Dong & John Riedl (2012): In search of the Ur-Wikipedia: universality, similarity, and translation in the Wikipedia inter-language link network. *Proceedings of the eighth annual international symposium on wikis and open collaboration, Linz (A)*. Retrieved from https://dl.acm.org/citation.cfm?id=2462959, accessed August 07, 2018.
Whaley, Lindsay J. (1997): *Introduction to typology: the unity and diversity of language*. London: SAGE.
Wray, Alison (2002): *Formulaic language and the lexicon*. Cambridge: Cambridge University Press.
Wray, Alison (2008): *Formulaic language: pushing the boundaries*. Oxford: Oxford University Press.
Wray, Alison & Michael R. Perkins (2000): The functions of formulaic language: an integrated model. *Language and Communication* 20 (1), 1–28.

Abdullah Eisa
Marḥaban: Reconsidering the Criteria of an Arabic Phraseme

Abstract: This paper deals with the difficulties that face Arabic phraseology when the established criteria of phraseology as defined by Gries (2008) are applied. The paper focuses especially on the number of elements involved in a phraseme and here we introduce the concept of one-word + zero-element phrasemes in Arabic.

1 Introduction

Studies on Arabic phraseology focus on empirical applications of Arabic phrasemes. Scholars adopted the definition already established in the research to define an Arabic phraseme (Müller 1993, 2001; Ghariani Baccouche 2007). However, an Arabic phraseme challenges the established criteria for a phraseme. In order to illustrate this, we base our discussion of Arabic phraseology on the criteria for a phraseme as defined by Gries (2008: 6):
1. Natural elements are lexemes or lemmas (words)
2. The number of elements is two or more
3. Frequency of co-occurrence is greater than expected
4. The distance between elements is usually short (interrupted by just one word) or nonexistent
5. The flexibility of elements should not exceed more than one element
6. A phraseme should function as one semantic unit

The six parameters criteria "underlie most phraseological work" (Gries 2008: 5) and provide a precise definition that would help phraseologists and researchers from other fields to identify a phraseme in general and an Arabic phraseme in particular.

Gries suggested that his first criterion (the nature of the elements) included not only lexical items, but also grammatical patterns (Gries 2008: 5). He further argued that lexical items and lemmas should be accepted as phraseological (Gries 2008: 5).

As to the second criterion (the number of elements), a phraseme must be created from two or more elements. The minimum number of elements in the case of

---

ǝ Open Access. © 2020 A. Eisa, published by De Gruyter. [CC BY] This work is licensed under the Creative Commons Attribution 4.0 License.
https://doi.org/10.1515/9783110669824-006

Arabic should be the focus of more scholarly attention, since the morphological concepts *manḥūt* and *al-murakkab al-mazjī* – both of which originally contained two or more lexical items – are dealt with as single lexemes in dictionaries.

With regard to the third criterion (the number of occurrences), Gries claims that a phraseme can be identified as such "if its observed frequency of occurrence is larger than its expected one" (Gries 2008: 5). Although the strong tendency of two items to co-occur has been mentioned in most of the published definitions of phrasemes, such a method requires a well-established corpus, which does not exist for classical Arabic.

Regarding the fourth criterion (the permissible distance between the elements), Gries adopted a "widespread broader perspective" that allowed word collocations that contained discontinuous items to be identified as phrasemes (Gries 2008: 5). Arguments in favour of this criterion can be found in papers based on N-gram studies of natural language processes (Gries 2008: 5).[1] However, applying this criterion to Arabic would tend to conflict with Arabic's syntactic nature as a free-order language.

The fifth criterion (the degree of flexibility of the elements) revolves around the question of how flexible a phraseme ought to be. What tenses can it contain and still be considered a phraseme? What is the level of lexical flexibility for a phraseme? Completely inflexible forms, i.e. full-phrasemes are accepted, but the criterion also allows "relatively flexible patterns", such as phrases that allow multiple tenses but exclude one particular tense (Gries 2008: 5). Also, the criterion includes "partially lexical-filled patterns".

Lastly, the sixth criterion (semantic unity) is a semantic one, acting as the core of the definition of a phraseme: any word combination deemed a phraseme should function as one semantic unit (Gries 2008: 6). However, a debate has arisen over whether a phraseme should be semantically non-compositional. Gries argued that this was unnecessary, but advocated unity of meaning (Gries 2008: 6). The final definition of a phraseme he arrived at, based on the foregoing six criteria, was as follows:

> [A] phraseologism is defined as the co-occurrence of a form or lemma of [a] lexical item and one or more additional linguistic elements of various kinds which function as one semantic

---

[1] N-grams, bigrams, and trigrams are the extracted results of a study that statistically analyses "recurrent continuous sequences of two or more words". Phraseological studies based on N-gram analysis have usually advocated the continuity of the items of a phraseme (Granger and Paquot 2008: 38–39).

unit in a clause or sentence and whose frequency of co-occurrence is larger than expected on the basis of chance[.]

(Gries 2008: 6)

The six parameters and definitions discussed above provide us with six clear criteria for the definition of a phraseme. These criteria focus on three main concepts: the individual elements, the occurrence of the elements as a single unit, and the semantic unity of the phraseme. Although this definition provides a comprehensive definition of a phraseme within the frame of the European languages, it needs to be examined within Classical Arabic, the object of this study.

In this paper I will investigate the challenges that applying the criteria of a phraseme provides, aiming to redefine a phraseme within the context of Arabic.

2 Investigating the Criteria

2.1 The Nature of a Phraseme Element

According to the definition proposed by Gries and adopted in this paper, all elements of a phraseme should be words. Words, according to Gries, are "a form or lemma of lexical items and any kind of linguistic element" (Gries 2008: 5). The term 'word', however, requires further discussion. In Arabic tradition, 'word' is defined as a letter (ḥarf), a noun, or a verb (Ibn ʿAqīl 1980: 14). A noun is thus a word with an independent meaning but no tense; a verb is a word with an independent meaning and a tense; and a letter is a word with neither (Ibn ʿAqīl 1980: 15).[2] Also, given that pronouns in Arabic are considered to be nouns, as they refer to a meaning by themselves and function as nouns grammatically (al-Nīlī 1999: 596; Ibn ʿAqīl 1980: 15), a suffix pronoun – e.g., kāf al-khiṭāb [second person singular] – is considered an independent element of a phraseme and can, with another lexeme, form a phraseme (Ibn ʿAqīl 1980: 31). As a result, any word of any word-class, whether a noun, pronoun, verb, or ḥarf, can form a phraseme under certain conditions as in ḥanānay-ka (your [dual] mercies) = be patient. The second element of the phraseme ḥanānay-ka is the second person pronoun kāf al-

---

2 In traditional Arabic grammar, conjunctions and determiners are included in the ḥarf word-class, while pronouns are included in the noun word-class (Ibn ʿAqīl 1980: 15).

khiṭāb [second person singular], which with the first element *ḥanānayn* forms the phraseme.[3]

Additionally, the Arabic definition of 'word' implies that there is no distinction between lexical items and grammatical patterns in terms of fulfilling the requirements of phraseme elements; i.e., the granularity level of the element can be either a lemma or a morphological form (Gries 2008: 15).

2.2 The Number of Elements

A phraseme, by definition, comprises a phrase. An English phrase, for instance, is defined as "any syntactic unit which includes more than one word and is not an entire sentence" (Matthews 1997: 255). Applying this criterion to the Arabic language calls for further investigation, however, due to the existence of what I will term 'one + zero elements' phrasemes. In the following, I will discuss how the word *marḥaban* is actually a phrase, in the deep structure, and a phraseme made up of one explicit element and a zero element.

Some Arabic phrasemes are made up of two elements, one explicit and the other implicit, i.e., understood from context. The words *marḥaban* [to be in a spacious place] = to be welcome, and *ahlan* [to be among one's people] = to be welcome, are two good examples of this phenomenon. *Marḥaban* is a word used for greeting, and has the original meaning 'wide' (Ibn Manẓūr 2005: 1472–1473). *Marḥaban* is classified as a cognate object, or what is known in Arabic as *mafʿūl muṭlaq*. The cognate object is a verbal noun derived from the main verb (Taha 2011: 1), used after a verb to either describe or emphasize it (Ibn ʿAqīl 1930: 169). Given the grammatical class to which *marḥaban* belongs, we can surmise that the phrase has a missing element. That element can be defined as a zero element on both a syntactic and a semantic level. Syntactically, the accusative case (*naṣb*) requires a verb from which the cognate object is derived. *Marḥaban* is therefore in the accusative case as it is influenced *al-ʿāmil* (the governor) by *taqdīr*. The concept of *taqdīr* can be explained as follows:

> The speaker 'hides' things in speech, and it is the grammarian's task to reconstruct these hidden elements in order to explain the surface structure of the sentences. The most important aim of Arabic grammar is the explanation of the case endings (*iʿrāb*) in the sentences that are produced by the action (*ʿāmil*) of a visible element in the sentence. If no such

---

[3] The *-n* at the end of *ḥanānayn* is dropped in the formation of the merging of the word and the pronoun.

element is available, the grammarian must have recourse to an underlying structure in which these elements are made explicit.

(Versteegh 2011: 1)

In the case of *marḥaban*, the implicit element is the ʿ*āmil*, which is the verb *arḥaba*. It is crucial to mention here that the implicit element can be either a zero element or a semantic ellipsis. These two potential explanations are both considered below.

First, with regard to ellipsis, an elliptical phrase is one in which some elements are omitted, especially if its meaning is supplied by its context (Matthews 1997: 111). Linguists distinguish between different kinds of ellipsis.[4] In Arabic, there are a number of linguistic phenomena considered to be ellipsis, including sluicing, verb-phrase (VP) ellipsis, and noun-phrase (NP) ellipsis (Mughazy 2011: 2). In sluicing, the omitted element is preceded by a wh-question tool, as in example (1a), where an omission can be understood from the antecedent, thereby allowing the phrase to be interpreted as *arāda ʿAlī an yadhhaba ilā l-bayti* in (1b). Sluicing therefore contrasts with NP ellipsis, illustrated in example (2), in which the missing element is not a phrase but a single noun. The quantifier can be *tanwīn*: the suffix *n*, or the prefix *al-* (Mughazy 2011: 2).[5] In example (2), the omitted noun can be interpreted as *al-muwaẓẓafīn*, as in (2b). Lastly, in VP ellipsis, the omitted element is the head verb and its internal object the argument (Mughazy 2011: 2). This type of ellipsis only occurs after auxiliary verbs. No examples of VP ellipsis have been identified in classical Arabic, other than in ʿ*āmiyyah* (colloquial), which is beyond the scope of this research (Mughazy 2011: 2).

(1a) ʿAlī arāda dh-dhahāba ila l-bayti wa lā adrī limādhā.
 'Ali wanted to go home, and I don't know why.'
(1b) [s ʿ*Alī*[ı[ıpast., Sing., 3rd person][vp[v*arāda*₁] obj*dh-dhahāb*₂]] conj*wa* negl*ā* sΔ[pres., sing., 1st person][vp*adrī*]][q *limāthā*][sΔ [vp Δ]NPΔ]]]
(2a) *al-mudīru qābala l-muwaẓẓafīna illa l-baʿḍ/baʿḍa-n*
 'The manager met all the employees except for a few.'
(2b) [*al-mudīru* [ı[ıpast., Sing., 3rd person][vp *qābala*] obj *l-muwaẓẓafīna*] excep.*illa* [obj *l-baʿḍ*] [npΔ]]]

The above examples, although they are not formulaic, refer to the syntactic subsentential level, and in the case of a one-element phraseme like *marḥaba-n*, none

---

4 There is no agreement about the typology of ellipses. Nevertheless, VP ellipsis, NP ellipsis, and sluicing, albeit under various names, are widely acknowledged.
5 Mughazy (2011: 2) does not mention the suffix *al-* as a quantifier, although it can be used in *al-baʿḍ* for the same purpose, as in example (2).

of the ellipsis types can be applied. Linguists have proposed two rival explanations for this phenomenon. Haddar and Ben Hamadou (1998: 271) referred to it as "false ellipsis", which can be understood without constructing the complete form. The same authors claimed that false ellipses "can be resolved at the lexical level" (Haddar and Ben Hamadou 1998: 271) and gave two examples of it: *ʿīda-n saʿīda-n* (Happy New Year), and *an-nāra n-nāra!* (Fire, fire!). The elliptical element in the first example is the verb *atamannā* (I wish), and in the second, the verb *iḥdhar* (be careful). Although their examples indicate more than one lexeme, both demonstrate the concept of omitted *ʿāmil* (action) – the case with which we are specifically concerned. It may thus be claimed that ellipsis can be understood on a lexical level, but further investigation into the syntactic level is nevertheless required.

Stainton discussed two potential modes of analysing/explaining the phenomenon: a pragmatics-oriented approach, and semantic ellipsis (Stainton 2005: 386). The first requires that an utterance's "face value" be the main focus of analysis, while its pragmatics – i.e., gestures and context – treated as the responsibility of the utterance's receiver, who reconstructs missing elements and fills in gaps (Stainton 2005: 387).[6] Crucially, however, it is not the non-sentential phrases that this approach intends to reconstruct; it has no interest in filling in *linguistic* gaps (Stainton 2005: 387). Rather, the non-linguistic context in which the elliptical phrase occurs fills the *semantic* gap in the utterance.

Analysing the phenomenon of one-word Arabic phrasemes using Stainton's pragmatics-oriented approach therefore leads us to either a) accept or b) reject the idea that single words can be phrasemes. The first option, however, must be rejected as contradicting the definition of phraseology and its units: for a phraseme, by definition, is formed from a phrase, which cannot comprise fewer than two elements (in the case of the Arabic language, lexemes and pronouns). And in considering the second option, we cannot overlook the fact that one-word expressions function as phrasemes in Arabic, and syntactically reflect a missing element – the *ʿāmil* (action) – which changes their grammatical case from nominative to accusative. These cases are marked by case-endings: *ḍammah* [suffix *u*],

---

6 Stainton provides two "competing views" of how to explain how the gap is filled. The first view, advocated by Barton (2005: 386), "postulates (i) a sub-module of linguistic context, that operates exclusively on the sub-sentence uttered plus prior explicit discourse, (ii) a sub-module of conversational context, that takes the output of the first sub-module as input, and uses non-linguistic context [...] to derive what the speaker meant to convey". The other view, advocated by Stainton himself, is that while gap-filling does occur "via non-deductive inference", there are no pragmatics modules at work, but rather "central system progresses, inferential processes not specific to language, [that are used] to bridge the gap".

wāw [suffix *ū*], *alif* [suffix *ā*] and *nūn* [suffix *n*] for nominative, and *fatḥah* [suffix *a*], *yā'* [suffix *i*], *alif* [suffix *ā*], and *ḥadhf* [deletion] for accusative.

Semantic ellipsis occurs when a sentence is elliptic, but the ellipsis can be reconstructed by applying the syntactic rules of the language in the absence of an uttered antecedent. It differs from the previously described varieties of ellipses in that it could potentially explain one-word phrasemes. Although *marḥab-ta*, the omitted verb of *marḥaba-n*, does not exist (or at any rate has not been detected) in lexicons of the Arabic language, it must still be reconstructed – especially in combination with the cognate object *marḥaba-n* – to justify the accusative case ending (al-Farāhīdī 2005: 342).[7] Stainton defended the pragmatics-oriented approach by arguing that the reconstructed phrases may not suit the elliptic phrase, and cited the following example. If someone asks 'Who loves Michael Jackson?', the answer could be 'Me'. The elliptic part of the phrase 'Me' does not suit the reconstructed phrase 'I love Michael Jackson', since the pronoun in the elliptic phrase is in the accusative case, whilst in the reconstructed phrase it is in the nominative case. Stainton gives another example in German. A German speaker would say 'mein Vater' [my [nom.] father], whilst pointing at someone that reminds him of his father; however the reconstructed phrase would be 'Das erinnert mich an meinen Vater' [that reminds me of my [acc.] father]. However, in the case of Stainton's first example, answering the question posed with 'I' or 'I do' would be more grammatically correct English than answering with 'Me', even though the latter is generally accepted in colloquial usage; i.e., the elliptic phrase could originally have been composed with the pronoun in the nominative case. Alternatively, we can view the reconstructed phrase as being the (likewise grammatically correct) 'It is me who likes Michael Jackson'. Similar arguments can be applied to Stainton's German example. It should also be noted that ellipsis can be used to simplify an utterance, and that therefore, an elliptic phrase can be understood when the simplest case is used, even if it does not agree with the original/reconstructed phrase.

The example of *marḥaban* can be better explained via the concept of a zero element in a phraseme, given that a phraseme is a set phrase and a phrase by definition is more than one word (McGregor 2003: 77–78, 82).[8] However, a one +

---

[7] "When al-Khalīl (2003: 105) was asked about the accusative case of *marḥaban* he said "in it a hidden verb"; he meant: dwell or stay, so it became accusative by a hidden verb, then it became dead when its [the verb's] meaning became well-known" (al-Farāhīdī 2005: 342).

[8] McGregor (McGregor 2003: 77–119) provides a detailed account of the historical background of the concept of the zero-element. Hel also differentiates between 'zero' and 'nothing', for zero should fulfill two conditions provided by Haas (1962: 49): a) distinctive omission of overt forms,

zero element phraseme is not to be confused with a lexeme + pronoun phraseme, in which the second element is a suffix pronoun, e.g., ḥananayka [your [dual] mercies] = slowly. Though the zero element is the element that does not exist in some linguistic cases of a given language, its visible equivalent does exist in the majority of language cases (Haas 1962: 34). However, the zero element has an impact on its linguistic context (Haas 1962: 34). For example, the suffixes -ed and -t are morphemes that indicate the past tense in verbs in English, although such morphemes do not exist in verbs like *cut* and *put* (Haas 1962: 34). However, these verbs' tenses can be understood from context; and the absence of an element signifying the tense is the zero-element. In Arabic, the zero-element applies to *sukūn* (Bishr 1998: 187; Firth 1957: 180–189):[9] the case-ending used in the absence of any of the three case endings *fatḥah* \a\, *ḍammah* \u\, and *kasrah* \i\ (Bishr 1998:187). *Jazm* is a syntactic case in which the case-ending is a zero-element (*sukūn* ∅) because it demonstrates an absence of the uttered morphemes. In the case of a one-uttered-word phraseme, the second non-pronounced element is a zero-element of the phraseme. For instance, the verb *marḥb-ta*, which functions as the action of the cognate object *marḥaban*, constitutes the zero-element in the phrase that forms the phraseme *marḥaban*.

In conclusion, applying the second criterion of phraseology to Arabic phrasemes creates a difficulty that needs to be overcome insofar as Arabic includes one-word phrasemes in which one element is uttered and the other is elliptic. This phenomenon is best classified as semantic ellipsis for two reasons. Firstly, the uttered element is a cognate object that needs an governor (*'āmil*) to justify its grammatical case. Therefore, a verb that coheres with it is reconstructed (*taqdīr*) – as *arḥab-ka allāhu* [[may] God [have] you in a spacious [place]], in the case of *marḥaban*. Secondly, a one word Arabic phraseme, e.g. *marhaban*, does not constitute a syntactic ellipsis, since in such an ellipsis, the uttered element requires a reference to an uttered antecedent, but the action/verb has never actually been found in classical Arabic in the context of *marḥaban*. Finally, the application of the concept of the zero-element to one-word phrasemes allows them to meet the established definition of a phrase. The elliptic element of the phraseme *marḥaban* is a zero-element, as it exists only in parallel phenomena, and it has an effect – i.e., the formation of a phraseme – on the existing element. The one-

---

and b) overt alternates to this operation. If the potential zero element loses one of those conditions, it becomes 'nothing' rather than 'zero'.

9 The concept of a zero-element in Arabic was first introduced by Firth (1957: 180–189) then further explored by Bishr (1998: 187).

word phraseme can thus be defined as a single word that is part of an elliptic phrase and therefore functions as a phraseme on its own.

Another issue that emerges when attempting to apply the second criterion to Arabic phraseology is the polylexical phenomenon of *naḥt*: two or more words that are merged into one, losing some of their letters in order to cohere with the structure of the quadrilateral root.[10] For instance, *ḥawqalah* is derived from *lā ḥawla wa lā quwwata illā bi-llāh* [there is no might nor power except in God]: a sentence used in prayer or in response to an unpleasant situation. Such words function as phrasemes since they adhere to the other criteria; however, they require some further explanation. Semantic ellipses and zero-elements cannot be applied to the phenomenon of *naḥt*, since there is neither any ellipsis nor are there any non-pronounced elements. However, the original words are merged via contraction. Hence, *manḥūt* is a phraseme written as one word, but composed of fragments of other words that together formed a sentence-long phrase (al-Khaṭīb 2003: 439).

2.3 The Number of Co-Occurrences Required before a Phrase can be Considered a Phraseme

Counting the instances of co-occurrence of a particular phraseme in classical or Modern Standard Arabic would normally require the existence of a corpus of relevant text. In its absence, classical collections of idioms and proverbs including *Amthāl al-ʿArab* by al-Mufaḍḍal al-Ḍabbī (d. 784), *al-Durrah al-Fākhirah fī al-Amthāl al-Sāʾirah* by Ḥamzah al-Aṣfahānī (d. 961), *Majmaʿ al-Amthāl* by al-Maydanī (d. 1124), and collections of non-figurative set phrases like *Thimār al-Qulūb fī al-Muḍāf wa al-Mansūb* by al-Thaʿālibī (d. 1038) and *Mā Yuʿawwal ʿalayh fī al-Muḍāf wa al-Muḍāf Ilayh* by al-Muḥibbī (d. 1699), are key repositories of phrasemes for Classical Arabic and for MSA, which contains a large number of Classical Arabic phrasemes. Collections of Classical Arabic books such as Islamport.com or Shamila could be referred to, in order to measure the number of occurrences of the phraseme in Classical Arabic works. Also, the International Arabic Corpus is useful for MSA. Additionally, collections of eloquent phrases are an important source of phrasemes, reflecting prevalent metaphorical phrases. Two examples of this type of lexicon will be referred to: the *Jawāhir al-Alfāẓ* of Qudamah Ibn Jaʿfar (d. 949), and the *al-Alfaẓ al-Kitabiyyah* of al-Hamathānī (d.

---

10 The root in Arabic consists of either three letters 1-2-3 (a-k-l) or four letters 1-2-1-2 (w-s-w-s)/1-2-3-4 (ḥ-n-ẓ-l).

939). However, with Gries (2008: 5) stating only that this number should be "larger than [...] expected", as previously noted in reference to Gries's work, the lack of a well-established corpus of Classical Arabic does not support the corpus-based method of identifying a phraseme.

Accordingly, analyses of the idiomatic level and referring to the previous collections would be the potential methodology used to identify Arabic phrasemes. However, distinguishing idiomatic from literal meaning in Arabic can at times be problematic because of the lexemes that are affected by dead metaphors. Two conditions will merit the use of dictionaries for the purpose of tracking original meaning. First, the source should be written before the target era. Secondly, the original meaning, i.e. literal if it occurs in a secondary meaning, of the phraseme's elements should be indicated. For example, for phrasemes that occur in late Andalusi works, e.g. the works of Ibn al-Khaṭīb, the dictionaries that can possibly be used for this purpose are the *Al-ʿAyn* of al-khalīl (d. 736), the *Tahthīb al-Lughah* of al-Azharī (d. 981), the *Maqāyīs al-Lugah* of Ibn Faris (d. 1004), and the *Tāj al-Lugah wa Ṣiḥāḥ al-ʿArabiyyah* of al-Jawharī (d. 1003). Additionally, the original source domains of the phrasemes would be traced to their possible sources, with the aim of gaining a clear indication of their primary semantic level.

2.4 The Permissible Distance between the Elements of a Phraseme

A phraseme is a set phrase in which the elements cannot be substituted. These elements function as one semantic unit by being attached to each other (Gries 2008: 6). In a restricted-order language, the order in which an element occurs in a phrase is important to the reader's understanding of that word's grammatical class. Arabic is a free-order language, meaning that the grammatical class of a word is not affected by the order of the elements in the phrase in which it appears (al-Sīrāfī, 2008: 263).[11] This raises an important question: What are the limits of order-change in an Arabic phraseme? To arrive at a definitive answer will require thorough analysis. It is reasonable to claim that a set phrase can be considered a

---

11 In some cases in Arabic, order is important for the identification of the grammatical class of a word: for instance, when a case-ending does not appear because it would render a long vowel at the end of a word un-pronounceable. One example of this is *ḍaraba ʿĪsā Mūsā* [Isa hit Musa]. Both Musa and Isa end with long vowels that cannot be pronounced alongside either the case-ending of the nominative case /u/, or the case-ending of accusative case /a/. Thus, only word-order reveals the meaning of the sentence, based on grammarians' agreement that the subject comes before the object.

phraseme as long as order-changes do not affect its metaphorical meaning. For instance, in the case of the phraseme *as-salāmu ʿalaykum wa raḥmatu l-lāhi wa barakātuhu* (may the peace, mercy, and blessings of God be with you), although the literal meaning of the phrase's element does not express the meaning of greeting, the phrase is commonly used as a greeting. It can be found in various orders, such as *salāmu l-lāhi ʿalayka wa raḥmatuhū wa barakātu* and *ʿlayka wa raḥmatu l-lāhi s-salāmu*. In all three of these versions, despite changes to word-order, the phrase retains both the same metaphorical meaning and the same function as a greeting.

The second issue that must be addressed under this criterion is the size of any gap between the elements of a phraseme. As discussed earlier, in a broad sense and up to a certain point, a gap between the elements of a phraseme can be accepted. To identify the specifics of such limits in Arabic, a survey study would be required. However, as noted above the metaphorical meaning of a phrase is the main criterion for accepting a phrase, regardless of whether it is a phraseme or has lost its phraseological identity. For instance, *ʿalā qawmihā janat barāqish* [Barāqish has harmed her people] is a phraseme used to describe anyone who hurts their people unwillingly. In the context of an own-goal in a football match, for instance, the commentator might say *wa barāqishu hunā narāhā janat li-l'asafi ʿalā qawmihā* [and Barāqish, we can see her here, harmed, unfortunately, her people]. Although the phraseme has been changed syntactically – with Barāqish this time not a subject, but an object functioning as an antecedent of the omitted pronoun in the verb *janat* [harmed] – it still reflects its original metaphorical meaning. This, of course, works with sentence-long phrasemes but not with one-word phrasemes or with lexical idioms (e.g. compounds such as *manḥūt* or *tarkīb mazjī*).

2.5 The Lexical and Syntactic Flexibility of Phraseme Elements' Non-Substitutability

The concept of fixedness of an Arabic phraseme can be examined on two main linguistic levels: the syntactic and the lexical. Syntactically, phrasemes that "break the conventional grammatical rules" (Moon 1998: 21), known as ill-formed collocations, are completely fixed. Ill-formed collocations can be idioms, proverbs or even pragmatic phrasemes. A clear example of an Arabic pragmatic phraseme that is an ill-formed collocation is *murghamu-n akhāka lā baṭal* [your brother is forced (to do what he has done) not a hero]. Under the conventional grammatical rules of Arabic, *akhāka* should be written in the nominative case (*akhūka*) as the subject of a passive-voice sentence, or as it is known in Arabic, *nāʾib fāʿil*. In this pragmatic phraseme, the two conditions of free phrases are violated (Melʾčuk 1998: 30). Pronouns in Arabic are mostly morphemes,[12] so in phrasemes that contain a pronoun, the pronoun changes with context. For instance, *ḥanānay-ka* [your (dual) mercies] is grammatically fixed in the accusative case, and its pronoun changes depending on the person(s) to whom it is addressed, as follows:

2MUS-ḥanānay-ka, 2FEM-ḥanānay-ki, 2DUL-ḥanānay-kuma, 2PLUR.FEM-ḥanānay-kum, 2PLUR-MAS ḥanānay-kunna.

Thus, the fixedness percentage of an Arabic phraseme can either be complete (in the case of ill-formed collocations/pragmatic phrasemes) or semi-flexible; and its status as completely fixed or semi-flexible affects whether its pronoun morpheme varies with context.

The lexical flexibility of an Arabic phraseme depends on the number of elements it has. Phrasemes with two elements, regardless of whether both are uttered or one is a zero-element, are completely fixed. *Marḥaba-n* (a lexeme + zero-element phraseme) and *subḥāna l-lāh* [exalted is God] (both elements of which are uttered) are both examples of two-element phrasemes that are completely lexically fixed. However, the lexical flexibility of phrasemes that are formed of more than two lexemes is merely restricted, due to the ability of the receiver/audience to comprehend the metaphorical meaning intended by the phraseme's formation. Take the phraseme *ḍaraba ʿuṣfūrayni bi ḥajari-n wāḥidi-n* [(he) hit two birds with one stone]. If a speaker means to refer to finishing two or more tasks by performing just one action, he can either use the phraseme as it is, or change the word *ʿuṣfūrayn* [two birds] to *ʿamalayn* [two tasks], yielding *ḍaraba ʿamalayni bi ḥajari-n wāḥidi-n*. His audience will comprehend the reference to the metaphorical meaning because the semantic metaphorical meaning is still preserved in the remaining elements of the phraseme. Similarly, if the element *ʿuṣfūrayn* remains while *ḥajari-n* [a stone] is changed to another lexeme, such as *tawqīʿ* [signature] in the context of, say, paperwork, the phrase now being *ḍaraba ʿuṣfūrayn bi tawqīʿ wāḥidi-n*, the intended metaphorical meaning of the phraseme will still be obvious to the Arabic audience. In other words, the lexical flexibility of an Arabic phraseme is dependent on two conditions: 1) the phraseme must be formed of more than two elements, and 2) its metaphorical meaning must remain intact.

---

12 Unless the pronoun in the accusative case, it is either separated from the action or placed before the action. In these two situations, the pronoun is *iyyā* + (second-person or third-person pronoun). Pronouns in the nominative case are treated as separate lexemes.

2.6 The Semantic Unity and Unpredictability of a Phraseme

Fully fixed phrasemes are defined by the third and the fourth cases of the formula provided by Mel'čuk (1998: 30–31):

> A [phraseme] AB of a language L is a semantic phraseme of L such that its signified 'X' is constructed out of the signified of one of its two constituent lexemes—say, of A— and a signified 'C' ['X' = 'A⊕C'] such that the lexeme B expresses 'C' only contingent on A.
>
> (Mel'čuk 1998: 30)

The third case:

> 'C' = 'B', i.e. B has (in the dictionary) the corresponding signified; and 'B' cannot be expressed with A by an otherwise possible synonym of B.
>
> (Mel'čuk 1998: 31)

As in the Arabic phraseme: *Baytu l-Māl* 'the house of money' (ministry of finance in the medieval era).

The fourth case:

> 'C' = 'B'; 'B' includes (an important part of) the signified 'A', that is, it is utterly specific, and thus B is 'bound' by A.'
>
> (Mel'čuk 1998: 31)

As in the Arabic phraseme: *kharīru l-mā'i* 'the sound of falling water'.

Mel'čuk's (1998: 30) formulae illustrate fully fixed phrasemes in which neither element can be substituted, at a semantic level. In the first formula, *bayt* as an individual lexeme means 'house', while *al-māl* means 'money'. Yet the individual meanings of the lexemes do not add up to or predict the overall meaning of their phraseme: 'ministry of finance'. Moreover, substituting a synonym for either of these elements will obscure the metaphorical meaning of the original phraseme. The same phenomenon can be observed with other figurative metaphors, and to a certain extent with non-figurative ones, e.g., *kharīru l-mā'i* [the voice of falling water] = a specific term for the sound of water like in a waterfall.

In the case of *khariru l-mā'i*, the first element of the phraseme does not co-occur with any other lexeme, since the semantic field of the first element is included in the semantic field of the second element. This leads us to deem it a 'cranberry collocation': i.e., one of the elements – *kharīr*, in this instance – is unique to that collocation (Moon 1998: 21). Nevertheless, this unique element can be replaced by another synonym that gives a broad sense of the target meaning. *Kharīr* is a special term to indicate the sound of falling water, but if a speaker uses *ṣawt* [sound] in the same context, it will be understood, provided that the hearer recollects the meaning of the original substituted element, *kharīr*.

In short, Arabic phrasemes occur as single semantic units, and their meanings cannot be predicted from the individual meanings of their elements. In non-figurative phrasemes, and in figurative ones (albeit with more difficulty), one of the elements can have a synonym substituted for it. However, when this happens, the resultant phrase 1) does not act as a phraseme, and 2) requires the audience to recall the original element of the phraseme, in order to understand the semantic unit that the collocation seeks to provide.

3 Conclusion

This paper has explored the challenges that emerge when the established criteria for phrasemes are applied to the Arabic language. The first criterion is affected by the fact that pronouns in Arabic are considered to be one-letter nouns; and the second, by the existence of numerous one-word Arabic phrasemes. The theory of the zero-element was found useful in overcoming the latter issue, insofar as a one-word phraseme can be construed as having two elements, one of which is a zero-element lexeme that was important in the formulation of the phraseme, but which no longer explicitly exists.

With regard to the third criterion, a lack of corpora prevents direct counting of the co-occurrence of the elements of a given phraseme in Arabic. We will therefore utilise metaphorical fixedness as a key parameter of the phrasemes sampled from that literature, supported by comparison with collections of fixed collocations in Arabic. In terms of the fourth criterion, the question of the distance between the elements of an Arabic phraseme will require further investigation. However, this chapter established that Arabic phrasemes exhibit a degree of flexibility based on the context, as long as the sixth criterion is fulfilled.

As to the fifth criterion, an Arabic phraseme can have some flexibility as regards accepting a substitute element, when the phraseme is formed of more than one uttered element and its semantic unity remains intact. Finally, Arabic phrasemes fit the sixth criterion in the sense that they occur as single semantic units. This criterion also supports the fifth one, by demonstrating the possibility of substituting one or more of the elements in a phraseme – but only if the audience recalls the original element(s).

References

al-Farāhīdī, al-Khalīl Ibn Aḥmad (2005): *Kitāb al-ʿAyn*. Beirut: Dār Iḥyāʾ al-Turāth al-ʿArabī.
Al-Khaṭīb, ʿAbd. Al-Laṭīf (2003): *al-Mustaqṣā fī ʿIlm al-Taṣrīf*. Kuwait: Dār al-ʿUrūbah.
al-Nīlī, Ibrāhīm (1999): *Ṣafwat al-Ṣafiyyah Fī Sharḥ al-Durrah al-Alfiyyah*. Mecca: Jamiʿah Um al-Qurā.
al-Sīrāfī, Abū Saʿīd (2008): *Sharḥ Kitāb Sībawayhi*. Beirut: Dār al-Kutub al-ʿIlmiyyah.
Baccouche, Moufida Ghariani (2007): Arabic Phraseology. In Harald Burger, Dmitrij Dobrovol'skij, Peter Kühn & Neal R. Norrick (eds.), *Phraseology: An International Handbook of Contemporary Research*, 752–758. Berlin, New York: De Gruyter.
Bishr, Kamaal (2003): *Dirāsāt fī ʿIlm al-Lughah*. Cairo: Dār al-Kutub al-ʿIlmiyyah.
Firth, John R. (1957): *Papers in Linguistics*. Oxford: Oxford University Press.
Gries, Stefan Th. (2008): Phraseology and Linguistic Theory: A Brief Survey. In Sylviane Granger & Fanny Meunier (eds.), *Phraseology: An Interdisciplinary Perspective*, 3–26. Amsterdam, Philadelphia: John Benjamins.
Haas, William (1962): Zero in Linguistic Description. In John R. Firth (ed.), *Studies in Linguistics*, 33–53. Oxford: Basil Blackwell.
Haddar, Kais & Abdmajid Ben Hamadou (1998): An Ellipsis Detection Method Based on a Clause Parser For Arabic Language. In Diane J. Cook (ed.), *Proceedings of the Eleventh International FLAIRS Conference*, 270–274. California: The AAAI Press.
Ibn ʿAqīl, Bahāʾ al-Dīn ʿAbdullāh (1980): *Sharḥ Alfiyyat Ibn Mālik*. Cairo: Dār al-Turāth.
Ibn Manẓūr, Muḥammad (2005): *Lisān al-ʿArab*. Beirut: al-Aʿlamī li-l-Maṭbūʿāt.
Karabekyan, Samvel (2011): Ḥarf'. In Lutz Edzard & Rudolf de Jong (eds.), *Encyclopedia of Arabic Language and Linguistics*. Leiden: Brill. Retrieved from http://dx.doi.org/10.1163/1570-6699_eall_EALL_SIM_vol2_0015, accessed July 2, 2017.
Kees, Versteegh (2011): Taqdīr'. In Lutz Edzard & Rudolf de Jong (eds.), *Encyclopedia of Arabic Language and Linguistics*. Leiden: Brill. Retrieved from http://dx.doi.org/10.1163/1570-6699_eall_EALL_SIM_0134, accessed July 2, 2017.
Matthews, Peter (1997): Ellipsis. In Peter Matthews (ed.), *The Concise Oxford Dictionary of Linguistics*, 111. Oxford: Oxford University Press.
McGregor, William (2003): The Nothing That Is, The Zero That Isn't. *Studia Linguistica* 57 (2), 77–87.
Mel'cuk, Igor (1998): Collocation and Lexical Functions. In Anthony Paul Cowie (ed.), *Phraseology: Theory, Analysis, and Applications*, 23–54. Oxford: Clarendon Press.
Moon, Rosamund (1998): *Fixed Expressions and Idioms in English: A Corpus-Based Approach*. Oxford: Clarendon Press.
Mughazy, Mustafa (2011): Ellipsis. In Lutz Edzard & Rudolf de Jong (eds.), *Encyclopedia of Arabic Language and Linguistics*. Leiden: Brill. Retrieved from http://dx.doi.org/10.1163/1570-6699_eall_EALL_COM_vol2_0003, accessed July 2, 2017.
Müller, Kathrin (1993): *Und der Kalif lachte, bis er auf den Ruecken fiel. Ein Beitrag zur Phraseologie und Stilkunde des klassischen Arabisch*. München: C. H. Beck.
Müller, Kathrin (2001): *Da war ihm, als müsse er fliegen vor Freuden. ‚Tausendundeine Nacht' als Fundus für arabische Phraseologie*. München: C. H. Beck.
Stainton, Robert. J. (2005): In Defense of Non-Sentential Assertion. In Zoltan Gendler Szabo (ed.), *Semantics Versus Pragmatics*, 383–458. Oxford: Clarendon Press.

Taha, Zeinab Ahmed (2011): Mafʿūl. In Lutz Edzard & Rudolf de Jong (eds.), *Encyclopedia of Arabic Language and Linguistics*. Leiden: Brill. Retrieved from http://dx.doi.org/10.1163/1570-6699_eall_EALL_COM_vol3_0201, accessed July 2, 2017.

Muhammad A. Badarneh
Formulaic Expressions of Politeness in Jordanian Arabic Social Interactions

Abstract: This study explores the use of politeness formulaic expressions in everyday social interaction in colloquial Jordanian Arabic. Analysis of ethnographically observed data of ninety-four formulaic expressions within the framework of Brown and Levinson's (1987) classical politeness theory reveals that these formulae are of two types: positive politeness formulae which are used in interactional and transactional contexts and emphasize solidarity and communal belonging; and negative politeness formulae concerned with showing deference and non-imposition. The use of these formulae reflects speakers' greater concern with positive rather than negative politeness. It further displays the fixity and continuity of social norms and traditions transmitted through these formulae. As many of these formulae involve reference to God, such formulaicity further emphasizes the religious and fatalistic nature of the community.

1 Introduction

This paper investigates formulaicity in colloquial Jordanian Arabic, specifically in the domain of everyday social interaction from the perspective of politeness theory. Although everyday spoken colloquial Jordanian Arabic is rich in formulaic expressions, these expressions have not received sufficient attention. This study, therefore, seeks to address and redress this gap by considering formulaic expressions as used in everyday social interactions in this variety of Arabic.

Formulaic expressions are exploited as 'conversational routines', defined by Coulmas (1981: 2) as "highly conventionalized prepatterned expressions whose occurrence is tied to more or less standardized communication situations". The formulaic expressions examined in this paper constitute "routine formulae" in line with Coulmas's (1994: 1292) definition, that is, they are 'fixed' both in form, compared to other expressions in the language which are created anew every time, and in function, in that they fulfil specific highly recurrent communicative tasks. They are conventionalized linguistic formulae triggered by specific communicative settings where their use is expected and deemed appropriate because they are seen as part of the speaker's communicative competence as well as his/her everyday politeness behavior. As Bardovi-Harlig (2012: 207) explains, formulaic expressions "often succinctly capture the illocutionary force of a contribution by virtue of the fact that the speech community in which they are used has tacitly agreed on their form, meaning, and use". According to her review of recent findings on formulaic language, definitions of formulaic expressions in pragmatics research usually contain three elements: they are recurrent sequences, they occur in specified social contexts, and they are known by members of a speech community (Bardovi-Harlig 2012: 207). These criteria will be shown to apply to the politeness formulae used in everyday Jordanian Arabic.

The meanings and uses of some formulaic expressions can be particularly appreciated when they are translated into English, showing the sociocultural specificity of Arabic as well as the values and beliefs of the speech community. While the use of these formulae is not obligatory, failure to use them in the appropriate context will result in socially negative conversational 'implicatures' (Grice 1975) and consequently constitute a threat to the interlocutor's 'positive face' or 'negative face' (Brown and Levinson 1987), which is another reason why these conversational formulae deserve attention.

Formulaic expressions are described as having a stereotyped, routinized, or fixed form; conventionalized meanings that include attitudinal and affective connotations; and specialized usage conditions (Hallin and Van Lancker Sidtis 2017: 69). The use and prevalence of such formulaic expressions in spoken discourse has been highlighted by different scholars (e.g. Coulmas 1981; Aijmer 1996; Kecskés 2003; Wray 2008; Bladas 2012). Formulaic expressions differ from newly created, grammatical utterances in that they are characterized by familiarity and predictability, are closely related to communicative-pragmatic context, and are widely regarded as crucial in determining the success of social interaction in many communicative aspects of daily life (Van Lancker Sidtis and Rallon 2004; Van Lancker Sidtis 2010). Native speakers can recognize and complete such formulaic expressions (when words are omitted) as well as demonstrate knowledge of their specialized meanings and appropriate contexts (Van Lancker Sidtis and Rallon 2004: 208). Tactical use of speech formulae is even honored in some languages, as reported by Tannen and Öztek (1981) regarding Turkish and Greek. This value and special status of formulaic expressions in social interaction has led to renewed interest in formulaic language as a large and vibrant part of language competence (Coulmas 1994; Kuiper 2004; Pawley 2007; Wray 2008), leading to increased interest in formulaicity in diverse discourse contexts, mainly as a result of the burgeoning interest in pragmatics, and the embracing of spoken text by sociolinguists and discourse analysts. The present study is carried out in the spirit of this interest and in light of the use of spoken discourse as an important source for investigating formulaic language and speech.

While formulaic expressions have been studied in different languages (e.g. Dogancay 1990; Takekuro 1999; Overstreet and Yule 2001; Terkourafi 2002; Saberi 2012; Levin 2014), they have not received as much attention in Arabic, and despite the prevalence of formulaic expressions in everyday Arabic social interactions, only a limited number of studies have investigated their communicative and pragmatic functions. A pioneering study in this area is Ferguson's (1983) work on the pragmatic features of what he called 'God-wishes' in Syrian Arabic, which are formulaic expressions that begin or are assumed to begin with 'God', and whose semantics is only peripherally related to their actual uses.

A number of studies have focused on the use of other God-related formulae that are originally religious expressions but have undergone pragmatic transformation, thus acquiring new discourse pragmatic functions in everyday Arabic speech, notably the two expressions that have an iconic status in spoken Arabic: *inšallah* (Gregory and Wehbe 1986; Farghal 1995; Clift and Helani 2010) and *māšāallah* (Migdadi et al. 2010). These expressions are prototypically illustrative of a unique language feature that the Arabic language possesses, namely the so-called 'Allah Lexicon', which is a rich and varied body of religious expressions invoking the Almighty (Morrow 2006). Other researchers have analyzed broader and diverse aspects of Arabic formulaic expressions, such as their literary and textual sources (Müller 2000; Baccouche 2007), their use in relation to body parts in colloquial Arabic (Kotb 2002), their translation (Al-Qinai 2011), their transfer in cross-linguistic contexts (Ramajo Cuesta and Ainciburu 2015), and their sociolinguistic and pragmatic functions (Kamel 1993; Badarneh 2016).

The present study approaches Arabic formulaic expressions from a politeness theoretical perspective. It attempts to answer the following research questions:
– What role do Jordanian Arabic formulaic expressions play in social interaction in general and politeness in particular?
– What do these formulae tell us about the politeness orientation and face concerns of Jordanians?
– What do these formulae reveal about interactants' local sociocultural and religious values and assumptions?

2 Theoretical Framework

The interpersonal meanings of formulaicity have been regarded as a discourse phenomenon because they can only manifest themselves within some concrete context (Norrick 2003: 86). Since such interpersonal meanings affect the alignment of conversational participants and their interpersonal relationships, the use of formulaic expressions as part of the poetics of everyday talk can be approached from the perspective of politeness behavior (Norrick 2003: 86). Relevant to this concern is the politeness theory of Brown and Levinson (1987) that is predicated on the sociological and highly abstract notion of 'face', derived from Goffman (1967) and from the English folk term linking face with embarrassment or humiliation. This 'face' is defined as "the public self-image that every member wants to claim for himself", which makes face "emotionally invested" (Brown and Levinson 1987: 61). This concept of face consists of two aspects: *positive* and *negative* face. Positive face refers to participants' "perennial desire that [their] wants (or the actions/acquisitions/values resulting from them) should be thought of as desirable" (Brown and Levinson 1987: 101). Preserving the positive face of others would thus result in *positive politeness*, which involves the choice of strategies that emphasize solidarity with the addressee. These include claiming 'common ground' with the addressee and satisfying the addressee's wants (Brown and Levinson 1987: 101–129). *Negative face* refers to an individual's "want to have [their] freedom of action unhindered and [their] attention unimpeded" (Brown and Levinson 1987: 129). Maintaining this negative face of others would thus lead to *negative politeness*, which is linguistically realized through strategies that emphasize deference for the addressee, such as the use of conventional indirectness, hedges on illocutionary force, polite pessimism, e.g. about the success of a request, and emphasizing the relative power of the addressee (Brown and Levinson 1987: 130). Thus, negative politeness constitutes "rituals of avoidance" (Brown and Levinson 1987: 129) in polite interaction. In this theory, face is taken to be a universal notion in all human societies, and conversational participants are assumed to be rational agents who will ideally seek to preserve both their own face and their interlocutor's face in a verbal interaction. While stressing this universality of face, Brown and Levinson (1987: 13) recognize that in any particular society face can be "subject to cultural specifications" and naturally links up to "fundamental cultural ideas about the nature of the social persona, honor and virtue, shame and redemption and thus to religious concepts".

In such verbal interaction, different speech acts used by conversational participants intrinsically threaten face, such as criticisms, requests, and disagreements, referred to as 'face-threatening acts' (FTAs). A variety of FTAs can threaten the addressee's positive face, such as accusations, disagreements, and disapproval, while other FTAs can threaten the addressee's negative face, such as orders, advice, and warnings. A number of FTAs can be damaging to the speaker's own positive face, such as apologizing, while other FTAs can threaten the speaker's own negative face, such as accepting apologies. Given that both the speaker and the addressee seek normally to preserve face, an FTA that is damaging to the addressee's face will be also a potential threat to the speaker's face, and vice versa (Brown and Levinson 1987: 65–68). To minimize the threat of such FTAs, Brown and Levinson (1987) propose a set of strategies that are ordered along a continuum of remedial action, suggesting that the more threatening an FTA is, the more polite strategy one must use to reduce its damaging effects. In this case, the speaker uses a 'face-saving act' that involves either positive politeness redress or negative politeness redress, with negative politeness redress ranked higher than positive politeness redress. In contrast with negative politeness where "the sphere of relevant redress is restricted to the imposition itself, in positive politeness the sphere of redress is widened to the appreciation of alter's wants in general or to the expression of similarity between ego's and alter's wants" (Brown and Levinson 1987: 101).

Although Brown and Levinson (1987: 43) play down the importance of politeness routines by stressing the 'generative' production of linguistic politeness, they nonetheless state that polite formulae clearly form an important focal element in folk notions and in the distinction between 'personal' tact and 'positional' politeness, where the latter is associated with formulaic decorum (Coulmas 1979, 1981), of the type that is investigated in this paper.

This approach to linguistic politeness, which is pragmatic, is contrasted with a recent approach, described as post-pragmatic or 'discursive' (Watts 2003: 9), which constitutes a non-contextual paradigm of politeness and a complete departure from the static classical view of politeness adopted by Brown and Levinson (1987). This approach is based on a dynamic view of politeness, arguing that politeness is negotiated by the speaker and the hearer. Accordingly, politeness becomes discursive and negotiable, to the extent that "no linguistic expression can be taken to be inherently polite" (Locher and Watts 2005: 16), and hence politeness is theorized as the product of the evaluations of interactants in a particular speech event rather than assessment based on context. However, as argued by Schlund (2014: 5), this assumption may be suitable to a general theory of social practice, but it is not sufficient in linguistic terms because it does not provide a theoretical framework for the analysis of the structure of linguistic politeness devices, like the formulaic expressions examined here. Moreover, "the speakers of a given language would simply learn and thus know that certain linguistic politeness patterns stereotypically occur in certain speech situations" (Schlund 2014: 277).

3 Data

The data on which this paper is based consist of 94 formulaic expressions that were ethnographically observed in different everyday interactions in Jordanian Arabic. These formulae were collected by the researcher in naturally occurring interactions and exchanges involving native speakers of Jordanian Arabic. The observed interactions in which the formulaic expressions were used involved talk in a variety of conversational settings, such as interactions in supermarkets, grocery stores, restaurants, coffee shops, and shopping malls, interactions on private and public occasions, and interactions among family members, in-laws, friends, acquaintances, and strangers, which involved both interactional and transactional talk. The instances of formulae were checked against the researcher's own sociocultural background knowledge, expertise and repertoire as a native speaker and as a member of the community, as well as against the knowledge and expertise of other native-speaker community members who were consulted regarding the use and accuracy of each formula. All formulae collected were verified as authentic expressions that are recognized and used in actual social interaction. No formula displayed *cross-functioning* (Moon 1992: 21–22), that is, no formula was found to be "used with a function other than and additional to its primary one".

A number of the formulaic expressions collected behave like an 'adjacency pair' (Schegloff and Sacks 1973). That is, the formula becomes the first part of an automatic sequence where the utterance of the formula immediately creates an expectation of the utterance of a second part, i.e. a second formulaic response. In contrast, a number of formulaic expressions in the data do not create this expectation of a second-part formulaic response, and the addressee has thus the option to respond in a non-formulaic way. Given that these routine formulae are "situation-bound utterances" (Kecskés 2003), they are standardly taken to have a specific meaning and use in a specific context, beyond which they cannot be used. The occurrence of a formula, and thus its function, is therefore predetermined by a specific context that is communally agreed upon by the interactants.

It is important to point out that there are no corpora, electronic or otherwise, available for spoken Jordanian Arabic. This represents a methodological obstacle in the study and analysis of formulaic expressions and patterns in the spoken data of this Arabic variety. Ethnographical observation was chosen, therefore, to obtain the data. While this method has disadvantages such as time constraints, reliability, and access, it has a variety of advantages, especially direct observation of how the formulae are used, the ability to have a holistic view of these formulae, validity of the data as first-hand evidence, and being ecologically sound as the author is a member of the community where these formulae are used. Ethnographical observation would thus provide an effective method for the study of formulaic patterns in a given community as the researcher would better understand how such patterns are used in naturally occurring exchanges and be able to explicate the sociocultural meanings involved in their use.

4 Analysis

As stated above, each formula in Jordanian Arabic is situation-bound and context-specific. Accordingly, each formulaic expression was approached and analyzed according to the function it performs in the given (predetermined) communicative context. In addition to providing the predetermined context, the analysis of these formulae involved explicating their semantics, use and function, the typical response to the formula by the addressee, how the formulae reflect the sociocultural values and assumptions of the community at large, and the aspect of politeness with which these formulae are concerned, namely, positive or negative face of the speaker, the addressee, or both. Literal translations of these formulae are provided in order to capture their local sociocultural meanings and flavor, which are then explicated in more detail in the analysis.

The analysis of the data reveals that formulaic expressions used in Jordanian Arabic fall into two categories. The first category is oriented toward the positive face of the addressee or audience to communicate solidarity and common ground, and this category consists of two types: interactional formulae and transactional formulae. The second is concerned with the negative face of the addressee or audience to emphasize deference and non-imposition.

4.1 Positive Politeness Formulae

The great majority (= 76) of the formulaic expressions in the data (80.9%) were found to be oriented toward positive politeness, which is in line with the observation that Arab societies tend to favor positive politeness (e.g. Davies 1987). Formulae oriented toward the addressee's positive face are designed to communicate that the speaker and the addressee are familiar to one another. Thus, these formulae serve as an inclusive, in-group membership marker whereby the addressee is considered to be an insider treated as someone who belongs to the same community and shares the same sociocultural values. Positive politeness formulae in Jordanian Arabic attending to different aspects of the addressee's positive face can be categorized in terms of situational appropriateness into two types of contexts: *interactional* and *transactional*.

4.1.1 Interactional Formulae

Almost all formulaic expressions in the current data (N = 91) are employed in primarily *interactional* (Brown and Yule 1983: 1) contexts, including social occasions involving festive and celebratory social bonding, such as public or private invitations to food on occasions such as weddings, graduation, house-warming, and child's birth invitations. In such interactional contexts, formulaic expressions are oriented toward focusing on the participants and their social needs, they are interactive, requiring two-way participation, and they reflect the participants' sociocultural and religious identity. Being interactionally oriented, these formulaic expressions can thus serve to "establish and maintain social relationships" and "negotiate role-relationships, peer-solidarity, the exchange of turns in a conversation, [and] the saving of face for both speaker and hearer" (Brown and Yule 1983: 3).

One of the domains where positive politeness formulaicity is exploited is *hospitality*, which is considered an inherent and hallowed ritualized tradition of Jordanian society (Shryock 2004: 35). Consider the following instances of hospitality-based formulae[1]:

(1) Host: *ahlan wa-sahlan*
              أَهْلاً وَسَهْلاً
              'Family and smooth land'
    Guest: *bi-l-mahlli*
              بِلْمَهَلِّيْ
              '(Same) to one who says 'welcome''

(2) Host: *nawwarat*
              نَوَّرَتْ

---

1 All translations are the author's unless otherwise indicated.

	Guest:	'(Our home) has lightened' mnawrah bi-ṣḥāb-ha مْنَوْرَةْ بِصْحَابْهَا '(It is already) lightened with its owners'
(3)	Guest: Host: Guest:	(Praises guest's food) ṣiḥtayn w-ᶜāfiyeh صِحْتَينْ وْعَافِيهْ '(May the food be) double health and healthiness (to you)' ᶜalā qalb-ak عَلَى قَلْبَكْ '(Same) to your heart'
(4)	Host: Guest:	(to someone shows up while one is eating): inṭaḥ fāl-ak إنْطَحْ فَالَكْ 'Hit your good omen' (accepts or declines)

In (1), the speaker, i.e. the host, uses the traditional greeting formula *ahlan wa-sahlan*, typically functionally translated as 'welcome', and sometimes reinforced by *wa-marḥaban* 'and hello', upon seeing the addressee, i.e. the guest. This formula is a prototypical politeness device in Arabic that is patently oriented toward the addressee's positive face, specifically his/her need to feel *welcome* upon being seen by the host. This can be further appreciated when considering the original expression from which the present formula derives, namely *atayta* **ahlan wa-waṭi'ta sahl-an**, which literally means 'You have come upon *family* and treaded on *smooth land*'. Thus the now shortened formula carries the meaning 'You are among people who are (like) your family and in a place that is hospitable to you'. The guest's one-word response *bilmahlli* 'same to one who says *welcome*' is equally formulaic and is designed to communicate equal positive politeness toward the host. Hospitality is thus formulaically shown to be central to the *habitus* (Bourdieu 1991: 37) of the local culture and its assumptions about the rights, needs and obligations of the host and the guest, and at the same time the importance attached to 'verbal generosity', combined of course with 'food generosity', toward one's guest or visitor is demonstrated.

In example (2), the host formulaically greets and welcomes the guest using the expression *nawwarat*. This formula metaphorically treats the guest as a source of 'light' that has eliminated 'darkness' in the host's home, which invokes the host's conceptualization and evaluation of the guest's visit and presence as highly desirable and conducive to joy. As *nawwarat* constitutes a compliment formula, the guest responds with another formulaic expression that is designed to reflect the guest's modesty and deflect the compliment by attributing such metaphorical 'light' to the host, that is, the owner and inhabitant of the house, which reduces the force of the compliment and shows the guest's appreciation of the host's invitation.

The health-wishing formula ṣiħtayn uᶜāfiyeh in (3) is invariably used to convey the speaker's wish that the food has a salubrious effect on the guest, typically after food is served. The fact that the formula consists of the dual ṣiħtayn 'literally, two healths' and reinforced by its synonym ᶜāfiyeh 'healthiness' reflects the formulaic aspect of home hospitality ritual, showing the strong emphasis placed on and the importance assigned to this ritual in the local culture. The guest's response ᶜala qalbak 'lit. (same) to your heart' is equally formulaic and reflects the guest's similar health wish for the host. However, through metaphorical reference to the host's 'heart', the guest shifts the emphasis from his/her own physical health to the host's psychological well-being to reciprocate the host's positive politeness toward the guest.

Formulaicity thus iconically plays an important role in the realization of hospitality (and other traditions of the society). That is, the fixedness that comes with such hospitality formulae seems to reflect the permanence and endurance of this ritual in society, whereby these formulae are constantly reproducible in any context of hospitality. This can further be seen in example (4) where the formula inṭaħ fālak 'literally, hit your good omen' is used as an invitation to someone who shows up unexpectedly while the speaker is eating. The words of the formula, and their literal meaning, reflect its Bedouin origin, taken to be the provenance of the tradition of Arab hospitality. More importantly, the metaphorical nature of the formula shows a concern with avoiding directness in inviting or asking an unexpected guest to join the host while eating. Through such metaphorical formulaicity, the host implies that the unexpected guest has not come for the sole or primary purpose of eating food, something that is very much avoided in local culture. It shows the speaker to be a competent community member who shows awareness of the addressee's face.

Another area where positive politeness formulaicity operates in everyday Jordanian Arabic is death-related discourse. While they show respect to the deceased, such 'death formulae' display solidarity with and provide solace to the audience affected, directly or indirectly, by the death event, such as family, relatives, and friends of the deceased (see e.g. Parvaresh and Capone 2017). While some of these formulae are inextricably linked to religious (i.e. Islamic) beliefs about death, other formulae constitute a colloquial form of prayer for the addressee or audience to live a longer life than the deceased, hence their positive politeness value in discourse:

(5) Speaker: ʿaḍḍama allāh-u ajra-kum
عَظَّمَ اللهُ أجْرَكُمْ
'May Allah increase your reward!'

Addressee: šakara allāh-u saʿya-kum
شَكَرَ اللهُ سَعْيَكُمْ
'May Allah thank your efforts!'

(6) Speaker: yirḥam mā faqadit
يِرْحَمْ مَا فَقَدِتْ
'May mercy be upon the one you lost!'

Addressee: mā tufqud ġāli
مَا تُفْقُدْ غَالِيْ
'May you not lose a loved one!'

(7) Speaker: yislam rās-ak
يِسْلَمْ رَاسْكَ
'May your head be safe!'

Addressee: allah yisalm-ak
اللهُ يِسَلْمَكَ
'May Allah keep you safe!'

(8) Speaker: (Name of deceased) aʿṭā-k ʿumr-uh / ʿumr-ha
(إسْمُ الْمُتَوَفَى) أَعْطَاكَ عُمْرُهُ / عُمْرُها
'(The deceased) has given you his/her life'

As can be seen, in addition to reflecting sociocultural assumptions about death, these death formulae are adjacency pairs characterized by their reciprocal nature, where the use of one formula requires the obligatory use of a specific, fixed response. The formula in (5) is the formal Classical Arabic expression of offering condolences, still used today especially when the setting is public. It is purely religious as it involves a prayer to Allah to multiply the divine reward, or *ajr*, for the person affected by death in his/her family. This divine reward is believed to be given to the person who patiently endures, rather than expresses dissatisfaction with, the pain of losing someone. The addressee reciprocates by praying that the speaker be 'thanked' by Allah for their efforts of coming and offering condolences, so the act of thanking is metaphorically made by God rather than the speaker him/herself. Example (6) is a colloquial, and hence less formal, formula. It is predicated on the two concepts of 'loss' and 'mercy' where divine mercy is invoked upon the deceased, and where the second part is a prayer that the speaker will not go through similar loss of a loved one.

The formulaic expression in (7) moves away from the divine and the religious toward a colloquial, socioculturally grounded mode of expression. More specifically, positive politeness toward the addressee is communicated metonymically by wishing that the addressee's 'head' be safe. The choice of this part of the body to refer to the person is motivated by the status of the 'head' in the Arab culture as a symbol of life itself (being alive). Focusing on these meanings shows how the formula is oriented toward the positive face of the addressee.

While the death formulae in (5–7) are solace-providing, the one in (8) is used when communicating a death event to someone. Rather than using a neutral term, e.g. *twaffa* 'passed away', the formula *aʿṭāk ʿumruh / ʿumrha* figuratively transforms the death of someone into an extended new life given to the bereaved or the news recipient, as if the lost life of the deceased will result in a longer life given to the news recipient. The formulaic transformation of death into a new life for the addressee thus becomes a positive politeness strategy, clearly implicating solidarity with the addressee and wishing that he/she lives a longer life. Such formulaicity in delivering news of death thus avoids mention of death terms, and at the same time offers emotional support to the recipient of the news of death.

Apart from the major discourses of hospitality and death above, formulaic expressions are employed as compliment speech acts in mundane everyday talk by way of orienting toward the addressee's or audience's positive face, as in the following examples:

(9) Speaker: *naʿīman!*
نَعِيمًا
'(May it be) a bliss!'
Addressee: *allah yinʿim ʿalayk!*
اللهُ يِنْعِمْ عَلِيكْ
'May Allah give you bliss (too)!'

(10) Speaker: *šarwa man ʿindi / šarwa il-ḥāḍrīn*
الخَاضْرِينْ شَرْوَىْ / شَرْوَىْ مَنْ عِنْدِيْ
'As praiseworthy as those sitting with me / As praiseworthy as the audience'
Addressee / Audience: *wa-la t-hūn*
وَلَا تْهُونْ
'May you not be belittled'

(11) Speaker: *tihri w-tjaddid*
تِهْرِيْ وتْجَدَّدْ
'May your clothes wear out and you renew them'
Addressee: *tislam / tʿīš / w-ilgāyil*
تِسْلَمْ / تْعِيشْ / وَالْقَايِلْ

'(May you) be safe / (May you) live (a long life) / (Same to) the speaker'

In these examples, the formulae serve either as a compliment or a compliment response in a predetermined context. In (9), the formula *naʿīman!* '(May it be) a bliss!' is used when meeting someone who has had a new haircut or has just taken a shower, and the absence of these formulae in these two contexts may be interpreted as a threat to the positive face of the referent in question. The formula *šarwa man ʿindi* or its variant *šarwa il-ḥāḍrīn* 'As praiseworthy as you / as the audience' in (10) is an obligatory formula that must be used by the speaker when complimenting an absent third party in front of the addressee or audience. The formula is used to eliminate any suggestion or hint that the speaker is criticizing, underestimating, or negatively evaluating the addressee/audience by implicit comparison with that absent third party. Thus, the formula preemptively shows the speaker's awareness of the audience/addressee's positive face, communicating the implicature 'no critical comparison is intended' and 'you are equally good'.

The formula *tihri w tjaddid* 'May your clothes wear out and you renew them' in example (11) is used as a compliment toward someone who has just bought new clothes. This compliment formula is not directed toward the new clothing item itself, but rather toward the person wearing it. By wishing that the addressee's new clothes wear out fast so that the addressee can buy yet more new clothes in the future, the formula expresses the wish that the addressee live a long life in which he/she can and will always buy and put on new clothes. This in turn implies that the speaker asks for constant renewal in the addressee's life, a renewal symbolized by the act of getting new items of clothing, so new clothes become a metaphor for renewal, i.e. prolonging, of the complimentee's life. The latter's understanding of 'prolonged and renewed life' is reflected in the three possible responses to the formula: *tislam*, which wishes the speaker safety and protection; *tʿīš*, which wishes the speaker a long life; and *wilgāyil* which is functionally similar to English 'right back at you', suggesting a more casual and easygoing tone. In these examples, the addressee shows agreement about praiseworthiness but with praise formulaically shifted back to the speaker in order to express common ground with, and mutual liking toward, the speaker.

4.1.2 Transactional Formulae

In contrast with interactional positive politeness formulae, only three formulaic expressions in the data were found to be used in *transactional* contexts that are intrinsically concerned with the transmission of information, e.g. price, rather than the maintenance of social relationships (Brown and Yule 1983). Brown and Levinson (1987: 103) insightfully argue that "positive politeness utterances are used as a kind of metaphorical extension of intimacy, to imply common ground or sharing of wants to a limited extent even between strangers who perceive themselves, for the purposes of the interaction, as somehow similar". The transactional formulae discussed here are illustrative of this point. Through using such formulae, the speaker, i.e. the salesperson or shopkeeper, implies that, despite the business-oriented nature of the transactional talk, the salesperson still cares about the social dimension of the transactional relationship with the addressee, i.e. the customer. By using such formulae, the speaker will imply to the customer that the transaction is not purely materialistic or driven by mere financial gain, and that the salesperson is interested in establishing or maintaining a social relationship with the customer. This is illustrated by the following two commonly used transactional formulae:

(12) *xallīha ᶜalayna*
خَلِّيها عَلَيْنا
'Make it on us'

(13) *mᶜawwadāt / mᶜawwadīn*
مُعَوَّضاتْ / مُعَوَّضِينْ
'May (what you paid) be compensated'

The formula in (12) is commonly used by a salesperson or shopkeeper when the customer hands over the money to pay for the goods or service. Although the formula is of course understood by the customer as an "ostensible speech act" (Link and Kreuz 2005: 227) of suggesting that the customer take the goods for free and therefore cannot be taken seriously, its use is widespread among shopkeepers, barbers, and local service providers in Jordan as a way of establishing or maintaining a social relationship with the customer, thus merely serving as a positive politeness gesture toward the customer. Realizing the nonserious and insincere (Isaacs and Clark 1990: 493–494) nature of this formula, the response of the customer would be, of course, something to the effect of *šukran* 'thank you'. The formula thus becomes a positive politeness technique used as a kind of 'social accelerator' whereby the speaker indicates that he/she wants to 'come closer' to the addressee (Brown and Levinson 1987: 103).

In contrast with (12), which is uttered *before* taking money from the customer, the formula in (13), *mᶜawwadāt*, or its variant *mᶜawwadīn* 'May (what you paid) be compensated' is commonly uttered by the shopkeeper *after* the customer has paid for the goods. It is essentially an invocation (to God) that the customer may earn new money to replace the money he/she has just spent. While the speaker does not have to say this formula, uttering it will communicate that the speaker, even if not uttering the formula with total sincerity, at least sincerely wants to satisfy the customer's positive face (Brown and Levinson 1987: 101). Using the formula gives the transaction an interactional flavor and shows interest in the customer as a social actor rather than just a paying customer.

4.2 Negative Politeness Formulae

Formulaic expressions in everyday Jordanian Arabic constitute an important resource for satisfying the addressee's negative face wants by showing respect toward and non-imposition on the addressee or audience, and communicating the speaker's concern not to invade their private space. Although these negative politeness formulae constitute only 19.1% of the data collected (total 18), they cover different interactional aspects, as illustrated by (14–19) below:

(14) *ba-la zuġrah*
بَلا زُغْرَة
'Without smallness'

(15) *w-inta b-karāmah*
وإنْتَ بْكَرامَة
'And you are in dignity'

(16) *w-inta l-kabīr*
وإنْتَ الكْبيرْ
'And you are the big one'

(17) *w-inta l-ṣādig*
وإنْتَ الصّادِقْ
'And you are the truthful one'

(18) *wa-la taᶜlīm ᶜalayk*
ولا تَعْليمْ عَليكْ
'And no teaching of you'

(19) *harjak ᶜala rāsi*
هَرْجَكْ على راسي
'Your talk is on my head'

As these formulae are addressed to negative face, they lie at "the heart of respect behavior" (Brown and Levinson 1987: 129). The formula *bala zuġrah* in (14) is invoked when asking someone about his/her name or identity. The function of the formula is to minimize or eliminate the addressee's sense of being unknown or insignificant. That is, asking the addressee about their name or identity socioculturally communicates that the addressee is not known (hence *zuġrah* 'smallness') in the community, so the formula serves to redress or eliminate that implicature.

The formula in (15) is called upon whenever a speaker mentions something that is socioculturally deemed offensive or evocative of unpleasant images. The mention of such a thing without using the hedging formula *w-inta b-karāmah* 'and you are in dignity' is considered an invasion of the listener's auditory space and hence a threat to their negative face, interestingly signified by the word *karāmah* 'dignity'. Examples of topics with which this formula must be used include mention of or reference to shoes, the toilet, feces, urine, and certain animals such as dogs, donkeys, and mules as these entities socioculturally symbolize, or are associated with, inferiority.

The formula *w-inta l-kabīr* in (16) is used in a requesting context whereby the speaker (i.e. the requester) communicates to the requestee that the request made does not in any way mean or suggest that the requester has any power over, or has a higher status than, the requestee or that the requestee is under any obligation to comply with the request. In fact, the formula shifts a higher status onto the requestee ('you are the big one'), thus eliminating any sense of imposition upon, or intention of disrespect toward, the requestee. The appeal to *kabīr* 'big' shows how the formula is used as a strategy for softening requests in a kinship-based society like the Jordanian one (see Brown and Levinson 1987: 117–118) where there is a strong sense of social hierarchy.

The formula *w-inta l-ṣādig* 'and you are the truthful one' in (17) is employed in disagreement, an act typically seen as confrontational and are therefore dispreferred, and should therefore be mitigated or avoided (but see Sifianou 2012). The use of this formula stems from the need to minimize the face-threatening act of disagreement. Thus when the speaker disagrees with, contradicts, or corrects something that a participant has said, he/she softens such disagreement, contradiction or correction by formulaically communicating the message 'although what you said is inaccurate or incorrect, you *are* a truthful person and it is not my intention to accuse you of lying'.

The use of the formula *wa-la taʿlīm ʿalayk* 'lit., and no teaching of you' in (18) constitutes a sociopragmatic norm in the specific context of giving of advice or making a suggestion (see DeCapua and Dunham 2007). In local Jordanian culture, giving advice or instructing the addressee on how to perform a specific action or how to behave in a certain situation is considered highly face-threatening as it implies lack of knowledge or expertise on the part of the advisee. Therefore, this formula is used in such contexts as a preemptive strategy to deny any intention of arrogance or condescension on the part of the speaker. By using this formula, the speaker conveys that he/she is not assuming epistemological superiority over the addressee.

Finally, the formula *harjak ʿala rāsi* 'lit. 'your talk is on my head' in (19) is used in interruptions, often perceived as intrusive as they involve blocking of the flow of the current speaker's talk. This formula can be described as a meta-interruptive speech act whose use signals interruption of the current speaker, and as a palliative offered by the interrupter showing recognition that some infringement of the current speaker's rights has occurred. As the interruption is initiated, the formula is immediately invoked to communicate lack of intention to cause any threat to the current speaker's negative face, specifically the right to be heard and listened to. The formula is based on a metaphorical positioning of the current speaker's talk 'on the head' of the interrupting speaker where 'head' here symbolizes the highest degree of respect in Jordanian culture (cf. example 7). While the act of interruption occurs, the formula signals a preservation of negative face to communicate that no threat to the current speaker's autonomy and control over their talk turn is intended, thus making the act of interruption sound less disaffiliative and more affiliative.

5 Conclusion

The present chapter has provided a pragmatic account of the use of formulaic expressions in everyday Jordanian Arabic, grounded in the classical face-based politeness theory of Brown and Levinson (1987). These formulae constitute an integral part of everyday communication. They are so important because they are oriented towards preserving the participants' both positive and negative faces, thus ensuring the smooth flow of communication and adherence to fundamental sociopragmatic principles and rules.

Given the important and sensitive aspects of managing both the speaker's and the addressee's face in social interaction, the present study shows how formulaicity has come to play an important role in polite social interaction. As emphasized by Terkourafi (2002: 196), formulaic expressions "provide ready-made solutions to the complex and pertinent problem of constituting one's own and one's addressee's face while simultaneously ensuring that one's immediate goals in interaction are achieved". The use of Jordanian everyday formulae as discussed in this paper support the notion that formulaic expressions have an important role in the speaker effectively assuming the role of social actor as these formulae "embody accepted ways of responding verbally to a variety of situations" and therefore their use becomes "a strong indication of belonging, social identity or acculturation" (Coulmas 1994: 1293). As Terkourafi (2002: 196) maintains, this characteristic of formulaic speech makes it conducive to maintaining one's face through demonstrating familiarity with the norms of the community to which the speaker belongs. The present study thus supports the argument that formulaic speech carries the burden of polite discourse and the prediction that "the use of formulae may be a prominent feature of polite discourse in any culture", which needs "further quantitative studies of polite discourse across cultures" (Terkourafi 2002: 197). The present study has sought therefore to demonstrate this connection between formulaicity and politeness by examining formulae whose use is oriented towards preserving the participant's face in the underexplored language and culture of Jordanian society.

Formulaicity in social interaction as explored in this paper across specified, socially recognized and ratified communicative contexts suggests that such formulaicity reflects the fixedness of the norms and traditions of Jordanian society. This formulaicity further reflects the positive politeness leanings of Jordanians, as the majority of these formulae are oriented toward positive rather than negative face. Accordingly, through these formulae one can see more concern with solidarity and acquaintance, collectivist satisfaction, and communal belonging, as opposed to individualism and personal space.

References

Aijmer, Karin (1996): *Conversational routines in English*. London: Longman.
Al-Qinai, Jamal B. S. (2011): Translating phatic expressions. *Pragmatics* 21, 23–39.
Baccouche, Moufida Ghariani (2007): Arabic phraseology. In Harald Burger, Dmitrij Dobrovol'skij, Peter Kühn & Neal R. Norrick (eds.), *Phraseology: An international handbook of contemporary research*, 752–759. Berlin, New York: De Gruyter.
Badarneh, Muhammad A. (2016): Proverbial rhetorical questions in colloquial Jordanian Arabic. *Folia Linguistica* 50 (1), 207–242.
Bardovi-Harlig, Kathleen (2012): Formulas, routines, and conventional expressions in pragmatics research. *Annual Review of Applied Linguistics* 32, 206–227.
Bladas, Òscar (2012): Conversational routines, formulaic language and subjectification. *Journal of Pragmatics* 44 (8), 929–957.
Bourdieu, Pierre (1991): *Language and symbolic power*. Cambridge: Polity Press.

Brown, Gillian & George Yule (1983): *Discourse analysis*. Cambridge: Cambridge University Press.
Brown, Penelope & Stephen Levinson (1987): *Politeness: Some universals in language usage*. Cambridge: Cambridge University Press.
Clift, Rebecca & Fadi Helani (2010): *Inshallah*: Religious invocations in Arabic topic transition. *Language in Society* 39 (3), 357–382.
Coulmas, Florian (1979): On the sociolinguistic relevance of routine formulae. *Journal of Pragmatics* 3 (3/4), 239–266.
Coulmas, Florian (1994): Formulaic language. In Ron Asher (ed.), *Encyclopedia of language and linguistics*, 1292–1293. Oxford: Pergamon.
Coulmas, Florian (ed.) (1981): *Conversational routines*. The Hague: Mouton.
Davies, Eirlys (1987): A contrastive approach to the analysis of politeness formulas. *Applied Linguistics* 8, 75–88.
DeCapua, Andrea & Joan Findlay Dunham (2007): The pragmatics of advice giving: Cross-cultural perspectives. *Intercultural Pragmatics* 4-3, 319–342.
Dogancay, Seran (1990): Your eye is sparkling: Formulaic expressions and routines in Turkish. *Penn Working Papers in Educational Linguistics* 6 (2), 49–64.
Farghal, Mohammed (1995): The pragmatics of *inšallah* in Jordanian Arabic. *Multilingua* 14 (3), 253–270.
Ferguson, Charles (1983): God-wishes in Syrian Arabic. *Mediterranean Language Review* 1, 65–83.
Goffman, Erving (1967): *Interaction ritual: Essays on face to face interaction*. New York: Garden City.
Gregory, Stanford Jr. & Kessem Wehbe (1986): The contexts of *inshaallah* in Alexandria Arabic. *Anthropological Linguistics* 28 (1), 95–105.
Grice, Paul (1975): Logic and conversation. In Peter Cole & Jerry L. Morgan (eds.), *Speech acts*, 41–58. New York: Academic Press.
Hallin, Anna Eva & Diana Van Lancker Sidtis (2017): A closer look at formulaic language: Prosodic characteristics of Swedish proverbs. *Applied Linguistics* 38 (1), 68–89.
Isaacs, Ellen & Herbert Clark (1990): Ostensible invitations. *Language in Society* 19, 493–509.
Kamel, Abdulaziz Mustafa (1993): *A sociolinguistic analysis of formulaic expressions in Egyptian Arabic*. Ph.D. thesis, Georgetown University.
Kecskés, István (2003): *Situation-bound utterances in L1 and L2*. Berlin: Mouton de Gruyter.
Kotb, Sigrun (2002): *Körperteilbezogene Phraseologismen im Ägyptisch-Arabischen*. 'Body part phraseology in Egyptian Arabic'. Wiesbaden: Reichert.
Kuiper, Koenraad (2004): Formulaic performance in conventionalised varieties of speech. In Norbert Schmitt (ed.), *Formulaic sequences: Acquisition, processing, and use*, 37–54. Amsterdam, Philadelphia: John Benjamins.
Levin, Magnus (2014): The Bathroom Formula: A corpus-based study of a speech act in American and British English. *Journal of Pragmatics* 64, 1–16.
Link, Kristen & Roger Kreuz (2005): The comprehension of ostensible speech acts. *Journal of Language and Social Psychology* 24 (3), 227–251.
Locher, Miriam & Richard Watts (2005): Politeness theory and relational work. *Journal of Politeness Research* 1 (1), 9–33.
Migdadi, Fathi, Muhammad A. Badarneh & Kawakib Momani (2010): Divine will and its extensions: Communicative functions of *maašaallah* in colloquial Jordanian Arabic. *Communication Monographs* 77 (4), 480–499.

Moon, Rosamund (1992): Textual aspects of fixed expressions in learners' dictionaries. In Pierre J. L. Arnaud & Henri Béjoint (eds.), *Vocabulary and applied linguistics*, 13–27. Basingstoke: Macmillan.

Morrow, John (ed.) (2006): *Arabic, Islam, and the Allah lexicon: How language shapes our conception of God*. Lewiston, NY: Edwin Mellen Press.

Müller, Kathrin (2000): „Da war ihm, als müsse er fliegen vor Freude": 'Tausendundeine Nacht' als Fundus für arabische Phraseologie. 'Thousand and One Nights as a source for Arabic phraseology'. München: C.H. Beck.

Norrick, Neal (2003): Discourse and semantics. In Deborah Schiffrin, Deborah Tannen & Heide Hamilton (eds.), *The handbook of discourse analysis*, 76–99. London: Blackwell.

Overstreet, Maryann & George Yule (2001): Formulaic disclaimers. *Journal of Pragmatics* 33, 45–60.

Parvaresh, Vahid & Alessandro Capone (eds.) (2017): *The pragmeme of accommodation: The case of interaction around the event of death*. New York: Springer.

Pawley, Andrew (2007): Developments in the study of formulaic language since 1970: A personal view. In Paul Skandera (ed.), *Phraseology and culture in English*, 3–45. Berlin, New York: De Gruyter.

Ramajo Cuesta, Ana & María Cecilia Ainciburu (2015): Transfer of Arabic formulaic courtesy expressions used by advanced Arab learners of Spanish. *Procedia – Social and Behavioral Sciences* 173, 207–213.

Saberi, Kourosh (2012): *Routine politeness formulae in Persian: A socio-lexical analysis of greetings, leave-taking, apologizing, thanking and requesting*. Ph.D. thesis, University of Canterbury.

Schegloff Emanuel & Harvey Sacks (1973): Opening up closings. *Semiotica* 8, 289–327.

Schlund, Katrin (2014): On form and function of politeness formulae. *Journal of Politeness Research* 10 (2), 271–296.

Shryock, Andrew (2004): The new Jordanian hospitality: House, host, and guest in the culture of public display. *Comparative Studies in Society and History* 46 (1), 35–62.

Sifianou, Maria (2012): Disagreements, face and politeness. *Journal of Pragmatics* 44, 1554–1564.

Takekuro, Makiko (1999): *Formulaic speech and social conventions in linguistic politeness of Japanese*. Paper presented at the International Symposium for Linguistic Politeness, Bangkok, 7–9 December 1999.

Tannen, Deborah & Piyale Cömert Öztek (1981): Health to our mouths: Formulaic expressions in Turkish and Greek. In Florian Coulmas (ed.), *Conversational routines*, 37–54. The Hague: Mouton.

Terkourafi, Marina (2002): Politeness and formulaicity: Evidence from Cypriot Greek. *Journal of Greek Linguistics* 3, 179–201.

Van Lancker Sidtis, Diana & Gail Rallon (2004): Tracking the incidence of formulaic expressions in everyday speech: Methods for classification and verification. *Language & Communication* 24, 207–240.

Watts, Richard (2003): *Politeness*. Cambridge: Cambridge University Press.

Wray, Alison (2008): *Formulaic language: Pushing the boundaries*. Oxford: Oxford University Press.

Part III: **Linguistic Varieties Used in Spoken Domains and/or Regarded as 'Conceptually Oral'**

Joanna Szerszunowicz
New Pragmatic Idioms in Polish: An Integrated Approach in Pragmateme Research

Abstract: The general aim of the paper is to discuss the purposefulness and usefulness of the adoption of an integrated approach in research on pragmatic idioms, i.e. conventional expressions used in recurrent situations, also called *routine formulae, pragmatic idioms* or *pragmatemes*. Used mostly in spoken language, such units tend to be neglected in phraseological analyses, although they are very important from a communicative perspective. In order to provide a comprehensive analysis of this group of idioms, one needs to analyze not only the linguistic aspects, but also to take into consideration other factors, for instance, the cultural background. The specific aim is to analyze the implementation of the proposed approach in the studies of selected recent Polish idioms of pragmatic character which came into existence after 1989, the year of Poland's political and economic transformation.

1 Pragmatic Idioms as Objects of Phraseological Research

Recent years have witnessed an increase in interest in phraseology understood in the broad sense of the term. The expression *phraseological unit* tends to be used as an umbrella term encompassing a variety of fixed constructions: collocations, idioms, proverbs, winged words and routine formulae. The last group is composed of units whose indirectness, i.e. non-literal character, is rooted in the form, not in mental imagery (Dobrovol'skij and Piirainen 2005: 21).

As observed by Dobrovol'skij and Piirainen (2005: 20), one of the main problems encountered while dealing with indirect utterances consists in the fact that there are many fixed multiword combinations which resemble conventional expressions, but which still remain textual units, not lexical ones. Yet it has to be admitted that it is rather difficult to draw a definite borderline for all candidate units, so a vast transitory area can be assumed. Although routine formulae are very useful from a communicative perspective, they tend to be given less scope in phraseological analyses than figurative idioms. Therefore, it is very important to focus on pragmatic multiword units used in spoken language to offer insight into their specifics.

1.1 Pragmatic Idioms: Properties and Classifications

In modern research on phraseology, as observed by Pawley (2007), since the 1970s, there has been an increasing interest in situation-bound expressions – pragmatic formulae. These are known by a number of different terms such as *routine formulae*, *communicative phrasemes*, *pragmatic phrasemes* or *pragmatemes*, *functional idioms*, *interpersonal idioms* or *pragmatic idioms* (Aijmer 1996; Burger 2010; Coulmas 1979; Cowie et al. 1983; Fernando 1996; Fléchon et al. 2012; Lüger 2007; Mel'čuk 1988; Roos 2001).

Basically speaking, pragmatic idioms are conventionalized multiword expressions which are used in recurrent situations (Fiedler 2007: 50; Lüger 2007: 444). Although the need for studies on pragmatic aspects of idioms was noticed by Fillmore et al. (1988), Pawley (2007: 19) draws attention to the fact that "there have been surprisingly few studies of the full array of attributes exhibited by pragmatic formulae".[1] Such expressions perform various functions in the realization of speech acts; they are used for instance as greetings (*How are you?*), leave-taking formulae (*Take care!*), encouragements (*Keep smiling!*), replies (*You're welcome*), congratulations (*Happy birthday!*) etc. Selected Polish expressions belonging to this group will be analyzed in the analytical part of the paper (2).

Fernando (1996) draws attention to the fact that pragmatic idioms differ significantly from ideational ones, which is important from the research perspective. First of all, pragmatic idioms are "overtly or covertly marked for interaction" (Fernando 1996: 154). Being discourse-oriented, they contribute greatly to structuring the conversation and ensuring its coherence. To a great extent, the realization of stereotyped speech acts relies on conventional phrases (Kauffer 2013). In fact, although some of the expressions in question are fixed and lexically invariant, like *After you* or *Say when*, others are embedded in variant forms. *Happy birthday* is an example of this latter group: it can appear on its own as well as in variants, for

---

[1] As for the attributes of pragmatic idioms, it is worth mentioning the contributions of Pawley (1991, 2001), Coulmas (1981) and Aijmer (1996). Ruusila (2015), who focuses on the lexicographic description of pragmatic fixed expressions, also offers an insight into their specifics (Ruusila 2015: 25–112).

instance, *Have a happy birthday*, *Have a very happy birthday*, *Wishing you a very happy birthday* etc. (Fernando 1996: 154).

Adopting the function as the main criterion, Granger and Paquot (2008) propose an extended version of Burger's classification of fixed expressions (2010: 36-42), which is adopted for the purpose of the present study. They distinguish three main groups of phrasemes: referential, textual (extending Burger's structural phraseme category), and communicative. Referential phrasemes are carriers of content messages, i.e. they refer to persons, objects, phenomena etc. According to Granger and Paquot (2008: 42), this group comprises the following kinds of units: lexical and grammatical collocations, idioms, irreversible bi- and trinomials, similes, compounds, and phrasal verbs. Textual phrasemes include: complex prepositions, complex conjunctions, linking adverbials, and textual sentence stems. As for the last group, it can be said that

> Communicative phrasemes are used to express feelings or beliefs toward a propositional content or to explicitly address interlocutors, either to focus their attention, include them as discourse participants or influence them.
>
> (Granger and Paquot 2008: 42)

Communicative phrasemes constitute a large and varied group which includes several kinds of units. Coulmas (1981) offers a classification comprising five classes of pragmatic idioms (discourse structuring formulae, formulae of politeness, metacommunicative formulae, formulae expressing the speaker's emotional attitude, delaying formulae), with a further subdivision into 17 subtypes. Fernando (1996) proposes four categories of interpersonal idiomatic expressions: markers of conviviality, institutionalized good wishes and sympathy, information-oriented units, and markers of conflict, subdividing each of the groups.

As for the main interactional functions of formulae, Wray (1999) and Wray and Perkins (2000) distinguish the following three: manipulation of others, including such subtypes as politeness markers, commands, requests etc.; asserting separate identity, comprising for instance personal turns of phrase and turn claimers; asserting group identity, with such subtypes as, *inter alia*, proverbs and hedges.

Granger and Paquot (2008: 44) list the following main kinds of pragmatic expressions:
1. Speech act formulae or routine formulae – phrasemes which are stereotyped ways of performing given functions, for instance, greetings, farewells, compliments etc.
2. Attitudinal formulae – units expressing language users' attitude towards their utterances and their interlocutors.

3. Commonplaces – non-metaphorical sentences expressing tautologies, truisms and sayings reflecting everyday experience, observations etc.
4. Proverbs – sentence-like units expressing widely accepted ideas in a figurative way.
5. Slogans – short phrases of directive character which have been made popular as a result of their repeated use in advertising texts or political discourse.

It should be emphasized that many formulae can fulfil several pragmatic functions in communication. An illustrative example is the English phrase *you know*, which can be used as a filler, an attention-seeking formula and an appeal for shared knowledge (Moon 1998: 188). Similarly, as observed by Inoue (2007: 163–167), *here we go* is a multifunctional unit.[2] It can be employed to capture attention, to rouse people to do something, to express irritation, to show agreement, to indicate that the speaker has found something, to show something to the interlocutor.

1.2 Key Issues in Research on Pragmatic Idioms

As already mentioned, there has been a constant interest in pragmatic idioms over the last decades. Scholars adopt different perspectives, both diachronic and synchronic, to analyze various issues concerning pragmatic idioms. Since formulaic language contributes greatly to fluent speech production and comprehension, the role of conventionalized multiword expressions has been analyzed from this perspective by a number of people, including Wray and Perkins (2000). Special attention is paid to the importance of prefabricated language including pragmatic idioms both in mother tongue acquisition and foreign language teaching (Nattinger and DeCarrico 2001; Nosowicz and Szerszunowicz 2004). Yet one of the main research questions remains how to identify formulaic language (Dobrovol'skij and Piirainen 2005: 20; Wray 2009: 27–51), a problem that is closely related to the general definition of formulaicity.

In terms of linguistic analysis of multiword expressions, the construction grammar approach offers a methodological basis for analyses. Adopting this approach (Croft 2001) allows for viewing constructions as partially arbitrary symbolic units, i.e. pairings of form (syntactic, morphological and phonological properties) and meaning (semantic, pragmatic and discourse-functional properties).

---

[2] In her book, Inoue (2007) also offers detailed analyses of the units *you know what* and *let's say* including their variant forms.

This perspective offers an appropriate basis for conducting a multiaspectual analysis of constructions (cf. Richter and Sailer 2014; Ziem 2014)

In fact, as already mentioned, fixed word combinations can be analyzed from various angles. While discussing the developments in the study of formulaic language since 1970, Pawley draws attention to several research problems. One of the most important aspects is the presence of pragmatic idioms in oral genres. All kind of genres, including the oral ones, can be analyzed from a phraseological viewpoint. For example, Brown (1987) investigates radio sports commentaries on rugby, Kuiper (1996) offers an analysis of auctioneers' sales talk and Hickey and Kuiper (2000) discuss the highly formulaic character of the New Zealand meteorological weather forecasts.

Another important issue is the relation between pragmatic idioms and culture. In fact, as emphasized by Piirainen (2008: 215), "only few routine formulas are figurative in the sense that elements of culture can be found in their source domain". One of them is the expression *Touch wood!*, which is a gesture-based idiom used after the speaker has said that something is going fine and by using the idiom he/she wishes it continues in this way. The gesture comes from old folk beliefs, according to which "woods and trees have good spirits" (Piirainen 2016: 452).

Yet, as observed by Piirainen (2008: 215), pragmatic idioms are "part of a larger complex of stereotyped action patterns and social interaction". If this perspective is adopted, then communicative phrasemes can be analyzed in terms of culturally conditioned communication. Therefore, it can be concluded that linguo-cultural analyses of pragmatic idioms may reveal many interesting facts regarding the ethnic community in which they developed.

From a linguo-cultural perspective, it is also worth analyzing such idioms diachronically, observing the development of formulaic language over centuries. For instance, Filatkina and Hanauska (2010) discuss formulaic language in material excerpted from a corpus of German historical texts from 750 to 1750, with a focus on how routine formulae were used in Old High German texts and which functions they performed. The studies of different periods, even not so distant ones, are likely to offer interesting findings, as is the case with the comparison of communication styles and style-related phraseology in Poland before and after the transformation of 1989 analyzed in the present paper.

In the same vein, i.e. taking into consideration the cultural aspect, pragmatic idioms have been analyzed from a cross-linguistic perspective: one such study was conducted by Jakubowska (1998, 1999), who looked into cross-cultural dimensions of good wishes and – in a broader perspective – politeness, discussing many fixed expressions which function as exponents of politeness in Polish and

English. The inclusion of this component facilitates the understanding of changes occurring in the sphere of pragmatic phraseology, which is attested by the observations regarding Polish pragmatic idioms coined in the post-transformation period. Such analyses can reveal similarities and differences, and can detect cross-linguistic lacunae in pragmatic phraseological stock.

All these approaches contribute greatly to developments in the field of formulaic language, since they enable researchers to analyze pragmatic idioms from various angles. Adopting a linguo-cultural perspective, one can assume that as a result of cultural developments, new oral genres will develop, which involves the coinage of new pragmatic idioms. Significant cultural changes may trigger the creation of new expressions, including those of pragmatic character. This phenomenon will be discussed on the basis of Polish phrasemes coined after the political transformation of 1989.

2 Polish Phraseology after the Transformation of 1989

In his article on Poland, French sociologist Alain Touraine commented on the 1989 transformation, saying that

> Kraj oderwał się od Wschodu i stał się częścią Zachodu [...] Zrobił to z niezwykłą polską brawurą, powtórzę, skok na konia i galopem! [lit. The country got disconnected from the East and became part of the West. [...] It did it with incredible Polish bravery, I'll repeat, on horseback and at a gallop!].
>
> ("Gazeta Wyborcza", 7–8.08.1999)

This observation reflects very concisely on the importance of the transformation, emphasizing the dimension of its consequences.

The notions of the East and the West are the key ones from a Polish perspective: in fact, Poland is a country with a turbulent past and a special location described by Mrożek, a Polish writer, as a country to the east of the West and to the west of the East.³ The year 1989 is momentous in the history of the country, since

---

3 Sławomir Mrożek (1930–2013) was a Polish dramatist and writer. His works belong to the Theatre of Absurd. He shocked his audience with non-realistic elements and political and historical references in order to present the absurdity of real socialist life. His most famous works are *Tango* (*Tango*) and *Emigranci* (*The Emigrants*). The sentence quoted, "*Pochodzę z kraju położonego na*

it marks the beginning of the political and economic transformation, often referred to as a turning point. The changes which occurred were fundamental and influenced all spheres of life in Poland.

2.1 The Transformation of 1989 as a Turning Point in Polish History

The year 1989 was of great importance not only to the Polish, but also to the other Central European nations. It was then that the transformation began – a transformation that was caused by the fact that the political system did not function and

> Both the governed and governors of these countries almost commonly accepted that the economic system based on central management and state ownership lost in the competition with the system based on private property and individual entrepreneurship, market competition, coordinating role of prices and regulatory role of law.
>
> (Gomułka 2016: 19)

In June 1989, the anti-communist party "Solidarity" won the first partially free election. The two main areas in which changes occurred were politics and the economy. In January 1990, the old political system collapsed completely: the Polish United Workers' Party (PZPR) was dissolved, democracy was adopted, a multi-party system was introduced and different party organizations were set up (Banaszkiewicz-Zygmunt and Olendzki 2000: 407).

In the economic sphere, there were several goals: the first was to restore a sustainable macroeconomic equilibrium, the second to fully liberalize prices and foreign trade, the third to restore the development potential of the Polish economy so that the difference in the standard of living in relation to Western Europe could be reduced and – in the end – eliminated (Gomułka 2016: 19). In 1990, the government introduced broad economic reforms to curb hyperinflation and to thoroughly restructure the country (Banaszkiewicz-Zygmunt and Olendzki 2000: 407).

The changes were pervasive: the transformation influenced Poles' perception of Europe (Bartmiński 2001: 45–49). Furthermore, certain differences occurred in the perception of nationalities: for example, the image people have of a German has improved, while that of a Russian has deteriorated – modifications which

---

wschód od Zachodu i na zachód od Wschodu" [lit. I come from a country situated to the east of the West and to the west of the East], comes from *Kontrakt* (*Contract*, 1986).

correspond to the re-evaluation of the oppositions: East–West, Asia–Europe, Communism–Capitalism (Bartmiński 2001: 39).

The turning point of 1989 also had an impact on the hierarchy of values: work and climbing up the career ladder became much more important than before, with new opportunities offered by various companies and branches of foreign corporations. Being successful became the main objective, which involved changes in the creation of the self-image (Szerszunowicz 2007: 43). The excessive modesty imposed by Polish culture was no longer useful at job interviews, which were a new phenomenon on the Polish labor market.[4] Achieving success, Poles' new priority (cf. Ożóg 2004: 237), involved the conscious creation of one's own image: the awareness of having appropriate soft skills increased greatly. These changes serve as examples showing how the transformation influenced Polish society.

2.2 Language Changes in the Post-Transformation Period

The transformation of 1989 influenced all spheres of life including that of language. First of all, there was a significant increase in the creation of new words and the coinage of idiomatic expressions. It resulted from a period of growth in the lexicon triggered by this important event in Polish history.[5] The political and economic changes brought about led to the creation of many new phenomena which had to be named. Consequently, many neologisms entered the language at that time. The adoption of the new system required new terms for institutions, organizations, positions, forms of activity etc.

Another way of expanding the Polish lexicon was borrowing. After the transformation of 1989, contact with other countries was much more intensive: the Polish began to travel freely and many foreign companies started to operate on the Polish market. As in other languages, English, the modern lingua franca, was

---

4 Galasiński (1992: 58) emphasizes that there is a contradiction between a person's wish to present himself/herself at his/her best and others' negative evaluation of all such efforts. The existence of this contradiction results in developing means which allow a person to boast and at the same time to avoid punishment for doing so.

5 According to Chlebda (2001: 159), two kinds of phraseological stock growth can be distinguished, i.e. a constant growth and a periodic one. The former is related to the development of science, technology and culture, due to which there is a constant need to create new words and expressions. The latter is caused by a very important event such as the political and economic transformation of Poland in 1989 in this case, which results in greater nomination needs than in the case of constant growth (Szerszunowicz 2015).

the main donor language. Many words and idioms were borrowed during the post-transformation period. Loans were very common in those areas which were either non-existent or poorly developed in Communist times, such as computing, marketing and advertising. In the case of these three, mainly English terminology was adopted (Ożóg 2004: 237–238).

From a broader perspective, the new post-transformation reality called for different means of communication from those used in the previous system (Marcjanik 2007; Szerszunowicz 2007). The changes concerned both the public sphere and the private one. In terms of public communication, Newspeak had disappeared and new forms such as public debate, were created (Fras 2005). The language of politics changed considerably: after 1989, Wałęsa, the first Polish president in the post-transformation period, used informal language rich in figurative expressions, which was completely different from the style of communication of Communist dignitaries, and this had an influence on the language of politics.

As for everyday conversation, the American style of communication had an impact on Polish language behaviour.[6] For instance, American small talk influenced to some extent the way the Polish communicate (Szerszunowicz 2007: 41–47; Grybosiowa 2003). In everyday informal and semi-formal language contact, more exponents of a positive attitude are attested than before, which to a great extent is related to speakers' self-image creation efforts (Szerszunowicz 2007). Informality has become a desirable quality (Ożóg 2004: 237), which is reflected, *inter alia*, in interviews on television and radio programs in which people who have never met before often prefer to use their first names – a custom not typical of Polish culture (Marcjanik 2007). This behavior can be classified as a violation of Polish norms resulting from the adoption of a foreign model of communication (Dąbrowska 2001: 188; Grybosiowa 2003; Marcjanik 2007).

---

6 The West, comprising the western European countries and the USA, is perceived as attractive from the Polish perspective. It can be assumed that the American everyday routines shown in films influenced the style and manner of communication of the young generation. Moreover, since the transformation, foreign travel has become common, which has also contributed to the adoption of certain new communicative behaviors (Ożóg 2004; Skowroński 2007).

3 An Integrated Approach to Pragmatic Idioms: A Case Study of New Polish Pragmatic Idioms

Pragmatic idioms are important tools in the process of communication and their main function is to constitute speech acts, thus revealing "aspects of culture-based social interaction" (Piirainen 2008: 215). Since their nature is complex, a multiaspectual analysis is required to determine their properties. The proposed approach integrating different aspects permits an in-depth analysis of the complexity and specificity of pragmatic idioms. The study will encompass not only linguistic aspects, but also those related to extralinguistic issues. The presentation of the proposed model will be followed by three case studies of Polish pragmatic idioms. All the units came into use after the transformation of 1989 and are used in the spoken variety of Polish.

Pragmatic idioms are language units which exhibit various different features. Analyzing the idiomatic expressions in question involves a comprehensive study of all aspects related to their linguistic characteristics and properties, status and functions in a given language. For instance, apart from lexico-grammatical characteristics, the stylistic value of pragmatic idioms should be analyzed, since pragmatic idioms and their variants may have different markedness. A comprehensive approach ensures a true and fair picture of a particular unit, allowing the full set of its properties to be revealed.

Furthermore, the cultural aspect is of importance, as will be attested by the examples to be analyzed. In the case of the Polish post-transformational reality, the new culturally-conditioned situations generated many pragmatic idioms (Grybosiowa 2003; Marcjanik 2007; Szerszunowicz 2015). To fully understand them, the inclusion of the cultural background is necessary. For example, the changes in Poles' perception of the new reality (e.g. success as a well-deserved award, the awareness of positive self-presentation) caused by the influence of the English-speaking world, especially the USA and Australia, resulted in the coinage of new pragmatic idioms, suited to the post-transformation conditions (Grybosiowa 2003: 180).[7] Cultural changes influence communication strategies

---

[7] The American influence is observed in many spheres of life, not only communication (Marcjanik 2007; Ożóg 2004; Szerszunowicz 2007), but also in others, such as, *inter alia*, culinary culture (Skowroński 2007). As observed by Skowroński (2007: 362), it may be hard to determine the border between the phenomenon of Americanization and that of globalization, yet, it can be assumed that from the Polish post-transformational perspective it is the USA which sets the standards for what is desired. The rule that what is American is better than our own results in the ease of adoption of American models of communication, behavior etc. Skowroński (2007:

and styles, which gives rise to new units – in the case of the Polish language, the exponents of positive thinking (e.g. *Będzie dobrze* lit. It will be good, *Damy radę* lit. We will make it).

A comprehensive analysis may include other elements: the quality and quantity of parameters depend on the unit itself. An interdisciplinary approach is taken and includes such disciplines as marketing. For instance, after the transformation, many shops began to introduce their own marketing policy, which comprised a standardized way of addressing clients. In one of the Polish chain stores, PPS Społem, a specially designed set of pragmatemes was launched: for example, when the client has paid, while giving him/her the receipt, the shop assistant always says: *Dziękujemy, zapraszamy!* (lit. Thank you [and] we invite [you]). Analysis of such units involves the inclusion of elements of marketing and customer loyalty studies.

In the case of pragmatic idioms, a multiaspectual analysis is necessary to determine their properties and functions. The analysis should comprise various factors to ensure that the specific character of a given unit will be detected. Considering the cultural background in a broad sense may be of importance, too. The adoption of the integrated approach results in a comprehensive description of the analyzed units.

The proposed approach will be implemented in the case studies of selected Polish pragmatic idioms which came into use after the transformation of 1989. The units chosen for the analysis reflect the cultural changes related to the new post-transformational political and economic situation. Analyses of three expressions will be conducted to show how this approach can be applied in practice in the study on recent units.

3.1 *Miłego dnia!* (lit. 'Have a nice day!')

Pragmatic idioms should also be viewed from the point of view of genre studies. Such expressions have an act-constituting potential, thus it is of importance to determine in which genre they tend to be used. Fixed multiword units of pragmatic character appear in various genres, both spoken and written. The genre perspective relates to discourse analysis, which should also form part of studies of pragmatic idioms. They are used in various forms of discourse, for instance,

---

363) draws attention to the fact that in Poland, the statement *It is like that in the USA* may function as an argument in a discussion. It means that the solution followed by this comment is the best possible one.

live speeches, demotivators etc. Furthermore, due to the act-constituting potential of the units in question, situational aspects should be included (Filatkina 2007: 137–138). For instance, it has to be determined who usually uses a given expression when talking to whom, in which situations, and which functions the units may perform. A corpus of the spoken variety is useful in such analyses, offering many examples of use of given units, as shown by Inoue (2007).

The first pragmatic idiom chosen for analysis belongs to the category "greetings and farewells". Goffman (1971: 79) calls such expressions "access rituals" and states that "greetings mark the transition to a condition of increased access and farewell to a state of decreased access" (Goffman 1971: 47). The expression *Miłego dnia!* (lit. Have a nice day!) belongs to the latter group, since it is a leave-taking formula.

The unit *Miłego dnia!* started to be used in Polish after 1989: the phrase was introduced by American corporations which brought their own communication model with many ready-made expressions (Marcjanik 2007: 53). In fact, in English, this expression is commonly used and by no means limited to one sphere of communication – it is universal and may occur in various contexts (Grybosiowa 2003: 182). The English pragmatic idiom *Have a nice day!*, calqued into Polish as *Miłego dnia!*, was introduced at staff training sessions (Marcjanik 2007: 53). In such companies, using this expression was a way of finishing the conversation with the customer recommended by the firm (Marcjanik 2007: 53). The function of the unit is to warm up relations between persons who either know each other on a client-staff basis or have never met before.

Initially, the idiom aroused doubts among Polish normative linguists, who perceived it as "foreign", unrelated to Polish culture and not compliant with Polish standards of politeness (Grybosiowa 2003: 182; Marcjanik 2007: 53–54).[8] It was viewed as too informal and as interfering in the interlocutor's private life, in some way imposing a good mood on the addressee. Another aspect which might have raised objections is the fact that in Polish informal discourse more sincerity is expected.[9] For instance, answers to the Polish question *Jak się masz?* [lit. How

---

[8] In fact, as observed by Marcjanik (2007: 53), wishes are part of Polish farewell formulae, for instance, wishing somebody a good journey. However, wishing the interlocutor a good day is not rooted in the Polish tradition. In the past, as observed by Grybosiowa (2003: 182), there were some farewell formulas of performative character, like *Zostań z Bogiem* ('Remain with God') or *Bądź zdrów* ('May you be healthy'), which are no longer in use.

[9] The reactions to the question *Jak się masz?* ('How are you?') may vary in Polish, depending on the interlocutor's mood (Grybosiowa 2003: 178). However, over recent decades, the responses have been shifted towards the creation of a more positive self-image on the part of the speaker

are you?] may vary, including complaining and expressing negative feelings (Wojciszke and Baryła 2001: 45–64). Thus, taking into consideration the cultural differences in this respect, in many communicative situations in which unrelated persons are involved, *Miłego dnia!* may sound unnatural.

Marcjanik (2007: 54) observes that the use of the expression is limited to the sphere of services and trade: *Miłego dnia!* is a phrase used by shop assistants, bank clerks and hairdressers. The clients may respond using the same idiom (*Miłego dnia!* 'Have a nice day!'), replying *Wzajemnie/Nawzajem* ('The same to you') or by thanking the employee (*Dziękuję* 'Thank you'). Since it is limited to services and trade, according to Marcjanik (2007: 54), its use is not recommended in other spheres of life.

Irrespective of normativists' opinions, the borrowing gradually began to be used outside the branches of American corporations – for instance, in everyday informal conversations (Grybosiowa 2003: 182).[10] In one of Tomasz Jastrun's novels, a character describes the phrase after using it at the end of his utterance in the following way: "Życzę miłego dnia (ten zwrot upowszechnia się w Polsce i pewnie zrobi taką karierę jak słowo dokładnie na przełomie lat 80. i 90)". (lit. 'I wish a nice day' (the expression is becoming widespread in Poland and is bound to make a career like the word *exactly* at the turn of the 80s and 90s)) (NKJP)[11]. This statement does justice to the status of the phrase in question in the spoken variety of Polish.

As for the linguistic properties of a formula, the expression has to be analyzed from the point of view of its fixedness and variance: Does it appear in other forms? If it does, which constituents are substituted and which factors condition the alterations – maybe it is a pattern which freely generates realizations. The canonical form has to be determined, which in some cases may be problematic, especially due to the units being used in spoken language. The problems may be related not only to the wording itself, but also to the graphic form.[12]

(Jakubowska 1999: 58), which is also confirmed by a study of the small talk genre from a Polish-English perspective (Szerszunowicz 2007).

10 In fact, the unit is not mentioned in the monograph on cross-cultural dimensions of politeness in Polish and English (Jakubowska 1999).

11 A detailed presentation of the Polish national corpus (NKJP) is given in a monograph available online (Przepiórkowski et al. 2012).

12 For instance, in 2005, *Poradnia językowa PWN*, an online language advisor, received a question regarding the graphic form of a common informal greeting *siema* with alternative spellings (*sie ma/się ma*)[12]. The consulting linguist (Grzenia 2005) answered: "najlepiej napisać *siema*, jest to zresztą już powszechnie stosowany zapis" (lit. 'the best spelling is *siema*, this spelling is common'). In the case of some units, phonetic features, such as intonation, are also important.

In modern Polish, a phraseological pattern has developed in which the noun *dzień* 'day' can be substituted with another noun. In fact, the phrase *Miłego dnia!* generated the model [*Życzę*] X *miłego* Y (lit. '[I wish] X a nice Y]' in which X is the addressee of the speaker's wishes, for instance *Panu/Pani/Państwu/ci/wam* (lit. 'Sir/Madam/Sir' and 'Madam/you') etc., and Y is the period meant to be nice, like *dzień* 'day', *popołudnie* 'afternoon', *weekend* 'weekend' or *tydzień* 'week'.

To verify the status of the expressions in question, *Narodowy Korpus Języka Polskiego* (NKJP), was consulted. The corpus search was conducted for the canonic unit *Miłego dnia!* and three derived forms, i.e. *Miłego popołudnia!, Miłego wieczoru!* and *Miłego weekendu!* with the PELCRA search engine. It shows a fairly high frequency with 142 occurrences of the unit *Miłego dnia!* and several uses of the variant forms: *Miłego wieczoru!* – 19 occurrences, *Miłego weekendu!* – 19, *Miłego popołudnia!* – 6. A WebCorp search allowing for analyzing the distribution of the usage of a given phrase in a wide spectrum of genres shows that the expressions in question (*Miłego dnia!, Miłego popołudnia!, Miłego wieczoru!, Miłego tygodnia!*) also function in different contexts: for instance, these phrases are included as a category in an online catalogue of pictures accompanied by wishes for a nice day, afternoon, evening or week to be sent via email (*Obrazki Online*).

The phrase *Miłego dnia!* is used in various communicative contexts, ranging from clerk-client conversations to friendly chats. It is becoming a universal conversation-ending formula. The widespread use of the unit *Miłego dnia!* reflects the changes occurring in the style of Polish conversation, and, from a broader perspective, in Poles' communicative behavior. The English-speaking world's communication standards oblige the speaker to use exponents of positive attitude, encapsulated in the saying *If you don't have anything nice to say, don't say anything.* Many of the exponents of positive attitude and being nice are pragmatic idioms, such as *How nice to see you, I'm fine, Well done!* etc. To some extent, the increasing popularity of the analyzed phrase and its variants shows that this tendency is being adopted in modern Polish communicative culture.

3.2 *Ja panu nie przerywałem* (lit. 'I didn't interrupt you, sir')

After the transformation of 1989, the changes in the sphere of Polish politics were fundamental. The adoption of the new system resulted in the creation of different

---

Moreover, extralinguistic aspects may be of importance, too: for example, certain pragmatic idioms tend to be used with a particular gesture, for instance, *Touch wood!* or *I'll keep my fingers crossed!*

communicative situations. The new genres, such as political debate, provided the opportunity to voice opinions freely in public. In the budding democracy, politicians had to work out their own ways of discussing issues in public. Since many political discussions were televised after the downfall of Communism, viewers were able to witness the development of the genre.

Fras (2005: 97) draws attention to the fact that in Poland, there is no tradition of such public debate where participants presenting views unacceptable to others would be treated with due respect. Until 1989, the ability to participate in public discussion had been of little importance and consequently these skills had not developed. Under Communism, communication was not based on interaction – it was one-directional, with censorship and police restrictions. As a result, there is no model for participation in public debate.

The post-transformational situation was a new one and there was a shortage of fully professional politicians skilled at public speaking and creating a positive self-image so that viewers were rather disappointed by the quality of the televised debates. The language used in the debates varied from informal, sometimes even aggressive and vulgar, to formal, official, with an inclination towards using specialized terminology. Moreover, in the post-transformation period, after the Newspeak period, public discourse was rich in colloquial expressions, in many cases even too informal, and thus rude (e.g. *Pani jest śmieszna!* ('You are ridiculous!'), *Pani jest chyba chora!* ('[Maybe] You are ill!'); Grybosiowa 2003: 183–184).

What immediately captured viewers' attention was a phrase *Ja panu nie przerywałem* (lit. 'I did not interrupt you, sir'), overused by many public speakers who participated in political discussions. The constituent *panu* 'sir' can be substituted with *pani* 'madam' or the plural form comprising representatives of both sexes – *państwu* 'sirs and madams'.

The formula can be described as a single-sentence speech act performing two main functions: phatic and persuasive. In political discourse in the media, it is extremely frequent: occurring in almost all television or radio programs where the representatives of various parties meet (Zimny and Nowak 2009: 91). In order to create an emotional dispute, the host of the program stirs up a pseudo-conflict in which the phrase tends to be used frequently.

As a result of having been used so frequently, this phrase has now become an element of political communicative ritual in Polish debates. Politicians tend to employ it in their utterances, since using the pragmatic idiom *Ja panu nie przerywałem* implies that the speaker is a well-behaved, tactful and collected person, who is able to contribute to the discussion in an appropriate way, open, cooperative and skilled at starting a dialogue and conducting it (Kampka 2009: 162).

This image is desired by politicians and using this kind of idiom is meant to contribute to conveying to the viewers a positive picture of the speaker. At the same time, the opponent to whom the expression is addressed is presented as one devoid of good manners, impolite and unable to participate in public debate.

In fact, the idiom *Ja panu nie przerywałem* has already begun to be perceived as a kind of phatic gesture. Its status is attested by the presence of the unit in various cultural texts such as demotivators or cabaret shows. The phrase is used as an element of the satirical image of a politician (Zimny and Nowak 2009: 91), for example, in one of Tym's editorials:

> Dzieci, które nie nauczą się słuchać innych, zostają parlamentarzystami zapraszanymi do dyskusji telewizyjnych. I oto mamy czwórkę dzieci, każde z innym logo na śliniaczku, które mówią jednocześnie "Ja panu nie przerywałem", a pan Rymanowski próbuje im zadać pytanie.
> [lit. Children who have not learnt to listen to others become members of parliament invited to television discussions. And here we have four children, each with a different logo on his bib, who are all saying at the same time, "I didn't interrupt you", and Mr Rymanowski is trying to ask them a question.] [13]

(NKJP)

The phrase is underrepresented in the corpus with only 7 occurrences, which results from the contents of the NKJP. Yet, after analyzing the results from the Web-Corp search, it can be concluded that the expression has become part of the lexicon of the Polish language. The phrase is multifunctional: performing both phatic and persuasive functions. Occasionally, the expression is used in informal discourse to introduce humor into the conversation or as an element of memes, which also confirms its well-established status in the modern Polish language.

3.3 *Byle do piątku!* (lit. 'Only till Friday!')

Although the results of the 1989 transformation were most noticeable in the areas of politics and the economy, they also occurred in other spheres. One of them is everyday life. Multiword units of pragmatic character should also be viewed from

---

[13] The excerpt comes from the editorial titled *Pustka* ('emptiness') published in a Polish magazine Polityka. The author, Stanisław Tym, is a Polish satirist who has also written film scripts. Bogdan Rymanowski is a Polish journalist and the host of a television program *Kawa na ławę* (the title is an idiomatic expression similar to the English idiom, *Don't beat about the bush*) shown on the TVN24 channel in which politicians representing different parties meet and discuss important issues.

a sociolinguistic perspective. Pragmatic idioms differ depending on the age group, whether they belong to a particular subculture and other factors. For instance, after the transformation of 1989, as the awareness of the importance of being fit increased, numerous fitness and bodybuilding centers sprang up: the people who went to them developed their own lexicon with idiomatic expressions, including pragmatic units like *Nie napinaj się, bo pęknie lustro* (lit. 'Don't try so hard, or the mirror will break') – used to ironically suggest that somebody is trying too hard (Piekot 2000: 53).

The transformation brought many changes, one of which was that Saturdays were work and school free so that Poles now had a longer weekend. After this change, as in most western countries, Friday was the last working day of the week in the vast majority of the companies. It meant that the transformation increased the number of free days, thus giving Polish people more leisure time.

The new situation resulted in a change in perception of the free weekdays: the weekend began to gain in importance and it started to play an important role in the collective minds of Poles.[14] Its status attained after 1989 is reflected in the Polish language of recent decades: new words and phrases have come into use, for example, *od piątku do piątku* (lit. from Friday to Friday). It is not surprising, since all kinds of weekend activities, socializing and going out are of great importance, in particular for the young.

In youth jargon, the day preceding Friday, *czwartek* 'Thursday', is figuratively named *mały piątek* 'little Friday', whereas the word *piątek* 'Friday' is used interchangeably with its diminutive form *piąteczek* 'little piątek', which can be classified as a term of endearment. Another phrase showing the attitude towards the weekend is the unit *piątek, piąteczek, piątunio* (lit. 'Friday, little Friday, very little Friday'), used to express the happiness resulting from the fact that it is already Friday – a phrase similar to the *TGIF – Thank God/goodness it's Friday* (Peeters 2007: 94).[15]

The phrase *Byle to piątku!* (lit. 'Only till Friday!'), meaning 'May we survive till Friday' and suggesting 'afterwards it will be all downhill', is a variant form of phrases attested before the transformation in which seasons of the year appeared

---

[14] Peeters (2007) offers a study of the Australian perception of the weekend, presenting both linguistic and cultural data to show that it is one of the key words in Australian culture.
[15] A Google Graphics search produced a modification containing even more diminutive forms: *Piątek, piąteczek, piątunio, piątuś, piącieczek, piątuniek – znajdziesz tysiące słów, by opisać to, co kochasz* (lit. 'Friday, then five diminutive forms derived from the word Friday followed by a comment: You will find thousands of words to describe what you love'). Unlike English, the Polish language is rich in diminutive suffixes, so that many diminutives of the word *piątek* can be formed.

such as *Byle do wiosny!* (lit. 'Only till spring!') and *Byle do lata!* (lit. 'Only till summer!').[16] The expressions were used in spoken discourse to cheer the interlocutor up, inspire hope, bring encouragement, suggest improvement in the course of time etc. In certain communicative situations, they can be used as leave-taking formulae optimistic in character.

The use of the name *piątek* ('Friday') is significant. Viewed from a linguocultural perspective, it can be concluded that the presence of the constituent *piątek* corroborates the gradual development of Polish weekend culture. Friday afternoon is the start of the weekend and thus the day is the indicator of the off-work period.

The Polish corpus contains as few as 5 occurrences, but the WebCorp search brought more information on the use of the unit in question. For example, like the pragmatic idiom *Miłego dnia!*, the phrase accompanies pictures to be sent electronically – for instance, one of them shows Bugs Bunny working in a quarry (*Jeja*). Numerous examples of its use were attested in the Google Graphics search. As shown by the analysis of the corpus search and the analysis of the findings retrieved by means of WebCorp, the pragmatic idiom *Byle do piątku!* tends to be used in the spoken variety of Polish as well as in internet communication such as blogs, chats, demotivators etc.

4 Conclusions

The transformation of 1989 changed Poland in many respects: a new political system was adopted and the economy was replaced with another model, so society was now adapting to a transformed reality, rich in new phenomena, processes and situations. This state of affairs forced language users to deal with the post-transformation environment and develop appropriate communicative strategies. It involved finding ways of functioning linguistically in the new situations: either borrowing, for instance, from English, modifying Polish language units or coining new ones.

In many of the situations, language users needed pragmatic idioms, since the old means of expression were now inappropriate or inadequate. After 1989,

---

16 The frame *Byle do X*, in which X is the moment after which life should be much easier may be modified. An example of such a modification is observed in a demotivator which contains the following string of realizations: *Byle do 15... Byle do piątku... Byle do wypłaty... I tak jeszcze przez 30 lat* (lit. 'Only till 3 p.m.... Only till Friday... Only till pay day... And like this for the next 30 years').

many idioms were coined as a result of the period of growth following the transformation. Moreover, the constant growth also contributed to an increase in the stock of pragmatic idioms. A multiaspectual analysis of selected examples shows that the study of such units involving various parameters offers an insight into their complex character.

First of all, pragmatic idioms reveal a considerable amount of cultural information, i.e. facts regarding post-transformation Poland. The first of the idioms analyzed confirms the influence of the English-speaking world on the Polish communicative style. It reflects the changing language behaviors in the new reality, in which being pleasant and friendly gains a new dimension. From the linguistic perspective, it can be concluded that the canonical form borrowed from English, *Miłego dnia!*, is easily modified and it can be seen that a pattern based on it now has a place in the Polish language.

The origins of the second unit can be traced back to the problems of budding Polish democracy in which public debate still leaves a lot to be desired. A multifunctional phrase *Ja panu nie przerywałem* began to be used not only in the language of politics but also in other varieties. Found in various cultural texts, memes or press articles, it developed a connotative potential which is also important from the communicative perspective.

The third expression, *Byle do piątku!*, which in fact exploited a pattern known before 1989, illustrates the changes in social perception of the weekend. It is indicative of the increasing importance of having free time at the end of the week: Friday is the day one is looking forward to since it starts the weekend period. The frequent use of the expression as a text accompanying visual material which can be sent to an addressee is indicative of new ways of cheering somebody up.

In conclusion, it should be emphasized that as important tools of communication, pragmatic idioms should be analyzed from various perspectives. A multiaspectual analysis of pragmatemes reveals their properties and their potential, which is important from both a theoretical perspective and a practical one. As for the former, such analyses contribute to a better understanding of formulaic language, while in terms of the latter, the research studies in question may improve lexicographic descriptions of pragmatic idioms and the quality of their presentation in the process of language teaching.

References

Aijmer, Karin (1996): *Conversational Routines in English*. London: Longman.
Banaszkiewicz-Zygmunt, Edyta & Krzysztof Olendzki (2000): *Poland. An Encyclopedic Guide*. Warsaw: Polish Scientific Publishers PWN.
Bartmiński, Jerzy (2001): O językowym obrazie świata Polaków końca XX wieku [On the linguistic picture of the world of Poles at the end of 20th century]. In Stanisław Dubisz & Stanisław Gajda (eds.), *Polszczyzna XX wieku. Ewolucja i perspektywy rozwoju*, 27–53. Warszawa: Dom Wydawniczy ELIPSA.
Brown, Dennis (1987): *New Zealand radio rugby commentary in English: an analysis of non-standard features*. Auckland: University of Auckland, Department of Anthropology.
Burger, Harald (2010): *Phraseologie. Eine Einführung am Beispiel des Deutschen*. 4. Auflage. Berlin: Erich Schmidt.
Chlebda, Wojciech (2001): Frazeologia polska minionego wieku [Polish phraseology of the last century]. In Stanisław Dubisz & Stanisław Gajda (eds.), *Polszczyzna XX wieku. Ewolucja i perspektywy rozwoju*, 155–165. Warszawa: Dom Wydawniczy ELIPSA.
Coulmas, Florian (1979): On the sociolinguistic relevance of routine formulae. *Journal of Pragmatics* 3, 239–266.
Coulmas, Florian (1981): *Routine im Gespräch*. Wiesbaden: Akademische Verlagsgesellschaft Athenaion.
Cowie, Anthony P., Roland Mackin & Isabel R. McCaig (1983): *Oxford Dictionary of Current Idiomatic English*. Volume 2. Oxford: Oxford University Press.
Croft, William (2001): *Radical Contrastive Grammar. Syntactic Theory in Typological Perspective*. Oxford: Oxford University Press.
Dąbrowska, Anna (2001): O sposobach zmniejszania dystansu między rozmówcami [On the ways of shortening the distance between interlocutors]. In Grażyna Habrajska (ed.), *Język w komunikacji*. Volume 1, 187–194. Łódź: Wyższa Szkoła Humanistyczno-Ekonomiczna w Łodzi.
Dobrovol'skij, Dmitrij & Elisabeth Piirainen (2007): *Figurative Language: Cross-cultural and cross-linguistic Perspectives*. Amsterdam: Elsevier.
Fernando, Chitra (1996): *Idioms and Idiomaticity*. Oxford: Oxford University Press.
Fiedler, Sabine (2007): *English Phraseology. A Coursebook*. Tübingen: Narr.
Filatkina, Natalia (2007): Pragmatische Beschreibungsansätze. In Harald Burger, Dmitrij Dobrovol'skij, Peter Kühn, Neal R. Norrick (eds.), *Phraseology. An International Handbook of Contemporary Research*. Volume 1, 132–158. Berlin, New York: De Gruyter.
Filatkina, Natalia & Monika Hanauska (2010): Wissensstrukturierung und Wissensvermittlung durch Routineformeln: Am Beispiel ausgewählter althochdeutscher Texte. *Yearbook of Phraseology* 1, 45–71.
Fillmore, Charles, Paul Kay & Mary C. O'Connor (1998): Regularity and idiomacity in Grammatical Constructions: The Case of Let Alone. *Language*, 64 (3), 501–538.
Fléchon, Genviève, Paolo Frassi & Alain Polguére (2012): Les pragmatèmes ont-ils un charme indéfinissable? In Pierluigi Ligas & Paolo Frassi (eds.), *Lexiques. Indetités. Cultures*, 81–104. Vèrone: QuiEdir.
Fras, Janina (2005): *Komunikacja polityczna. Wybrane zagadnienia gatunków i języka wypowiedzi* [Political communication. Selected issues of genres and language]. Wrocław: Wydawnictwo Uniwersytetu Wrocławskiego.

Galasiński, Dariusz (1992): *Chwalenie się jako perswazyjny akt mowy* [Boasting as a persuasive speech act]. Kraków: Instytut Języka Polskiego Polskiej Akademii Nauk.
Goffman, Erving (1971): *Relations in Public*. New York: Harper.
Gomulka, Stanisław (2016): Poland's economic and social transformation 1989–2014 and contemporary challenges. *Central Bank Review* 16, 19–23. Retrieved from http://dx.doi.org/10.1016/j.cbrev.2016.03.005, accessed August 15, 2017.
Granger, Sylviane & Magali Paquot (2008): Disentangling the phraseological web. In Sylviane Granger & Fanny Meunier (eds.), *Phraseology: An interdisciplinary perspective*, 27–49. Amsterdam, Philadelphia: John Benjamins.
Grybosiowa, Antonina (2003). *Język wtopiony w rzeczywistość* [Language melted into reality]. Katowice: Wydawnictwo Uniwersytetu Śląskiego.
Grzenia, Jan (2005): *Siema*. Retrieved from https://sjp.pwn.pl/poradnia/haslo/siema;5924.html, accessed August 17, 2017.
Hickey, Francesca & Koenraad Kuiper (2000): A deep depression covers the South Tasman Sea: New Zealand Met Office weather forecasts. In Allan Bell & Koenraad Kuiper (eds.), *New Zealand English*, 279–296. Wellington: VUW Press and Amsterdam, Philadelphia: John Benjamins.
Inoue, Ai (2007): *Present-Day Spoken English. A phraseological Approach*. Tokyo: Kaitakusha.
Jakubowska, Ewa (1998): Good wishes in a cross-cultural perspective. In Janusz Arabski (ed.), *Studies in Foreign Language, teaching and Learning*, 232–246. Katowice: Wydawnictwo Uniwersytetu Śląskiego.
Jakubowska, Ewa (1999): *Cross-Cultural Dimensions of Politeness in the Case of Polish and English*. Katowice: Wydawnictwo Uniwersytetu Śląskiego.
Jeja. Retrieved from www.obrazki.jeja.pl/127651,byle_do_piatku.html, accessed August 11, 2017.
Kampka, Agnieszka (2009): *Perswazja w języku polityki* [Persuasion in political language]. Warszawa: Wydawnictwo naukowe Scholar.
Kauffer, Maurice (2011): Actes de langage stéréotypes en allemand et en français. Pour une redéfinition du stéréotype grâce à la phraséologie. *Nouveaux Cahier d'Allemand* 1, 35–53.
Kauffer, Maurice (2013): Le figement des 'actes de language stéréotypés' en français et en allemand. *Pratiques* 159/160, 42–45.
Kuiper, Koenraad (1996): *Smooth Talkers. The Linguistic Performance of Auctioneers and Sportscasters*. Mahawah, NJ: Lawrence Erlbaum.
Lüger, Heinz-Helmut (2007): Pragmatische Phraseme: Routineformeln. In Harald Burger, Dmitrij Dobrovol'skij, Peter Kühn, Neal R. Norrick (eds.), *Phraseology. An International Handbook of Contemporary Research*. Volume 1, 444–459. Berlin, New York: De Gruyter.
Marcjanik, Małgorzata (2007): *Grzeczność w komunikacji językowej* [Politeness in language communication]. Warszawa: Wydawnictwo Naukowe PWN.
Mel'čuk, Igor (1988): *Dependency Syntax: Theory and Practice*. Albany, NY: SUNY Press.
Narodowy Korpus Języka Polskiego [National Corpus of the Polish Langauge]. Retrieved from www.nkjp.pl, accessed July 15, 2017.
Moon, Rosamund (1998): *Fixed Expressions and Idioms in English*. Oxford: Clarendon Press.
Nattinger, James R. & Jeanette S. DeCarrico (2001): *Lexical Phrases and Language Teaching*. Oxford: Oxford University Press.
Nosowicz, Jan F. & Joanna Szerszunowicz (2004): Interpersonal Idioms in Teaching Foreign Languages. In Jan F. Nosowicz (ed.), *Edukacja dla przyszłości*, 184–190. Białystok: Wydawnictwo Wyższej Szkoły Finansów i Zarządzania w Białymstoku.

Obrazki Online. Retrieved from www.obrazkionline.pl, accessed August 12, 2017.
Ożóg, Kazimierz (2004): *Polszczyzna przełomu XX i XXI wieku. Wybrane zagadnienia* [The Polish language at the turn of the 20th and 21st centuries. Selected problems]. Rzeszów: otwarty Rozdział.
Pawley, Andrew (1991): How to talk cricket: On linguistic competence in a subject matter. In Robert Blust (ed.), *Currents in Pacific Linguistics: Papers on Austronesian Languages and Ethnolinguistics in Honour of George Grace*, 339–368. Canberra: Pacific Linguistics.
Pawley, Andrew (2001): Phraseology, Linguistics and the Dictionary. *International Journal of Lexicography* 14 (2), 122–134.
Pawley, Andrew (2007): Developments in the study of formulaic language since 1970: A personal view. In Paul Skandera (ed.), *Phraseology and Culture in English*, 3–45. Berlin, New York: Mouton de Gruyter.
Peeters, Bert (2007): Australian perception of the weekend: Evidence from collocations and elsewhere. In Paul Skandera (ed.), *Phraseology and Culture in English*, 79–107. Berlin, New York: Mouton de Gruyter.
Piekot, Tomasz (2000): Problem analizy frazeologii socjolektalnej (na przykładzie socjolektu kulturystów nieprofesjonalnych) [The analysis of sociolectal phraseology (on the example of amateur body builders)]. *Poradnik Językowy* 4, 50–56.
Piirainen, Elisabeth (2008): Figurative phraseology and culture. In Sylviane Granger & Fanny Meunier (eds.), *Phraseology: An interdisciplinary perspective*, 207–228. Amsterdam, Philadelphia: John Benjamins.
Piirainen, Elisabeth (2016): *Lexicon of Common Figurative Units. Widespread Idioms in Europe and Beyond*. Volume 2. New York: Peter Lang.
Przepiórkowski, Adam, Mirosław Bańko, Rafał L. Górski & Barbara Lewandowska-Tomaszczyk (eds.) (2012): *Narodowy Korpus Języka Polskiego* [National Corpus of the Polish Language]. Warszawa: Wydawnictwo Naukowe PWN. Retrieved from http://nkjp.pl/settings/papers/NKJP_ksiazka.pdf, accessed February 10, 2018.
Richter, Frank & Manfred Sailer (2014): Idiome mit phraseologisierten Teilsätzen: eine Fallstudie zur Formalisierung von Konstruktionen im Rahmen der HPSG. In Alexander Lasch & Alexander Ziem (Hrsg.), *Grammatik als Netzwerk von Konstruktionen. Sprachwissen im Fokus der Konstruktionsgrammatik*, 291–312. Berlin, Boston: De Gruyter.
Roos, Eckart (2001): *Idiom und Idiomatik: ein sprachliches Phänomen im Lichte der kognitiven Linguistik und Gestalttheorie*. Aachen: Shaker.
Ruusila, Anna (2015): *Pragmatische Phraseologismen und ihre lexikographische Darstellung. Am Beispiel eines mehrsprachigen elektronischen Spezialwörterbuch für Übersetzer*. Frankfurt am Main, Berlin: Peter Lang.
Skowroński, Krzysztof P. (2007): Amerykanizacja polskiej kultury kulinarnej [Americanization of Polish culinary culture]. In Katarzyna Łeńska-Bąk (ed.), *Pokarmy i jedzenie w kulturze. Tabu, dieta, symbol*, 361–381. Opole: Wydawnictwo Uniwersytetu Opolskiego.
Szerszunowicz, Joanna (2007): A Comparative Analysis of Small Talk. In Lawrence N. Berlin (ed.), *Theoretical Approaches to Dialogue Analysis. Selected Papers from the IADA Chicago 2004 Conference*, 39–48. Tübingen: Max Niemeyer.
Szerszunowicz, Joanna (2015): Periodic growth of phrasemes from a linguo-cultural perspective: Polish phraseology after the political transformation of 1989. *Yearbook of Phraseology* 6, 103–124.
Wojciszke, Bogdan & Wiesław Baryła (2001): Kultura narzekania i jej psychologiczne konsekwencje [The culture of complaining and its psychological consequences]. Bralczyk,

Jerzy and Katarzyna Mosiołek-Kłosińska (eds.), *Zmiany w publicznych zwyczajach językowych*, 45–64, Warszawa: Rada Języka Polskiego przy Prezydium PAN.
Wray, Alison (1999): Formulaic language in learners and native speakers. *Language Teaching* 32 (4), 213–231.
Wray, Alison (2009): Identifying formulaic language: Persistent challenges and new opportunities. In Roberta Corrigan, Edith A. Moravcsik, Hamid Ouali & Kathleen Wheatley (eds.), *Formulaic Language. Volume 1: Distribution and historical change*, 27–51. Amsterdam, Philadelphia: John Benjamins.
Wray, Alison & Michael R. Perkins (2000): The functions of formulaic language: An integrated model. *Language and Communication* 20 (1), 1–28.
Ziem, Alexander (2014): Von der Kasusgrammatik zum FrameNet: Frames, Konstruktionen und die Ideen eines Konstruktikons, In Alexander Lasch & Alexander Ziem (Hrsg.), *Grammatik als Netzwerk von Konstruktionen. Sprachwissen im Fokus der Konstruktionsgrammatik*, 263–290. Berlin, Boston: De Gruyter.
Zimny, Rafał & Paweł Nowak (2007): *Słownik polszczyzny politycznej po roku 1989* [A dictionary of political Polish after 1989]. Warszawa: Wydawnictwo Naukowe PWN.

Mareike Keller
Compositionality: Evidence from Code-Switching

Abstract: The storage and processing of phrasemes has been discussed many times over the past decades, with varying results. Researchers still disagree as to the degree to which phrasemes are stored and processed holistically or compositionally. This paper approaches the topic of compositionality through bilingual data, which is rarely discussed in theoretical work on phraseology. It provides a qualitative analysis of verb-based phrasemes, highlighting the structural and semantic features of code-switching patterns in and around phrasemes which serve as clues to underlying production processes. The study is based on recordings of German-English informal conversation. The language-mixing patterns are presented in the framework of the MLF model (Myers-Scotton 2002; Myers-Scotton and Jake 2017). The mixing patterns inside collocations and the resistance to mixing of more idiomatic phrasemes suggest that the surface realization of phrasemes in bilingual speech is determined both by morphosyntactic code-switching constraints and by the semantic impact of nominal and verbal phraseme components on the meaning of the phraseme as a whole. The findings support both the Superlemma Theory of phraseme processing (Sprenger et al. 2006) and the MLF model of code-switching, as they provide empirical evidence for the unitary storage of phrasemes at the conceptual level as well as for their compositional assembly in accordance with structural code-switching constraints during language production.

1 Introduction

One of the much-discussed but still unresolved questions related to multi-word sequences like idioms, semi-idioms and collocations (henceforth referred to as *phrasemes*) concerns the way they are stored in the mental lexicon: Are they stored and retrieved holistically or are they assembled compositionally from individual words each time they are produced? A traditional approach to compositionality is the investigation of variation and modification in monolingual canonical data (Moon 1998; Langlotz 2006: 175–224). Further insights have been drawn

∂ Open Access. © 2020 M. Keller, published by De Gruyter. This work is licensed under the Creative Commons Attribution 4.0 License.
https://doi.org/10.1515/9873110669824-009

from the analysis of non-canonical data like language acquisition, aphasia, attrition, or slips of the tongue (Häcki-Buhofer 2007; Paradis 2004; Kuiper et al. 2007). More recently, psycholinguistic experiments have been conducted measuring processing speed, mostly in comprehension, but also in production (Havrila 2009; Wray 2012). In this paper the subject of compositionality is approached via a largely unexplored type of data: phrasemes in naturally occurring code-switching produced by balanced bilinguals.[1] The approach builds on the assumption that language switching or mixing alongside or within phrasemes can be employed as an indicator for chunking or parsing during language processing (Backus 2003; Wray and Namba 2003; Namba 2012). As differences between monolingual and bilingual language processing concern areas like speed of access or executive control rather than basic processing mechanisms (Paradis 2004; Bialystok and Craik 2010), the conclusions are not restricted to bilingual contexts but could also provide explanations for monolingual storage and processing of complex lexical items.

Phrasemes are a highly heterogeneous group of lexicalized word-strings and the information a phraseme can reveal with respect to language processing depends on the lexical category of its syntactic head as well as on its internal syntactic structure. This paper is devoted exclusively to phrasemes in the form of syntactic constituents with a verb as syntactic head.[2] Verb-based phrasemes were chosen because their comparatively complex argument structure provides more opportunities for internal language mixing than e.g. nominal phrasemes. All examples were extracted manually from a 50-hour corpus of German-English spontaneous speech.[3] The paper provides empirical evidence of the mixing patterns in and around phrasemes and explores the ways in which language contact phenomena can be related to syntactic and semantic properties of phrasemes. The findings provide clues to the mental representation of phrasemes, including the

---

1 *Balanced bilingualism* is defined here as a native-like level of proficiency in both languages.
2 The phraseological terminology used in this paper is based primarily on Burger (2015). The term *phraseme* will be used as a cover term for idioms, semi-idioms and collocations. Verb-based phrasemes, which are the focus of the study, fall into Burger's category of referential phrasemes in the form of syntactic constituents (*nominative referentielle Phraseme*, Burger 2015: 32).
3 The data were collected between 1999 and 2005 as part of the project "Sprachkontakt Deutsch-Englisch: Code-switching, Crossover & Co." funded by the Deutsche Forschungsgesellschaft (DFG) and headed by Rosemarie Tracy (University of Mannheim) and Elsa Lattey (University of Tübingen). Further details on the speakers and data collection process are given in Tracy and Lattey (2010). My sincere thanks go to Rosemarie Tracy for access to the recordings and the transcripts.

level at which language selection takes place and will hopefully inspire further research into a complex but highly promising type of data.

The structure of the paper is as follows. As most readers will be more familiar with phraseology than code-switching, basic assumptions concerning storage and processing of phrasemes are outlined only very briefly (section 2), before the structural approach to code-switching is introduced in more detail (section 3). Then the empirical data are presented and analysed (section 4). In section 5 the findings are discussed with respect to theoretical issues concerning the compositionality of phrasemes. Section 6 concludes the paper with a short summary and suggestions for future research.

2 Conceptual Unity – Compositional Processing

The observation that different types of phraseme exhibit different degrees of fixedness or compositionality has been widely discussed among phraseologists, and over the past decades various taxonomic approaches placing different types of phraseme along a continuum have been proposed and refuted (Wray and Perkins 2000). The one characteristic uniting all types of phraseme, from true idioms to collocations, seems to be that they are recurrently co-occurrent sequences of lexemes which appear to be reproduced rather than creatively assembled. Some of them express meaning beyond the sum of the meaning of their individual components, some are peculiar in their syntactic make-up – but the vast majority do not show any semantic or syntactic characteristics which clearly set them apart from free combinations of words. How, then, can we tell that one string of words is a phraseme and another one is not? One indispensable precondition for recognizing phrasemes as such in actual discourse seems to be their representation as conceptual units at some level in the mental lexicon (Backus 2003: 92). However, unitary representation does not necessarily entail holistic storage and processing all the way from the conceptual level to actual phonological realization. The question that remains is: Which aspects or components of a phraseme are stored in long-term memory, and what can be assembled online during production (see Jackendoff 2002, 152–195)?

It is widely assumed that phrasemes have their own entries in the mental lexicon (Levelt 1989: 186–187; de Bot 1992: 10), but there is no agreement on what this entry actually looks like.[4] To describe the representation of a phraseme in the mental lexicon, Levelt and Meyer (2000: 442) introduce the term *superlemma*, which "represents the idiom's restricted syntax and points to a set of simple lemmas." This idea is expanded by Sprenger, Levelt and Kempen (2006) into their Superlemma Theory. The theory supports a hybrid view of phraseme processing (Cutting and Bock 1997) and claims that "[f]ixed expressions and idioms and literal language only differ with respect to the *source* of word activation: while the words of a literal phrase are activated by their own lexical concepts, the words of a fixed expression will benefit from a common idiom node" (Sprenger et al. 2006: 167). This means that in a phraseme, the individual lexemes are selected from the lexicon via the superlemma entry for the phraseme. The Superlemma Theory is attractive because it treats the production of phrasemes similarly to the production of free combinations, and it elegantly aligns production and comprehension. In addition, the contradiction between conceptual unity on the one hand and syntactic compositionality on the other is resolved by postulating the superlemma as a conceptual unit and the component lexemes as syntactically related but individually accessed pieces.

As long as we are dealing with monolingual data, we can use e.g. speed of access in experimental settings, or performance errors in spontaneous and elicited speech as indicators of chunking or parsing of phraseological units. When we look at bilingual data, the contrast between the two languages involved offers an additional clue to the way in which conceptual units are assembled into actual phonetic strings. One might assume that a string of words which appears as a unit on the level of conceptual representation should be barred from internal language mixing in order to preserve the exact meaning or pragmatic function of the unit. The relevance of phrasemes in contrast to simplex lexemes for the study of code-switching patterns was already noticed in a very early study by Hasselmo (1970: 196), who writes about the data he analysed: "Purely lexical conditioning of switching is obviously an important factor, but throughout this discourse it appears that larger preformulated segments play a role as well." Later code-switching research has mentioned in passing that phrasemes are often inserted as whole constituents (e.g. Myers-Scotton 2006: 263), supporting the view that phrasemes are processed as units all the way from the mental lexicon/phrasicon to the phonetic level. However, this blanket view does not hold for all types of

---

[4] One problem with previous research on the topic is the definition of the target structures. Earlier works focus mainly on pure idioms, or idioms in a narrow sense. The authors cited in the following paragraphs may not all have had phrasemes in the wider sense in mind, but their findings are applicable nevertheless.

phraseme. Backus (2003) cites examples of phraseme-internal language mixing, which suggest that under specific conditions phrasemes can be broken up into their sub-components at some point in the production pipeline.[5] Furthermore, it shows that not all phraseme components are language-specific on all levels of language production. I believe that the propensity or resistance of a phraseme to internal language mixing can be used as a clue to how phrasemes are assembled during language production. The following section provides a short introduction to the structural study of code-switching. This will serve as the theoretical background against which the behaviour of phrasemes in code-switching is analysed.

3 Bilingual Code-Switching

Over the past decades, code-switching has been studied from various angles, such as sociolinguistics, psycholinguistics or syntax, with the goal of finding out which factors influence or constrain mixed utterances. Contrary to early beliefs, mixing languages is neither a sign of incompetence, nor does it occur randomly. Instead, it seems to be governed by social as well as syntactic constraints, the nature of which has not been fully understood. What we can say for sure is that code-switching constraints, just like any other grammar rule, are probabilistic rather than absolute.[6] This paper focuses on the morphosyntactic aspect of language mixing and attempts to link it to semantic factors influencing the surface form of complex lexical items which are the object of investigation of phraseological research. Myers-Scotton's Matrix Language Frame Model (MLF model) (1993 and following) serves as the theoretical framework for the account of bilingual phraseme processing developed in the following pages. For reasons of space the account must remain somewhat superficial. Readers new to the topic are referred to Myers-Scotton and Jake (2009) for a concise but detailed overview.

    The MLF model is cognitively based and lexically driven, which means it is focused on processes originating in the mental lexicon. It was devised in accordance with basic assumptions of generative grammar and aims to explain how language production is linked to linguistic competence (Myers-Scotton 2002: 14). At

---

5 Namba (2012) also deals with the topic of mixed phrasemes in code-switching. However, as his analysis is based on bilingual acquisition data from two young children, his examples are very few and cover only a small section of frequent phraseological structures.
6 See Mindt (2002: 210–211) who argues that any descriptive grammatical rule will have about 5% exceptions due to online processing errors, idiosyncrasies or variation/language change.

the core of the MLF model lies the claim that the distribution of languages in bilingual clauses is asymmetrical. One language, the *matrix language (ML)*, provides the morphosyntactic frame of a bilingual clause.[7] Into this ML frame, elements from a second language, called the *embedded language (EL)*, can be inserted. The MLF model's unit of reference is the bilingual clause (Myers-Scotton and Jake 2017: 3).[8] This means that the two principles restricting the surface realization of morphemes in code-switching are only applicable to bilingual clauses. They are not aimed at syntactic units bigger than one clause. Also, the terms ML and EL only refer to one clause at a time. According to the MLF model, the surface realization of morphemes[9] in a bilingual clause is constrained by two principles. These two principles state that in mixed-language constituents, word order and particular grammatical morphemes (e.g. morphemes transporting information on agreement or case) have to come from the ML:

> The Morpheme-Order Principle: In ML+EL constituents consisting of singly occurring EL lexemes and any number of ML morphemes, surface morpheme order (reflecting surface syntactic relations) will be that of the ML.
>
> (Myers-Scotton 1997: 83)

> The System Morpheme Principle: In ML+EL constituents, all system morphemes which have grammatical relations external to their head constituent (i.e. which participate in the sentence's thematic role grid) will come from the ML.
>
> (Myers-Scotton 1997: 83)

The MLF model has been revised several times in order to make its predictions more precise. One crucial step in clarifying which morphemes are affected by the System Morpheme Principle was the introduction of the 4-M-Model (Myers-Scotton and Jake 2000). Myers-Scotton and Jake (2017: 2) state explicitly that the 4-M-Model is not itself a model of code-switching but a general model of morpheme processing, applicable equally well to other types of data. It relates to the MLF

---

[7] This assumption is made only about so-called classic code-switching "in which empirical evidence shows that abstract grammatical structure within a clause comes from only one of the participating languages" (Myers-Scotton and Jake 2009: 337). For mixed languages, Myers-Scotton (2002: 100) proposes a composite matrix as the grammatical basis. The term ML should not be mistaken for or confused with the dominant language of a speaker or a discourse. It is a grammatical abstraction, applicable only within one clause (Myers-Scotton 2002: 58).
[8] In terms of generative syntax: "Our unit of analysis is the clause, or CP, the projection of complementizer, or COMP" (Myers-Scotton and Jake 2015: 418).
[9] The term *morpheme* is used for surface realizations (phonetic form in the actual utterance) as well as for the underlying lemma entry (abstract form in the speaker's mind) (Myers-Scotton 2002: 106).

model only insofar as it can help to explain the morphosyntactic regularities observed in bilingual clauses. The model assumes four different types of morpheme (hence the name, 4-M[orpheme]-Model): 1. content morphemes, 2. early system morphemes (e.g. plural affixes), 3. bridges (e.g. possessive markers) and 4. outsiders (e.g. case and agreement markers).[10] Content and early system morphemes together transport the meaning of an utterance. They are accessed at the conceptual level. The two types of late system morpheme, bridges and outsiders, make the utterance grammatical in terms of the morphosyntactic structure projected by the matrix language. Their exact phonological form is selected only at the level of the formulator, once the thematic grid of the utterance has been laid out.[11] In short, "[c]ontent morphemes and early SMs satisfy the speaker's intentions, while late SMs provide grammatical structure" (Myers-Scotton and Jake 2017: 3). According to the System Morpheme Principle, only the late outsider system morphemes must be supplied by the ML in bilingual constituents. Their function in a clause lies in "disambiguating grammatical roles and providing argument struc-

---

10 Explanatory note: The 4-M-Model assumes an asymmetry between content and system morphemes, which is crucial for language processing. In crude terms, content morphemes are conceptually activated lexical items (which assign or receive theta-roles; Myers-Scotton and Jake 2015: 425), whereas system morphemes are structurally assigned functional elements. The system morphemes are subdivided into early and late. Early system morphemes are accessed along with content morphemes from the mental lexicon. They are functional affixes which add to the semantic content but do not affect the grammaticality of the sentence. The sentences *Paul likes Anna's sister* and *Paul likes Anna's sisters* are equally grammatical, but the plural affix on the word *sister* in the second one changes the meaning of the proposition. The late system morphemes are subdivided again, into bridges and outsiders. Both help to make the sentence grammatical. A bridge establishes a grammatical relation between lexical items within the systactic constituent in which it occurs. In *Paul likes Anna's sister* the possessive marker expresses the grammatical relation between Anna and the sister, which in the given sentence are both components of the same object NP. An outsider establishes a grammatical relation with a lexical item outside the systactic constituent in which it occurs. In *Paul likes Anna's sister* the agreement marker on the verb expresses the grammatical relation between the subject NP and the verb under INFL (Myers-Scotton and Jake 2017: 7). A particular grammatical morpheme is not necessarily assigned to the same group crosslinguistically (Myers-Scotton and Jake 2017: 4). Its type depends on the kind of grammatical information the morpheme carries. In Modern English, the article only carries information about definiteness and is classified as an early system morpheme. In Modern German the article also carries information about case and is thus a late outsider system morpheme.
11 The processing components referred to by Myers-Scotton are based on Levelt's model of language processing (Levelt 1989; Levelt et al. 1999). The model was adapted to bilingual speech by de Bot (1992) and Wei (2009); see also Myers-Scotton (2005).

ture" (Myers-Scotton and Jake 2017: 7). The intuition that different types of morpheme are accessed at different levels during language production will prove crucial for understanding which types of phraseme, or which phraseme components, are uttered in which language in code-switching discourse.

The MLF model does not make any predictions about the processing of phrasemes. Nevertheless, the following comment shows how the model relates to the question of phraseme storage and processing:

> I also see my work as recognizing that explanations lie in linking a theory of language with a theory of language processing in a manner similar to the views expressed in Jackendoff (2002). Jackendoff stresses the need to consider what aspects of an utterance are in long-term memory (content morphemes in my framework) and what aspects can be constructed online with working memory.
>
> (Myers-Scotton 2002: 310)

Myers-Scotton has not published any work focusing on phrasemes specifically but in her discussion of so-called EL-islands (full syntactic constituents from the EL inserted into an ML clause) she mentions that these islands often show phraseological characteristics:

> Many of the Embedded Language islands can be considered collocations, combinations of words that often appear together as a single phrase.
>
> (Myers-Scotton 2006: 263)

> [M]any Embedded Language islands are either formulaic or routine collocations, perhaps making them similar to the activation required to access singly occurring forms.
>
> (Myers-Scotton 2002: 162)

These comments suggest that phrasemes are likely to be inserted as chunks of lexemes from only one language into bilingual utterances. At first glance my data seem to confirm this. Most phrasemes are inserted as EL chunks and do not show internal mixing at all, among them the vast majority of adverbial and nominal phrasemes:

(1)   KL: *Not anymore. And* **{in} einer Hinsicht** *it's-äh I think it is is it's more hygienic.*

[K6:730][12]

---

12 Most of the examples used in this paper are taken from the database compiled for the research project presented in Keller (2014). Transcription conventions: "In order to ensure readability of examples, we added punctuation marks and adopted the following conventions: German items are roman, English are italic; a slash signals a word- or sentence-break, a dash con-

(2) AS: ...jetzt is des Tor net zugangen. Und **all of a sudden** hat der g'schrien ja geh halt rei', du Depp!

[AlMI1b:722]

(3) LK: Weil wenn ma', wenn ma' sieben Jahr' lang nicht nicht redet/ **first of all**, damals war's no' net so wie heut', dass du...

[L2:401]

(4) KL: *That keeps me going. I'm pretty sure. And* **der gute Wille**. *And that's about it.*

[K9:467]

(5) KL: *Things were then better over here, too, you know?* Naja. *But* **der liebe Gott**, *h-he-he evened it out.*

[K16:58]

(6) TG: ...da ham se bloß das Essen gekriegt und 'n- **place to stay**!

[T29:949]

However, especially among verb-based phrasemes there is a significant number of items that do show internal language mixing:

(7) TG: ...because- *he* **made himself** {so} **wichtig**, *you know*.

[T29:278]

Here, the German phraseme *sich wichtig machen* (Engl. *act the big shot*, literally 'make oneself important') is rendered partly in English and partly in German. Examples like (7) suggest that at least verb-based phrasemes are not necessarily accessed as completely prefabricated, language-specific strings of lexemes. Maybe they are accessed as strings of lemmas, or as superlemmas, at the conceptual level – but somewhere along the production process the superlemma must be decomposed and reassembled drawing on lexemes/morphemes from two different languages. This raises the question of which elements of a mixed phraseme appear in which language in a bilingual utterance. Or more precisely: Which elements of a mixed phraseme are realized in the language the phraseme is drawn from and which elements are translated, or calqued?

---

nects iterated items. Curly brackets mark ambiguous language affiliation. Round brackets indicate incomprehensible sections, square brackets set off meta-linguistic comments and indicate passages left out; [...] Note that we consistently – even within English utterances – employed German orthography for hesitation expressions, i.e. *äh(m)* (Tracy and Lattey 2010: 57). I added curly brackets to mark homophonous diamorphs, i.e. elements which could be English or German. Square brackets following examples contain file and line identification.

In the pursuit of possible constraints regulating the language distribution in the surface realization of phraseme components, Backus (2003: 92) suggests that "ML morphemes will have semantically basic meanings." Unfortunately, Backus (2003) leaves it to the reader to decide what does and what does not qualify as semantically basic meaning. Unrelated to the topic of phraseological units, Wei (2009: 280–283) regards lemma congruence, i.e. the degree of similarity between word forms from different languages expressing the same lemma, as the organizational principle guiding the production of mixed utterances. For him the main reason for inserting EL content morphemes into an ML frame seems to be insufficient semantic or pragmatic congruence between lemmas. Likewise, Myers-Scotton (2002: 20) suggests that "lack of sufficient congruence may explain why certain structures are avoided or impossible in switching between specific language pairs." However, what is sufficient and what is insufficient congruence remains unclear. Nevertheless, studying code-switching data might shed more light on the question of which elements are central and which peripheral in lexical entries, simplex or complex ones:

> [H]ow an EL content morpheme is accommodated by an ML frame tells us something about which features characterizing that morpheme (ultimately characterizing its supporting lemma) are critical and which may be peripheral in lexical entries. At this stage, we only aim to have shown the effects on CS [=codeswitching] of different aspects of lexical structure, but we do think it is clear how studying congruence in CS has implications far beyond the nature of CS itself.
>
> (Myers-Scotton and Jake 1995: 1019)

This is to say that the study of morphosyntactic details in code-switching data and its implications is more than just a source for understanding more about the possible compositionality of phrasemes. It holds valuable clues to the make-up of entries in the mental lexicon. With this theoretical introduction in mind, the goal of the study presented in the following section is to show how balanced bilinguals integrate verb-based phrasemes in their everyday conversations.

4 A Study of Verb-Based Phrasemes in German-English Code-Switching

The examples presented in this paper are based on 732 utterances containing various types of phraseme of the size of a syntactic constituent, extracted manually from 50 hours of informal interviews with seven German Americans (see footnote

3). Six of the interviewees emigrated to the US as adults, one at the age of fourteen. At the time of recording they were 65–87 years of age and had lived in an English-speaking environment for 42–66 years. After their emigration from Germany some of the speakers continued to use their variety of German on a regular basis, others experienced phases with no or hardly any interaction with other native speakers of German.

The close typological relatedness of English and German, which might pose an obstacle to some areas of linguistic research, is a definite advantage for an investigation of mixing patterns targeting phraseological material, because the high number of cognates and (near-)homophones along with the large overlap on the morphosyntactic level provokes a variety of mixing phenomena less likely to be found in bilingual data based on typologically more distant languages.

Phrasemes are notoriously hard to define, and the decision as to whether or not a combination of words is phraseological or not is always to a certain degree a subjective one (see Howarth 1998: 29). I cannot guarantee that I did not miss items that another phraseologist would have wanted to include. To confer a certain degree of objectivity, I included only phrasemes listed in major printed and online dictionaries of idioms and collocations.

Out of a total of 732 utterances containing phrasemes in the form of a syntactic constituent (verb-based and other), 146 (i.e. about 20%) exhibit obvious traces of the speaker's bilingualism, either in the form of code-switching in the vicinity of the phraseme or as phraseme-internal language mixing (table 1).

Tab. 1: The frequency of mixing vs. switching (N=146)

	mixing		switching	
verb-based phrasemes	59	75%	18	27%
other	20	25%	49	73%
total	79	100%	67	100%

My argumentation builds on the hypothesis that language mixing inside a phraseme is suggestive of a compositional process. Phraseme-internal language mixing can be observed primarily inside verb-based phrasemes. Therefore, the present paper focuses on verb-based phrasemes (N=451) and refers to other syntactic types of phraseme only for comparative reasons. Very early on during the research process it became clear that the semantic impact of the verb itself appears to be a crucial factor in determining the mixing patterns in utterances containing verb-based phrasemes. Consequently, the target utterances were divided into two groups. The first group consists of 236 utterances, each containing a phraseme headed by a verb that adds a clearly discernible semantic component to the overall meaning of the phraseme (Example: _live in the lap of luxury_). These phrasemes will be referred to as *VPhr*. The second group consists of 215 utterances, each containing a phraseme headed by a light verb. These phrasemes will be referred to as *vPhr*. In a vPhr, the semantic core of the phraseme is carried by the nominal component (Example: _be sorry_).[13] The verb does not add clearly discernible meaning to the overall meaning of the utterance but rather serves the syntactic function of turning the expression into a predicate (Pottelberge 2007; see also Allerton 2001; Butt 2003, 2010; Winhart 2005).[14] For the present paper I included the verbs *be, have, make, get* from English and *sein, haben, machen* from German as heads of light-verb phrasemes. The choice is undoubtedly arbitrary, and more verbs could be included in this group.

4.1 Phrasemes with a Semantically Salient Verbal Head

All seven informants produce phrasemes with a semantically salient verbal head (VPhr) in both their languages with equal ease and there are hardly any cases of transfer or interlanguage forms of the kind found in contexts of foreign language acquisition. In monolingual English utterances the speakers use idiomatic VPhr that do not have a word-for-word translation (8) as well as idioms which can be expressed using the same image in German (9, *Sterne sehen*). In monolingual German utterances the speakers use a wide variety of standard and dialect idioms, some of which they may not have encountered anymore at all after settling in the United States (10 and 11). This shows that all speakers have a well-developed active repertoire of idiomatic expressions in both their languages.

---

13 The German tradition uses the term *Funktionsverbgefüge* mostly for combinations of light verb + noun. As I could not find a difference in mixing behavior between light verb + noun and light verb + adjective combinations, I have decided to treat them as one group, focusing on the semantic lightness of the verb instead of on the syntactic category of the nominal complement. I have also included more complex combinations like *be close with s.o.*, containing a light verb, an adjective, a preposition and an external valency slot.

14 The light verb constructions discussed in this paper should not be confused with the dummy verb constructions frequently mentioned in works on language contact (Myers-Scotton and Jake 2015: 428; González-Vilbazo and Lopez 2011). Light verb constructions are lexicalized phraseological units listed in monolingual dictionaries. Dummy verb constructions are a type of contact phenomenon where a light verb is used to integrate foreign lexical material from one language into another.

(8) KL: *I'm- you know, I'm **keeping my fingers crossed***.

[K3:16]

(9) KL: *I walked right into that door, and fast, because I was in a hurry. **I saw stars***.

[K22:523]

(10) TG: En Abstecher hier und da und/ **den Rahm** überall **abschöpfen**, ne?

[T20:954]

(11) TG: San aa die die, wo die arme Leit alle/ ois abnehme und dann **leben wie Gott in Frankr-Frankreich.**

[T1:890]

In addition to phrasemes in a monolingual context the speakers produce various forms of overt and covert language mixing in and around VPhr. One form of covert language mixing is spontaneous or idiosyncratic calquing, where a phraseme (mostly a collocation rather than a true idiom) is rendered as a word-by-word translation.

(12) TG: Wenn ma nach *California* g'flogen san, des **hat** ja aa **lang g'numme**.

[T16:1144]

In (12) the Bavarian German *hat lang g'numma* is a calque of the English collocation *take long*. Spontaneous calques are unidiomatic in monolingual standard usage and are not listed in idiomatic dictionaries.[15] The calques that are produced by the speakers are limited to a few recurring items which seem to have become established within the speaker community. Apart from those few established calques, the speakers seem to notice their own spontaneous calques and make an effort to repair them:

(13) TG: *Because, for the children's sake you have **to bring a- a little sa/** you have to sacrifice something.*

[Tel:1121]

In (13) the speaker first begins to translate the German phraseme *ein Opfer bringen* (lit. *bring a sacrifice*). The attempt is abandoned, and the speaker starts the sentence over, using the simplex verb *sacrifice*, thus achieving a non-phraseological but native-like wording.

---

15 Traditionally the term *calque* refers to lexicalized items (English *skyscraper* → German *Wolkenkratzer*). The spontaneous word-for-word translations described here are mostly idiolectal nonce formations.

Especially if a VPhr has no translation equivalent, we could assume that it would most likely be embedded as a whole into a clause from another language. In her code-switching studies Myers-Scotton refers to the insertion of a full EL constituent into an ML frame as an *EL island*. She assumes that phrasemes are frequent triggers for EL islands (2002: 157, 162 and 263). From studies of lexical borrowing we know that noun phrases and adverbials are borrowed quite easily. The data confirm this kind of insertion for phrasemes with a noun head or in the function of an adverbial (see examples (1)–(6) above). The borrowing of verbs is more complex, as it usually requires the borrowed item to be adapted to the morphosyntactic requirements of the recipient language (tense, word-order, etc.). With simplex verbs, borrowing along with morphosyntactic adaptation is still quite common (*to google s.th.* < *etw. googeln* < *Er hat etwas gegoogelt*). Yet, when a verb can express its meaning only in combination with at least one lexically predetermined argument, insertion in the form of an EL island does not occur. What we do find is a number of code-switches which in all likelihood are anticipational and triggered by a VPhr (14–15):

(14) TG: Aber ich bin froh. *They **keep an eye on her**, too.* Wenn wie/ irgendwie was wär, die würden ihr helfen.

[T28:22]

(15) KL: ...*but the situation in Osoppo, I think **that really/ that-** des is ma sehr nahe gegangen, I mean I couldn't understand anybody wanting to live like that.*

[K1:164]

In each case the language is switched not only for the VPhr but for the entire clause. In (14) the switch-point coincides with the beginning of a new independent clause. Planning and production difficulties are obvious in (15), where the anaphoric subject *that* of the switched clause is first uttered in the ML, repeated in the ML and then uttered in the EL as *des*. The decision as to whether a language switch was triggered by a phraseme or was due to other factors is undoubtedly subjective. Reasonable cues are hesitation[16], self-correction, hedges or metalinguistic comments, and maybe also the lack of a translation equivalent.

---

16 Code-switching per se is not concomitant with an increase in hesitation phenomena compared to monolingual speech (Ehinger 2003). However, in my corpus phrasemes in bilingual utterances show significantly more hesitation than those in monolingual utterances. This is particularly noticeable around verb-based phrasemes (bilingual utterances: VPhr 56% and vPhr 41%; monolingual utterances: VPhr 18% and vPhr 16%). This suggests significantly higher production costs.

The corpus contains a handful of VPhr where the phraseme as a conceptual unit is clearly attributable to language A but some components of it are realized through words or morphemes from language B. The result is a form of overt language mixing which, for lack of an established term, we will for now refer to as *partial calque*. This is rare and produced only by the speaker TG who, compared to other members of her German-American social group, is most at ease with mixing her languages:

(16) TG: Und dann war's f- für Freudenmädchen. Sin' se *{in}* **line gestanden**! Die Soldaten, die Fl- die die Flotte, die amerikanische, war im Hafen.
[T6:284]

(17) TG: Und mein Vater, der ging mal zur Bank in {New York} **und hat sich *{i-in}-äh line* ge-gestanden**, *to- get to the teller...*
[T29:259]

In both (16) and (17) the underlying phraseme seems to be the English *stand in line*. The verb is realized in German, the perfect tense is selected in accordance with German colloquial norm. The nominal component, *line*, appears in English. It is preceded by the preposition *in*, which in German-English language mixing cannot be assigned to either of the two languages. Such elements are referred to as *homophonous diamorphs* (following Clyne 1967) and are often found at switch points.

The last example in this section is a rare and curious form of covert language mixing which we can call *bilingual contamination*. Contamination is a well-documented phenomenon affecting phrasemes in monolingual contexts where two phrasemes are merged into one (Cutting and Bock 1997; Burger 2015: 26). In our case, one of the phrasemes comes from English, the other one from German:

(18) KL: Ah, des is nett, *well*, dann **gibst ihr viele Grüsse**.
[K8:51]

In (18) the verb from the German phraseme *jmdm. viele Grüße sagen* is replaced by a translation of the English *give*, which is most probably a transfer of the verbal component from the English phraseme *give s.o.'s love to s.o.* The surface lexicalization is entirely monolingual. What makes this example interesting in the given context is that just as in the overtly mixed examples it is the verbal component which is calqued.

So far, we have established that the speakers have a well-developed repertoire of VPhr in both their languages. They use them in monolingual as well as in bilingual turns. If during a turn a speaker wants to use a phraseme from the language which is currently not the ML, he or she switches the language, possibly in anticipation of the phraseme, for the entire clause. The use of VPhr in bilingual clauses in the form of overt mixing is rare and often accompanied by hesitations and repairs. In the following section we will look at verbal phrasemes with a semantically light verb. These show more overt phraseme-internal mixing and thus provide more interesting evidence with respect to the question of compositional processing.

4.2 Phrasemes with a Semantically Light Verbal Head

In this section we zoom in on verb-based phrasemes with *be, have, make, get* from English and *sein, haben, machen* from German as their syntactic head. Some of the phenomena and findings described in the section on VPhr are also applicable to vPhr. The speakers use them with equal ease in both their languages, in monolingual as well as in bilingual turns. Most vPhr occur in monolingual clauses:

> (19) LK: Un' na sag i, *well*, i wollt'- **Mittag** mit dir **mache** heut, un' i hab Zeit.
>
> [L2.518]

> (20) KL: *And afterwards she* **was sorry** *that she didn't buy it.*
>
> [K9.118]

As with VPhr, insertions limited to a vPhr alone do not occur. However, in contrast to VPhr, anticipational switching is not frequent either. There are a few switches following abandoned calques of more idiomatic vPhr:

> (21) KL: Na, aber die war nicht/ *She* **was not** *what we call here* **my cup of tea**.
>
> [K16:38]

In (21) the entire clause is repaired and also the phraseme is flagged as an item specific to American culture by the meta-comment *what we call here*. Although there are no obvious complete calques, there are also a few cases of attempted calquing, abandoned mid-sentence. In these cases, it is not the complete clause that is started over; rather, the repair is limited to the nominal component of the vPhr:

> (22) TG: **Is'** die Elsie Eigel noch **in gut/ {in}** **good shape**, Elsa?
>
> [T28:200]

In (22) the English *be in good shape*[17] is first translated but abandoned at the point where the speaker would have to assign a German gender-specific adjective ending to *gut*. The repair begins with the homophonous diamorph *in*. In the repaired version the verb still remains in the ML, whereas the complete NP is inserted in the EL.

Overt phraseme-internal language mixing in the form of partial calques is found with significant frequency (17% of 215 targets) and across speakers (6 out of 7 speakers):

(23) LK: ...und deshalb si/ **bin** i ja {so} *close* **mit denen**.

[L2:454]

(24) TG: Hätt's ihn grad' runterschlagen können, *because- he* **made himself** {so} **wichtig**, *you know!*

[T29:278]

In (23) the verb of the English vPhr *be close with s.o.* is calqued, as is the preposition *with*. The semantically most salient component, the adjective *close* remains in its original English form. Before the English insertion we have the intensifier *so* as a homophonous diamorph. In (24) the verb of the German vPhr *sich wichtig machen* is calqued, as is the reflexive pronoun *sich*, whereas the adjective *wichtig* remains in its original language. Again, the homophonous diamorph *so* appears between the calqued components and the EL insertion.

All mixed verbal phrasemes appear to follow one consistent mixing pattern: the verb is calqued and the semantic core (mostly a noun or an adjective) appears in the original language of the phraseme. The mixing pattern is not dependent on the language of the phraseme, English or German. The partial calque in (25) will now be discussed in more detail in order to relate this recurrent pattern to the theoretical assumptions about code-switching and language processing outlined in sections 2 and 3.

(25) LK: ...wie mer unser/ uns die Häuser angschaut ham, da wollte mer *sure* **mache**, dass mer e Haus kriege, wo mer e Eckbank neistelle kann.

[L1:42]

The underlying phraseme appears to be the English collocation *make sure*. A possible German translation equivalent is *sichergehen* (literally: *go sure*). Thus, a conflict on the level of lexical congruence could be expected with respect to the

---

17 Whether or not to include the copula verb in the phraseme is a complex issue which for reasons of space is not addressed in this paper (see Fix 1971: 72 and Keller 2014: 195–198).

semantically non-congruent verb rather than the congruent adjective. However, this is the reverse of what we actually see happening: the speaker chooses to calque the semantically incongruent verb *make* as German *machen* and to leave the semantically congruent adjective *sure* in its original form. This suggests that in partial calques superficial lexical equivalence is not the primary force at work. So, what exactly is motivating lexical selection during the production of mixed vPhr?

If there were no morpho-syntactic constraints governing the production of mixed utterances, one could imagine the following alternative renderings of the phraseme *make sure* in a bilingual clause with German as the ML (note: for ease of explication the dialect from the original is adapted to standard German):

(a)   Da wollten wir *make sure*, dass…
(b)   Da wollten wir *sure make*, dass…
(c)   Da wollten wir sicher *make*, dass…
(d)   Da wollten wir *sure make*-en, dass…
(e)   Da wollten wir *sure* machen, dass…

The MLF model provides arguments for why versions (a)–(c) should be dispreferred by a balanced bilingual. The complete EL insertion of the phraseme as in the hypothetical realization given in (a) violates the morpheme order principle, which states that word order must come from the ML. According to the rules of German word-order, the non-finite verb *make* should be preceded by the adjective *sure*. The EL insertion in (b) fixes this problem and follows ML word order. However, it still violates the system morpheme principle: the non-finite EL verb *make* doesn't carry the ML infinitive suffix *-en*.[18] The same holds for the mixed option in (c), which calques only the semantically congruent adjective and retains the original but non-congruent light verb. Option (d) is in line with both

---

18 Myers-Scotton and Jake (2017: 10) refer to French infinitive suffixes as early SMs, based on the observation that in their data French infinitives appear to be inserted along with their French infinitive suffixes. This does not seem to be so for the inserted German and English infinitives in the corpus I used. There are instances where the German infinitive suffix is omitted, e.g. in "Na, *let's* fahr-ø nach England, wegen deine Geschwister und die alle" (Keller 2014: 219). Conversely, when an English infinitive is adapted to German, an infinitive ending is added, e.g. "Zwei *languages* zusammen-*put*-en!" (Münch and Stolberg 2005: 74). Therefore, I am inclined to assume that the German infinitive suffix is a late outsider, which – as all other outsiders – conveys grammatical rather than semantic information.

MLF principles (word-order and outsiders from the ML) but includes word-internal language mixing.[19] The combination in (e), i.e. the one actually produced by the speaker, is the one that optimally solves or integrates congruence issues on the morphosyntactic as well as on the semantic level: word-order and the infinitive marker on the light verb come from the ML (German), satisfying the MLF constraints. The adjective, which carries the semantically salient core of the phraseme, is retained in its original language and inserted as an EL element into the clause. It does not carry any late outsider system morphemes and occurs in a position which does not violate ML syntax.

5 Discussion

The examples provided in section 4 show that the code-switching constraints proposed by Myers-Scotton in her MLF model also hold for phraseological units. So, the study of phrasemes in code-switching lends further support to the model. However, as the subject of this paper is the processing of phrasemes rather than the predictive power of a code-switching model, the crucial question is: what can the behaviour of phrasemes in code-switching tell us about the internal make-up and processing of phrasemes?

Mixed vPhr all show the same distribution of languages: The (light) verb is calqued and produced in the ML of the clause. The nominal component is inserted in its original language.[20] The order of the elements follows the syntactic requirements of the ML. This pattern integrates two challenges in an optimal way. First, retaining the nominal element carrying the semantic weight of the phraseme in its original language serves as a cue for the language-specific multi-word sequence stored in the mental lexicon and helps to convey the intended propositional content to the hearer. Second, calquing of the semantically light verb allows integration of a phraseme from language A into a clausal frame from language B in a manner that does not violate the grammatical rules of language B as

---

[19] Word-internal mixing resulting from the addition of a language-B system morpheme to a language-A content morpheme is commonly observed among early bilinguals during simultaneous acquisition (Lanza 1997). The adult speakers who participated in our study seem to avoid word-internal mixing and use it mainly to achieve a comic effect.
[20] This distribution of languages matches findings presented by Marian (2009: 172), who, without reference to phrasemes, writes that in her data verbs tend towards covert mixing (calquing), whereas nouns are more often overtly inserted. She attributes this to the stronger syntactic relations of verbs with other syntactic constituents in a clause.

proposed in the MLF model. The pattern is repeatedly produced by six out of the seven speakers and is thus not an idiosyncratic feature. The mixing pattern leads to the following hypothesis concerning the roles of semantics and syntax in the production of mixed phrasemes in classic code-switching:

> The lexeme carrying the semantic core of an EL phraseme needs to be produced in its original language as a cue to the language-specific superlemma stored in the mental lexicon. Semantically lightweight elements can be calqued in order to satisfy ML morphosyntactic requirements.

This hypothesis is an empirically derived synthesis of Myers-Scotton's (2002: 240) assumption that the primary function of an EL is to supply content morphemes in mixed constituents and Backus's (2003: 92 and 123) claim that in mixed constituents based on conceptual units ML elements will have semantically basic meanings. It also supports the claim that "basic vocabulary" tends to be calqued whereas "specific vocabulary" will be inserted as an EL form (Backus and Dorleijn 2009: 92).

With respect to language processing, the question now is: How do we get from a language-specific superlemma entry to a mixed phonological realization? With no explicit reference to phrasemes, De Bot proposes the following – fairly vague – suggestion concerning language-sensitivity or -specificity of the levels of speech production:

> [The conceptualizer] is probably partly language-specific and partly language-independent. Further it is hypothesized that there are different formulators for each language, while there is one lexicon where elements from different languages are stored together. The output of the formulator is sent to the articulator, which makes use of a large set of non-language specific speech motor plans.
>
> (De Bot 1992: 1)

Also without reference to phrasemes, Myers-Scotton and Jake (1995: 987) suggest that at the conceptual level, language-specific lemmas are selected and sent to one of the language-specific formulators, which then adds the required predicate-argument structure, word-order and inflections.

Let us assume that the initial[21] step is the same for lemmas and superlemmas: Guided by the intent of the speaker, a language-specific superlemma is selected

---

21 We can avoid the unresolved question of relative timing of the sub-processes if we adopt Jackendoff's Parallel Architecture model, according to which lexical/semantic and morphosyntactic processes run in parallel and influence each other (Jackendoff 1998: 39).

at the conceptual level. According to Sprenger et al. (2006: 167), each component of the superlemma is accessed individually from the mental lexicon, but through one common idiom node. This complex of individual but connected lemmas is sent to one of the language-specific formulators. As we want to explain the language distribution in mixed EL phrasemes, we are interested in the case where an EL phraseme is sent to an ML formulator.[22] The formulator is supposed to project ML argument structure onto the elements it receives from the conceptualizer and to convert lemmas into lexemes and then word forms which can be sent on to the articulator. Under the current assumption that bilinguals might have two separate grammars but only one joint lexicon, it might not be all that surprising that a lemma from one language could be realized by a word-form from the other language, even if this lemma is part of a phraseme. However, the choice of surface language does not appear to be random. Judging from the mixing patterns we find in the data, the choice of word-forms at the formulator level appears to be subject to two constraints, one conceptual-semantic and one morphosyntactic in nature (Tab. 2).

Tab. 2: Assigning surface language to phraseme components

Conceptualizer	A superlemma representing a complete language-specific phraseme is selected from the mental lexicon.	
Formulator	**Morphosyntactic constraint** (Myers-Scotton's SMP) Phraseme components which host late outsider system morphemes activated only at the level of the formulator must come from the ML	**Conceptual-semantic constraint** Semantically salient phraseme components must come from the language with which the phraseme is affiliated in monolingual speech

The morphosyntactic constraint, Myers-Scotton's System Morpheme Principle, holds for classic code-switching in general. The semantic constraint is specifically formulated for phrasemes in code-switching. The two constraints, applicable in parallel rather than consecutively, offer a theoretical explanation for the

---

[22] If an ML phraseme is sent to the ML formulator, we will get a monolingual utterance. If an EL phraseme is sent to the EL formulator, the result will be an EL island. An ML phraseme sent to an EL formulator would not be an option, as it renders the basic idea of having an ML completely mute.

recurring overt language mixing pattern in vPhr. Also, they can help to explain the apparent resistance of VPhr to internal mixing. When an EL vPhr is inserted into an ML clause, the semantically salient element (mostly a noun or an adjective) must be realized in the original language of the phraseme in order to satisfy the semantic constraint. The semantically light verb, which in the actual phonetic string carries a late outsider, can be adapted to ML morphosyntactic requirements by way of calquing (or "literal translation") to satisfy the syntactic constraint. However, if a speaker wants to make use of a VPhr which is not part of the language he or she is currently using as the ML, the verb is semantically salient and thus needs to be realized in the original language of the phraseme. But it also carries a late outsider. Without word-internal mixing the verb cannot be adapted to ML morphosyntactic well-formedness conditions. Therefore, the only solution appears to be anticipational switching of the entire clause. The observed resistance of VPhr to internal mixing might suggest that more idiomatic phrasemes are processed holistically. I don't think this is the case. Rather, the "grammar" of classic code-switching (outsiders have to be supplied by the ML) prevents overt mixing of idiomatic VPhr.[23] The few instances where the speakers start with the production of a mixed or calqued VPhr are quite instructive: The observation that these attempts are often abandoned and rephrased indicate that the speakers are aware of the "unlawfulness" of such translations of phrasemes. And it suggests that the bilingual language monitor checks for idiomaticity not necessarily <u>before</u> but rather <u>while</u> assembling a phraseological unit from individual language-specific lexemes. The abandoned calques show that more idiomatic elements of a phraseme can be calqued individually as well but that the result is rejected by the language monitor.

6 Conclusion

Of 451 verb-based phrasemes analysed for the present study, 20% show overt or covert language contact phenomena, either inside the phraseme (language mixing) or in its direct vicinity (language switching). The analysis has shown that phrasemes are subject to the same morphosyntactic constraints as free combinations of words proposed in the MLF model and the 4-M-Model (Myers-Scotton

---

23 If we look at cases of attrited (or attriting) phrasemes, which for reasons of space have been left out of the discussion, we can observe that in cases where an automatized production route is no longer available, VPhr also appear to be assembled from individual components (Keller 2014: 251–253).

2002; Myers-Scotton and Jake 2017): word order and late outsider system morphemes, i.e. the inflectional morphemes, which only serve a grammatical function, have to be supplied by the ML of the clause. Consequently, the verb, which in German and English carries a late outsider, has to be realized in the ML, at least in speaker groups where word-internal mixing is dispreferred. In contrast to the verb, nominal or adjectival complements can appear in the EL. This distribution of languages based on word-class is reflected in a recurring mixing pattern which is mostly found with inserted EL phrasemes containing a light verb but is also occasionally observable in more idiomatic phrasemes: the noun or adjective which carries the semantic core of the phraseme is realized in the EL, whereas the verb is calqued and produced in the ML of the clause.

The observation that phrasemes in code-switching can be composed of elements from different languages also supports the Superlemma Theory (Sprenger et al. 2006), which claims that the components of a phraseme are accessed individually, but through one common idiom node at the conceptual level. The findings suggest that at the level of the formulator, the production of phrasemes is determined not only by morphosyntactic code-switching constraints but also by phraseme-specific semantic considerations: The semantic core of a phraseme must be produced in the original language of the phraseme, while functional elements, including light verbs, can also be realized in a different language.

A promising next step to test the theoretical modelling of language distribution or language assignment to surface lexemes in mixed phrasemes proposed in this paper would be an extended analysis of more utterances with semantically light verbs as their syntactic head. But of course, there is a lot more to explore in the context of phrasemes and code-switching, for example the status of the copula verb (included in or excluded from the phraseme) or de-automatisation as observable in attrition of phrasemes. Also, the influence of internal and external valency or of semantic compositionality could be analysed in more detail in order to further enhance our understanding of storage and processing of phrasemes.

References

Allerton, David J. (2001): *Stretched verb constructions in English*. Oxford: Routledge.
Ayto, John (2010): *Oxford dictionary of English idioms*. Oxford: Oxford University Press.
Backus, Ad (2003): Units in Codeswitching: evidence for multimorphemic elements in the lexicon. *Linguistics* 41 (1), 83–132.
Backus, Ad & Margreet Dorleijn (2009): Loan translations versus code-switching. In Barbara Bullock & Almeida Jaqueline Toribio (eds.), *The Cambridge Handbook of Linguistic Code-switching*, 75–93. Cambridge: Cambridge University Press.

Bialystok, Ellen & Fergus I. M. Craik (2010): Cognitive and linguistic processing in the bilingual mind. *Current Directions in Psychological Science* 19, 19–23.
Burger, Harald (2015): *Phraseologie: Eine Einführung am Beispiel des Deutschen*. 5., neu bearbeitete Auflage. Berlin: Erich Schmidt.
Butt, Miriam (2003): The Light Verb Jungle. *Harvard Working Papers in Linguistics* 9, 1–49.
Butt, Miriam (2010): The Light Verb Jungle: Still Hacking Away. In Mengistu Amberber, Brett Baker & Mark Harvey (eds.), *Complex Predicates: Crosslinguistic Perspectives on Event Structure*, 48–78. Cambridge: Cambridge University Press.
Clyne, Michael (1987): Constraints on code-switching: how universal are they? *Linguistics* 25 (4), 739–764.
Cutting, J. Cooper & J. Kathryn Bock (1997): That's the way the cookie bounces: Syntactic and semantic components of experimentally elicited idiomatic blends. *Memory & Cognition* 25, 57–71.
De Bot, Kees (1992): A bilingual production model: Levelt's 'Speaking' model adapted. *Applied Linguistics* 13, 1–24.
Ehinger, Anja (2003): *Simultaneous activation of languages: Investigating co-production and hesitation phenomena in bilingual speech*. Tübingen, Univ., MA Thesis.
Fix, Ulla (1971): *Das Verhältnis von Syntax und Semantik im Wortgruppenlexem*. Leipzig: Diss., Karl-Marx-Universität.
González-Vilbazo, Kay & Luis Lopez (2011): Some properties of light verbs in code-switching. *Lingua* 121 (5), 832–850.
Häcki-Buhofer, Annelies (2007): Phraseme im Erstspracherwerb. In Harald Burger, Dmitrij Dobrovol'skij, Peter Kühn & Neal R. Norrick (eds.), *Phraseology: An International Handbook of Contemporary Research*, 854–869. Berlin, New York: De Gruyter.
Havrila, Marek (2009): Idioms: Production, Storage and Comprehension. *philologica.net*. Retrieved from http://philologica.net/studia/20091107224500.htm, accessed September 28, 2019.
Howarth, Peter (1998): Phraseology and second language proficiency. *Applied Linguistics* 19 (1), 24–44.
Jackendoff, Ray (2002): *Foundations of Language: Brain, Meaning, Grammar, Evolution*. Oxford: Oxford University Press.
Keller, Mareike (2014): *Phraseme im bilingualen Diskurs: All of a sudden geht mir ein Licht auf*. Frankfurt am Main: Peter Lang.
Kuiper, Koenraad, Marie-Elaine van Egmond, Gerard Kempen & Simone Sprenger (2007): Slipping on superlemmas: multi-word lexical items in speech production. *The Mental Lexicon* 2 (3), 313–357.
Langlotz, Andreas (2006): *Idiomatic creativity: A cognitive-linguistic model of idiom-representation in English*. Amsterdam, Philadelphia: John Benjamins.
Lanza, Elizabeth (1997): *Language Mixing in Infant Bilingualism: A Sociolinguistic Perspective*. Oxford: Clarendon.
Levelt, Willem J.M. (1989): *Speaking: From Intention to Articulation*. Cambridge, Mass.: Massachussetts Institute of Technology Press.
Levelt, Willem J. M. & Antje Meyer (2000): Word for word: Multiple lexical access in speech production. *European Journal of Cognitive Psychology* 12 (4), 433–452.
Levelt, Willem J. M., Ardi Roelofs & Antje Meyer (1999): A theory of lexical access in speech production. *Behavioral and Brain Sciences* 22 (1), 1–75.

Marian, Viorica (2009): Language interaction as a window into bilingual cognitive architecture. In Ludmila Isurin, Don Winford & Kees De Bot (eds.), *Multidisciplinary Approaches to Code Switching*, 161–185. Amsterdam, Philadelphia: John Benjamins.

Mindt, Dieter (2002): What is a grammatical rule? In Leiv Egil Breivik & Angela Hasselgren (eds.), *From the COLT's mouth ... and others: Language corpora studies - in honour of Anna-Brita Stenström*, 197–212. Amsterdam, New York: Rodopi.

Moon, Rosamund (1998): *Fixed Expressions and Idioms in English*. Oxford: Oxford University Press.

Münch, Alexandra & Doris Stolberg (2005): "Zwei languages zusammenputten": Bilingual ways of expressing bicultural identities. In Bent Preisler, Anne H. Fabricius, Hartmut Haberland, Susanne Kjærbeck & Karen Risager (eds.), *The Consequences of Mobility*, 71–79. Roskilde: Roskilde University: Department of Language and Culture.

Myers-Scotton, Carol (1997): *Duelling languages: Grammatical structure in codeswitching*. Oxford: Clarendon.

Myers-Scotton, Carol (2002): *Contact linguistics: Bilingual encounters and grammatical outcomes*. Oxford: Oxford University Press.

Myers-Scotton, Carol (2005): Supporting a Differential Access Hypothesis: Code switching and other contact data. In Judith F. Kroll & Annete M. B. deGroot (eds.), *Handbook of bilingualism. Psycholinguistics approaches*, 326–358. New York: Oxford University Press.

Myers-Scotton, Carol (2006): *Multiple Voices: an introduction to bilingualism*. Oxford: Wiley-Blackwell.

Myers-Scotton, Carol & Janice Jake (1995): Matching lemmas in a bilingual language competence and production model: evidence from intrasentential code switching. *Linguistics* 33, 981–1024.

Myers-Scotton, Carol & Janice Jake (2000): Four types of morpheme: evidence from aphasia, code switching, and second-language acquisition. *Linguistics* 38, 1053–1100.

Myers-Scotton, Carol & Janice Jake (2009): A universal model of code-switching and bilingual processing and production. In Barbara Bullock & Almeida Jaqueline Toribio (eds.), *The Cambridge Handbook of Linguistic Code-switching*, 336–357. Cambridge: Cambridge University Press.

Myers-Scotton, Carol & Janice Jake (2015): Cross-language asymmetries in code-switching patterns: Implications for bilingual language production. In John W. Schwieter (ed.), *The Cambridge Handbook of Bilingual Processing*, 416–458. Cambridge: Cambridge University Press.

Myers-Scotton, Carol & Janice Jake (2017): Revisiting the 4-M model: Codeswitching and morpheme election at the abstract level. *International Journal of Bilingualism* 21 (3), 340–366.

Namba, Kazuhiko (2012): *English-Japanese Code-Switching and Formulaic Language: A Structural Approach to Bilingual Children's Interactions*. Saarbrücken: Lambert Academic Publishing.

Paradis, Michael (2004): *A neurolinguistic theory of bilingualism*. Amsterdam, Philadelphia: John Benjamins.

Pottelberge, Jeroen van (2007): Funktionsverbgefüge und verwandte Erscheinungen. In Harald Burger, Dmitrij Dobrovol'skij, Peter Kühn & Neal R. Norrick (eds.), *Phraseology: An International Handbook of Contemporary Research*, 436–444. Berlin, New York: De Gruyter.

Röhrich, Lutz (2010): *Lexikon der sprichwörtlichen Redensarten*. Freiburg: Herder.

Scholze-Stubenrecht, Werner (2013): *Duden – Redewendungen*. Berlin: Dudenverlag.

Sinclair, John (2011): *Collins COBUILD idioms dictionary*. Glasgow: Harper Collins.
Spears, Richard (2005): *McGraw-Hill's dictionary of American idioms and phrasal verbs*. New-York: McGraw-Hill.
Sprenger, Simone A., Willem J. M. Levelt & Gerard Kempen (2006): Lexical access during the production of idiomatic phrases. *Journal of Memory and Language* 54, 161–184.
Tracy, Rosemarie & Elsa Lattey (2010): '*It wasn't easy but* irgendwie äh da hat sich's rentiert, net?': a linguistic profile. In Michaela Albl-Mikasa, Sabine Braun & Sylvia Kalina (eds.), *Dimensionen der Zweitsprachenforschung/Dimensions of Second Language Research. Festschrift für Kurt Kohn*, 53–73. Tübingen: Narr.
Wei, Longxing (2009): Code-switching and the bilingual mental lexicon. In Barbara Bullock & Almeida Jaqueline Toribio (eds.), *The Cambridge Handbook of Linguistic Code-switching*, 270–288. Cambridge: Cambridge University Press.
Winhart, Heike (2005): *Funktionsverbgefüge im Deutschen: zur Verbindung von Verben und Nominalisierungen*. Tübingen, Univ., Diss.
Wray, Alison (2012): What do we (think we) know about formulaic language? An evaluation of the current state of play. *Annual Review of Applied Linguistics* 32 (1), 231–254.
Wray, Alison & Kazuhiko Namba (2003): Use of formulaic language by a Japanese-English bilingual child: a practical approach to data analysis. *Japan Journal for Multilingualism and Multiculturalism* 9 (1), 24–51.
Wray, Alison & Michael R. Perkins (2000): The functions of formulaic language: an integrated model. *Language & Communication* 20, 1–28.
Wörterbuch für Englisch-Deutsch und andere Sprachen (2002–2018). Retrieved from https://www.dict.cc, accessed September 28, 2019.
Wörterbuch für Redensarten, Redewendungen, idiomatische Ausdrücke, Sprichwörter, Umgangssprache (2001–2018). Retrieved from https://www.redensarten-index.de, accessed September 28, 2019.

Part IV: Earlier/Historical Stages of Language Development

Marie-Luis Merten
Insights into a Changing Communal Constructicon

Legal Writing in the Late Middle Ages and Early Modern Period

Abstract: The paper examines legal writing in the Late Middle Ages and Early Modern Period from a diachronic perspective. The underlying corpus consists of Middle Low German law codifications of the period from 1227 until 1567. Applying a constructionist approach, the focus lies on evolving and changing constructions (of legal writing). The corpus-based examination reveals insights into the changing communal constructicon. This communal constructicon can be seen as a repertoire of constructions shared by legal writers (of that time). Due to observable language elaboration processes, this repertoire – modelled as a socio-cognitive network – becomes increasingly complex and literate over time. Language elaboration is a type of language change closely linked to written usage. In this context, the obvious nexus between legal writing and language elaboration plays a crucial role.

1 Introduction

From a diachronic point of view, the paper aims to discuss (vernacular) legal writing in the Late Middle Ages and Early Modern Period. Thereby, focusing on e-merging and evolving form-meaning pairs – constructions in the sense of Croft (2001) – as literate entities. From the perspective of corpus analysis, form-meaning pairs can appear as formulaic patterns in different corpora. Literate constructions emerge via processes of language elaboration (Maas 2008: 333). This type of language change is closely linked to writing and contexts surrounding the production of written documents. Especially legal texts – e. g. urban law codifications – can reveal interesting insights into this phenomenon. Within the period of investigation (1200–1600), legal texts have to meet growing requirements: They need to be as explicit and unambiguous as possible (Hiltunen 2012), but they must also construe an increasing number of varying legal situations and circumstances in a schematic and often compacted way (Tophinke 2009: 175–176,

2012). Subsequently, numerous literate form-meaning pairs coping with these demands evolve. Obvious examples are prepositional constructions (propositional integration) or different types of complex sentences (linking propositions to one another). Here, constructional changes and constructionalizations can be seen. Moreover, they serve as markers for a changing communal constructicon, a sociocognitive network of form-meaning pairs shared by legal writers of that period. Since the focus of research is on Middle Low German legislative documents, the paper not only deals with new data but also takes into account a much neglected historical language (Hundt and Lasch 2015: 3). Around the year 1600 – before the written language shift towards Early New High German was completed –, this historical stage of contemporary and nowadays (mostly) only spoken Low German had been highly elaborated. Following Maas (2009: 170), Middle Low German in those days was "fit to replace Latin in all linguistic domains". In the Early Modern Period, Middle Low German was a far-reaching and wide-spread written language: It functioned as the *lingua franca* of the Hanse area.

To capture the historical-diachronic dimension of elaboration processes, the corpus underlying this study consists of 13 urban law codifications from between 1227 and 1567. Overall, it includes 244,140 words, whereby the shortest legal text (statutes of Werl of 1324) consists of only 1,400 words, the longest one (the urban law of Cleve from 1424/40) of about 70,000 words (for further infomation about the corpus cf. Merten 2018: 286–289). The qualitative research design includes the following steps and sub-objectives: (1) exploring the texts in their structural character and specific functionality (to regulate urban life), (2) identifying form-meaning pairs (in their function in legal texts) and (3) tracing their development over time (constructional change). Although the study is primarily qualitative in nature, frequencies of occurrence and changes of frequency can serve as important indicators: They indicate which recurrent patterns are most likely to have constructional status and where/when changes have presumably taken place. Beyond that, identified constructions and formulaic patterns – e. g. multiword expressions as construction evoking elements – are investigated regarding their social dimension. Here, it is relevant to consider an evolving legal style (Schwyter 1998: 190; Coupland 2007), for example, providing an explanation for retaining complex constructions that remain unchanged (e. g. theme indicating constructions).

The structure of this paper is as follows: Section 2 introduces language elaboration as a fundamental process of language change brought about by written usage. Cultural, cognitive and structural aspects of textualization phenomena are discussed and, in so doing, the language-historical setting is recapitulated. Section 3 provides an overview of key aspects of (diachronic) Construction Grammar research. The focus lies on (1) processes of constructionalization and constructional change and (2) the emergence and nature of communal constructica. In this context, pragmatic associations between certain linguistic entities – constructions – and typical usage events play a crucial role. Section 4 offers a closer look at the evolvement of Middle Low German legal writing (constructions) during the period of investigation. Selected examples are presented and discussed: firstly, restrictive constructions to construe exceptions to previous legal norms (section 4.1), and, secondly, theme indicating constructions (section 4.2). Section 5 briefly summarizes main aspects of the paper and gives an over- and preview of ongoing and further work (DFG-funded research project InterGramm).

2 Cultural, Cognitive and Structural Textualization: Language Elaboration and Legal Writing

The Late Middle Ages and Early Modern Period are mainly characterized by a growing importance of (vernacular) writing and written documents. Written texts play an increasingly integral role in cultural memory (Assmann 1992: 52). As a pivotal form of mediation, written records preserve knowledge detached from contexts of its production. Not only are written texts essential for recording knowledge but also for its transmission and dissemination.[1] Law serves in this context as the domain par excellence: In the (Late) Middle Ages, urban life becomes increasingly complex, social relations grow and more and more legal claims are made. At this point, law serves as an (establishing) institution to control and regulate social situations and legal matters – e. g. how to behave as heir, seller, purchaser and so forth and what kind of punishment to expect when committing different crimes. Consequently, the older Latin law (not tailored to urban needs) is replaced by vernacular legal writing (Deutsch 2013; Wallmeier 2013; Warnke 1999).[2] A rising number of urban communities starts to write down their

---

[1] See Ong (1986: 38) in this context: "Knowledge itself is not object-like: it cannot be transferred from one person to another physically even in oral communication, face-to-face, or a fortiori in writing. [...] Since knowledge cannot be physically transferred verbally from one human person to another but must always be created by the hearer or reader within his or her own consciousness, interpretation is always in play when one listens or when one reads."
[2] Maas (2009: 169) points out the following: "It took a long time to elaborate the vernacular languages so that they could articulate complex literate texts, and Latin served as the model:

own municipal law, using already existing codifications of other cities as model. This growing use of the vernacular language for formal occasions and functions marks the starting point for the gradual rise and conventionalization of literate form-meaning pairs – viewed as processes of constructionalization and constructional changes as they are discussed in the following section in greater detail.

However, several further developments need to be pointed out as they have an impact on the constructional/structural dimension of legal writing, e. g. changing practices of reception: While the oldest Middle Low German law texts were meant to be read out to the public, the newer ones were meant to be read in silence to oneself (Erben 2000: 1585). This development from being read out to the urban community towards silent reading – as an adjustment of perspective – is accompanied by several structural developments (Szczepaniak 2015: 109). It becomes increasingly important to produce texts "that will be consistent and defensible when read by different people at different times in different places" (Chafe 1982: 45). Correspondingly, structures supporting the independent comprehension of face-to-face contexts (have to) evolve (Maas 2009: 166): complex sentence types (e. g. subordinate constructions), modifying prepositional schemata, written text organizing constructions, several attributive techniques resulting in complex noun phrases and so on:

> Written discourse develops more elaborate and fixed grammar than oral discourse does because to provide meaning it is more dependent simply upon linguistic structure, since it lacks the normal full existential contexts which surround oral discourse and help determine meaning in oral discourse somewhat independently of grammar.
>
> (Ong 1982: 37)

Moreover, legal writing undergoes a noticeable professionalization within the period of investigation: Legal writers become experienced practitioners sharing their established and further elaborating routines of producing legislative texts. Urban chancelleries turn progressively into institutions of professional writing. At the same time, the proportion of citizens able to read increases over the Late Middle Ages (Maas 2001: 85; von Polenz 2000).

Consequently, numerous textualization phenomena at different levels start to emerge. The interwoven and corresponding dimensions are: the cultural, the cognitive-conceptual and the structural level (Schwyter 1998; Raible 1998). Structural textualization relates to the language-internal dimension. It manifests itself

---

Latin texts were 'sparring partners' for writers struggling to cope with these tasks. They had to calque Latin structures until a flexible literate grammar was also available in languages like German."

in the shape of grammatical and lexical elaboration (Koch and Oesterreicher 2007; Weber 2010), but is linked to the higher cognitive-conceptual textualization. Cognitive-conceptual textualization phenomena present themselves as (1) a "conceptual change of a whole discourse tradition from spoken to written" (Schwyter 1998: 190), but they also refer to (2) an increase in literate thinking (Raible 1998: 175). Writing makes a huge impact on thinking, it enables an intensive reflection on the text being produced, its planning and revision without communicative pressure. On the whole, structural and cognitive-conceptual textualization are driven by but also function as driving forces for a superordinate cultural textualization as "a culture's increasing use and acceptance of writing and literate modes" (Schwyter 1998: 190). As a consequence, literate societies (Goody 1986: 26) emerge, a form of community mainly based on and shaped by literacy (manuscript culture).

In sum: As has already been stated at several points, language elaboration is closely linked to writing and is a continuous development. Already existing constructions change and new literate form-meaning pairs emerge. From a grammatical point of view, constructionally complex schemata belonging to the formal register appear and evolve. The term *literate* refers to a linguistic coding in the form of sentences, the (functional) focus is on "addressing a generalized 'other', e. g. not presupposing a cooperative other for making sense of what is said, not relying on the situational context" (Maas 2009: 165–166).[3] When we look at the range of evolving construction types, we can distinguish at least three phenomena of grammatical language elaboration (Merten 2018: 273): (1) the genesis of complex sentences/subordination (syntactically complex constructions), (2) the evolvement of integrating constructions (propositional integration, text compression) and (3) the gradual rise of constructions supporting the organization of written text (e. g. several coordinating constructions).

---

3 Maas (2001: 94) differentiates between orate and literate structures as follows: "One dimension of these style differences is explicitness or formality. At one extreme it is a strictly context-bound structure of utterances under control of face-to-face interaction, leaving most of what is said implicit. At the other extreme it is context-free articulation of an utterance, submitted to the formal demand of completeness with every piece to be articulated as a grammatical sentence, and permitting the reproduction of identical utterances in different context."

3 The Emerging Communal Constructicon: Constructionalization and Constructional Changes

Before discussing the rise and change of constructions within Middle Low German legal writing, I will briefly introduce what constructions are and give a short summary of the most important aspects concerning constructions in use. Constructions are (cognitively stored) pairings of a meaning with a (mainly verbal) form. Moreover, their idiomaticity and/or high frequency in usage has to be emphasized:

> Any linguistic pattern is recognized as a construction as long as some aspect of its form or function is not strictly predictable from its component parts or from other constructions recognized to exist. In addition, patterns are stored as constructions even if they are fully predictable as long as they occur with sufficient frequency.
>
> (Goldberg 2006: 5)

Modelled as "formulaic, fixed sequences" (Bergs and Diewald 2008: 1), constructions differ in terms of complexity, schematicity and productivity (Goldberg 2006: 5). They range from single lexical entities (words) or morphemes with grammatical meaning to complex constructions with several schematic slots (e. g. argument structure constructions) being filled in usage. In this regard, not only does their form vary from simplex to complex but their meaning or function can also be to a greater or lesser extent specific/abstract (Ziem 2018: 9; Croft 2001: 17). Ziem and Boas (2017: 275) point out that so-called CEEs (construction evoking elements) can make up the lexical anchors of varying constructions. In view of partially specific constructions – the focus of section 4 –, CEEs often fill those slots that are lexically fixed. In some cases, complex multiword expressions serve as evoking elements (Merten 2018: chapter 4). Overall, CEEs – whether lexical or grammatical/schematic – assume a decisive role in the constitution of constructional gestalts. They can thus project subsequent components or lead to a reinterpretation of preceding elements.

New form-meaning pairs arise due to (changing) communicative needs and are formed by communicative circumstances. Through language use, both form and meaning of a construction are subject to variation and change (Hoffmann and Trousdale 2011; Hilpert 2011, 2013; Filatkina 2014). In this regard, the majority of constructionist approaches – e. g. Cognitive Grammar, Radical Construction Grammar and Cognitive Construction Grammar – can be described as usage-based models (Hoffmann and Trousdale 2011: 4), following the guiding maxim that usage of a language shapes its structure and engenders change (Bybee 2010: 194; Langacker 2010: 94):

> Unlike most other modern theories of linguistics, cognitive linguistics is a usage-based model of language structure (Langacker 1987: 46; 2008: 220). In other words, we posit no fundamental distinction between 'performance' and 'competence', and recognize all language units as arising from usage events. Usage events are observable, and therefore can be collected, measured, and analyzed scientifically (Glynn 2010: 5-6). In this sense, cognitive linguistics has always been a 'data-friendly' theory, with a focus on the relationship between observed form and meaning.
>
> (Janda 2013: 2)

Consequently, realized constructions – constructs – are the "locus of linguistic innovation and subsequent change" (Trousdale 2013: 511). Emerging constructions may allow for a varying construal. This notion from Cognitive Grammar highlights the ability to construe one situation in different (linguistic) ways (Langacker 2015: 120). Linguistic meaning always encompasses both conceptual content and construal:

> Content and construal are equally important aspects of the processing activity that constitutes linguistic meaning. They cannot be neatly separated (indeed, the selection of content is itself an aspect of construal). The rationale for distinguishing them is that the apprehension of a situation is more than just a representation of its elements. While content and construal are ultimately indissociable, the distinction draws attention to the flexibility of conception and the variability of expression even in regard to the same objective circumstances.
>
> (Langacker 2015: 121)

For example, one conceptual content (CELEBRATE) can be construed as process (*celebrate*) or thing (*celebration*); a shift in profile[4] takes place:

(a) *We celebrated all night.*
(b) *The celebration was great.*

Depending on the communicative intentions, propositions and their relations can be construed differently – e. g. as a complex prepositional phrase (thing profile) or as a subordinate clause (process profile) – with the result that divergent images emerge (Langacker 2008: 55). Construal has to be viewed as a "multifac-

---

4 Cf. Langacker (2008: 98): "[W]hat determines an expression's grammatical category is not its overall conceptual content, but the nature of its profile in particular."

eted phenomenon" (Langacker 1999: 5), encompassing the dimensions of specificity, focusing, prominence and perspective. All of these conceptual factors have in fact "manifestations in other sensory modalities" (Langacker 2015: 121), they rely on fundamental perceptive phenomena. In this context, Langacker (2015: 121) underlines the "primacy of vision and the grounding of cognition in perceptual and motor interaction".

Back to constructional change: In a diachronic perspective, as has already been pointed out, new constructions emerge and already existing ones are used in new contexts or change with regard to frequency, form or function. They are adapted to changing communicative circumstances (Tomasello 2003: 14). These processes can be accompanied by changes in degree of schematicity, productivity and compositionality. According to Traugott and Trousdale (2013: 20–21), two types of processes can be distinguished in this context: Constructional change has to be differentiated from processes of constructionalization. Whilst constructional change only affects one dimension of a construction (Hilpert 2011: 69, 2013), constructionalization involves the creation of a new form-meaning pair. Newly emerged constructions can make a huge impact on the overall boundary structure of the linguistic system. Viewing this structure as a (mental) network of related constructions – the so-called constructicon (Goldberg 2003: 220) –, emerging entities (form-meaning pairings) form new nodes and can thus change the whole network architecture. Both processes have in common that they are gradual in nature. Normally, only one constructional feature changes at a time and the observable steps are (very) small.[5]

> A succession of small discrete steps in change is a crucial aspect of what is known as 'gradualness' (Lichtenberk 1991b). We understand 'gradualness' to refer to a phenomenon of change, specifically discrete structural micro-changes and tiny-step transmission across the linguistic system [...]. Synchronically it is manifest in small-scale cariation and 'gradience' [...]. This means that at any moment in time changing constructions contribute to gradience in the system.
>
> (Traugott and Trousdale 2013: 74–75)

Focusing on the underlying corpus, it has to be pointed out that within one single text (as a synchronic form of the language/practice under investigation), the different stages of constructional change can surface as contextually determined variants (Heine and Narrog 2010: 409). Constructions of different ages exist side

---

[5] "While there is no predetermined order for reanalyses at different constructional levels, the hypothesis is that pragmatic changes precede semantic changes; and these meaning changes precede formal changes" (Trousdale 2012: 543).

by side and may be realized by one legal writer in one textual record. Hence, the distinction between synchrony and diachrony is not sharp, rather, synchrony and diachrony have to be viewed as an integrated whole (Bybee 2010: 105; Langacker 2010: 94). Here, the frequency of related constructions can reveal which variants are more or less entrenched and conventionalized at a given time. Generally speaking, a (relatively) high frequency of occurrences mirrors the typicality of the respective structure. From a cognitive point of view, high frequency (on token and/or type level) indicates a high degree of (constructional) entrenchment. A construction is very likely to be an entrenched and conventionalized entity at the time of its frequent usage (Bybee 2010: 81; for a further discussion concerning the connection of frequency, entrenchment and conventionalization see Schmid 2010, 2015). However, Traugott and Trousdale (2013: 5) note that the decision "what level of frequency is sufficient for pattern storage and entrenchment is problematic" and has to be modelled as relative and gradual (see also Langacker 2010: 94). This is particularly the case "in historical work where the textual record is often minimal" (Traugott and Trousdale 2013: 5).

Especially in the framework of usage-based Construction Grammar, constructions as schematized (often formulaic) patterns of language use can be thought of as entities also including information about the communicative usage events they are abstracted from (Langacker 2008: 458; Cienki 2015).[6] Constructions can be enriched by pragmatic associations (Schmid 2014: 253). Repetitive language use contributes to the routinization of pragmatic associations: Due to the recurrent usage of form-meaning pairs in relatively stable communicative circumstances, a linkage between linguistic structures and "occasions when they were uttered" (Schmid 2014: 253) is established and becomes entrenched. This coinedness in discourse complies with the notion of "pragmatische Prägungen" discussed by Feilke (1996). Certain constructions can be "fitted to particular social actions" (Fox 2007: 312) performed linguistically, e. g. headline constructions in the context of (written) text production (Merten 2018: 443–451). In this respect, linguistic entities – single words, complex constructions, etc. – act as "keys adapted to different social contexts" (Maas 2001: 94). Inversely, they function as contextualization cues (Gumperz 1982: 131), evoking different contexts of speaking and writing when realized in actual usage events. They serve, for example, as key components for *doing legal writing* in the Late Middle Ages and Early Modern Period.

Legal writers in the Late Middle Ages and Early Modern Period – as (historical) community of practice – make use of a shared (and evolving) repertoire of

---

6 Cf. also Kristiansen and Dirven (2008); Hollmann (2013).

constructions that are more or less enriched by pragmatic associations. These form-meaning pairings are linked to the usage event of creating legislative texts. As the circumstances and communicative constellations of the production and reception of legal texts alter, the repertoire of legal writing constructions undergoes a change as well. As pointed out in section 2, it becomes more complex and literate. A growing number of literate construal techniques evolves and the communal[7] constructicon – the socio-cognitive network of form-meaning pairs shared by legal writers – is elaborated.

By using these constructions, legal writers present themselves as members of a (professional) community and enact a certain social identity[8]. In this view, community membership is based on shared expertise/skills (Clark 1996: 102; Croft 2000: 939) referring to "the same in different individuals" (Schatzki 2002: 18):

> The term community does not imply necessarily co-presence, a well-defined, identifiable group or socially visible boundaries. It does imply participation in an activity system about which participants share understanding concerning what they are doing and what that means in their lives and for their communities.
>
> (Lave and Wenger 1991: 98)

4 Legal Writing in the Late Middle Ages and Early Modern Period: Examples and Insights

The main function of legal texts, especially of urban law codifications, lies in regulating and controlling urban life. Primarily, they have to construe what happens or has to be considered if a specific act is committed (e. g. murder, robbery, adultery, etc.) or an event has taken place (e. g. death resulting in an inheritance case). Accordingly, conditionality (if X then Y) is a highly relevant semantic relation in this context. Several conditional construal techniques in their usage and change are discussed in Merten (2017, 2018) or Tophinke (2009, 2012). But an evolving distinctive legal style seems also to appear in the form of restrictive (sec-

---

7 See Croft (2000: 94) for the similar notion of communal lexicon as a "specialized vocabulary for a particular domain of shared expertise".

8 Social identities are co-constructed within communities of practice: "In this view, as individuals interact with others in shared social practice, their actions – including common ways of speaking – shape and are shaped by their social identities" (Mallinson and Childs 2005: 1).

tion 4.1) and so-called theme indicating constructions (section 4.2). In the following sections, the focus will be on partially specific constructions and formulaic[9] expressions such as *it si denn (dat)* ('unless') or *were it sake dat* ('was it the case that') that serve as construction evoking elements (section 3). While the different slots of the respective constructions can be filled with varying contents/propositions depending on the legal scenario to construe/to regulate, these CEEs are relatively stable entities – 'relatively stable', because they are – on closer inspection – (also) subject to change.

4.1 Construing Restrictive Relations: *it ne si dat-* and *it si denn (dat)*-Constructions

Restrictive relations concern exceptions to (often) previously coded content. The oldest restrictive construal possibility realized in the (older) investigated legal texts is the exceptive clause. It is also discussed for Middle High German by Paul et al. (2007: 402). Structural properties evoking this construction (type) are the mononegation – often expressed by the negation particle *ne/en* – and the subjunctive (finite verb of the respective clause). These features are highlighted by bold print in the following examples:

(1) he heuet sine hant verloren he **ne moge** se weder kopen weder dat gerichte
'he has lost his hand, unless he can buy/purchase it against the law court'

(Braunschweig 1227)

(2) Dhes ne scal ene de uoghet nicht weldeghen . he **ne winne** it mit rechte
'Therefore, the bailiff shall not put him into possession, unless he wins it with law (justifiably)'

(Stade 1279; I:7)

In (early) Middle Low German, the mononegation can serve as a marker for restriction/exceptions because the contemporary negation of propositions is commonly realized by polynegation (cf. Breitbarth 2014 for the change of negation in Middle Low German). This exceptive clause as a restrictive construal technique is much more grammaticalized but less explicit than the emerging *it ne si dat*-construction – whereby *si* can be replaced by *were* ('was'). The *it ne si dat*-construc-

---

9 Cf. Wray (2002, 2008).

tion gradually evolves during the 13th/14th centuries as the polynegation for negating (propositions and so forth) is replaced by mononegation. In consequence, the *it ne si dat*-construction represents an increasingly used linguistic option for construing an exception to preceding legal norms.

The multiword string *it ne si/were dat* – as lexical component of the relational construction – can be classified as a formulaic entity. Needless to say, the writing/spelling variation in historical times has to be considered in this context. The lexical entity encompasses the expletive *it*, the negation particle *ne/en*, a (mainly) subjunctive finite form of the copular verb *sin* ('to be') and the primary subjunction *dat*. Presumably, due to repetition in usage and thus frequency effects, chunking and fixing of a specific form of the exceptive clause – the recurrent instantiated predicative structure *it **ne si** dat* X – has taken place here:

> Once word sequences such as *be going to* or *in spite of* have become frequent enough to be accessed from cognitive storage and produced as units, they begin to become autonomous from the words or morphemes that compose them. Both chunking and increase in autonomy are gradual processes, and the formation of a chunk (a storage and accessing unit) does not necessarily mean that speakers are no longer aware of the component parts and their meanings. That is, a sequence of words can become automated as a chunk through usage while a transparent relationship with the words in other contexts is maintained.
> (Bybee 2011: 71)

The formulaic expression *it ne si/were dat* is used as a relating entity. Owing to its fixing and (presumable) reinterpretation, we can assume one overarching and non-compositional grammatical meaning that is undoubtedly more than the sum of its component parts (expletive *it* + negation particle + copular verb + subjunction *dat*). This functional word group construes the constraining relation between a (previous) content X (schematic slot I) and the content Y following this multiword string (schematic slot II). Subsequently, the syntagma *it ne si/were dat* + content Y (exception) is typically placed at the end of more or less complex paragraphs and articles (example 3). Sometimes, modifying adverbs are integrated into this multiword string, for example the form *also* ('therefore/thus', example 4):

> (3) Hebbet lude lengu+ot in samender ha(n)t · sterft der en / de len eruen heuet · de binnen iren iaren sin · wat men van ireme gu+ode vp nemet · dat scal men in weder gheuen wanne se to iren iaren komet · **It ne were dat** kost vp dat gu+ot ghe draghen were · de men redeliken bewisen mochte · der men nicht vmme ghan ne mochte · des scolen se ire del ghelden
> 'If people have fief together: If one of them dies who has fief heirs who are under their years: What one takes from their property, one shall give them back this property,

when they come to their years. **Unless (it is the case that)** costs for the property incurred, one can prove in accordance with the legal norm, one could not avoid, they have to pay their share of it'

(Goslar 1350; Guardianship, § 9; Lehmberg 2013: 155)

(4) Hebben ſe ouer nene kyndere to ſamende. vnde is de man voruluchtich. ſo nemet ſe ere medegyft to voren vt. van deme anderen ſchal me ghelden de ſchult. **It en ſi alzo dat ſe mede ghelouet hebbe**. Wante denne mo+et ſe mede ghelden
'If they have no children together and the man is volatile, then, she removes her dowry afore. One shall pay the debt by the other. **Unless (it is thus the case that)** she has promised. Because then she has to pay'

(Oldenburg 1400; § 46)

It ne si/were dat provides not only the lexically fixed content of this restrictive form-meaning pair, it also serves as a construction evoking element (discussed in the previous section 3). Furthermore, *it ne si/were dat* can function as the profile determinant of a conditional construal technique: Legally recorded exceptions are often accompanied by construing what has to happen when the exceptional case comes to pass. In this way, *it ne si/were dat* relates a causing entity (exceptional case) and a thereby caused/initiated entity (consequence of the exceptional case) – both part of the construction[10] – as can be seen in both examples 3 and 4.

We can also find evidence for *it ne si/were dat*-constructs combined with the exceptive adverb *denne/dan* ('except/but'). To be precise, these instances show a fusion of the two form-meaning pairs – the *it ne si dat*- and the *denne*-construction. Accordingly, the restrictive meaning is intensified as two restrictive techniques fuse:

(5) Ersloghe auer vser borghere en enne gast dod, dat scholde in sodanem rechte bliuen, alse dat wente her to ghestan heft · also dat de rad dar nene veste vmme don scholde · **it en were denne dat** de rad den gast ghe velighet hedde
'But, if one of our citizens slays a visitor, that has to remain in such a law as this has remained until now, namely, that the council therefore should undertake no fortification. **Unless (it is the case that)** the council had protected the visitor'

(Goslar 1350; Breach of the Peace, § 146; Lehmberg 2013: 325)

(6) Item Soe wylch(er) vand(en) ii vand(en) Raide dye sy dan dair inne wroegeden(n) dye en sall dan dair voir nyet neen seggen(n) **then we(re) dan dat** sy wroegeden(n) van segge worden offt van hoer(e)n seggen(n)

---

10 These more or less schematic entities – e. g. causing entity and caused entity – are part of the complex construction. They (can) show a specific word order (verb-final, verb-second, etc.) that can alter over time.

> 'Item Which one of the two council commissioners, who they reprimand then, he cannot make an appeal to it, **unless (it is the case that)** they reprimanded for a complaint or due to hearsay'
>
> (Duisburg 1518; plate 3, section 12; Mihm and Elmentaler 1990: 116)

Examples like these can be found until the early 16th century. In retrospect, they illustrate an intermediate stage in the ascent of the *it si denn*-construction – the most recent restrictive form-meaning pair relating two processual entities. Its constructionalization "can be seen to have arisen from a number of small local changes" (Traugott and Trousdale 2013: 29), so-called "pre-constructionalization constructional changes" (Traugott and Trousdale 2013: 36). According to the observations presented, a multiple inheritance leads to the creation of this (new) form-meaning pair (Trousdale 2013: 511): For at least two functionally related constructions (*it ne si/were dat-* and *denne*-construction) are involved in this constructionalization and they transmit formal and functional characteristics. In addition, the final stage is characterized by (i) the loss/elimination of the negation particle and (ii) the primary subjunction *dat* becoming only an optional element. It can be realized (examples 7 and 8), but it can also be left out (example 9):

(7) Wat averst syn liggende Gru+ende / und stahnde Erve / de mach ein Vormunder nicht verkopen / **yt sy denn / dat** der Kinder u+eterste Noht datsu+elvige erforderde
'But what his lying properties and standing bequest, a guardian is not allowed to sell those, **unless** the children's extreme misery requires it'

(Dithmarschen 1567; Article 71, § 2)

(8) §.4. It schall averst neen Vormunder der Unmu+endigen Huse / Ho+efe / Ackere / und andere liggende Gru+ende verkopen;
§.5. **It ys denn / dat** der Unmu+endigen Vader den Kindern so vele Schu+elde nahgelahten / dat de beweglyken Gu+eder tho betalinge dersu+elven nicht konden tholangen
'§.4. No guardian shall sell the house, courtyard, field and other lying property of the underaged;
§.5. **Unless** the underaged's father left the children so much debt that the moveable property was not enough for its payment'

(Dithmarschen 1567; Article 22, § 4 and 5)

(9) NEEn Koep ys vo+er besta+endich tho holden / **yt sy denn** darby ein gewis Koepgeld bestemmet
'No purchase is valid, **unless** a certain purchase money is defined thereby'

(Dithmarschen 1567; Article 62, Introduction)

The *it si denn (dat)*-construction can very likely be categorized as a form-meaning pair typical of (historical) legal writing (Paul et al. 2007: 403). In this regard, it contributes to a legal style evolving in the period of investigation. As pragmatic association, this form-meaning pair is part of the (contemporary) communal constructicon (16th century). The development described from the exceptive clause to the *it si denn (dat)*-construction mirrors the changing repertoire of the legal writers. At different periods in time, different construal techniques serve as preferred strategies to construe exceptions – a highly relevant function in the production of legislative texts.

4.2 Indicating an Overall Theme: the *were it sake dat*-Construction and Related Form-Meaning Pairs

In the more recent urban law codifications investigated, a certain construction type (cluster of related constructions) indicating and introducing an overall (text/article) theme is used frequently. Here, the literate entity 'two-dimensional written text' plays a crucial role. The evolved constructions are tailored to this medial form designed for silent reading (as a visual-cognitive practice). From a diachronic viewpoint, a primarily conditional construal technique serves as source for (one micro-construction of) this construction type/construction cluster. But, with regard to the conditional usage, its text position is less restricted (source construction). This conditional form-meaning pair – with the CEE *were it/dat sake dat* meaning 'if' – can occur at different places in the article/paragraph.

> (10) Vortmer **wer dat sake dat** eyn dem anderen scult gheue vor rychte eder vor den borgheren, [...] bu+ode dey eyn eyt, so eyn solde de andere vort den ghynen vor eyme anderen reychte vmme dey sake nicht mer sculdeghen
> 'Further, **is it the case that** one accuses the other in court or in front of the citizens [...], does he take an oath, then, the other shall henceforth not accuse this one for that issue in another court anymore'
>
> (Werl 1324; § 24)

In constrast, theme introducing/indicating constructions have a relatively fixed position, which is restricted solely to the beginning of a new article or paragraph: At the beginning of the new article/paragraph the lexically fixed entity occurs as CEE (e. g. *were it sake dat*) followed by the theme/topic-slot that can be filled by diverging propositions (processual profile). This constructional characteristic can be viewed as textual coinedness (Feilke 1996: 281–282) implying that this formal feature of theme introducing/indicating constructions – their fixed position – is coined with respect to the written text and its characteristics. In addition, an expansion of function can be seen in these cases. Especially in the land law of Dithmarschen – the most recent legislative text investigated –, the *were it sake dat*-construction (see examples 11 to 13) not only construes a conditional relationship but marks the beginning of diverging articles and introduces their topic(s). Lehmann (1988: 187) has already pointed out that initial position usually indicates the topic of sentences:

> Just as elsewhere, sentence-initial position usually identifies the topic (more precisely, the exposition, in the terms of Lehmann, 1984: ch. V.5) of the sentence. This is well-known from left-dislocated NPs. It is perhaps not so well known that a whole subordinate clause may also provide a topic for the following main clause.
>
> (Lehmann 1988: 187)

In our context, this observation refers not only to sentences but also to more complex textual entities. Moreover, the recurrent multiword string *were it sake dat* (= lexically fixed elements) serves as a salient entity in view of its visual perceptibility; it can be easily perceived (and found in texts when searching for new paragraph beginnings). All in all, this construction type – besides serial numbering of the articles and so forth – is an aid to quick orientation in different parts of comprehensive text. This functional extension is brought about by writing and the two-dimensionality of written records. In the following examples from the land law of Dithmarschen, modifying adverb constructions (e. g. *ok-* ('also') and *aver-* constructions ('but')) can be combined with this complex form-meaning pair:

(11) SO ener Schaden lede dorch syne Kleder / he worde gesteken / effte gehowen / so schall men ehm den Schaden behteren und nicht de Kleder.
§.1. **Were yt Sake / dat** Se ehm ock anders syne Kleder thorehten hedden / dat bewyslyk were / so scho+elen Se ehm desu+elven betahlen / wat se wehrt syn.
§.2. Und de Kleder scho+elen tho der Behoef / ...
'So/when one suffers harm through his clothes, he was stung or hit, then, one shall pay for his damage and not for the clothes.
§.1. **Is it the case that** they also have to refund his clothes in another way, what is proven, then, they shall pay him these, what they are worth.
§.2. And, for this purpose, the clothes shall ...'
(Dithmarschen 1567; Article 101)

(12) §.1. **Were yt ock Sake / dat** dar wol synem Volcke Schuld geve / u+emme jennig Guht / dat ehm entfehret were / dat schall he dohn / ...
'§.1. **Is it also the case that** there [one] likely blames his folks, for that property that was stolen from him, he shall do this ...'
(Dithmarschen 1567; Article 83, § 1)

(13) §.1. **Were yt averst Sake / dat** he yt nicht bewysen konde / scho+elen beyde Ko+eper und Verko+eper schweren / dat eer Koep recht und redelyk / su+ender allen falsch und bedreechlicheit gegahn sy / so hoch alse se seggen ...

'§.1. **But is it the case that** he cannot prove it, both, buyer und seller, shall swear that their purchase has happened fairly and honestly without any falsehood and deception/imposture, as high as they say ...'

(Dithmarschen 1567; Article 67, § 1)

Although at first glance not closely related to each other, other multiword expressions evoking theme indicating constructions in the land law of Dithmarschen (1567) are *begeve yt sick dat* ('does it come to pass that'), *droge yt sick to dat* ('does it happen that') and *befunde it sick dat* ('does it take place that'). However, on closer inspection, they have a number of things in common: Typically, they share a finite verb in initial position (with the meaning potential 'happen/come to pass'), the subsequent expletive *yt/it*, the reflexive pronoun *sick* and the primary subjunction *dat*. On this schematic level, these CEEs are in fact identical and in turn related to the more common *were it sake dat* as a fixed entity. The difference lies in the use of a construction with full verb(s) (*zutragen* ('happen'), *befinden* ('happen'), etc.) and processual profile vs. the use of one with a copular verb and the (legal) noun *sake* ('legal case') that allows a thing profile (section 3).

Interestingly, conditional construal techniques such as the *efft*-construction ('if'-meaning, a conditional relationship is profiled) merge with theme indicating/introducing constructions on the construct level. These fusion examples can be interpreted as supporting evidence for the specific functionality of the latter constructions. As has already been pointed out, it highlights the beginning of a new paragraph and is not only responsible for construing a conditional relationship. This function is realized by the *efft*-construction (examples 15 and 16):

(14) Effte ein Tu+ege Kranckheit halven tho Rechte nicht kamen konde.
Begeve yt sick / dat einer de tu+egen scholde / so schwack und kranck werde / dat he uht syner Behu+osinge vor Recht nicht kamen konde / so schalde Vaget...
'If a witness could not come to the court due to illness.
Does it come to pass that one who shall testify becomes so weak and ill that he cannot leave his house in order to come to court, then, the bailiff shall ...'

(Dithmarschen 1567; Introduction into Article 11)

(15) §.10. **Efft yt sick ock begeve / dat** enner / de Schaden gewunnen hadde / tweerley Worde fo+ehrede / alse / dat he den Schaden des Avendes geve up eenen / und des Morgens up enen andern / ys dat bewyslyk / so schall he ...
'§.10. **If it also comes to pass that** one who suffered damage conducts twofold words, such as that he attributes the damage to one person in the evening and to another in the morning, if this can be proven, then, he shall ...'

(Dithmarschen 1567; Article 94, § 10)

(16) §.3. **Effte sick denn befunde dat** se ehres Gelovens nicht rein / und in ungo+ettlyker Schwermery steken / sick ock eines beteren nicht underwysen / und vanehren Erdohm wolden affleiden lathen / de scho+elen ahne Middel des Landes verwyset werden.
'§.3. **If it takes place that** they [are] not pure of their belief and are found in ungodly rapture, [they] also do not want to be open to conviction and disabused of their error, they shall be expelled from the country without funds.'

(Dithmarschen 1567; Article 2, § 3)

All in all, it is striking that these complex lexical entities are maintained and conserved although less complex alternatives – at least with a conditional meaning – exist. As Hoffmann and Trousdale (2011: 5) note, "if the same content can be expressed by two competing structures and one of these is easier to process than the other, then the simpler structure will be preferred in performance". This consideration supports the very likely assumption of functionally charged form-meaning pairs in the case of the *were it sake dat-*, *begeve it sick aver-*constructions etc. discussed above (theme indicating, visualizing beginning of paragraph/article). In addition, the dimension of social value/meaning (Elspaß 2015) within a language community seems to play a decisive role. In contrast to existing less complex alternatives (*efft-* or *wanne-*constructions), these multiword expressions as CEEs (*were it sake dat*, *befinde it sick dat*, etc.) seem to offer a socio-pragmatic added value (in their simply larger gestalt, their distance marking use of subjunctive verb forms and so forth).[11] In this context, legal writers are alluding to complex forms associated with skillful writing and prestigious language use in the Early Modern Period (Schwitalla 2002). In so doing, they underpin their professionality with the use of highly literate constructions that are part of their communal constructicon and which have evolved through the medium of writing.

5 Conclusion

The paper shed light on language elaboration processes in Middle Low German legal writing, whereby an underinvestigated historical language challenging (common) grammar theories became the central subject of investigation. Due to

---

[11] However, the conservative nature of law needs to be considered in this context: "The law has to be revised constantly so as to keep it up to date with social change. This need for revision, however, does not mean that the language of the law will automatically be updated at the same time. On the contrary: since the law is essentially a conservative institution, it follows that its language is relatively conservative as well. It is therefore not likely to change very quickly." (Hiltunen 2012: 50)

the diachronic research interest, an approach was adopted which was capable of coping with phenomena of language in transition and both formulaic (lexical) expressions and more complex form-meaning pairs between fixedness and variability: (Diachronic) Construction Grammar allows for the detailed description and explanation of changing form-meaning pairs, of observable relations between different constructions (as well as the development of these relations) and elements evoking those linguistic construal techniques (see also Filatkina 2018). Especially, the idiomatic/non-compositional nature of (grammatical) meaning was emphasized. Important processes in language change/usage such as reinterpretation and chunking as well as the idea of tiny-step transmissions played a crucial role. Source and target constructions were taken into account – whenever possible with regard to the underlying corpus – and a case of multiple inheritance where more than one form-meaning pair was involved in the creation of a new construction was discussed.

In particular, the focus was on the functionality of certain evolving constructions with regard to written text(s). Emerging constructions induced by writing can be viewed as literate entities and seem to be more complex than orate form-meaning pairs. They have to be interpretable independent of context and, thus, include all information necessary for comprehension. The nexus of language elaboration processes and legal writing was pointed out. Subsequently, attention was drawn to the adaption of vernacular language to literacy on the basis of urban law codifications produced over a period of more than 300 years (1227 to 1567). The evolving literate form-meaning pairs are increasingly tailored to (the production of) written texts structured for silent reading. In this legal context, important construal techniques concern conditional, causal or restrictive relations and so on. The combining of propositions and the changing ways of relating them linguistically are an interesting object of investigation. Certain constructions seem to be bound to legal writing, they can be modelled as pragmatic associations and are part of the changing communal constructicon of the historical community of legal writers.

InterGramm[12] – a Digital Humanities project at Paderborn University – continues this investigation of language elaboration processes in Middle Low German. Although the focus is on changing constructions, the underlying corpus consists of considerably more texts. Additionally, besides linguists, both computational linguists and computer scientists are part of the project team. By applying a human-in-the-loop approach, we combine phases of (human) expert annotation and machine learning. For the automatic construction tagging, we espe-

---

[12] For further information: https://www.uni-paderborn.de/forschungsprojekte/Intergramm/

cially use (lexical) construction evoking elements. These important elements are (relatively) easily identifiable and useful for hypothesising what kind of construction might be instantiated. Especially in the historical context, annotating linguists have to be aware of a comparative fallacy that emerges when researchers fall into the error of investigating one language by comparing it to another, for example, their native language. The historicity of the language under investigation has to be given serious consideration. Historical languages must be viewed on the basis of their own common structures/constructions, characteristics and functionalities.

References

Primary Sources (Cited Corpus Data)

1227 urban law of Braunschweig: Wilhelm, Friedrich (1932): *Corpus der altdeutschen Originalurkunden. Bis zum Jahr 1300*. Band I: 1200–1282 (Nr. 1-564), 1–5. Lahr: Moritz Schauenburg K. G.

1279 urban law of Stade: Korlén, Gustav (1950): *Das Stader Stadtrecht vom Jahre 1279*, 23–117. Lund: C.W.K. Gleerup.

1324 urban law of Werl: Retrieved from http://www.lwl.org/331-download/Texte/html/20009B.html, accessed August 20, 2018.

1350 urban law of Goslar: Lehmberg, Maik (2013): *Der Goslarer Ratskodex – Das Stadtrecht um 1350: Edition, Übersetzung und begleitende Beiträge*. Bielefeld: Verlag für Regionalgeschichte.

1400 urban law of Oldenburg: Korlén, Gustav (1951): *Das mittelniederdeutsche Stadtrecht von Lübeck nach seinen ältesten Formen*, 170–188. Lund: C.W.K. Gleerup.

1518 urban law of Duisburg: Mihm, Arend & Michael Elmentaler (1990): *Das Duisburger Stadtrecht 1518*. Duisburg: Walter Braun.

1567 land law of Dithmarschen: Retrieved from https://books.google.de/books?id=t88pAAAAYAAJ&pg=PA189&lpg=PA189&dq=Dithmarsisches+landrecht&source=bl&ots=-PyV-dAWXt&sig=Od1rEDzIbfcEvqJ2QDN0tsQTV-8&hl=de&sa=X&ved=0CC0Q6AEwAmoVChMIvInf6tqyxwIV551yCh0ffQAg#v=onepage&q=Dithmarsisches%20landrecht&f=false, accessed August 22, 2018.

Secondary Literature

Assmann, Jan (1992): *Das kulturelle Gedächtnis. Schrift, Erinnerung und politische Identität in frühen Hochkulturen*. München: C. H. Beck.

Bergs, Alexander & Gabriele Diewald (2008): Introduction: Constructions and Language Change. In Alexander Bergs & Gabriele Diewald (eds.), *Constructions and Language Change*, 1–12. Berlin, New York: De Gruyter.

Breitbarth, Anne (2014): *The History of Low German Negation*. Oxford: Oxford University Press.

Bybee, Joan (2010): *Language, Usage and Cognition*. New York: Cambridge University Press.
Bybee, Joan (2011): Usage-based theory and grammaticalization. In Heiko Narrog & Bernd Heine (eds.), *The Oxford Handbook of Grammaticalization*, 69–78. Oxford, New York: Oxford University Press.
Chafe, Wallace (1982): Integration and involvement in speaking, writing and oral literature. In Deborah Tannen (ed.), *Spoken and written language. Exploring orality and literacy*, 35–52. Norwood, New Jersey: Ablex.
Cienki, Alan (2015): Spoken language usage events. *Language and Cognition* 7 (4), 499–514.
Clark, Herbert H. (1996): *Using language*. Cambridge: Cambridge University Press.
Coupland, Nikolas (2007): *Style. Language Variation and Identity*. Cambridge, New York: Cambridge University Press.
Croft, William (2000): *Explaining Language Change. An Evolutionary Approach*. London: Longman.
Croft, William (2001): *Radical Construction Grammar: Syntactic Theory in Typological Perspective*. Oxford: Oxford University Press.
Deutsch, Andreas (2013): Historische Rechtssprache des Deutschen – Eine Einführung. In Andreas Deutsch (Hrsg.), *Historische Rechtssprache des Deutschen*, 21–80. Heidelberg: Universitätsverlag Winter.
Elspaß, Stephan (2015): Grammatischer Wandel im (Mittel-)Neuhochdeutschen – von oben und von unten. Perspektiven einer Historischen Soziolinguistik des Deutschen. *Zeitschrift für germanistische Linguistik* 43 (3), 387–420.
Erben, Johannes (2000): Syntax des Frühneuhochdeutschen. In Werner Besch & Anne Betten (Hrsg.), *Sprachgeschichte. Ein Handbuch zur Geschichte der deutschen Sprache und ihrer Erforschung*, 1584–1593. Berlin, New York: De Gruyter.
Feilke, Helmuth (1996): *Sprache als soziale Gestalt. Ausdruck, Prägung und die Ordnung der sprachlichen Typik*. Frankfurt am Main: Suhrkamp.
Filatkina, Natalia (2014): Constructionalization, Konstruktionswandel und figurative Sprache (sprach)historisch betrachtet. In Martine Dalmas & Elisabeth Piirainen (eds.), *Figurative Sprache – Figurative Language – Langage figuré*, 41–57. Tübingen: Stauffenburg.
Filatkina, Natalia (2018): Historische formelhafte Wendungen als Konstruktionen: Möglichkeiten und Grenzen der diachronen Konstruktionsgrammatik. *Linguistik-Online* 90 (3), 115–143.
Fox, Barbara (2007): Principles shaping grammatical practices. *Discourse Studies* 9, 299–318.
Goldberg, Adele (2003): Constructions: A new theoretical approach to language. *Trends in Cognitive Sciences* 7 (5), 219–224.
Goldberg, Adele (2006): *Constructions at work*. Oxford: Oxford University Press.
Goody, Jack (1986): Funktionen der Schrift in traditionalen Gesellschaften. In Jack Goody, Ian Watt & Kathleen Gough (Hrsg.), *Entstehung und Folgen der Schriftkultur*, 25–61. Frankfurt am Main: Suhrkamp.
Gumperz, John (1982): *Discourse strategies*. Cambridge: Cambridge University Press.
Heine, Bernd & Heiko Narrog (2010): Grammaticalization and Linguistic Analysis. In Bernd Heine & Heiko Narrog (eds.), *The Oxford Handbook of Linguistic Analysis*, 401–423. New York: Oxford University Press.
Hilpert, Martin (2011): Was ist Konstruktionswandel? In Alexander Lasch & Alexander Ziem (Hrsg.), *Konstruktionsgrammatik III. Aktuelle Fragen und Lösungsansätze*, 59–75. Tübingen: Stauffenburg.

Hilpert, Martin. (2013): Corpus-based approaches to constructional change. In Graeme Trousdale & Thomas Hoffmann (eds.), *The Oxford Handbook of Construction Grammar*, 458–477. Oxford: Oxford University Press.
Hiltunen, Risto (2012): The Grammar and Structure of Legal Texts. In Lawrence M. Solan & Peter M. Tiersma (eds.), *The Oxford Handbook of Language and Law*, 39–51. Oxford, New York: Oxford University Press.
Hoffmann, Thomas & Graeme Trousdale (2011): Variation, change and constructions in English. *Cognitive Linguistics* 22 (1), 1–23.
Hollmann, Willem B (2013): Constructions in cognitive sociolinguistics. In Thomas Hoffmann & Graeme Trousdale (eds.), *The Oxford Handbook of Construction Grammar*, 491–509. Oxford: Oxford University Press.
Hundt, Markus & Alexander Lasch (2015): Das Niederdeutsche im Rahmen einer Sprachgeschichte des Deutschen. *Jahrbuch für Germanistische Sprachgeschichte* 6 (1), 3–17.
Janda, Laura (2013): Quantitative methods in Cognitive Linguistics: An introduction. In Laura A. Janda (ed.), *Cognitive Linguistics: The Quantitative Turn. The essential reader*, 1–32. Berlin, Boston: De Gruyter.
Koch, Peter & Wulf Osterreicher (2007): Schriftlichkeit und kommunikative Distanz. *Zeitschrift für germanistische Linguistik* 35 (3), 346–375.
Kristiansen, Gitte & René Dirven (eds.) (2008): *Cognitive sociolinguistics. Language variation, cultural models, social systems*. Berlin, New York: De Gruyter.
Langacker, Ronald (1999): *Grammar and conceptualization*. Berlin, New York: De Gruyter.
Langacker, Ronald (2008): *Cognitive Grammar. A basic introduction*. New York: Oxford University Press.
Langacker, Ronald (2010): Cognitive Grammar. In Bernd Heine & Heiko Narrog (eds.), *The Oxford Handbook of Linguistic Analysis*, 87–110. Oxford: Oxford University Press.
Langacker, Ronald (2015): Construal. In Ewa Dabrowska & Dagmar Divjak (eds.), *Handbook of Cognitive Linguistics*, 120–142. Berlin, Boston: De Gruyter.
Lave, Jean & Etienne Wenger (1991): *Situated Learning. Legitimate Peripheral Participation*. New York: Cambridge University Press.
Lehmann, Christian (1988): Towards a typology of clause linkage. In John Haiman & Sandra A. Thompson (eds.), *Clause combining in grammar and discourse*, 181–225. Amsterdam, Philadelphia: John Benjamins.
Maas, Utz (2001): Literacy in Germany. In David R. Olson & Nancy Torrance (eds.), *The making of literate societies*, 82–100. Malden, Mass.: Blackwell.
Maas, Utz (2008): *Sprache und Sprachen in der Migrationsgesellschaft. Die schriftkulturelle Dimension*. Osnabrück: V&R unipress.
Maas, Utz (2009): Orality versus literacy as a dimension of complexity. In Geoffrey Sampson, David Gil & Peter Trudgill (eds.), *Language complexity as an evolving variable*, 164–177. New York, Oxford: Oxford University Press.
Mallinson, Christine & Becky Childs (2005): Communities of Practice in Sociolinguistic Description: African American Women's Language in Appalachia. *University of Pennsylvania Working Papers in Linguistics* 10 (2), 1–14.
Merten, Marie-Luis (2017): Sociocultural Construction Grammar: Historisches Schreiben. In Meike Glawe, Line-Marie Hohenstein, Stephanie Sauermilch, Kathrin Weber & Heike Wermer (Hrsg.), *Aktuelle Tendenzen in der Variationslinguistik*, 37–66. Hildesheim, Zürich, New York: Olms.

Merten, Marie-Luis (2018): *Literater Sprachausbau kognitiv-funktional. Funktionswort-Konstruktionen in der historischen Rechtsschriftlichkeit*. Berlin, Boston: De Gruyter.
Ong, Walter (1982): *Orality and Literacy*. London, New York: Taylor & Francis Group.
Ong, Walter (1986): Writing is a technology that restructures thought. In Gerd Baumann (ed.), *The written word. Literacy in transition. Wolfson College Lectures 1985*, 23–50. Oxford: Clarendon Press.
Paul, Hermann (2007): *Mittelhochdeutsche Grammatik*. 25. Auflage, neu bearbeitet von Thomas Klein, Hans-Joachim Solms & Klaus-Peter Wegera. Tübingen: Niemeyer.
Polenz, Peter von (2000): *Deutsche Sprachgeschichte vom Spätmittelalter bis zur Gegenwart*. Band I: 14. bis 16. Jahrhundert. Berlin, Boston: De Gruyter.
Raible, Wolfgang (1998): B5 & B12 Die Verschriftlichung der romanischen Sprachen (B5), Volkssprachliche Gattungen im europäischen Mittelalter (B12). In Wolfgang Raible (Hrsg.), *Medienwechsel. Erträge aus zwölf Jahren Forschung zum Thema ‚Mündlichkeit und Schriftlichkeit'*, 163–192. Tübingen: Narr.
Schatzki. Theodore (2002): *The Site of the Social. A Philosophical Account of the Constitution of Social Life and Change*. Pennsylvania: State University Press.
Schmid, Hans-Jörg (2010): Does frequency in text instantiate entrenchment in the cognitive system? In Dylan Glynn & Kerstin Fischer (eds.), *Quantitative methods in cognitive semantics: Corpus-driven approaches*, 101–133, Berlin, New York: De Gruyter.
Schmid, Hans-Jörg (2014): Lexico-grammatical patterns, pragmatic associations and discourse frequency. In Thomas Herbst, Hans-Jörg Schmid & Susen Faulhaber (eds.), *Constructions, Collocations, Patterns*, 239–293. Berlin, Boston: De Gruyter.
Schmid, Hans-Jörg (2015): A blueprint of the Entrenchment-and-Conventionalization Model. *Yearbook of the German Cognitive Linguistics Association* 3 (1), 3–26.
Schwitalla, Johannes (2002): Komplexe Kanzleisyntax als sozialer Stil. Aufstieg und Fall eines sprachlichen Imponierhabitus. In Inken Keim & Wilfried Schütte (Hrsg.), *Soziale Welten und kommunikative Stile. Festschrift für Werner Kallmeyer zum 60. Geburtstag*, 379–398. Tübingen: Niemeyer.
Schwyter, Jürg (1998): Syntax and Style in the Anglo-Saxon Law-Codes. In Christina Ehler & Ursula Schaefer (Hrsg.), *Verschriftung und Verschriftlichung. Aspekte des Medienwechsels in verschiedenen Kulturen und Epochen*, 189–231. Tübingen: Narr.
Szczepaniak, Renata (2015): Syntaktische Einheitenbildung – typologisch und diachron betrachtet. In Christa Dürscheid & Jan Georg Schneider (Hrsg.), *Handbuch Satz, Äußerung, Schema*, 104–124. Berlin, New York: De Gruyter.
Tomasello, Michael (2003): *Constructing a Language*. Cambridge, Massachusetts: Harvard University Press.
Tophinke, Doris (2009): Vom Vorlesetext zum Lesetext: Zur Syntax mittelniederdeutscher Rechtsverordnungen im Spätmittelalter. In Angelika Linke & Helmuth Feilke (Hrsg.), *Oberfläche und Performanz. Untersuchungen zur Sprache als dynamischer Gestalt*, 161–183. Tübingen: Niemeyer.
Tophinke, Doris (2012): Syntaktischer Ausbau im Mittelniederdeutschen. Theoretisch-methodische Überlegungen und kursorische Analysen. *Niederdeutsches Wort* 52, 19–46.
Traugott, Elizabeth Closs & Graeme Trousdale (2013): *Constructionalization and Constructional Change*. Oxford: Oxford University Press.
Trousdale, Graeme (2012): Grammaticalization, lexicalization and constructionalization from a cognitive-pragmatic perspective. In Hans-Jörg Schmid (ed.), *Cognitive Pragmatics*, 533–558. Berlin, New York: De Gruyter.

Trousdale, Graeme (2013): Multiple inheritance and constructional change. *Studies in Language* 37 (3), 491–514.
Wallmeier, Nadine (2013): *Sprachliche Muster in der mittelniederdeutschen Rechtssprache: Zum Sachsenspiegel und zu Stadtrechtsaufzeichnungen des 13. bis 16. Jahrhunderts.* Köln: Böhlau.
Warnke, Ingo (1999): *Wege zur Kultursprache. Die Polyfunktionalisierung des Deutschen im juridischen Diskurs (1200–1800).* Berlin, New York: De Gruyter.
Weber, Beatrice (2010): *Sprachlicher Ausbau. Konzeptionelle Studien zur spätmittelenglischen Schriftsprache.* Frankfurt am Main: Peter Lang.
Weber, Beatrice (2015): „the seid acte, statute or ordenaunve, or eny other made to the contrary, notwithstondyng": Zur Rolle der Faktoren 'Diskurstradition' und 'Sprachkontakt' bei der Etablierung der *notwithstanding*-Konstruktion im Englischen. In Alexander Ziem & Alexander Lasch (Hrsg.), *Konstruktionsgrammatik IV. Konstruktionen als soziale Konventionen und kognitive Routinen*, 225–241. Tübingen: Stauffenburg.
Wray, Alison (2002): *Formulaic Language and the Lexicon.* Cambridge: Cambridge University Press.
Wray, Alison (2008): *Formulaic Language: Pushing the Boundaries.* Oxford, New York: Oxford University Press.
Ziem, Alexander (2015): Desiderata und Perspektiven einer Social Construction Grammar. In Alexander Ziem & Alexander Lasch (Hrsg.), *Konstruktionsgrammatik IV. Konstruktionen als soziale Konventionen und kognitive Routinen*, 1–25. Tübingen: Stauffenburg.
Ziem, Alexander (2018): Construction Grammar meets Phraseology: eine Standortbestimmung. *Linguistik-Online* 90 (3), 3–19.
Ziem, Alexander & Hans C. Boas (2017): Towards a Constructicon for German. *Proceedings of the AAAI 2017 Spring Symposium on Computational Construction Grammar and Natural Language Understanding*, 274–277.

Christian Pfeiffer & Markus Schiegg
Religious Formulae in Historical Lower-Class Patient Letters

Abstract: This article examines the use and functions of religious formulae in historical lower-class letter writing. The data analysed are taken from the Corpus of Patient Documents (CoPaDocs), a new corpus of 19th- and early 20th-century texts written by patients from German psychiatric hospitals. An illustrative investigation of the occurrence and usage of religious formulae allows us to differentiate between explicit and implicit uses and to discuss instances of variation and modification. The functional analysis exhibits predominantly argumentative functions of religious formulae, but also parallelisation, expression of a shared ethos and a text-structural function. Finally, we discuss to what degree the formulae found are corpus specific, for example, resulting from the religious delusions of some patients, or whether they could also be connected to the idea of a cross-linguistic repertoire of formulaic writing.

1 Introduction

> Den gemeinen Mann in Deutschland hört man bei solchen Gelegenheiten, wo er sich besonders feierlich erheben möchte, häufig in den Bibelton verfallen. Bei dem Volke ist die Bibelsprache zur Sprache des täglichen Lebens, zur Sprache des innigeren Familienverkehrs, ja selbst zur Sprache der Liebe geworden, denn selbst in die Liebesbriefe des Volkes, gerade je ernsthafter es der ungeübte Schreiber meint, tritt um so leichter diese biblische Färbung ein […].
>
> (Mundt 1844: 159–160)[1]

In our paper, we discuss the results of a case study on the use and functions of religious formulae in 19th and early 20th century letters written by patients from psychiatric hospitals. In the past, the focus of research on formulaic language has

---

[1] Translation: 'On occasions where he wants to elevate himself in a particularly festive manner, one can hear the common German slipping into the biblical tone. For the common folk, biblical language has become the language of everyday life, the intimate language inside families, and even the language of love, hence even in the peoples' love letters, this biblical tone joins in, which happens, the more wholeheartedly the unroutined writer means it.'

∂ Open Access. © 2020 C. Pfeiffer, M. Schiegg, published by De Gruyter. This work is licensed under the Creative Commons Attribution 4.0 License.
https://doi.org/10.1515/9783110669824-011

mainly been on standard languages and close-to-standard varieties. As a consequence, we see a lack of studies based on text types from non-standard domains, even more so with regard to historical varieties. With the rise of new approaches to the history of language, such as the concept of a language history 'from below' (Elspaß 2005), private letters written by less-experienced writers are now regarded as a particularly valuable source of linguistic data. This is due to the writers' limited literacy: while they obviously do have a command of basic writing skills, they are usually not familiar with producing conceptually written language, or the language of distance in the sense of Koch and Oesterreicher (1985). Such letters hence provide a good opportunity to reconstruct the non-standard varieties of common people and to get "as close as we can [...] to authentic oral registers" (Elspaß 2012: 45). This also holds for investigations into formulaic language.

However, studies on the use of formulaic language in historical letters written by inexperienced writers are quite rare. This may be explained by the – already mentioned – dominant paradigms in the research on formulaic language, but also by a lack of available texts. Despite an increase in schooling and thus writing competence during the 19th century (Elspaß 2005: 76), lower-class people did not usually have a reason to write, either in their private lives or in their professions as farmers, craftsmen, etc. And if they ever wrote to each other, their texts would not usually be transmitted to us, but kept by their families and thrown away after some time.

Situations of separation, however, increased the amount of text production by lower-class people. Emigration played an important role in the 19th century and we have evidence of a large number of letters written by emigrants, especially emigrants to North America, sent home to their families (Elspaß 2005). Soldiers were also far away from their families and wrote home (Langer 2013). Another context of separation in which letter-writing became relevant were the psychiatric hospitals that were established systematically throughout Europe during the 19th century. After their hospitalisation, writing letters permitted the patients to continue personal communication with their spouses, relatives and acquaintances. Hence, patients at these institutions often wrote letters home, but also to the doctors of the hospitals and other recipients. These letters, however, were often not sent out but censored and put into the patients' files as proof of their mental illnesses (cf. Schiegg 2015). The research project 'Flexible Writers in Language History' in Erlangen, Germany, is currently compiling the first corpus of about

2,000 of those letters and other texts written by 19th- and early 20th-century patients from German psychiatric hospitals.[2] This corpus is the empirical basis of our study.

Taking into account the results of other studies, we expect the patients to often resort to formulaic language that, among other things, could support their text production and strengthen their arguments (Elspaß 2005: 174). Furthermore, as religion was a central part of 19th-century everyday life, particularly for rural people from the lower classes, we also assume that their texts will occasionally adopt religious elements (cf. the introductory contemporary quotation). The central purpose of our paper is thus to analyse the usage and functions of religious formulae in the CoPaDocs letters. Since research in the field of 'language in religion' generally shows a lack of studies with a pragmatic orientation (Lasch and Liebert 2014: 478), our study might also be relevant from this point of view.

The paper is structured in the following way. In section 2, we delimit our concept of a *religious formula* and summarise the results of existing research on religious formulaic writing by lower-class people. In section 3, we describe our corpus and the methods used to identify religious formulae in the letters. Sections 4 and 5 discuss the results of our case study. Section 4 gives an overview of the occurrence and usage of religious formulae in the corpus with regard to explicit versus implicit uses, to variation and creative modifications. In section 5, we analyse different functions of religious formulae in the CoPaDocs letters, with a focus on argumentative contexts. The paper ends with a summary of our main findings against the background of existing research on 19th century private letters.

2 Religious Formulaic Language in Lower-Class Letter Writing

2.1 Religious Formulaic Language

Before analysing the uses and functions of religious formulae, it is essential to define our concept of the term *religious formula*. Particularly when dealing with historical data, it is helpful to use a broad definition of formulaicity (Filatkina 2018: 164). We therefore take the often-cited working definition by Wray (2002: 9) as a starting point and consider formulaic any "sequence, continuous or discontinuous of words or other elements, which is, or appears to be, prefabricated: that

---

[2] See the Corpus of Patient Documents (http://copadocs.de, accessed July 5, 2019).

is, stored and retrieved whole from memory at the time of use, rather than being subject to generation or analysis by the language grammar". Expanding this approach, we additionally integrate the view advocated by Stein (1995: 57–58) that pragmatically fixed one-word-utterances can also be regarded as formulaic. The scope of formulaic language thus ranges from one-word-utterances with a specific pragmatic function over multi-word units and fixed sentences to formulaic texts (Filatkina 2018: 30).

A definition as such, however, does not permit a reliable extraction of formulaic material from a text corpus (cf. Wray 2009). To identify formulaic language in texts, we also need an operationalisation of the defining features, i.e. independent criteria that mark a given sequence as prefabricated and hence formulaic. In this context, Wray and Namba (2003: 28) offer eleven diagnostic criteria that can be derived from peculiarities of formulaic units in terms of the four dimensions form, meaning, function, and provenance. Most of these criteria, however, cannot be operationalised objectively either. Rather, it is their function to assist and support the researcher's introspective judgement, to help articulate the basis of his or her intuition and to provide insight into possible biases (Wray 2009: 41). The final decision on the status of an item, however, remains subjective and based on the researcher's intuition.

The second question to be addressed is under which circumstances a given formulaic item can be regarded as religious. A variety of approaches (semantic, discursive, intertextual etc.) could be chosen here.[3] For the purpose of our study, we will focus on the provenance aspect, regarding formulaic items as religious if they are associated with a particular religious source or context. Possible sources here include texts from the scriptures, but also popular textual sources from other religious contexts such as prayers, hymns, liturgies, rites, and texts from the catechism. From a theoretical point of view, the narrowing of the aspect of provenance is certainly simplifying; this reduction, however, is a necessity for a case study like ours.

To be classified as a religious formula in our article, it is not essential that the wording used in the patient letter should be completely identical with an available source text. We can assume that writers did not usually have the particular text at hand when writing. They normally quoted from memory rather than from the original text. Consequently, we also include cases in which the formulation

---

[3] According to Lasch and Liebert (2014: 477), characteristics of the religious domain are distinct objects, a reference to transcendence, and a more or less elaborated metaphysics.

itself is novel but clearly derived from or associated with something that is formulaic in its own right.[4] Thus, we have a continuum of usages, ranking from word-for-word formulae, fully identical with an available version of the original text, through formulae with individual deviations, to allusions and paraphrases, i.e. intertextual references which do not try to recapitulate the original text but merely refer to the content of a certain religious formula (cf. Lange 2012: 100–101; Bartolini 2012). In all these cases, the intertextual character of the formula can either be made explicit or remain implicit (see section 4).

2.2 Research Overview: Religious Formulaic Language in Lower-Class Letter Writing

Formulae are and have been essential parts of letters. In the nineteenth century, letter writing manuals enjoyed great popularity, and forms of address as well as closure formulae were considered the 'touchstone' (Baasner 1999: 23) of any official letter. These manuals, however, do not seem to have had significant influence on lower-class writers (Elspaß 2005: 195).[5] Nevertheless, comparative research on textual sources from different European countries has revealed that lower-class writers in particular relied heavily on textual routines and formulaic patterns acquired from model letters and other texts (Elspaß 2012: 45). Rutten and Van der Wal (2013) have identified a strong correlation between the frequency of formulae and the social class of a writer. They explain the increased use of formulae by 'ordinary people' by the fact that the use of formulae was "convenient to lesser-skilled writers" (2013: 45), for whom writing was not an everyday practice. It helped these writers solve communicative problems in the written code (Elspaß 2005: 192).

Several of the formulae that research has identified in lower-class letter writing contain religious elements. While Barton (1975: 5) states that most of his analysed emigrant letters written by Swedes in America "have in fact little of interest to relate" and consist, among other things, of "religious platitudes", more recent research has identified the textual functions of religious formulae beyond the mere informational function. In her analysis of 19th-century Scottish correspondence, Dossena (2013: 57) considers the religious element in letters to be a "highly meaningful device for the expression of involvement and psychological proximity between participants". Thus, religious formulae can be "network-reinforcing

---

4 Cf. the formulaicity criterion of 'deviation' discussed in Wray and Namba (2003: 28).
5 See a historical overview on the text type 'letter manual' in Schiegg (forthc.).

strategies" (2013: 50), by which a "writer expresses shared ethos with the recipient" (2013: 54). Similarly, Rutten and Van der Wal (2012: 181) have identified the 'Christian-ritual function' as one of the main functions of epistolary formulae in 17th- and 18th-century Dutch correspondence. Such formulae "usually place the writer and/or the addressee under divine protection, thereby manifesting the writer's religiosity". The authors connect this with Coupland's (2007) sociolinguistic theory of stylisation and interpret religious formulae as stylisations of "ethical reliability" (Rutten and Van der Wal 2012: 181). Elspaß's analysis of 19th-century German emigrants to America has revealed a large number of biblical quotations and proverbs, religious formulae and commonplaces that justify, excuse or support an argument. Writers trust in the approval of general religious 'truths' valid in their communities to avoid opposition. Thus, religious formulae can provide various aids in the formulation of letters (Elspaß 2005: 175–181).

3 Religious Formulaicity in the CoPaDocs Letters: Corpus and Methods

The Corpus of Patient Documents currently (March 2019) consists of about 2,000 texts written by more than 200 different writers born in the 19th century. Most of the writers can be classified as 'ordinary people' without much writing experience. They usually followed manual professions and had only attended primary school. Social data about these writers such as their professions, their provenance and family background as well as their financial circumstances can be retrieved from the patient files. The medical diagnoses given in the files, however, need to be treated with caution and can definitely not be equated with modern medical diagnoses. The great majority of their texts are letters, but in the patients' files, we also encounter other text types, such as autobiographic texts, poems, and diaries. Some patients wrote religious texts that can be identified by their title, for example: 'prayer before lunch' and 'evening prayer' (ans-34 Johann G. A.[6]) or 'prayer against blasphemous thoughts' (kfb-80 Hans A.). There is a 'sermon', written by the baker Franz O. (kfb-518), 'confessions' by the tailor Johann V. (kfb-775) and the miller Josef W. (kfb-2058) and even a 'prophecy' leading to a supposed apocalypse in 1888 by the nailer Johann H. (kfb-789). Johann H. was suffering from religious delusions, and a large number of references to religion

---

[6] Patient IDs are structured in the following way: institution (e.g. ans = Ansbach; see the reference section), file number (e.g. 34), first name, middle and last name.

are found, particularly in texts by patients with such a diagnosis. Apart from one example from a diary (see 14), however, in this article we only consider religious formulae that appear in letters.

A characteristic feature of the corpus and of historical letters in general is a large number of spelling variations, not only between different writers but also within one and the same person. Inexperienced writers in particular show this kind of variation, which is influenced by their degree of education, their regional varieties and by individual stylistic factors. The absence of a consistent orthography in our texts – along with a supposedly low frequency of individual formulae – obviates the application of corpus driven methods to automatically extract formulaic language, especially since corpus compilation is still in progress and lemmatisation has not yet been conducted. In addition, the CoPaDocs corpus currently comprises about 750,000 words – a size too large to be investigated on a manual basis alone. Consequently, the methodological approach used here does not aim at an exhaustive extraction of all religious formulae. However, this is not the ambition of our study in any case. Instead, we aim at an illustrative analysis of the uses and functions of religious formulae in the CoPaDocs letters. For this purpose, we applied a mixture of different methods to extract a sufficiently large sample of relevant text passages.

Our first approach was lexically based. We searched the corpus for single lexical items typical in religious contexts, assuming that these items should also frequently appear in formulae of religious provenance. Such key word searches were executed for the expressions *Amen* and *Kreuz* ('cross'). In both cases, we integrated a large number of spelling variants. The resulting hits were manually reviewed in order to identify those examples representing religious formulae in the sense of this paper. Afterwards, we also conducted key word searches for the items *Bibel* ('bible'), *sagen*, and *sprechen* ('say', including their morphological variants). The rationale was that some writers often use source-indicating routine expressions based on *verba dicendi*. By searching for the central constituents of such formulae, we were indeed able to identify a large number of explicit references to religious intertexts.

Besides these semi-automatic approaches, we examined the letters of one writer with regard to religious formulae using a traditional paper and pencil strategy: Martin B. (kfb-1621). Being a day-labourer and suffering from delusions, he is a prototypical example of an inexperienced writer who uses a lot of religious language in his letters. What is particularly interesting here is that Martin B. writes not only the relatively large number of 14 letters, but also letters to different addressees (his wife, his aunt, his brother-in-law, the mayor of his home town) in different social groups. Hence, in his letters he uses different registers (cf. Schiegg 2018), while the general function of his letters is relatively constant: appeals to be released from the hospital. We thus have plenty of intraindividual variation here that also appears in his formulaic language.

A difficulty in comparing the formulaic items with their possible sources results from the large number of Bible versions and other religious texts that were common in the 19th century – and of course the writers' own variations and modifications. It was not possible to find one 'best' Bible version for all cases, so we decided to quote different versions to achieve a maximum degree of accordance with the wording in the letter. With regard to the English translations of the formulae, we quote from the online-version of the Standard King James Bible (KJV).

4 Occurrence and Usage of Religious Formulae in Patient Letters

4.1 Explicit vs. Implicit Usage

In this section, we will illustrate different ways of how religious formulae appear and are integrated in the patients' letters. We can make a basic distinction between formulations which are explicitly marked as a religious formula on the one hand and implicit references to religious sources on the other.

In the letters, we find a variety of strategies used to explicitly mark the status of a text passage as a (religious) formula. In a number of cases, formulae are set apart from the rest of the text. Sometimes, this is realised by the arrangement of the page, e.g. by paragraphing and visible spaces between the body of the text and the formula and/or by explicit indications of the source text. This is illustrated by examples (1) to (4).

The farmer's daughter Magdalena S. (kfb-450) was suffering from religious delusions. Both of her letters, one to her sister (22.11.1857) and one to her friends (Christmas Day 1857; see example 1 and figure 1), begin with a biblical quote directly after the date and address, which span over 4 and 3 lines respectively and close with an identification of their sources. In each letter, the formula appears in an individual paragraph. The letter to her friends even has an empty line after the formula. Magdalena S. presumably copied both formulae from a Bible or another religious text that she had access to. A hint for a printed model text rather than her memory is the full capitalisation of 'HERRN' ('the Lord'; line 3), a common practice for nomina sacra in printing (Nübling et al. 2017: 265):

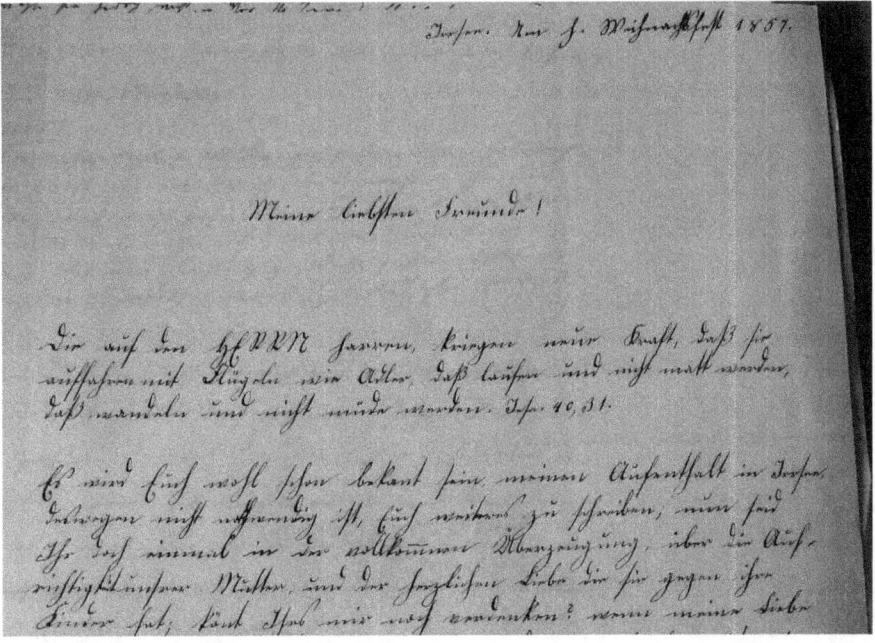

Fig. 1: Beginning of Magdalena S.'s (kfb-450) letter to friends (Christmas Day 1857) (example 1)

(1) Farmer's daughter Magdalena S. (kfb-450), letter to her friends (Christmas Day 1857):[7]
Irsee. Am h. Weihnachtsfest 1857.
Meine liebsten Freunde!
Die auf den HERRN harren, kriegen neue Kraft, daß sie auffahren mit Flügeln wie Adler, daß laufen und nicht matt werden, daß wandeln und nicht müde werden. Jesa. 40, 31.

The complexity and length of this quotation, the adherence to contemporary writing conventions (the capitalisation of *HERRN* 'the Lord') and the correct quotation of the source makes us assume that Magdalena S. did not cite this sentence by heart, but copied it from a written source. A search through the texts between 1800 and 1857 available as digital versions in the catalogue of the Bavarian State Library produces hundreds of results for this formula. None of them, however, has the exact wording used in the letter, so we do not actually know Magdalena S.'s textual version. Nevertheless, a fairly good correspondence can be found, for

---

7 In all cited examples, passages identified as religious formulae are printed in bold. Text in Latin script appears in italics, text in blackletter in roman font.

example, in a 48-page religious consolation book for the sick (Kindler 1848).[8] Both formulae are only slightly connected to the content of the letters, in which Magdalena S. complains about her situation in the psychiatric hospital, while the formulae convey a more positive mood: the temporality of all misery.

Other strategies to highlight formulaic language are punctuation (especially quotation marks), indications of the source, metalinguistic introductions and any combinations of these features. Such forms of highlighting, however, are rather rare in the CoPaDocs corpus, which consists mainly of texts by inexperienced writers. The rare examples we do find in the corpus generally come from more educated writers and mostly appear in more recent texts (beginning of the 20th century) at a time when orthographic standardisation had begun. Example (2) illustrates these strategies. In a letter to her mother, the deaconess Katharina S. uses a direct quote from the Psalms:

(2) Deaconess Katharina S. (kfb-3085), letter to her mother (01.05.1925):
Ds. Wort des Psalmisten: „**Freuet euch mit Zittern**", möchte ich Dir zurufen.

The formula is syntactically integrated into the context, but optically separated by two quotation marks, a colon at the start, and a comma at the end. In addition, the writer names the source, though not the exact place in the book (Psalms 2:11). She probably quotes the short sentence by heart, remembering it because of her religious profession.

Different languages and/or scripts, e.g. blackletter vs. Latin script (cf. Schiegg and Sowada 2019), can also be used to highlight religious formulae. This practice mainly occurs in contexts of code switching when religious formulae appear in foreign languages, especially, but not only (see example 4), in Latin. Lower class writers did not usually have any knowledge of foreign languages, so they had to transcribe phonetically from memory. The farmer Georg W. provides such an example (3; see figure 2) in a letter to his parents, where he closes with a Latin sentence that he probably remembered from the Catholic church services held in Latin before the Second Vatican Council in the 1960s. After his signature, *Johann Georg W.*, he finishes his letter by reciting the priest's absolution together with the response *Amen*, a common closure formula that we often found in patient letters (see section 5.2). Given that the writer does not have any command of the

---

[8] "Die auf den HERRN harren, kriegen neue Kraft, daß sie auffahren mit Flügeln wie Adler, daß sie laufen und nicht matt werden, daß sie wandeln und nicht müde werden. Jes. 40, 31." (Kindler 1848: 7).

Latin language, the quality of his phonetic transcription is all the more remarkable – and a strong indication of a high language competence, which is generally characteristic of his letters (cf. Schiegg 2015: 155–177).

(3) Farmer Georg W. (kfb-1720), letter to his parents (05.05.1890):
**Missereatur vestris n omnipets deus die misis
bekatus vestris vertukatvos im, 'vita met ternam
Amem**

Fig. 2: Closure of Georg W.'s (kfb-1720) letter to friends (05.05.1890) (example 3)

The original Latin text appears as follows: *Misereatur vestri omnipotens deus, et dimissis peccatis vestris, perducat vos ad vitam aeternam. – Amen* (Graeser 1829: 342). Although Georg W. writes his signature in Latin script, he uses blackletter for the Latin closure, such as he used in the rest of his letter.

The case is different in Maria R.'s letter to her siblings, where she adds the last words of Jesus on the cross, transmitted in Aramaic in the gospels of Mark and Matthew[9], in the left margin of her letter, using Latin script (example 4). She introduces this formula with the German *Bald heißt es* ('Soon, one can say') in blackletter.

---

9 See Mt 27:46: „um die neunte Stunde aber schrie Jesus mit lauter Stimme auf und sagte: Elí, Elí, lemá sabachtháni? Das heißt: Mein Gott, mein Gott, warum hast du mich verlassen?" (ELB) – 'And about the ninth hour Jesus cried with a loud voice, saying, Eli, Eli, lama sabachthani? that is to say, My God, my God, why hast thou forsaken me?'.

(4) Maria R. (no job specified) (kfb-994), letter to her siblings (28.03.1900):
Bald heißt es *Eli, Eli Lama Sabaktani*
eau sum nattum est

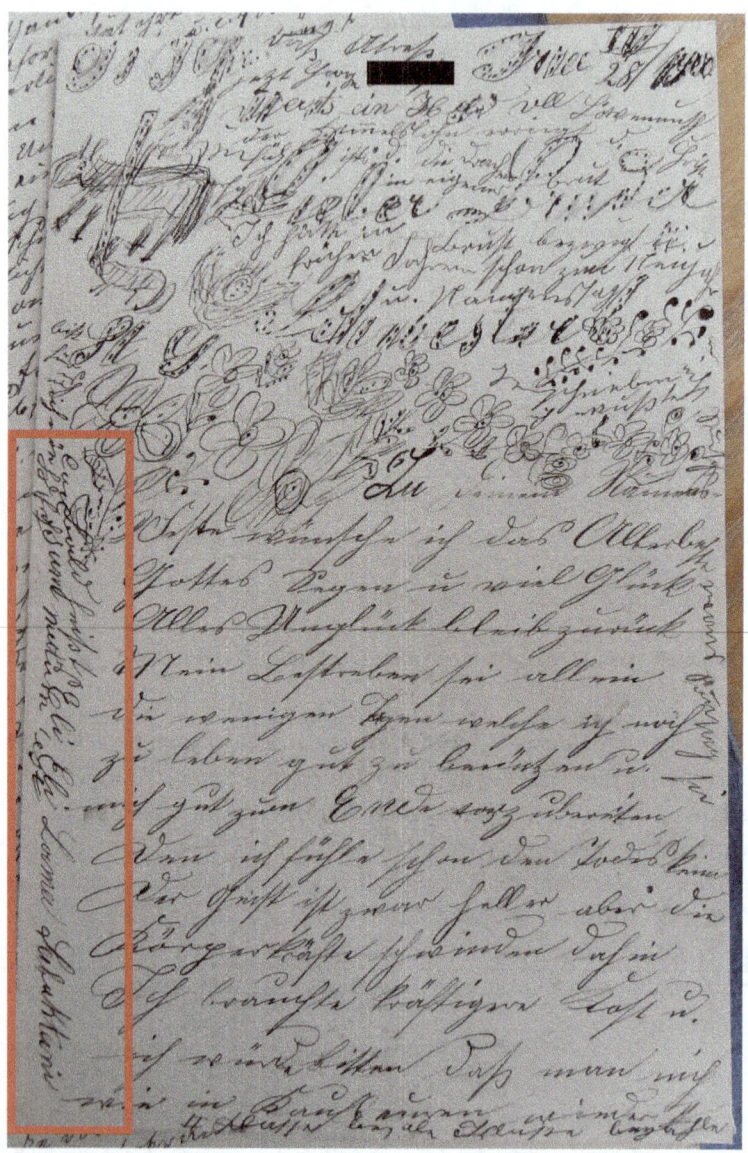

Fig. 3: Page 1 of Maria R.'s (kfb-994) letter to siblings (28.03.1900) (example 4); Aramaic and pseudo-Latin formula in the left margin

Fig. 4: Detail from figure 3 – Aramaic and pseudo-Latin formula in the left margin

Quoting Christ's final words, Maria R. draws a parallel between the last hours of Christ and her own poor health. She dies in the psychiatric hospital ten months after writing this letter. Using a religious formula to equate a biblical element with the patient's own situation is a practice that we commonly find in patient letters, particularly related to the passion of Christ. The words following (line 2) are also written in Latin script, but do not seem to be connected to the rest of the formula. We can recognise some elements of the Latin language (*sum* – 'I am'; *nattum* 'born (neuter)'; *est* 'he/she/it is') that Maria R. transcribes phonetically from memory (*nattum* usually has only one *t*), probably without knowing their precise meaning. These words do not seem to make much sense and Maria R. presumably inserts some text in the religious language of Latin to place emphasis on her previous formula.

While the examples cited so far provide explicit indications for the status as a (religious) formula, in the majority of cases in our corpus the use of the religious formula remains implicit. Such an example is the following:

(5) Day-labourer Martin B. (kfb-1621), letter to his wife (10.03.1896):
der Geist hat h aine Unsihbare Graft man mus es aus Füren **mit getangen Worten und Wergen** kain Mensch kans niht Ferstehen und weist niht wi noh was dan Baist di Maus Eher kainen Zwirn niht ab bis for bai ist

In a letter to his wife, day-labourer Martin B. includes a passage of the *Confiteor*, recited by Christians as part of the penitential act. In its German version, the *Confiteor* contains the trinomial *in Gedanken, Worten und Werken* ('in my thoughts and in my words, in what I have done [and in what I have failed to do]'). As part of the prayer, this formulation is extremely fixed and clearly an instance of formulaic language. In the letter, it is completely integrated into its syntactic context and is not marked in any way as a formula. This also holds for the other fixed phrases in the same passage: *weist niht wi noh was* ('he neither knows how nor what') and *dan Baist di Maus Eher kainen Zwirn niht ab* (literally: 'then, the mouse rather does not bite off no thread'). It is obvious that such unmarked uses of religious formulae are rather difficult to identify in texts. At the same time, the fact that the writers often see no need to explicitly mark religious formulae can be regarded as an indication of their status as highly familiar and commonly used units.

4.2 Variation and Modification

As already mentioned in section 3, formulaic language in the CoPaDocs letters reveals a high degree of variation. Example (5) illustrates peculiarities in several linguistic areas that can be explained as diastratic, diatopic and individual variation. In the (non-religious) formula *dan Baist di Maus Eher kainen Zwirn niht ab*, for example, we find a double negation in *kainen ... niht*, which is a syntactic structure that was highly stigmatised in the 19th century and only used in the written language of less-schooled writers (Elspaß 2005: 276). This construction is also diatopically marked, as it appears predominantly in southern German (Elspaß 2005: 281). In the same formula, we see the lexeme *Zwirn* ('twine'), while the formula usually has the near-synonym *Faden* ('thread') (Duden 2013: 498). Individual variation (cf. Barz 1995) also appears at the orthographic level, where we find individual characteristics for this writer, for example the phonetic spelling <ai> for /ai/ (*Baist, kainen*) instead of the conventional <ei> (see also examples 6a and 6b).[10]

Individual variation can particularly be observed when writers repeatedly use formulae. As Martin B.'s letters all have the same intention – being released from the hospital – their contents overlap and some of the (religious) formulae appear more than once:

> (6) Day-labourer Martin B. (kfb-1621), letters to his wife ([a] 28.01.1896 and [b] 10.03.1896) and letter to the mayor ([c] 07.05.1905):
> [a] **der Gaist Gottes ist ain langer warter aber ain sehr schtringer Bestrafer**
> [b] **Gott ist ain Langer Warter aber ain ser Strenger Bestrafer**
> [c] **Gott ist Ein Langer warter aber ein Strenger Bestrafer**

In three different letters, Martin B. uses a religious formula that is derived from Psalm 7:12 *Gott ist ein gerechter Richter und ein Gott, der täglich strafen kann.* (ELB) ('God judgeth the righteous, and God is angry with the wicked [...]'). All three instances have a common general inventory of lexical material, but at the

---

10 The <ai> spelling for the former /ei/ diphthong was a typical Upper German spelling in the 16th and 17th centuries (Schmidt 2013: 370). Afterwards, however, Upper German texts followed those from the rest of the German speaking area and switched to <ei> (name spellings remained <ai>). Thus, we can classify the <ai> spelling in 19th- and 20th-century letters as individual rather than diatopic variation.

same time show variation. Lexical variation can for example be observed in the particle *sehr* ('very') that intensifies the modifying adjective *streng* ('severe'), but only appears in the two letters to his wife (a and b) and not to the mayor (c). Similarly, the spelling variant <ai> instead of the conventional <ei> in *ain* and *Gaist* appears in all the five possible positions in the letters to his wife, but in neither of the two *ein* to the mayor. These differences between the first two formulae may appear by chance or because of the gap of almost ten years between Martin B.'s letters to his wife and that to the mayor. It may also result from the different addressees. Martin B. in general shows less conventional spellings in his private letters (cf. Schiegg 2018), and – as we will see in section 5.1 – the formulae to his wife have a more intense and threatening character, which is indicated by the intensifier *sehr*. Therefore this kind of variation may also be explained by his application of different linguistic registers. The phonetic spelling *schtringer* in (6a) supports that hypothesis. It appears only in one of the letters to his wife, and shows the palatalisation of /s/ in initial position before a consonant that is usually spelt <s> and not <sch>, as well as an assimilation of /e/ to /i/ resulting from the following velar consonant /ŋ/, which Martin B. writes as an <i>. If we assume that Martin B.'s variation here is intentional and has a communicative purpose, we approach the interface between variation and modification of formulaic language.

In phraseological research, modifications are usually defined as occasional, intentional and context-bound variations of formulaic items (Pfeiffer 2018: 51). The tendency to creatively modify formulaic language is often regarded as a characteristic development of media texts in the second half of the 20th century (e.g. von Polenz 1999: 381). Our corpus of letters by inexperienced writers at the turn of the 19th century, however, shows that this practice can also be found earlier and in other text types. A variety of religious formulae are indeed modified for their specific context. This will be illustrated in examples (7) to (9).

At the end of the following text excerpt (example 7), the tailor Pius G. uses the canonical form of the religious formula *ans Kreuz mit ihm* ('crucify him'), recorded in all four gospels (Mt 27:22–23; Mk 15:13–14; Lk 23:21; John 19:6, EU). These words are shouted by the crowds to demand that Jesus be crucified after his trial in the praetorium before Pontius Pilate. What is interesting here is the context of the formula, namely the continuous equation of the situation of the writer with the passion of Jesus Christ. A couple of lines before, the writer reports his own trial before a Bavarian court of justice. In his view, the trial was nothing but a show trial, ending with his condemnation and a sentence of acquittal for two fellow defendants. Already from a content point of view, the parallels to the passion of Jesus are evident. However, the parallelisation is also realised and even intensified by linguistic means, namely by modifying the formulaic item *ans Kreuz mit ihm* to *ins Narrenhaus Haus mit Ihm*. The writer substitutes the constituent *Kreuz* with *Narrenhaus* ('madhouse'), thus not only comparing his situation with the passion of Jesus but also establishing a link between the concepts of cross and 'madhouse'. This conceptual identification is quite frequent in the letters investigated (see section 5.1.2).

(7) Tailor Pius G. (kfb-936), letter to the local government (03.02.1890):
Wirkl. ᵂürklich zog sich der sogenannte Gerichtshof Zurük – und brachte die unzurechnungsfäghigkeit fertig Gegen einen Bürger u. Soldat von unbescholtenem Ruf Die zwei Meuhelmörder wurden Freihgesprochen, Und das *Wittelsbacher Haus* sammt seiner Schand Regierung war Gerettet. Jetzt **ins Narrenhaus Haus mit Ihm**! Dieses waren die ersten Worte welche ich hötrte, als ich heraus kam, ich aber ging ins *Hofbräuhaus*! Wo mir unwillkührlich die Geschichte eines Iesus einfiel dem auch sein Haupt Verbrechen darin bestand, weil Er den Banditten von Gottes Gnade, die Wahrheit sagte. **Ans Kreuz mit Ihm**! An dem Er noch heute hängt, zum Schreken für diejenigen welche es je wieder wagen sollten, Gegen derartige Verbrecher, und gedungene Knechte zu Zeugen!

The following two passages show further examples of modified religious formulae.

(8) Day-labourer Martin B. (kfb-1621), letter to his wife (10.03.1896):
du soltest fro froh sein wan ich zu dir nohmal gehen wirte dan wirte es Dir nohmal beser ᵍᵉʰᵉⁿ aber ich wil dihr niht mehr über lestig sein Du wirtest mih sofort wider hiher bringen ich hab in Krumbah auh witer kute Fraind di sich um meiner Annemmen ten ich kan noh Arbeiten **Der Mensch tengt und der Böse Geist lengt oft mer als der gute Geist**

(9) Day-labourer Martin B. (kfb-1621), letter to the mayor of his home town (06.01.1901):
Mein Weib und meine Tochter haben mich von der Anstald Kaufbeiren wider abgeholt! Es hat mich sehr gefreüt daß ich so gut wider entlaßen worden bin; **aber meine Freüde welche ich gehabt habe, ist wieder in Trauer verwandelt worden**;

In example (8), Martin B. refers to the formula *der Mensch denkt, Gott lenkt* ('man thinks, God directs'), which is not a direct quotation from the scriptures but can be traced back to the book of Proverbs 16:9: *Das Herz des Menschen plant seinen Weg, aber der HERR lenkt seinen Schritt.* (ELB) ('A man's heart deviseth his way: but the LORD directeth his steps.') and the derived and shortened middle-Latin phrase *Homo proponit, sed deus disponit* (Duden 2017: 382). Again, the writer does not use the formula in any canonical form, but rather adapts it to the specific context. In his letters, Martin B. often claims that his wife is possessed by an evil spirit, who has pushed aside her once good character. In his view, it is this evil spirit who prevents her from getting him out of the hospital. To express this view, he modifies the formula in a twofold manner: firstly, he substitutes the component *Gott* ('God') with *der Böse Geist* ('the evil spirit'). Secondly, he expands the formula with the comparative structure *oft mer als der gute Geist* ('often more than the good spirit'). Examples like this show that even less-experienced writers produce quite complex modifications to support their communicative goals.

The modification in (9) also adapts a biblical quotation to the context of the letter. The highlighted passage refers to John 16:20: *ihr werdet traurig sein, aber eure Trauer wird sich in Freude verwandeln* (EU) ('and ye shall be sorrowful, but your sorrow shall be turned into joy'). By substituting the possessive article (*eure* vs. *meine*), inserting the relative clause (*welche ich gehabt habe*) and permutating the constituents *joy* and *sorrow*, the formula is adapted to the writer's situation: shortly before, he had been released from the psychiatric hospital – only to find himself rehospitalised after a couple of days. So his joy about being released has indeed turned into sorrow again – the biblical promise of salvation has not come true but has rather been turned upside down for him.

5 Functions of Religious Formulae in Patient Letters

5.1 Argumentative Functions

From a text pragmatic perspective, the patients' letters are polyfunctional, serving appellative, contact-orientated and also informative functions. The dominant function of most letters is directive-appellative: the patients request the addressees to do something for them – often their release from the hospital, but also a visit or a parcel from home. This request is usually supported by the use of argumentative textualisation patterns, shaping major text parts and even whole letters. From the perspective of this paper, it is interesting to investigate which role religious formulae play in these contexts.

The typical argumentation in patient letters is deontic, with the thesis/conclusion being *I [the writer] should be released from hospital* and/or *you [the addressee] should help me be released from hospital*. To support this, the writers often claim that they were mistakenly hospitalised in the first place since they are not actually ill. The addressees are regarded as responsible for the writer's hospitalisation, so, from the writer's perspective, not only are they capable of effecting their release, but it is also their moral responsibility to do so. A possible strategy here is to WARN and THREATEN the addressees of what will happen if they do not fulfil this moral obligation. These acts are often realised or supported by the use of religious formulae. The day-labourer Martin B., for instance, uses this pattern in very similar ways in five of his letters:

(10) Day-labourer Martin B. (kfb-1621), letters to his wife ([a] 11.01.1895, [b] 28.01.1896, [c] 08.06.? and [d] 17.07.?) and to the mayor of his home town ([e] 05.07.1905):
[a] dengst du nih an das Sterben so wirst den Himmel mimals Erben u denge an das Gottes Keriht was unser Her Gott mit dihr dann sbirht
[b] tenge ainmal nah Das du Sterben must und Rehenschaft ab Legen must for Gottes Geriht
[c] dise heren solen auh Tengen an den Tot den unser Her Gott ist ain Stringer Rihter
[d] dengst du niht an das Sterben so wirst du auh den Himmel niht Erben d und denge an das lötzte Gehriht was unser Her Got mit dir dan Sbriht
[e] Dengen sie Daß sie auch einmal sterben müssen und Gottes Gericht rehen schaft ablögen müssen

The cited passages contain another interesting type of formulaic variation. While the concrete lexical realisation of the pattern varies, the individual units of argumentation and their sequence are remarkably constant. In a first step, the writer reminds the addressee of his or her own death, actualizing the famous vanity topos of *memento mori*. This topos can be traced back to Psalm 90:12: *Lehre uns bedenken, daß wir sterben müssen* (LU, 'So teach us to number our days'). In all five cases, the *memento mori* is followed by an explicit warning of the Last Judgement, where the addressees will have to account for their misconduct, especially for not supporting the writer's release.

5.1.1 Topical Argumentation

Referring to God and other religious authorities is an argumentative strategy the writers repeatedly use to prove and force their point. In these contexts, religious formulae are of particular relevance due to their status as *endoxa*, whose truth or validity is widely taken for granted as an effect of their source. Such source-based authority provides a specific potential for argumentation. In conventional argumentative contexts, speakers are pragmatically committed to proving the truth or validity of their thesis statement. Referring to the authority of a certain person or source, however, can obviate the need for actual argumentation. In these cases, we come across instances of *topical argumentation*, the general mechanisms of which were already described by Aristotle (cf. Aristoteles, *Topik*, 116a). Using the authority topos is probably the most typical form of topical argumentation. According to Klein (2001: 1317), the underlying pattern and conversational effect of the authority topos can be described as follows: *if a person or entity associated with high authority produces an utterance U or performs an action A, it is likely that U is true or valid / that A is appropriate.* In such cases, it is superfluous to support one's positions in a truly argumentative way.

Our key word search for *sagen* ('say'; and its morphological variants) yielded the following examples (11) to (14) that illustrate the usage of religious formulae in this form of topical argumentation:[11]

> (11) Plumber Friedrich Wilhelm S. (ham-20087), letter to diverse official addressees (29.02.1936):
> *Somit erklähre ich vor Gott und der ganzen Menschheit auf Erden alle Fahneneide und Treueeide für Ungültig da Gott seinen Heiligen Namen führ solche Sauereien nicht hergibt. Jesu sagte Deutlich* **wehr mit dem Schwert tötet wird durchs Schwert Umkommen** *Gott brauch keine Soldaten.*

> (12) Mill labourer Georg Sch. (kfb-1763), letter to Bavarian bishops (undated):
> *Da der Papst die Sache nicht versteht, hätte Er gar nicht verlangen sollen, daß man die Unfehlbarkeit glauben muß, ohne Belehrung u. Beweiß. Dazu erinnere ich an die Apostel. Jesus war, u. ist, eine höhere Person als der Papst, u. die Apostel haben nicht geglaubt, u. der Ap. Tomas sagte,* **wenn ich nicht meine Hand in seine Wunden lege, glaube ich nicht.** *Demnach wird es erlaubt sein, zu fragen, ob das recht ist, wenn man dieße welche auch nicht glauben ohne Beweiß, von der Kirche ausschlüßt. Ich erinnere auch, daß Jesus befohlen hat,* **das Unkraut nicht ausrotten.**

In the context of the first passage, plumber Friedrich Wilhelm S. sharply criticises the militarisation of Germany in the 1930s and the common practice of religiously motivating oaths of loyalty and allegiance. Instead, he pleas for demilitarisation and a pacifist attitude from the church and society. To support this, he refers to a famous quote from Jesus, uttered when one of his disciples violently tried to prevent his arrest after the betrayal of Judas Iscariot: *wer das Schwert nimmt, der soll durchs Schwert umkommen* (Mt 26:52, LU, 'all they that take the sword shall perish with the sword'). By quoting Jesus and the scriptures, the writer has recourse to the authority of the source. At least for fellow Christians, it is not easy to take the opposite view.

---

[11] The effects of the usage of religious formulae in topical argumentation have also been described for other text types, for example emigrant letters (see section 2.2).

This function can also be found in example (12). In a letter addressed to all Bavarian bishops, mill labourer Georg Sch. basically argues that he cannot be insane since he always acts according to Jesus's model. So if the writer were insane, Jesus would necessarily have been insane, too. The letter contains theoretical reflections on a number of theological issues, particularly on confessional schism. In the passage quoted, he requests the bishops not to excommunicate religious sceptics since Jesus had not expelled sceptics among his disciples either. The request is substantiated with reference to two biblical formulae: the well-known quote from the apostle Thomas ("doubting Thomas") *wenn ich meinen Finger nicht in das Mal der Nägel und meine Hand nicht in seine Seite lege, glaube ich nicht* (John 20:25, EU, 'except I shall [...] put my finger into the print of the nails, and thrust my hand into his side, I will not believe') and Jesus's verdict that the tares should not be rooted out to protect the wheat in the parable of the Wheat and Tares (Mt 13: 24–30).

A specific variation of the authority topos is characteristic for writers suffering from religious delusions. These patients often claim that they act in a particular way because God – or other persons or forces in his name – has explicitly told them to do so. The action is thus justified as God's will. In these contexts, too, religious formulae play an important role since the religious authority often uses words from the scriptures. This may be illustrated by the following examples:

(13) Farmer's daughter Magdalena S. (kfb-450), letter to friends (25.12.1857):
bei mir gillt das Wort auch, wie bei Abraham, als der allmächtige Gott sagte; **Gehe aus deinem Vaterlande, und aus deiner Freundschaft, und aus deines Vaters-Haus, in ein Land das ich dir zeuge; denn daselbst will ich dich zum großen Volk machen**. Gerade diese Worte hat Gott zu mir gesagt, ehe ich nach Neuendettesaus wanderte [...].

(14) Shop owner's daughter Anna K. (kfb-2585), diary (27.04.1852):
Mir war während des Schlafes als sei ich im Hause meiner Eltern und mein Bruder *Edmund* brachte mir zwei Briefe in denen ich Nachricht bekam: „Es sei unserm Könige *Maximilian* während der Nacht u. des Gebetes ein Engel erschienen der ihm gesagt, **dieses /:nämlich ich:/ ist die Maria die Jungfrau, die den Messias gebären soll**"! Als ich erwacht war sagte das Wesen in meinem Jnnern,: **fliehe! Sie werden Dich und mich zu tödten suchen! Nimm Dein Kind und gehe zu unserm Könige!** – Und dann ist mirs als müße ich mit Enzler fort!

In both passages, the use of the religious formula not only motivates and justifies a particular action of the patient's, but also establishes a parallel between the writers and the biblical persons who were the original addressees of the respective words (Abraham and Joseph) (see section 5.1.2).

In example (13), it is God himself who speaks to Magdalena S. with the same words he once used to call Abram (*Und der HERR sprach zu Abram: Gehe aus deinem Vaterlande und von deiner Freundschaft und aus deines Vaters Hause in ein Land, das ich dir zeigen will Und ich will dich zum großen Volk machen*; 1. Mose 12:1–2, LU – 'Now the LORD had said unto Abram, Get thee out of thy country, and from thy kindred, and from thy father's house, unto a land that I will shew thee: And I will make of thee a great nation').

While the wording in (13) widely conforms to the biblical source, the formulae in (14) exhibit more adaptions to the context. In her diary, written in 1852 in the hospital in Augsburg before she had been transferred to the psychiatric hospital in Irsee, Anna K. refers to Archangel Gabriel's Annunciation, whereby she herself is being addressed as Virgin Mary, who will give birth to Jesus (cf. Lk 1:31). However, the angel does not appear to the writer herself but to the then-king Maximilian II. of Bavaria, who forwards the angel's prophecy. The religious authority of the original source is enriched with the earthly authority of the king as the initial bearer and receiver of the message – an interesting "double" use of the authority topos. In a further instance of topical argumentation, Anna K. then recites a voice from inside her, adopting the words of Mt 2:13: *Steh auf, nimm das Kind und seine Mutter und flieh nach Ägypten; [...] denn Herodes wird das Kind suchen, um es zu töten* (EU, 'Arise, and take the young child and his mother, and flee into Egypt, [...] for Herod will seek the young child to destroy him'). These are the words of an angel of the Lord who appears to Joseph in a dream after Jesus's birth, and Anna K. interprets this as an instruction to leave with Dr Enzler, one of the hospital's doctors.

5.1.2 Affirmation by Parallelisation

As we have seen, the patient texts contain a large number of cases in which the writer parallelises his or her own situation with a religious event, person or topos. Our key word search for *Kreuz* ('cross') in CoPaDocs yielded several examples in which the writer's situation (being in the hospital) is metaphorically conceptualised as the cross he or she has to bear.[12] The farmer's daughter Marie V., for example, wrote the following letter (cited in full) from a psychiatric hospital in Lower Bavaria:

---

12 We have already discussed two of them: Maria R. (example 4) draws a parallel between the last hours of Christ and her own poor health by including Christ's last words in Aramaic in her letter; Pius G. (example 7) connects the passion of Christ and the cross with the asylum.

(15) Farmer's daughter Marie V. (mkf-987), letter to the institution (1932/33):
Sehr geerhter u~~n~~d liebe~~fe~~volste Direktion Ärzte Schwester Ihr seid mir die Stufe im Kreuzweg *N* 6 ich die Verronika Ihr der liebe Heiland tief trügt Ihr das Bildniß der Liebe in mein Herz aber ich muß wandeln die 2te Jesu **nimt das Kreuz auf seine Schuldern** Ich bitte Euch von Herzen verzeihet mir der liebe Got sol für Euerer Liebe z~~n~~u uns alles vergelten Ein iniges Vergelts Gott

In this letter, she thanks the institution's doctors and nurses and compares herself with Veronica, who, according to Christian legends, offered Jesus a piece of cloth to wipe blood and sweat from his face at the sixth station along his *Via Dolorosa*. The veil afterwards bore an imprint of Jesus's face that this letter interprets as a portrait of love that had been offered by Jesus (i.e. the institution's doctors and nurses) to Veronica (i.e. Marie V.). The perspective then changes and the writer calls herself "the second Jesus" who has to bear the cross (i.e. her illness) on her shoulders. These images have parallels with the Bible (cf. Mk 15:20, Mt 27:32, Lk 22:26, Joh 19:16), but the Stations of the Cross do not appear in detail in it. They are derived from late medieval developments in Christian liturgy, when the story of the *Via Dolorosa* became a central element of meditation (Köpf 1996: 728). In several religious publications, we find the story of Veronica and her veil, as well as the formula *Jesus nimmt das Kreuz auf seine Schultern* ('Jesus carries the cross on his shoulders.'), for example in a 19th-century meditation book on the *Via Dolorosa* for use in church in Passau, Lower Bavaria (Schmid 1855: 6). Marie V.'s use of Christian imagery and religious language allows her to draw parallels both to her state of health and to the doctors' and nurses' benignity.

5.1.3 Expression of a Shared Ethos

It has often been noticed that formulaic language plays an important role in addressing one's audience (cf. e.g. Fleischer 1997: 218). In argumentative contexts, for instance, writers often resort to formulaic language to express shared knowledge, assessments and values (Pfeiffer 2016: 227–234). In the CoPaDocs letters, too, writers allude to religious formulae to establish a connection and create a social community with their addressees. While Martin B. predominantly uses religious formulae to warn and threaten his addressees, mainly his wife – see the five letters cited in example (10) – his formulae are not restricted to this function. In the few religious formulae[13] to the other addressees, the mayor of his home

---

[13] There are only four religious formulae in letters addressed to people other than Martin B.'s wife, three in letters to the mayor and one in a letter to his aunt. In the letters to his wife, we have

town, his aunt and his brother-in-law, we can observe other functions. Example (9) has already demonstrated the use of religious formulae in a letter to the mayor in which he illustrated his sorrow at being brought back to the hospital, with a modified formula putting emphasis on his general argument that he should be released. He also includes a religious formula in a letter to his aunt:

> (16) Day-labourer Martin B. (kfb-1621), letter to his aunt (15.05.1899):
> du schreibst mir ich solle auf Gott vertrauen er sei der **Helfer in der Noth** ich werde dann immer beßer den Himmel verdinen wann es auf dieser Welt keine Barmherzigkeit giebt für ^(mich) dann ist mein langes warten vergebens die Barmherzigkeit muß ich von Menschen Hülfe erhalten

In this passage, Martin B. refers to a letter that he received from his aunt (not part of his file), in which she tried to calm him down by asking him to trust in God as an aide in any misery (cf. Psalm 124). He points to this shared knowledge but emphasises the importance of mercifulness on earth and thus the aunt's duty to help him. Although his text here is still appellative, the writer does not try to reach his goals by means of a threat, but by referring to a common knowledge and expressing a shared ethos with the recipient, a practice that has been observed in other contexts (Dossena 2013; see section 2.2). The threats only appear in the letters to his wife and his last letter to the mayor, when he may have realised that the politeness of his earlier letters would not lead to the goals envisioned.

5.2 Text-Structural Functions

While our analysis has up to this point focussed on functions of religious formulae with regard to the content of the letters, we can also find formulae that primarily help to structure letters (cf. Stein 2003: 123–132). As we have seen above, Magdalena S. (example 1) starts her letter with a religious formula, while Georg W. (example 3) closes his letter with a religious formula plus *Amen*. To find out whether this practice of closing letters with *Amen* also appears in other patient letters, we searched the corpus for *Amen*. In several cases, *Amen* is conventionally used to close prayers that are recited in the patients' texts. Some are similar to Georg W.'s example, where a text ends with a religious formula that closes with

---

observed 32 religious formulae. The number of tokens addressed to his wife is higher (about 5,100 words) than to the other addressees (together about 2,750 words), but the religious formulae are still clearly dominant in the letter to his wife. Religious lexis in general is significantly more frequent in the letters to his wife than to the other addressees.

Amen. Often, writers add references to a shared religious context (see section 5.1.3) to the end of their letters and close this section with *Amen*. This is the case in example (17), where Josefa M. asks her brother Martin to pray for her or have a mass read for her and closes this section with *Amen*. Afterwards, she adds two more conventional closure formulae ('I now close my letter…' and 'You are greeted cordially'; cf. Elspaß 2005: 163), her informal nickname *Babett*, and finally a short addition that Martin's saint's day is approaching (11th November), with which she again tries to establish a connection with him:

> (17) Seamstress Josefa M. (kfb-2211), letter to her brother (09.11.1913):
> […] bete auch für mich oder laß für eine schwer kranke eine hl. Messe lesen. **Amen**. Ich beschließe nun mein Schreiben u. hoffe daß Du mir nicht zürnst. Du seiest also aufs herzlichste von mir gegrüßt u. die Deinigen. Babett kommt jetzt auch bald der Namenstag.

The corpus search also produced cases, where the formula *Amen* is used in text structuring functions, but outside religious contexts. After closing and signing his letter, Anton H. (example 18) adds another few sentences in which he repeats his plea to be collected from hospital. He emphasises that he has turned into a different person, healthier and able to work and that he behaves decently. He closes this confirmation that is unconnected to any religious domain with *Amen*. This short formula thus helps to fulfill the communicative task of closing a letter:

> (18) Tailor Anton H. (kfb-1789), letter to his family (08.06.1900):
> Hollet mich balde ihr werdet sehen Ich bin auch ein andere Mensch geworden, gesunder und rechter ihn der Arbeit, Arbeiten thue Ich auch ihmer den Tagen, ganz mache meine Sache ihmerund recht. **Amen**.

Using *Amen* at the end of their text provided inexperienced writers with an option for marking the end of their letters with an affirmative formula. This secularised use of *Amen* in a text-structural function does not seem to have been described for German lower-class writing before. We find very similar uses of *Amen* as closure formula in the Dutch *Letters as Loot Corpus* (Rutten and Van der Wal 2014: 106, 182). To get a first impression whether this function can be found across individual corpora, we also searched for uses of *Amen* in the corpus of 19th-century emigrant letters from Germany.[14] Interestingly, we indeed found a number of similar uses in these letters, too. For example, farmers from Norwood in Cincinnati ended a letter to their family with greetings to all relatives, followed by *Amen*, place and date of writing and their signatures:

---

14 We thank Stephan Elspaß for his permission to use and quote from this unpublished corpus.

(19) Farmers Dedert and Johanna Farwick, letter to family (March 1851):
Wir grüßen Euch alle, Vater, Mutter, Bruders, Schwesters und Schwagers und alle unsere Verwandten. **Amen**. Cincinnati März 1851 Dedert und Jan Farwick

6 Conclusion and Outlook

Our paper has illustrated the spectrum of occurrences and functions of religious formulae in the CoPaDocs corpus, comprising letters from patients of psychiatric hospitals born in the 19th century. Since most of the letters were written by lower-class people with a low level of education, the letters permitted an insight into the use of formulaic language by ordinary people in the 19th century.

Some of our findings can be regarded as specific to the letters investigated here. This holds in particular for passages where patients suffering from religious delusions claim that God or other religious instances have told them to do something using religious formulae known from other contexts. Another interesting observation was that lower-class writers in the 19th century already exploited the potential of formulaic language for occasional modifications, often in a remarkably complex and creative manner. This shows that the tendency for creative use of formulaic items has a long tradition and is not a development of recent decades. Interestingly, the modifications we found do not seem to aim at wordplay but are most obviously produced to achieve particular communicative goals.

The majority of our findings, however, rather confirm observations that have already been made for 19th century lower class letter writing in previous studies. Prominent features such as a high degree of variation in formulaic language use, and a tendency to refer to religious formulae to express shared values and to utilise the advantages of topical argumentation are not specific to the corpus investigated, but seem to be characteristic of 19th century lower-class letter writing in general. This also seems to apply to the secularised use of *Amen* in a text-structural function.

This volume is dedicated to Elisabeth Piirainen, who in a number of papers and books has researched on widespread idioms in Europe and beyond (e.g. Piirainen 2012, 2015). Continuing this approach to formulaic language, contrastive studies – not only across the borders of single letter collections but also across different languages – might offer a variety of new insights, especially with regard to a "pan-European tradition of letter writing" (Rutten and Van der Wal 2013: 52) and the question of "whether there existed something like a central European stock of letter writing formulae and how they could have evolved or how they were transmitted into the different languages" (Elspaß 2012: 60). Our findings on the use of *Amen* could be related to this idea. However, the various writers' individual attempts at closing a letter by means of this formulae may as well have resulted from their shared European cultural and religious backgrounds.

In any case, religious formulae in historical lower-class writing have been shown to be a promising area for historical research on formulaic language. The corpus of historical patient documents provides new data that can shed light on the occurrence and functions of religious formulae in these letters, giving us valuable insights both into the writers' religious knowledge and into their competence in transforming this knowledge into a letter.

References

Primary Sources

ans= Staatsarchiv Nürnberg (Außenstelle Lichtenau), Historische Patientenakten der Heil- und Pflegeanstalt Ansbach, Patientenakten Männer, Nr. 34 (Johann Georg A.).

ham = Staatsarchiv Hamburg, Bestand Staatskrankenanstalt Langenhorn (352-8/7, Abl. 1995/2), Patientenakte Nr. 20087 (Friedrich Wilhelm S.).

kfb = Archiv des Bezirkskrankenhauses Kaufbeuren, Historische Patientenakten aus Kaufbeuren-Irsee, Akten Nr. 80 (Hans A.), Nr. 450 (Magdalena S.), Nr. 518 (Franz O.), Nr. 775 (Johann V.), Nr. 789 (Johann H.), Nr. 936 (Pius G.), Nr. 994 (Maria R.), Nr. 1621 (Martin B.), Nr. 1720 (Georg W.), Nr. 1763 (Georg Sch.), Nr. 1789 (Anton H.), Nr. 2058 (Josef W.), Nr. 2211 (Josefa M.), Nr. 2585 (Anna K.), Nr. 3085 (Katharina S.).

mkf = Archiv des Bezirksklinikums Mainkofen, Historische Patientenakten der Heil- u. Pflegeanstalt Mainkofen, Akte Nr. 1562/987 (Marie V.).

Secondary Sources

Aristoteles (1968): *Topik. (Organon V)*. Übersetzt und mit Anmerkungen versehen von Eugen Rolfes. Hamburg: Felix Meiner.

Baasner, Rainer (Hrsg.) (1999): *Briefkultur im 19. Jahrhundert*. Tübingen: Niemeyer.

Bartolini, Maria Grazia (2012): "Glava že vsěm Biblija". Le citazioni bibliche nell'opera di H.S. Skovoroda (1722–1794) tra tradizione slava ecclesiastica e cultura barocca. *Studi Slavistici 9*, 29–52.

Barton, H. Arnold (1975): *Letters from the Promised Land. Swedes in America, 1840–1914*. Minneapolis: University of Minnesota Press.

Barz, Irmhild (1995): Idiolektale Aspekte der phraseologischen Variation. In Gotthard Lerchner, Marianne Schröder & Ulla Fix (Hrsg.), *Chronologische, areale und situative Varietäten des Deutschen in der Sprachhistoriographie. Festschrift für Rudolf Große*, 345–356. Frankfurt am Main: Peter Lang.

Coupland, Nikolas (2007): *Style. Language variation and identity*. Cambridge: Cambridge University Press.

Dossena, Marina (2013): Mixing genres and reinforcing community ties in nineteenth-century Scottish correspondence: Formality, familiarity and religious discourse. In Joanna Kopaczyk & Andreas H. Jucker (eds.), *Communities of Practice in the History of English*, 47–60. Amsterdam, Philadelphia: John Benjamins.

Duden (2013): *Redewendungen. Wörterbuch der deutschen Idiomatik*. 4., neu bearbeitete und aktualisierte Auflage. Berlin: Dudenverlag.

Duden (2017): *Zitate und Aussprüche: Herkunft, Bedeutung und aktueller Gebrauch*. 4., überarbeitete und erweiterte Auflage. Berlin: Dudenverlag.

ELB = *Revidierte Elberfelder Bibel*. Rev. 26, 2008. Witten: SCM R. Brockhaus.

Elspaß, Stephan (2005): *Sprachgeschichte von unten. Untersuchungen zum geschriebenen Alltagsdeutsch im 19. Jahrhundert*. Tübingen: Niemeyer.

Elspaß, Stephan (2012): Between linguistic creativity and formulaic restriction. Cross-linguistic perspectives on nineteenth-century lower class writers' private letters. In Marina Dossena & Gabriella Del Lungo Camiciotti (eds.), *Letter writing in late modern Europe*, 45–64. Amsterdam, Philadelphia: John Benjamins.

EU = *Einheitsübersetzung der Heiligen Schrift*. Vollständig durchgesehene und überarbeitete Ausgabe 2016. Stuttgart: Katholische Bibelanstalt.

Filatkina, Natalia (2018): *Historische formelhafte Sprache. Theoretische Grundlagen und methodische Herausforderungen*. Berlin, Boston: De Gruyter.

Fleischer, Wolfgang (1997): *Phraseologie der deutschen Gegenwartssprache*. 2., durchgesehene und ergänzte Auflage. Tübingen: Niemeyer.

Graeser, Adolph H. (1829): *Die römisch-katholische Liturgie nach ihrer Entstehung und endlichen Ausbildung*. Zweiter Theil. Halle: Friedrich Ruff.

Kindler, J. P. (1848): *Gespräche des Herzens mit Gott: besonders zu Trost und Stärkung für Kranke und Angefochtene in Kernsprüchen der h. Schrift*. Nürnberg: J. P. Raw.

KJV = *The Holy Bible, King James Version*. Cambridge Edition, 1769. King James Bible Online, 2019. Retrieved from www.kingjamesbibleonline.org, accessed March 25, 2019.

Klein, Josef (2001): Erklären und Argumentieren als interaktive Gesprächsstrukturen. In Klaus Brinker, Gerd Antos, Wolfgang Heinemann & Sven F. Sager (eds.), *Text- und Gesprächslinguistik: Ein internationales Handbuch zeitgenössischer Forschung/Linguistics of Text and Conversation: An international handbook of contemporary research*, 2. Halbband, 1309–1329. Berlin, New York: De Gruyter.

Koch, Peter & Wulf Oesterreicher (1985): Sprache der Nähe – Sprache der Distanz: Mündlichkeit und Schriftlichkeit im Spannungsfeld von Sprachtheorie und Sprachgeschichte. *Romanistisches Jahrbuch* 36, 15–43.

Köpf, Ulrich (1996): Passionsfrömmigkeit. In Gerhard Müller (Hrsg.), *Theologische Realenzyklopädie*. Band 26: Paris–Polen, 722–764. Berlin, New York: De Gruyter.

Lange, Armin (2012): The text of Jeremiah in the War Scroll from Qumran. In Nóra Dávid (eds.), *The Hebrew Bible in light of the Dead Sea scrolls*, 95–116. Göttingen: Vandenhoeck & Ruprecht.

Langer, Nils (2013): Norddeutsches in holsteinischen Soldatenbriefen von 1848–1850. *Niederdeutsches Jahrbuch* 136, 73–95.

Lasch, Alexander & Wolf-Andreas Liebert (2014): Sprache und Religion. In Ekkehard Felder & Andreas Gardt (Hrsg.), *Handbuch Sprache und Wissen*, 475–492. Berlin, Boston: De Gruyter.

LU = *Die Bibel oder die ganze Heilige Schrift des Alten und Neuen Testaments*. Revidierte Fassung der deutschen Übersetzung Martin Luthers 1912. Stuttgart: Privilegierte Württembergische Bibelanstalt.

Mundt, Theodor (1844): *Die Geschichte der Gesellschaft in ihren neueren Entwickelungen und Problemen*. Berlin: Simion.

Nübling, Damaris, Antje Dammel, Janet Duke & Renata Szczepaniak (2017): *Historische Sprachwissenschaft des Deutschen. Eine Einführung in die Prinzipien des Sprachwandels*. 5. Auflage. Tübingen: Narr.

Pfeiffer, Christian (2016): *Frequenz und Funktionen phraseologischer Wendungen in meinungsbetonten Pressetexten (1911–2011)*. Baltmannsweiler: Schneider Verlag Hohengehren.

Pfeiffer, Christian (2018): Zur Identifikation modifizierter Phraseme in Texten: ein Vorschlag für die analytische Praxis. In Sören Stumpf & Natalia Filatkina (Hrsg.), *Formelhafte Sprache in Text und Diskurs*, 49–83. Berlin, Boston: De Gruyter.

Piirainen, Elisabeth (2012): *Widespread idioms in Europe and beyond: Toward a lexicon of common figurative units*. New York: Peter Lang.

Piirainen, Elisabeth (2015): Zur europaweiten Verbreitung von Idiomen. Ursachen und Hintergründe. In Tomislav Zelić, Zaneta Sambunjak & Anita Pavić Pintarić (Hrsg.), *Europa? Zur Kulturgeschichte einer Idee*, 361–382. Würzburg: Königshausen & Neumann.

Polenz, Peter von (1999): *Deutsche Sprachgeschichte vom Spätmittelalter bis zur Gegenwart*. Band 3. 19. und 20. Jahrhundert. Berlin, New York: De Gruyter.

Rutten, Gijsbert & Marijke Van der Wal (2012): Functions of epistolary formulae in Dutch letters from the seventeenth and eighteenth centuries. *Journal of Historical Pragmatics* 13 (2), 173–201.

Rutten, Gijsbert & Marijke Van der Wal (2013): Epistolary formulae and writing experience in Dutch letters from the seventeenth and eighteenth centuries. In Marijke Van der Wal & Gijsbert Rutten (eds.), *Touching the past. Studies in the historical sociolinguistics of egodocuments*, 45–65. Amsterdam, Philadelphia: John Benjamins.

Rutten, Gijsbert & Marijke Van der Wal (2014): *Letters as Loot. A sociolinguistic approach to seventeenth- and eighteenth-century Dutch*. Amsterdam, Philadelphia: John Benjamins.

Schiegg, Markus (2015): Der flexible Schreiber in der Sprachgeschichte. Grammatische Variation in süddeutschen Patientenbriefen des 19. Jahrhunderts. *Zeitschrift für Dialektologie und Linguistik* 82 (2), 169–205.

Schiegg, Markus (2018): Factors of intra-speaker variation in nineteenth-century lower-class writing. *Neuphilologische Mitteilungen* 119 (1), 101–120.

Schiegg, Markus (forthc.): Briefsteller. In Jochen Strobel, Marie I. Matthews-Schlinzig & Jörg Schuster (Hrsg.), *Handbuch Brief*. Berlin, Boston: De Gruyter.

Schiegg, Markus & Lena Sowada (2019): Script switching in nineteenth-century lower-class German handwriting. *Paedagogica Historica* (Special Issue: Education and the visual dimension of writing: Script systems and typefaces in educational history).

Schmid, Franz X. (1855): *Kreuzwegandacht, zunächst zum öffentlichen Gebrauche in der Kirche während der heiligen Fastenzeit*. 5. Auflage. Passau: Elsässer/Waldbauer.

Schmidt, Wilhelm (2013): *Geschichte der deutschen Sprache. Ein Lehrbuch für das germanistische Studium*. 11. Auflage. Stuttgart: Hirzel.

Stein, Stephan (1995): *Formelhafte Sprache. Untersuchungen zu ihren pragmatischen und kognitiven Funktionen im gegenwärtigen Deutsch*. Frankfurt am Main: Peter Lang.

Stein, Stephan (2003): *Textgliederung. Einheitenbildung im geschriebenen und gesprochenen Deutsch: Theorie und Empirie*. Berlin, New York: De Gruyter.

Wray, Alison (2002): *Formulaic language and the lexicon*. Cambridge: Cambridge University Press.
Wray, Alison (2009): Identifying formulaic language. Persistent challenges and new opportunities. In Roberta Corrigan, Edith A. Moravcsik, Hamid Ouali & Kathleen Wheatley (eds.), *Formulaic language*. Volume 1: Distribution and historical change, 27–51. Amsterdam, Philadelphia: John Benjamins.
Wray, Alison & Kazuhiko Namba (2003): Use of formulaic language by a Japanese-English bilingual child: a practical approach to data analysis. *Japan Journal of Multilingualism and Multiculturalism* 9 (1), 24–51.

www.ingramcontent.com/pod-product-compliance
Lightning Source LLC
Chambersburg PA
CBHW061935220426
43662CB00012B/1913